Alberta Plant Names
A Guide to Their Pronunciation, Meaning, and English Alternatives

by
Linda Kershaw

Copyright © 2019 Linda J. Kershaw

All rights reserved. No part of this book may be reproduced in any form or by any electronic or mechanical means without the prior written permission of the copyright holder, except for reviewers who may quote brief passages in a review. Any request for photocopying, recording, taping or storage on information retrieval systems of any part of this book shall be directed in writing to the copyright holder.

Kershaw, Linda, 1951 - Alberta Plant Names: A Guide to Their Pronunciation, Meaning, and English Alternatives

Includes bibliographic references

Cover photo: Broadleaf starflower (*Lysimachia latifolia*) by Linda Kershaw

Table of Contents

Introduction	1
The Derivation of Scientific Names	2
The Organization of Scientific Names	3
The Pronunciation of Scientific Names	4
Dividing Words Into Syllables	5
Vowel Sounds	5
Table 1: Pronunciation Symbols	6
Table 2: English/North American and Reconstructed Ancient Latin Pronunciation	7
Common Names	8
Pronunciation & Derivation	10
Alphabetical Scientific Names	136
Alphabetized Common Names	217
References	298
Table 1: Pronunciation Symbols	300

INTRODUCTION

Plants are among the most important parts of our environment. Look around you and imagine the place where you live without plants. The remaining moonscape of rock and soil would be bleak indeed! In urban settings, trees, grass and flowers are purposely added for their beauty and shelter. In the age of global warming, the expansion of urban forests can play a significant role in cooling roasting cities. Even more importantly, the beauty of plants along streets and in parks greatly improves the emotional quality of urban environments. In the countryside, plants are much more prevalent. Forests, prairies, wetlands and agricultural land are all blanketed in, and largely defined by plants.

There are many reasons for learning the names of plants. Naming something is a first step to recognizing and appreciating it. When we look at a crowd and see a mass of unknown faces, we perceive the group very differently than we would if we recognized our friends Liam, James, Emma and Sophie among them. The gathering takes on a different character when we recognize even a few of its components. The more 'faces' we recognize, the greater our appreciation of the gathering.

If we want to study biology, ecology or natural history in general, it is even more important to be able to recognize and name plants. Plants are the foundation supporting life, as we know it, on earth. They have the amazing ability to gather energy from the sun, carbon and nitrogen from the air and minerals from the soil, and then combine these to create sugars, starches and proteins, that can be passed on to other organisms. Animals depend on the food, shelter and oxygen provided by plants. To understand the biology of an animal, we need to identify and appreciate the contributions of the many plants that support it.

Plants are the basic components used to describe most ecosystems. This is partly because they are so visible and identifiable, and partly because they are wonderfully co-operative and don't run or fly away when we arrive. If we want to describe the vegetation of an area or start to understand some of the interactions among the organisms in different ecosystems, it is essential that we learn the names of the plants.

Plants provide us with a wide array of food, medicine, fibre and fuel. Over the centuries and around the world, a myriad of names have evolved to identify the plants we commonly use and recognize. The same common name may apply to different species in different places, especially if the plants are similar in appearance or have similar uses. For example, the names 'lettuce' and 'daisy' have been applied to dozens of different plants over the years. Alternatively, one species can have many different names, especially if it occurs over a wide range and is useful to humans. For example, trembling aspen (*Populus tremuloides*) is also called quaking aspen, American aspen, quakies, mountain aspen, golden aspen, trembling poplar, white poplar, popple, etc. It also has just as many French names in Canada (e.g. peuplier faux-tremble, peuplier tremble d'Amérique, tremble, tremble américain). On the other side of the world, its Eurasian counterpart, European aspen (*Populus tremula*) has an even greater variety of names over a much wider array of languages.

When studying plants, it makes sense to use scientific names, in order to avoid the confusion of common names. Once you know the scientific name for a plant, you can use it around the world. If you visit botanic gardens or refer to floras in Russia, Sweden or India, you may not understand the local lingo, but you'll be able to recognize the names of the plants.

Many people are intimidated by Latinized names, and hesitate to use them. Latin is a 'foreign' language. We don't recognize the words, and we don't know how to pronounce them. Hopefully, the following sections discussing the derivation and pronunciation of Alberta plant names will help to demystify some of these unusual words, and will provide a guide to their pronunciation.

The Derivation of Scientific Names

Most scientific names are Latinized words derived from either Latin or Greek words, or from the names of people commemorated by the naming of a new taxon. Usually one meaning is assigned to a name, but occasionally, 2, 3 or even 4 possible sources are attributed to a single name. This is especially true of ancient names that have been used for centuries (e.g. see *Taraxacum*). The meaning of specific epithets (species names/modifiers) can vary when applied to plants of different genera (e.g. 'rubra' may apply to a red stem in one case and to a red flower in another). Ideally, understanding the reason that a plant was given a particular name will help you to remember the name and to identify the plant when you come across it again.

The name derivations presented below have been compiled from a variety of sources, including books, articles and websites (see References). The information provided is an introduction, and has been kept to a minimum to reduce space. If you are interested in some of the historical figures that have been commemorated, the California Plant Names section of the Calflora website (Charters 2018) is a wonderful resource. Many of the photos are very entertaining. The World Dictionary of Plant Names (Quattrocchi 1999) also has an amazing amount of information. These and many other sources can provide detailed information about many of the people and places associated with the names of plant families, genera and species.

The Organization of Scientific Names

Scientific plant names are organized in a complex heirarchy, with many different levels. The broadest category is the Kingdom Plantae, which includes all plants (but excludes some things, such as mushrooms and lichens, that are often thought of as plants). Below the Kingdom level, come the Divisions (e.g. Pteridophyta = Ferns and Horsetails, Coniferophyta = Conifers, Magnoliophyta = Flowering Plants), followed by Classes, Orders, Families, Tribes, Genera, Species, Subspecies and Varieties. All of these categories are designed to reflect the relationships between different plants, and to help us organize them in our minds. The most commonly used categories within this hierarchy are Family, Genus and Species, and these are the names addressed in this book.

In terms of organization, a Family name could be likened to that of a Scottish clan (e.g., the Mackenzie Clan), which encompasses several related septs (e.g., Charleson, Cromarty, MacIvor, Murchie, etc.). A Genus name could be likened to that of a sept or a surname, and a species name would be analogous to a given name (e.g. Angus, Agatha, Edna, George, etc.). Like surname and given name, Genus and Species are the most commonly used names when referring to a particular plant. Unlike the names of people, these scientific names are written in italics, with the larger grouping (Genus) first and the smaller grouping (Species) second. *Rosa woodsii* (Genus *Rosa*, species *woodsii*) belongs to the Rosaceae Family. The organization of this name could be likened to that of MacIvor, Angus of the Mackenzie Clan. The combination of a genus name plus species name (the specific epithet) gives each species a unique scientific name. This is called the Binomial Nomenclature System.

The Pronunciation of Scientific Names

A lot of confusion and controversy surrounds the pronunciation of scientific names. On-line sites with computer-generated audio files of pronunciation are often unreliable and usually incorrect. Even the major floras can disagree about which syllable to stress and whether the vowel sound is long (hard) or short (soft). Latin has a long history of use in many European countries. Consequently, it has been repeatedly modified as users in each country pronounced the words as if they were in their own language. Around 1900, the pronunciation of Ancient Latin was reconstructed, and today there are four main methods of pronunciation:

(1) reconstructed Ancient Roman Latin, (2) Northern Continental European Latin, (3) Church Latin (from Italy) and (4) English Latin. English-speaking people still use English Latin to pronounce historical and mythological names, and Church Latin is widely (though not universally) used in the Catholic Church and in singing. English Latin is most widely used by scientists in North America.

Pronunciation can vary greatly from one method to the next. For example, using phonetic representations, Julius Caesar can be pronounced as follows:

English Latin	JOO-lē-us SĒ-zer
Reconstructed Ancient Roman Latin	YOO-lē-us KĪ-sar
Northern Continental European Latin	YOO-lē-us (T)SĀ-sar
Church Latin	YOO-lē-us CHĀ-sar

Capital letters indicate which syllable is stressed (e.g. banana = ba-NA-na). A bar over a vowel indicates that it is long (e.g. ē = e as in beet) rather than short (e.g. e = e as in bet). The symbols used to denote different sounds in phonetic representations are presented in **Table 1**, and the pronunciation of letters in English Latin and in Reconstructed Ancient Latin is presented in **Table 2**. Table 1 is also repeated on the last page of the book, for easy referencing when sounding out names with the pronunciation guides presented later in the book.

Here are a few general rules for pronunciation. Although the phonetic pronunciation of the current scientific names for Alberta plants is presented below, if you travel elsewhere you will find many plants that don't grow in Alberta. This will help you to decipher new names and to feel more comfortable using them.

Dividing Words Into Syllables

1. There are as many syllables as there are separate vowel sounds.
2. If a single consonant separates two vowels, the consonant is placed with the second vowel (e.g. acicularis = a-ci-cu-la-ris)
3. If two consonants separate two vowels, the first consonant goes with the preceding vowel, and the second goes with the following vowel (e.g. alaskanus = a-las-ka-nus). For simplification, double consonants have been omitted in the following phonetic representations (e.g. affinis = a-fi-nis).
4. If more than two consonants separate two vowels, the first consonant goes with the first vowel, and the rest go with the following vowel (e.g. obscurum = ob-scu-rum)
5. There are some exceptions to these rules.
   (a) The letter x always goes with the vowel preceding it (e.g. exalbescens = ex-al-bes-cens)
   (b) If the first consonant is b, c, d, g, k, p, or t, and the second is either l or r, both consonants go together with the second vowel (e.g. acris = a-cris, glabra = gla-bra).
   (c) If the two consonants are ch, ph or th, both go together with the second vowel (e.g. microcephala, mi-cro-ce-pha-la, polystachion, po-lys-ta-chi-on).

Vowel Sounds

1. Vowels at the ends of words have long vowel sounds (e.g. anemone = a-ne-mo-nē, bakeri = bā-ker-ī)
   The exception is the letter a, which is short (as in cat) (e.g. densa = den-sa)
2. Y is always a vowel with the quality of the letter i (e.g. Agropyron = a-gro-pī-ron).
3. Diphthongs (two vowels that join to produce one sound - ae, au, ei, oe, ui) are treated as long vowels. According to Latin rules, oi is not a dipthong, so o and i are both pronounced when they occur together, but the sound is run together so that o-i sounds like oy. The pronunciation of dipthongs is outlined in Table 1.
4. Two vowels together, that do not form a dipthong, are always sounded separately. (e.g. alnifolia, al-ni-fō-li-a).
   Traditionally, the first vowel has a short sound. However, this can be difficult to pronounce, so many botanists prefer to give the first vowel a long sound to ease pronunciation. For example, ia is pronounced ē-a or ī-a (I prefer ē-a) rather than i-a, and ea is pronounced ē-a rather than e-a, because these sounds are easier to enunciate.

Table 1: Pronunciation Symbols

Symbol	Pronunciation
a A	as in c**a**t
ä Ä	as in f**a**ther
ā Ā	as in d**a**te
b B	as in **b**at
ch CH	as in **ch**at
d D	as in **d**o**d**der
e E	as in b**e**t
ē Ē	as in f**ee**t
f F	as in **f**i**f**ty
g G	as in **g**a**g**
h H	as in **h**at
i I	as in k**i**t
ī Ī	as in k**i**te
j J	as in **j**ay
k K	as in **k**i**ck**
l L	as in **l**i**l**y
m M	as in **m**ur**m**ur
n N	as in **n**a**nn**y
o O	as in n**o**t
ō Ō	as in n**o**te
oo OO	as in n**oo**n
õõ Õ͂Õ͂	like u in p**u**t
ou OU	as in ab**ou**t
p P	as in **p**o**p**
q Q	as in **q**uit
r R	as in **r**a**r**e
s S	as in **s**a**ss**y
sh SH	as in **sh**e
t T	as in **t**a**tt**er
th TH	as in **th**in
ū Ū	as in c**u**te
v V	as in **v**al**v**e
w W	as in **w**o**w**
x X	as in e**x**am
y Y	as in **y**et
z Z	as in **z**ig
ēoo	as in **f**e**ud**
ooē	Like ooey in g**ooey**
tzē	Like tzy in ri**tzy**

6

Table 2: English/North American and Reconstructed Ancient Latin Pronunciation

	English Latin	Phonetic Symbol	Reconstructed Ancient Latin	Phonetic Symbol
Vowels				
à, ā (long a)	as in plate	ā	as in father	ä
á, a (short a)	as in cat	a	as in cat	a
è, ē (long e)	as in feet	ē	like a in plate	ā
é, e (short e)	as in pet	e	as in pet	e
ì, ī (long i)	as in kite	ī	as in machine	ē
í, i (short i)	as in pit	i	as in pit	i
i preceding another vowel	as in machine	ē	as in machine	ē
ò, ō (long o)	as in home	ō	as in home	ō
ó, o (short o)	as in not	o	as in not	o
ù, ū (long u)	as in duty	ū	as in rule	oo
ú, u (short u)	as in but	u	as in put	ŏŏ
ỳ, ī (long y)	like i in kite	ī	like i in machine	ē
ý, i (short y)	like i in pit	i	like i in pit	i
Diphthongs				
ae	like e in feet	ē	like ai in aisle	ī
au	like a in father	ä	like ou in about	ow
ei	as in height	ī	as in hey	ā
eu	as in feud	ēū	like ee-oo	ēoo
oe	like e in feet	ē	as in coin	oi
ui	like i in kite	ī	like ooey in gooey	ooē
Consonants				
b, d, f, h, k, l, m, n, p, q, r, t, w, x, z	as in English		as in English	
c before e, i, y, ae, oe	like s in sit	s	like k in kit	k
c elsewhere	like k in kit	k	like k in kit	k
g before e, i, y, ae, oe	as in gem	j	as in goose	g
g elsewhere	as in goose	g	as in goose	g
j in ja suffix & between vowels	like y in yet		like y in yet	
j elsewhere	as in jet	y	like y in yet	y
s in -es suffix	like z in zag	z	as in sit	s
s	as in sit	s	as in sit	s
v	as in vat	v	as in win	w
ch	like k in kit	k	like k in kit	k
ph	like f in fit	f	like p in pit	p
sh	as in shin	sh	like s in sin	s
th	as in thin	th	like t in tin	t
ti between vowels	like tzy in ritzy	tzē	like sh in she	sh
cn, ct, gn, mn, pn, ps, pt tm	n, t, n, n, n, s, t, m (1st letter silent)	n, t, n, n, n, s, t, m	n, t, n, n, n, s, t, m (1st letter silent)	n, t, n, n, n, s, t, m

Common Names

Despite the superiority of scientific names, there are times when it is helpful to know a common name for a plant. Many people don't understand Latinized words, and they need to hear something "in their own language" in order to remember a name and apply it to a plant. Many of us grew up calling plants by their common names, and it is often helpful to use this information to learn scientific names. For example, you may know that a tree is a 'European mountain-ash', so it would be helpful if you could use that information to find the scientific name, *Sorbus aucuparia*.

The 'Common Names' section provides an alphabetical list of standardized common names paired with their scientific names and an alphabetical list of scientific names paired with some of their common names. These are only a few of the hundreds of common names that are applied to these plants in Canada and around the world. Common names are a very sensitive issue for some. These are the first names we learn, so people often identify with them, and feel that the name they grew up with is the only 'right' one to use.

The common names presented here were not chosen on the basis of local popularity. Instead they were taken from widely used, published lists produced by provincial and national authorities. The national Database of Vascular Plants of Canada or VASCAN (Brouillet et al., 2018) lists 2-6 common names for most species, including both French and English names. The 'accepted' colloquial name at the top of the VASCAN English list appears in the following lists. Similarly, the Alberta Conservation Information Management System (ACIMS, 2018) has provided a common name for most species, and this name is also included. Both of these sources are widely used as standards for naming plants in Alberta.

When the VASCAN and ACIMS colloquial names are the same, that name is entered as the 'Suggested Common Name'. However, when these two sites suggest different common names, other sources [e.g. the Integrated Taxonomic Information System website (ITIS Canada, 2018), the Flora North America website (FNA, 2018) and the PLANTS Database (USDA, NRCS, 2018)] have been consulted, in an attempt to determine the most widely accepted common name.

In some cases, common names are misleading. For example a "northern" species might have a range extending south to Texas or a "marsh" species might prefer upland forest in Alberta. In these cases, an alternate name is given preference. Of course, spelling, spacing and hyphenation also vary greatly from one site to the next. The following lists minimize the use of hyphens and retain one-word names for genera whenever possible. However, alternative spelling and spacing and even alternate names are perfectly acceptable, because there are no standardized common names for plants in Alberta. Scientific names can help you to avoid a lot of confusion

PRONUNCIATION & DERIVATION

Scientific Name	English Latin Pronunctiaion	Reconstructed Latin Pronunciation	Root Source	Root 1
abbreviata	a-bre-vē-Ā-ta	a-bre-wē-Ä-ta	Latin	abbreviatus
Abies	A-bē-ēz	A-bē-ēs	name, plant	Abies
abortivus	a-BŌR-ti-vus	a-BŌR-ti-wŏŏs	Latin	abortivus
abrotanum	a-BRO-ta-num	a-BRO-ta-nŏŏm	Latin	abrotonum
absinthium	ab-SIN-thē-um	ab-SIN-tā-ŏŏm	Latin	absinthium
Abutilon	a-BŪ-ti-lon	a-BOO-ti-lon	name, plant	Abutilon
acanthicarpa	a-kan-thi-KAR-pa	a-kan-ti-KAR-pa	Greek	akanthias
acanthoides	a-kan-THŌĪ-dēz	a-kan-TŌĒ-dās	name, plant	Acanthus
acaule	a-KÄ-lē	a-KOW-lā	Latin	a
acaulis	a-KÄ-lis	a-KOW-lis	Latin	a
Acer	Ā-ser	Ä-ker	name, plant	Acer
acetosa	a-sē-TŌ-sa	a-kā-TŌ-sa	Latin	acetum
acetosella	a-sē-tō-SE-la	a-kā-tō-SE-la	Latin	acetum
Achillea	a-KI-lē-a, a-ki-LĒ-a	a-ki-LÄ-a	name, myth	Achilles
Achnatherum	ak-NA-the-rum	ak-NA-te-rŏŏm	Greek	achne
achoreum	a-KŌ-rē-um	a-KŌ-rā-ŏŏm	Greek	achor
acicularis	a-si-kū-LÄ-ris	a-ki-koo-LÄ-ris	Latin	acus
Aconitum	a-ko-NĪ-tum	a-ko-NẼ-tŏŏm	name, plant	Aconiton
Acoraceae	a-kō-RÄ-sē-ē	a-kō-RÄ-kā-ī	name, plant	Acorus
Acorus	A-kō-rus	A-kō-rŏŏs	name, plant	Akoras
acre	Ā-krē	Ä-krā	Latin	acre
acris	A-kris	A-kris	Latin	acris
acrostichoides	a-kro-sti-KŌĪ-dēz	a-kro-sti-KŌĒ-dās	name, plant	Acrostichum
Actaea	ak-TĒ-a	ak-TĪ-a	name, plant	Aktea
acuminata	a-kū-mi-NÄ-ta	a-koo-mi-NÄ-ta	Latin	acumen
acuminatum	a-kū-mi-NÄ-tum	a-koo-mi-NÄ-tŏŏm	Latin	acumen
acutiflorum	a-kū-ti-FLŌ-rum	a-koo-ti-FLŌ-rŏŏm	Latin	acutus
acutus	a-KŪ-tus	a-KOO-tŏŏs	Latin	acutus
Adenocaulon	a-de-nō-KÄ-lon	a-de-nō-KOW-lon	Greek	aden
Adiantum	a-dē-AN-tum	a-dē-AN-tŏŏm	Greek	adiantos
Adoxa	a-DŌK-sa	a-DŌK-sa	Greek	adoxos
Adoxaceae	a-dok-SÄ-sē-ē	a-dok-SÄ-kā-ī	name, plant	Adoxa
adscendens	ad-SEN-denz	ad-SEN-dens	Latin	ascendo
adunca	a-DUN-ka	a-DOON-ka	Latin	aduncus
adusta	a-DUS-ta	a-DOOS-ta	Latin	adusta

Root 1 Meaning	Root 2	Root 2 Meaning / (referring to)
shortened		
name for silver fir or the fir tree, Latin name of an Old World species		
prematurely born		of
southernwood, an aromatic, medicinal plant		
wormwood, a plant yielding a bitter extract used in flavoring wine		
Arabic name for a mallow-like plant		
a prickly, thorny thing	karpos	fruit
the plant whose leaves inspired the ornamentation of Corinthian columns	oides	like, resembling
without	caulis	stem, stalk
without	caulis	stem, stalk
ancient name of the maples		
sour wine, vinegar		
sour wine, vinegar	ella	diminutive
Greek warrior, leader in the Trojan War		
chaff, down, any light substance	ather	stalk, barb (awned lemmas)
scurf, dandruff		
needle, pin	aris	possessing (the sharply pointed leaves or numerous thorns)
ancient name for a poisonous herb		
the type genus		
ancient name for an unknown plant		
sharp, pointed, strong, pungent		
sharp, pointed, strong, pungent		
a genus of ferns	oides	like, resembling
ancient Greek name for the elder tree		
point, sharpness	atus	with, like
point, sharpness	atus	with, like
sharp, pointed	floris	flower
sharp, pointed		
gland	caulis	stem, stalk
unwetted, unwettable		(the way the leaves repel water)
obscure, insignificant		
the type genus		
climb or ascend		(the flowers or leaves turning upwards or rising gradually)
curved, hooked		(the spurred lower petal)
scorched		

PRONUNCIATION & DERIVATION

Scientific Name	English Latin Pronunctiaion	Reconstructed Latin Pronunciation	Root Source	Root 1
aequalis	Ē-kwa-lis	Ī-kwa-lis	Latin	aequalis
aestivum	Ē-sti-vum	Ī-sti-wõõm	Latin	aestivus
affine	a-FI-nē	a-FI-nā	Latin	affinis
affinis	a-FI-nis	a-FI-nis	Latin	affinis
Agastache	a-GA-sta-kē	a-GA-sta-kā	Greek	agan
Agoseris	a-GO-se-ris	a-GŌ-se-ris	Greek + name, plant	aix
agraria	a-GRĀ-rē-a	a-GRĂ-rē-a	Latin	agrarius
agrestis	a-GRE-stis	a-GRE-stis	Latin	agrestis
Agrimonia	ag-ri-MŌ-nē-a	ag-ri-MŌ-nē-a	Greek	argema
Agropyron	a-gro-PĪ-ron	a-gro-PĒ-ron	Greek	agros
Agrostemma	a-gro-STE-ma	a-gro-STE-ma	Greek	agros
Agrostis	a-GROS-stis	a-GRO-stis	Greek	agros
aizoides	ā-ZŌĪ-dēz	ä-ZŌĒ-dās	Latin	aizoon
alaskana	a-las-KĀ-na	a-las-KÄ-na	name, place	Alaska
alata	a-LĀ-ta	a-LÄ-ta	Latin	ala
alatus	a-LĀ-tus	a-LÄ-tõõs	Latin	ala
alaxensis	a-lak-SEN-sis	a-lak-SEN-sis	name, place	Alaska
alba	AL-ba	AL-ba	Latin	albus
albertina	al-ber-TĪ-na	al-ber-TĒ-na	name, place	Alberta
albertinus	al-ber-TĪ-nus	al-ber-TĒ-nõõs	name, place	Alberta
albicans	AL-bi-kanz	AL-bi-kans	Latin	albico
albicaulis	al-bi-KĂ-lis	al-bi-KOW-lis	Latin	albico
albida	AL-bi-da	AL-bi-da	Latin	albico
albidus	AL-bi-dus	AL-bi-dõõs	Latin	albico
albiflorum	al-bi-FLŌ-rum	al-bi-FLŌ-rõõm	Latin	albico
albiflorus	al-bi-FLŌ-rus	al-bi-FLŌ-rõõs	Latin	albico
albonigra	al-bō-NĪ-gra	al-bō-NĒ-gra	Latin	albico
album	AL-bum	AL-bõõm	Latin	albus
albus	AL-bus	AL-bõõs	Latin	albus
aleppicum	a-LE-pi-kum	a-LE-pi-kõõm	name, place	Aleppo
aleuticum	a-LĒŪ-ti-kum	a-LĒOO-ti-kõõm	name, place	Aleutian Is.
Alisma	a-LIZ-ma	a-LIS-ma	name, plant	Alisma
Alismataceae	u-lis-ma-TĀ-sē-ē	õõ-lēs-ma-TÄ-kā-ī	name, plant	Alisma
Alliaria	a-lē-Ā-rē-a	a-lē-Ä-rē-a	name, plant	Allium
Allium	A-lē-um	A-lē-õõm	name, plant	Allium
Almutaster	al-mu-TĀ-ster	al-mõõ-TÄ-ster	name, person + name, plant	Almut G. Jones
alnifolia	al-ni-FŌ-lē-a	al-ni-FŌ-lē-a	Latin	alnus

12

Root 1 Meaning	Root 2	Root 2 Meaning / (referring to)
equal, like, uniform		
summer		
neighboring, related to		
neighboring, related to		
very much	stachys	spike, ear of grain (many spikes)
goat	seris	chicory, a plant in the Aster Family (goats' love of this species)
agrarian, of the land		
rustic, of the country, wild		
an eye disease		(its use as a remedy for this)
field, country	pyros	grain, wheat
field, country	stemma	crown, garland, wreath
field, country		
an evergreen plant	oides	like, resembling
state of Alaska, USA	anus	from or of
wing	atus	with, like
wing	atus	with, like
state of Alaska, USA	ensis	of a place or country
white, bright		
province of Alberta, Canada	inus	pertaining to
province of Alberta, Canada	inus	pertaining to
white or whitish		
white or whitish	caulis	stem, stalk
white or whitish		
white or whitish		
white or whitish	floris	flower
white or whitish	floris	flower
white or whitish	niger	black, dark
white, bright		
white, bright		
city of Aleppo (now Halab), Syria	ica	belonging to
Aleutian Islands, Alaska	ensis	of a place or country
ancient name for waterplantain		
the type genus		
ancient name for garlic		
ancient name for garlic		
1923-2013, American Aster specialist	aster	the genus aster
alder	folium	leaf

PRONUNCIATION & DERIVATION

Scientific Name	English Latin Pronunctiaion	Reconstructed Latin Pronunciation	Root Source	Root 1
alnobetula	al-nō-BE-tū-la	al-nō-BE-too-la	name, plant	Alnus
Alnus	AL-nus	AL-nŏŏs	name, plant	Alnus
Alopecurus	a-lō-pe-KŪ-rus	a-lō-pe-KOO-rŏŏs	Greek	alopex
alpina	al-PĪ-na	al-PĒ-na	Latin	Alpes
alpinoarticulatus	al-PĪ-nō-ar-ti-kū-LĀ-tus	al-PĒ-nō-ar-ti-koo-LĂ-tŏŏs	Latin	Alpes
alpinum	al-PĪ-num	al-PĒ-nŏŏm	Latin	Alpes
alpinus	al-PĪ-nus	al-PĒ-nŏŏs	Latin	Alpes
altaica	al-TĀ-i-ka	al-TÄ-i-ka	name, place	Altai
altissima	al-TI-si-ma	al-TI-si-ma	Latin	altus
altissimum	al-TI-si-mum	al-TI-si-mŏŏm	Latin	altus
alyssifolia	a-li-si-FŌ-lē-a	a-li-si-FŌ-lē-a	name, plant	Alyssum
alyssoides	a-li-SŌĪ-dēz	a-li-SŌĒ-dās	name, plant	Alyssum
Alyssum	a-LI-sum	a-LI-sŏŏm	Greek	a
alyssum	a-LI-sum	a-LI-sŏŏm	Greek	a
amara	a-MĀ-ra	a-MÄ-ra	Latin	amarum
Amaranthaceae	a-ma-ran-THĀ-sē-ē	a-ma-ran-TÄ-kā-ī	name, plant	Amaranthus
amaranthoides	a-ma-ran-THŌĪ-dēz	a-ma-ran-TŌĒ-dās	Latin	amarantus
Amaranthus	a-ma-RAN-thus	a-ma-RAN-tŏŏs	Greek	amarantos
amarella	a-ma-RE-la	a-ma-RE-la	Latin	amarum
Amaryllidaceae	a-mi-ri-li-DĀ-sē-ē	a-mē-rē-lē-DÄ-kā-ī	name, plant	Amaryllus
Ambrosia	am-BRŌ-shē-a	am-BRŌ-sē-a	name, plant	Ambrosia
Amelanchier	a-me-LAN-kē-a	a-me-LAN-kē-er	name, plant	Amelanchier
americana	a-me-ri-KĀ-na	a-me-ri-KÄ-na	name, place	America
americanum	a-me-ri-KĀ-num	a-me-ri-KÄ-nŏŏm	name, place	America
americanus	a-me-ri-KĀ-nus	a-me-ri-KÄ-nŏŏs	name, place	America
amphibium	am-FI-bē-um	am-PI-bē-ŏŏm	Greek	amphibios
Amphiscirpus	am-fi-SKIR-pus	am-pi-SKIR-pŏŏs	Greek + name, plant	amphi
amplexicaule	am-plek-si-KĀ-lē	am-plek-si-KOW-lā	Latin	amplector
amplexicaulis	am-plek-si-KĀ-lis	am-plek-si-KOW-lis	Latin	amplector
amplifolius	am-pli-FŌ-lē-us	am-pli-FŌ-lē-ŏŏs	Latin	amplus
Amsinckia	am-SIN-kē-a	am-SIN-kē-a	name, person	Amsinck, Wilhelm
amygdaloides	a-mig-da-LŌĪ-dēz	a-mig-da-LŌĒ-dās	Latin	amygdala
Anacardiaceae	a-na-kar-di-Ā-sē-ē	a-na-kar-dē-Ä-kā-ī	name, plant	Anacardium
anagallidifolium	a-na-ga-li-di-FŌ-lē-um	a-na-ga-li-di-FŌ-lē-ŏŏm	Greek	anagallis
anagallis-aquatica	a-na-GA-lis a-KWA-ti-ka	a-na-GA-lis a-KWA-ti-ka	Greek	anagallis

Root 1 Meaning	Root 2	Root 2 Meaning / (referring to)
alder	Betula	birch
ancient name for alder		
fox	oura	tail (spikes likened to a fox's tail)
of high mountains, alpine	inus	pertaining to
of high mountains, alpine	atus	with, like
of high mountains, alpine	inus	pertaining to
of high mountains, alpine	inus	pertaining to
Altai (Altay) Mountains, Siberia	ica	belonging to
high, tall	issimus	superlative, very
high, tall	issimus	superlative, very
a genus in the Mustard Family	folium	leaf
a genus in the Mustard Family	oides	like, resembling
without, not	lyssa	madness (said to sooth madness and anger and cure rabies)
without	lyssa	madness (said to sooth madness and anger and cure rabies)
bitter, pungent		
the type genus		
amaranth, an imaginary flower that never fades	oides	like, resembling
unfading		(the papery, long-lasting flowers)
bitter, pungent	ella	diminutive form
the type genus		
ancient name for several plants, meaning "food of the gods"		very inappropriate, given its irritating pollen
Provençal name of a European species		
continent of North America	anus	from or of
continent of North America	anus	from or of
continent of North America	anus	from or of
with a double life in both water and land		
double, on both sides	Scirpus	bulrush, a genus in the Sedge Family
to embrace, hug or encircle	caulis	stem, stalk (clasping leaves)
to embrace, hug or encircle	caulis	stem, stalk (clasping leaves)
large, ample	folium	leaf
1752-1831, Burgomaster of Hamburg, patron of botanical gardens		
almond tree	oides	like, resembling
the type genus		
pimpernel, a Primrose Family genus	folium	leaf
pimpernel, a Primrose Family genus	aquaticus	living in or near water

PRONUNCIATION & DERIVATION

Scientific Name	English Latin Pronunctiaion	Reconstructed Latin Pronunciation	Root Source	Root 1
Anaphalis	a-NA-fa-lis	a-NA-pa-lis	name, plant	anaphalis
Andersonglossum	an-der-son-GLO-sum	an-der-son-GLO-sōōm	name, person	Anderson, W.R.
andina	an-DĪ-na	an-DĒ-na	name, place	Andes
Andromeda	an-DRO-me-da	an-DRŌ-me-da	name, myth	Andromeda
andromedea	an-dro-MĒ-dē-a	an-dro-ME-dā-a	name, myth	Andromeda
Androsace	an-DRO-sa-sē	an-DRO-sa-kā	name, plant	androsakes
androsaceum	an-dro-SĀ-sē-um	an-dro-SĀ-kā-ōōm	name, plant	Androsace
androsaemifolium	an-dro-sē-mi-FŌ-lē-um	an-dro-sī-mi-FŌ-lē-ōōm	Latin	androsaemum
Anemonastrum	a-ne-mo-NA-strum	a-ne-mo-NA-strōōm	name, plant	Anemone
Anemone	a-NE-mo-nē, a-ne-MŌ-nē	a-NE-mo-nā	Greek	anemos
Anethum	a-NĒ-thum	a-NĀ-tōōm	name, plant	Anethum
Angelica	an-JE-li-ka	an-GE-li-ka	Latin	angelus
anglica	AN-gli-ka	AN-gli-ka	name, place	England
angustifolia	an-gus-ti-FŌ-lē-a	an-gōōs-ti-FŌ-lē-a	Latin	angusti
angustifolium	an-gus-ti-FŌ-lē-um	an-gōōs-ti-FŌ-lē-ōōm	Latin	angusti
annotinum	a-NŌ-ti-num	a-NŌ-ti-nōōm	Latin	annotinus
annua	A-nū-a	A-noo-a	Latin	annuus
annuus	A-nū-us	A-noo-ōōs	Latin	annuus
anserina	an-se-RĪ-na	an-se-RĒ-na	Latin	anser
Antennaria	an-te-NĀ-rē-a	an-te-NÄ-rē-a	Latin	antenna
Anthemis	AN-the-mis	AN-te-mis	name, plant	Anthemis
Anthoxanthum	an-thō-ZAN-thum	an-tok-SAN-tōōm	Latin	anthos
Anthyllis	an-THI-lis	an-TI-lis	Latin	anthos
Anticlea	an-ti-KLĒ-a	an-ti-KLĀ-a	name, myth	Anticlia
antirrhina	an-ti-RĪ-na	an-ti-RĒ-na	Latin	antirrhinon
aparine	a-pa-RĪ-nē	a-pa-RĒ-na	Greek	aparine
aparinoides	a-pa-ri-NŌĪ-dēz	a-pa-ri-NŌĒ-dās	Greek	aparine
aperta	a-PER-ta	a-PER-ta	Latin	apertus
apetalus	ā-PE-ta-lus	ā-PE-ta-lōōs	Latin	a
Aphyllon	ā-FI-lon	ā-PI-lon	Greek	a
Apiaceae	a-pi-Ā-sē-ē	a-pē-Ā-kā-ī	name, plant	Apios
apiculatus	a-pi-kū-LĀ-tus	a-pi-koo-LÄ-tōōs	Latin	apicula
Apocynaceae	a-po-si-NĀ-sē-ē	a-pō-kē-NÄ-kā-ī	name, plant	Apocynum
Apocynum	a-PO-si-num	a-PO-ki-nōōm	Greek	apo

Root 1 Meaning	Root 2	Root 2 Meaning / (referring to)
ancient name of a similar plant *or* anagram of Gnaphalium		
1942-2013, professor, botanist	glossa	tongue (tongue-shaped leaves)
Andes Mountains, South America	inus	pertaining to
princess of Greek mythology, daughter of King Cepheus and Cassiope		like these plants, Andromeda spent a lot of time with her toes in the water)
Ethiopian princess in Greek mythology	ea	of, belonging to
ancient name for a polyp (a coelenterate, formerly believed to be a plant)		
rockjasmine, a Primrose Family genus	aceus	with, like, pertaining to
an early name for Hypericum androsaemum	folium	leaf
genus in the Buttercup Family	astrum	like, similar to
wind		(the flowers were believed to open only when the wind blew)
ancient name for dill		originally from *aithinos*, burning hot, due to the pungent seeds
angel	ica	belonging to
country of England	ica	belonging to
narrow	folium	leaf
narrow	folium	leaf
last year's, year-old		
lasting a year, annual		
lasting a year, annual		
goose	inus	pertaining to (the fondness of geese for these plants)
feeler, antenna		(the pappus of male flowers resembles insect antennae)
ancient name for chamomile		
flower	xanthos	yellow
flower	ioulous	downy
mother of Odysseus and granddaughter of the god Hermes		
snapdragon		
bedstraw		
bedstraw	oides	like, resembling
bare, exposed		
without	petalum	petal
without, not	phyllon	leaf
the type genus		
little bee, small-pointed	atus	with, like
the type genus		
from, off, after	kynos	dog (its use to poison wolves)

PRONUNCIATION & DERIVATION

Scientific Name	English Latin Pronunctiaion	Reconstructed Latin Pronunciation	Root Source	Root 1
appelianum	a-pe-lē-Ā-num	a-pe-lē-Ä-nŏŏm	name, person	Appel, Oliver
aptera	AP-te-ra	AP-te-ra	Greek	a
aquacervensis	a-kwa-ser-VEN-sis	a-kwa-ker-WEN-sis	Latin	aqua
aquatica	a-KWA-ti-ka	a-KWA-ti-ka	Latin	aquaticus
aquatilis	a-KWA-ti-lis	a-KWA-ti-lis	Latin	aquaticus
Aquilegia	a-kwi-LĒ-jē-a	a-kwi-LĀ-gē-a	Latin	aquila
aquilinum	a-kwi-LĪ-num	a-kwi-LĒ-nŏŏm	Latin	aquila
aquilonis	a-kwi-LŌ-nis	a-kwi-LŌ-nis	Latin	aquila
Arabidopsis	a-ra-bi-DOP-sis	a-ra-bi-DOP-sis	name, plant	Arabis
Arabis	A-ra-bis	A-ra-bis	name, place	Arabis
Araceae	a-RĀ-sē-ē	a-RÄ-kā-ī	name, plant	Arum
Aralia	a-RĀ-lē-a	a-RÄ-lē-a	French	aralie
Araliaceae	a-rā-li-Ā-sē-ē	a-rä-lē-Ä-kā-ī	name, plant	Aralia
arborescens	ar-bō-RE-senz	ar-bō-RE-skens	Latin	arbor
arbusculoides	ar-bus-kū-LŌĪ-dēz	ar-bŏŏs-koo-LŌĒ-dās	Latin	arbuscula
Arceuthobium	ar-sēū-THŌ-bē-um	ar-kēoo-TŌ-bē-ŏŏm	name, plant	Arkeuthos
arcta	ARK-ta	ARK-ta	Greek	arktos
Arctagrostis	ark-ta-GRO-stis	ark-ta-GRO-stis	Latin + name, plant	arktos
arctica	ARK-ti-ka	ARK-ti-ka	Greek	arktos
arcticus	ARK-ti-kus	ARK-ti-kŏŏs	Greek	arktos
Arctium	ARK-tē-um	ARK-tē-ŏŏm	Greek	arktos
arctogena	ark-to-JĒ-na	ark-to-GĀ-ne	Greek	arktos
Arctostaphylos	ark-tō-STA-fi-los	ark-to-STA-pi-lŏŏs	Greek	arktos
Arctous	ARK-tus	ARK-tŏŏs	Latin	arktos
arcuata	ar-kū-Ā-ta	ar-koo-Ä-ta	Latin	arcus
Arenaria	a-re-NĀ-rē-a	a-re-NÄ-rē-a	Latin	arena
arenosa	a-rē-NŌ-sa	a-rä-NŌ-sa	Latin	arena
Arethusa	a-re-THŪ-sa	a-re-TOO-sa	name, myth	Arethusa
argentea	ar-JEN-tē-a	ar-GEN-tā-a	Latin	argentum
argenteus	ar-jen-TĒ-us	ar-gen-TĀ-ŏŏs	Latin	argentum
argophyllum	ar-go-FI-lum	ar-go-PI-lŏŏm	Greek	argos
arguta	ar-GŪ-ta	ar-GOO-ta	Latin	argutus
arida	A-ri-da	A-ri-da	Latin	aridus
aristata	a-ris-TĀ-ta	a-ris-TÄ-ta	Latin	arista
Aristida	a-ris-TI-da	a-ris-TI-da	Latin	arista

Root 1 Meaning	Root 2	Root 2 Meaning / (referring to)
fl. 1996, German botanist, studied Brassicaceae in China & Germany		
without	pteron	wing, feather
water	cerva	deer (the common name, Elkwater hawthorn)
growing in water		
growing in water		
eagle		(the petal resembled an eagle's claw)
eagle		(the petal resembled an eagle's clawe)
eagle		(the petal resembled an eagle's clawe)
rockcress, a genus in the Mustard Family	opsis	appearance, resembling
Arabia		(perhaps because it thrives in dry areas)
the type genus		
aralia		(the local name aralie in Quebec)
the type genus		
tree	escens	in the process of becoming
small tree, shrub	oides	like, resembling
juniper	bios	life (its similarity to a juniper)
northern		
northern	Agrostis	bentgrass genus
northern	ica	belonging to
northern	ica	belonging to
northern		
northern	genus	born in
northern	staphule	a bunch of grapes ()
northern		
bow	atus	with, like (bent like a bow)
sand		(the sandy habitat of many spp)
sand	ose	with, like (the sandy habitats)
the wood nymph who changed into a spring while fleeing the river-god Alpheus		
silver		
silver		
bright, white, silver	phyllon	leaf
clear-cut, bright, distinct		
dry, parched		
awn	atus	with, like
awn		(the awned lemmas)

PRONUNCIATION & DERIVATION

Scientific Name	English Latin Pronunctiaion	Reconstructed Latin Pronunciation	Root Source	Root 1
Aristolochiaceae	a-ris-tō-lō-ki-Ā-sē-ē	a-rēs-tō-lō-kē-Ä-kā-ī	name, plant	Aristolochia
arkansana	ar-kan-SĀ-na	ar-kan-SÄ-na	name, place	Arkansas
armeria	ar-MĒ-rē-a	ar-MÄ-rē-a	name, plant	Armeria
Armoracia	ar-mō-RĀ-shē-a	ar-mō-RÄ-kē-a	name, plant	Armoracia
Arnica	AR-ni-ka	AR-ni-ka	Greek	ptarmica
aromatica	a-rō-MA-ti-ka	a-rō-MA-ti-ka	Latin	aromatica
Artemisia	ar-te-MI-shē-a	ar-te-MI-sē-a	name, myth	Artemis
artemisiifolia	ar-te-mis-sē-i-FŌ-lē-a	ar-te-mis-sē-i-FŌ-lē-a	name, plant	Artemisia
Aruncus	a-RUN-kus	a-RŎŌN-kŏŏs	name, plant	aryngos
arundinacea	a-run-di-NĀ-sē-a	a-rŏŏn-di-NÄ-kā-a	Latin	arundo
arundinaceum	a-run-di-NĀ-sē-um	ā-rŏŏn-di-NÄ-kā-ŏŏm	Latin	arundo
arundinaceus	a-run-di-NĀ-sē-us	ā-rŏŏn-di-NÄ-kā-ŏŏs	Latin	arundo
arvense	ar-VEN-sē	ar-WEN-sā	Latin	arvus
arvensis	ar-VEN-sis	ar-WEN-sis	Latin	arvus
asarifolia	a-sa-ri-FŌ-lē-a	a-sa-ri-FŌ-lē-a	name, plant	Asarum
Asarum	A-sa-rum	A-sa-rŏŏm	name, plant	Asaron
ascendens	a-SEN-denz	a-SKEN-dens	Latin	ascendo
Asclepias	as-KLĒ-pē-as	as-KLÄ-pē-as	name, myth	Asklepios
asiatica	ā-sē-A-ti-ka	ä-sē-A-ti-ka	name, place	Asia
Askellia	as-KE-lē-a	as-KE-lē-a	name, person	Löve, Áskell
Asparagaceae	as-pa-ra-GĀ-sē-ē	as-pa-ra-GÄ-kā-ī	name, plant	Asparagus
Asparagus	a-SPA-ra-gus	a-SPA-ra-gŏŏs	name, plant	Asparagus
asper	AS-per	AS-per	Latin	asper
asperifolia	a-spe-ri-FŌ-lē-a	a-spe-ri-FŌ-lē-a	Latin	asper
Asperugo	a-spe-RŪ-gō	a-spe-ROO-gō	Latin	asper
Asperula	a-SPE-rū-la	a-SPE-roo-la	Latin	asper
asperum	A-spe-rum	A-spe-rŏŏm	Latin	asper
Aspleniaceae	as-plē-ni-Ā-sē-ē	as-plā-nē-Ä-kā-ī	name, plant	Asplenium
Asplenium	a-SPLĒ-nē-um	a-SPLÄ-nē-ŏŏm	Greek	a
Aster	A-ster	A-ster	Greek	aster
Asteraceae	as-te-RĀ-sē-ē	as-te-RÄ-kā-ī	name, plant	Aster
Astragalus	a-STRA-ga-lus	a-STRA-ga-lŏŏs	Greek	astragalos
athabascensis	a-tha-bas-KEN-sis	a-ta-bas-KEN-sis	name, place	Athabasca
atherodes	a-the-RŌ-dēz	a-te-RŌ-dās	Greek	ather
athrostachya	ath-rō-STA-kē-a	at-rō-STA-kē-a	Greek	athroos
Athyriaceae	a-thi-ri-Ā-sē-ē	a-tē-rē-Ä-kā-ī	name, plant	Athyrium

Root 1 Meaning	Root 2	Root 2 Meaning / (referring to)
the type genus		
state of Arkansas, USA	anus	from or of
leadwort, a genus in the Leadwort Family		
ancient name for horseradish		
sternutator, that which causes sneezing		
spice, flavoring		
a Greek goddess		
wormwood, a genus in the Aster Family	folium	leaf
classical name used by Pliny for herbs known as 'goat's beard'		
reed, cane	aceus	with, like, pertaining to
reed, cane	aceus	with, like, pertaining to
reed, cane	aceus	with, like, pertaining to
arable, ploughed land, a field	ense	of a place or country
arable, ploughed land, a field	ensis	of a place or country
wild-ginger, a Birthwort Family genus	folium	leaf
ancient name for wild-ginger		
climb or ascend		
Greek god of medicine		
continent of Asia	ica	belonging to
1916-1994, an Icelandic botanist		
the type genus		
ancient name for species of this genus		
rough, uneven, harsh		
rough, uneven, harsh	folium	leaf
rough, uneven, harsh		
rough, uneven, harsh	ula	diminutive
rough, uneven, harsh		
the type genus		
without, not	splynos	spleen (used as medicine for the spleen)
star		(star-like flowerheads)
the type genus		
ankle bone		(the shape of seeds, pods or leaves was likened to an ankle-bone)
region around Lake Athabasca, nAB-SK	ensis	of a place or country
spike or ear of wheat	odes	like, resembling
crowded, assembled	stachys	spike, ear of grain (crowded spikes)
the type genus		

PRONUNCIATION & DERIVATION

Scientific Name	English Latin Pronunctiaion	Reconstructed Latin Pronunciation	Root Source	Root 1
Athyrium	a-THI-rē-um	a-TI-rē-õõm	Greek	a
Atocion	a-TŌ-shē-on	a-TŌ-kē-on	unknown	unknown
atratiformis	a-tra-ti-FOR-mis	a-tra-ti-FOR-mis	Latin	atra
atribarba	a-tri-BAR-ba	a-tri-BAR-ba	Latin	atra
Atriplex	A-tri-pleks	A-tri-pleks	name, plant	Atriplex
atrocinctus	a-trō-SINK-tus	a-trō-KINK-tõõs	Latin	atro
atropurpurea	a-trō-pur-PŪR-rē-a	a-trō-põõr-POO-rā-a	Latin	atro
atrosquama	a-trō-SKWÂ-ma	a-trō-SKWÂ-ma	Latin	atro
atrovirens	a-trō-VI-renz	a-trō-WI-rens	Latin	atro
aucuparia	ä-kū-PÂ-rē-a	ow-koo-PÂ-rē-a	Latin	aucupo
aurantiaca	ä-ran-TĒ-a-ka	ow-ran-TĒ-a-ka	Latin, New	aurantium
aurea	Ä-rē-a	OW-rā-a	Latin	aureus
aureum	Ä-rē-um	OW-rā-õõm	Latin	aureus
aureus	Ä-rē-us	OW-rā-õõs	Latin	aureus
austiniae	ÄS-ti-ni-ē	OWS-ti-ni-ī	name, person	Austin, R.
australis	äs-TRÄ-lis	ows-TRÄ-lis	Latin	australis
austriaca	äs-TRĒ-a-ka	ows-TRĒ-a-ka	name, place	Austria
austromontana	äs-trō-mon-TÄ-na	ows-trō-mon-TÄ-na	Latin	australis
autumnale	ä-tum-NÄ-lē	ow-tõõm-NÄ-lā	Latin	autumnalis
Avena	a-VĒ-na	a-WÄ-na	name, plant	Avena
aviculare	a-vi-kū-LÄ-rē	a-wi-koo-LÄ-rā	Latin	avicula
axillaris	ak-si-LÄ-ris	ak-si-LÄ-ris	Latin	axillaris
Axyris	AK-si-ris	AK-si-ris	Greek	axyros
backii	BA-kē-ī	BA-kē-ē	name, person	Back, Sir George
Bacopa	ba-KŌ-pa	ba-KŌ-pa	name, plant	Bacopa
baffinensis	ba-fi-NEN-sis	ba-fi-NEN-sis	name, place	Baffin
balsamea	bol-SÄ-mē-a	bal-SÄ-mā-a	Latin	balsameus
balsamifera	bol-sa-MI-fe-ra	bal-sa-MI-fe-ra	Latin	balsameus
Balsaminaceae	bal-sa-mi-NÄ-sē-ē	bal-sa-mē-NÄ-kā-ī	name, plant	Balsamina
Balsamorhiza	BOL-sa-mō-RĪ-za	bol-sa-mō-HRĒ-za	Greek	balsameus
balticus	BAL-ti-kus	BAL-ti-kõõs	name, place	Baltic
banksiana	bank-sē-Â-na	bank-sē-Â-na	name, person	Banks, Joseph
Barbarea	bar-ba-RĒ-a	bar-ba-RÄ-a	name, person	St. Barbara
barbarum	BAR-ba-rum	BAR-ba-rõõm	Latin	barbarus
barbatus	bar-BÄ-tus	bar-BÄ-tõõs	Latin	barba

Root 1 Meaning	Root 2	Root 2 Meaning / (referring to)
without, not	thurium	shield (the enclosed sori or the non-peltate indusium)
black	forma	shape, form
black	barba	beard
the ancient name for orache		
very dark	cinctum	girdle, belt
very dark	purpureus	purple
very dark	squama	scale
very dark	vireo	to be green
catching birds	ia	pertaining to
orange	ica	belonging to
gold, golden		
gold, golden		
gold, golden		
1832-1919, a self-taught botanist	ae	of, belonging to
southern		
country of Austria	iaca	belonging to
southern	montanus	of mountains, mountainous
autumn	alis	of, like
ancient name for oats		
little bird	aris	relating to, possessing
of an axil, from *axilla*, armpit	aris	relating to, possessing
unshorn		
1796-1878, British naval officer, explorer of the Canadian Arctic, naturalist, artist	ii	of, belonging to
taken from the aboriginal name used by natives in French Guiana		
Baffin Island, NWT, Canada	ensis	of a place or country
fragrant balsam resin		
fragrant balsam resin	fera	bearing, carrying
the type genus		
fragrant balsam resin	rhiza	root
Baltic Sea, Europe	us	of
1743-1820, KEW director, on Captain Cook's 1st circumnavigation	anus	from or of
a saint of the 4th century A.D.		(the seed was traditionally sown on her feast day, Dec. 4)
foreign and therefore outlandish		
beard	atus	with, like (the long, weak hairs)

PRONUNCIATION & DERIVATION

Scientific Name	English Latin Pronunctiaion	Reconstructed Latin Pronunciation	Root Source	Root 1
barclayi	BAR-klā-ī	BAR-klā-ē	name, person	Barclay, George
barrattiana	ba-ra-tē-Ā-na	ba-ra-tē-Ä-na	name, person	Barratt, Joseph
Bassia	BA-sē-a	BA-sē-a	name, person	Bassi, Ferdinando
bebbiana	be-bē-Ā-na	be-bē-Ä-nĂ	name, person	Bebb, Michael Schuck
bebbii	BE-bē-ī	BE-bē-ē	name, person	Bebb, Michael Schuck
Beckmannia	bek-MA-nē-a	bek-MA-nē-a	name, person	Beckmann, Johann
beeringianum	bē-rin-jē-Ā-num	bē-rin-gē-Ä-nŏŏm	name, place	Bering
bellidifolia	be-li-di-FŌ-lē-a	be-li-di-FŌ-lē-a	Latin	bellis
Berberidaceae	ber-be-ri-DĀ-sē-ē	ber-be-rē-DÄ-kā-ī	name, plant	Berberis
Berberis	BER-ber-is	BER-ber-is	name, plant	Berberys
berchtoldii	berk-TŌL-dē-ī	berk-TŌL-dē-ē	name, person	Berchtold, (Count) F. von
berlandieri	ber-lan-dē-E-rī	ber-lan-dē-E-rē	name, person	Berlandier, Jean Louis
Berteroa	ber-te-RŌ-a	ber-te-RŌ-a	name, person	Bertero, Carlo Giuseppe
berteroi	BER-ter-rō-ī	BER-ter-rō-ē	name, person	Bertero, Carlo Giuseppe
Betula	BE-tū-la	BE-too-la	name, plant	Betula
Betulaceae	be-tū-LĀ-sē-ē	be-too-LÄ-kā-ī	name, plant	Betula
bicknellii	bik-NE-lē-ī	bik-NE-lē-ē	name, person	Bicknell, Eugene P.
bicolor	BĪ-ko-lor	BĒ-ko-lor	Latin	bi
Bidens	BĪ-denz	BĒ-dens	Latin	bi
biennis	bī-E-nis	bē-E-nis	Latin	bi
biflora	bī-FLŌ-ra	bē-FLŌ-ra	Latin	bi
bifolia	bī-FŌ-lē-a	bē-FŌ-lē-a	Latin	bi
bifoliata	bī-fō-lē-Ā-ta	bē-fō-lē-Ä-ta	Latin	bi
bifolium	bī-FŌ-lē-um	bē-FŌ-lē-ŏŏm	Latin	bi
biglumis	bī-GLŪ-mis	bē-GLOO-mis	Latin	bi
bimundorum	bī-mun-DŌ-rum	bē-mŏŏn-DŌ-rŏŏm	Latin	bi
bipinnatifida	bī-pi-na-TI-fi-da	bē-pi-na-TI-fi-da	Latin	bi
bipinnatum	bī-pi-NĀ-tum	bē-pi-NÄ-tŏŏm	Latin	bi

Root 1 Meaning	Root 2	Root 2 Meaning / (referring to)
naturalist on the ship Sulphur	i	of, belonging to
1796-1882, a Connecticut and Pennsylvania geologist	anus	from or of
1710-1774, Italian botanist and Prefect of the Bologna Botanical Garden		
1833-1895, a distinguished American specialist on willows	anus	from or of
1833-1895, a distinguished American specialist on willows	ii	of, belonging to
1739-1811, German scientific and author, coined the word 'technology'		
Bering Sea, west of Alaska, USA	anus	from or of
daisy	folium	leaf
the type genus		
ancient Arabic name for the berries of barberry		
1781-1876, wrote Oekonomischtechnische Flora Bohmens	ii	of, belonging to
1805-1925, Swiss botanist, collected in Texas	i	of, belonging to
1798-1831, Italian botanist/physician		
1798-1831, Italian botanist/physician	i	of, belonging to
ancient name for a birch		
the type genus		
1858-1925, a New York banker, amateur botanist	ii	of, belonging to
two, twice	color	hue, tint
two, twice	dens	tooth (2 bristles on achene tips)
two, twice	annus	year
two, twice	floris	flower
two, twice	folium	leaf
two, twice	folium	leaf
two, twice	folium	leaf
two, twice	gluma	bract, hull, husk two-glumed)
two, twice	mundus	neat, elegant
two, twice	pinnatus	feathered
two, twice	pinnatus	feathered

PRONUNCIATION & DERIVATION

Scientific Name	English Latin Pronunctiaion	Reconstructed Latin Pronunciation	Root Source	Root 1
Bistorta	bī-STŌR- ta	bē-STŌR- ta	Latin	bi
bistortoides	bī-stor-TŌĪ-dēz	bē-stor-TŌĒ-dās	name, plant	Bistorta
bisulcatus	bī-sul-KĀ-tus	bē-sõõl-KĀ-tõõs	Latin	bi
blitoides	bli-TŌĪ-dēz	blē-TŌĒ-dās	name, plant	Blitum
Blitum	BLĪ-tum	BLĒ-tõõm	Latin	blitum
Blysmopsis	blis-MOP-sis	blis-MOP-sis	name, plant	Blysmus
bodinii	bō-DIN-ē-ī	bō-DIN-ē-ē	name, person	Bodin, J.E.
Boechera	BŌ-ke-ra, BĒ-ke-ra	BOI-ke-ra	name, person	Boecher, Tyge W.
bolanderi	BO-lan-de-rī	bo-LAN-de-rē	name, person	Bolander, Henry N.
Bolboschoenus	bōl-bō-SKĒ-nus	bōl-bō-SKOI-nõõs	Greek + name, plant	bolbos
boothii	BOO-thē-ī	BOO-tē-ē	name, person	Booth, William B.
Boraginaceae	bō-ra-ji-NĀ-sē-ē	bō-ra-gē-NĀ-kā-ē	name, plant	Borago
Borago	bō-RĀ-gō	bō-RĀ-gō	Latin	burra
boreale	bo-rē-Ā-lē	bo-rā-Ä-lā	Latin	borealis
borealis	bo-rē-Ā-lis	bo-rā-Ä-lis	Latin	borealis
Boschniakia	bosh-nē-Ā-kē-a	bosk-nē-Ä-kē-a	name, person	Boschniak, A.K.
Botrychium	bō-TRI-kē-um	bō-TRI-kē-õõm	Greek	botrys
Botrypus	bō-TRI-pus	bō-TRI-põõs	Greek	botrys
bourgovii	bur-GŌ-vē-ī	bõõr-GŌ-wē-ē	name, person	Bourgeau, E.
Bouteloua	boo-te-LOO-a	boo-te-LOO-a	name, person	Bouteloua, C. & E.
brachyantherum	bra-kē-AN-the-rum	bra-kē-AN-te-rõõm	Greek	brachy
brachycarpa	bra-kē-KAR-pa	bra-kē-KAR-pa	Greek	brachy
brachycarpum	bra-kē-KAR-pum	bra-kē-KAR-põõm	Greek	brachy
brachyphylla	bra-kē-FI-la	bra-kē-PI-la	Greek	brachy
brachypodum	bra-kē-PO-dum	bra-KI-po-dõõm	Greek	brachy
bracteata	brak-tē-Ā-ta	brak-tā-Ä-ta	Latin	bractea
bracteosa	brak-tē-Ō-sa	brak-tā-Ō-sa	Latin	bractea
Brasenia	bra-SĒ-nē-a	bra-SĀ-nē-a	name, person	Brasen, Christoph
Brassica	BRA-si-ka	BRA-si-ka	name, plant	Brassica
Brassicaceae	bra-si-KĀ-sē-ē	bra-sē-KĀ-kā-ē	name, plant	Brassica
Braya	BRĀ-ya	BRĀ-ē-a	name, person	de Bray, F.G.
brevicaudatus	bre-vi-kä-DĀ-tus	bre-wi-kow-DĀ-tõõs	Latin	brevis
brevifolia	bre-vi-FŌ-lē-a	bre-wi-FŌ-lē-a	Latin	brevis
brevior	BRĒ-vē-or	BRĀ-wē-or	Latin	brevio
brevissimus	bre-VI-si-mus	bre-WI-si-mõõs	Latin	brevis

Root 1 Meaning	Root 2	Root 2 Meaning / (referring to)
two, twice	tortus	twisted (twisted roots)
bistort, a genus in the Buckwheat Family	oides	like, resembling
two, twice	sulcus	furrow, groove
old name for strawberry blite or spinach	oides	like, resembling
a kind of spinach		(its similarity to spinach)
saltmarsh flat-sedge	opsis	appearance (resembling Blysmus)
botanist/collector in California	ii	of, belonging to
1909–1983, Danish botanist, biologist, plant ecologist, and phytogeographer		
1831-1897, California Botanist, collected in Yosemite National Park	ii	of, belonging to
a bulb, onion	Schoenus	a genus in the Sedge Family
1804-1874, close friend of Scottish collector David Douglas	ii	of, belonging to
the type genus		
rough hair, a shaggy cloak		(the hairy leaves)
north wind, northern		
north wind, northern	alis	of, like
1786-1831, Russian botanist		
a bunch of grapes		(the form of the fertile spike)
a bunch of grapes	pous	foot
1813-1877, French Canada plant collector	ii	of, belonging to
1774-1842 & 1776-1813, Claudio & Estéban professors of horticulture in Madrid, Spain		
short	anther	pollen-bearing part of a stamen
short	karpos	fruit
short	karpos	fruit
short	phyllon	leaf
short	podos	foot (the short-stalked spikelets)
scale, small leaf	atus	with
scale, small leaf	osus	with the quality or nature of
1738-1774, Danish surgeon, started Moravian Mission of Nain in Labrador		
ancient name for cabbage		
the type genus		
1765-1832, of Rouen		
short, little	cauda	tail
short, little	folium	leaf
to shorten		
short, little	issimus	superlative, very

PRONUNCIATION & DERIVATION

Scientific Name	English Latin Pronunctiaion	Reconstructed Latin Pronunciation	Root Source	Root 1
brevistyla	bre-vi-STĪ-la	bre-wi-STĒ-la	Latin	brevis
breweri	BROO-er-ī	BRE-we-rē	name, person	Brewer, William H.
Brickellia	bri-KE-lē-a	bri-KE-lē-a	name, person	Brickell, John
britannica	bri-TA-ni-ka	bri-TA-ni-ka	Latin	Brittanus
Briza	BRĪ-za	BRĒ-za	name, plant	Briza
Bromus	BRŌ-mus	BRŌ-mōōs	name, plant	Bromos
brunnescens	bru-NE-senz	brōō-NE-skens	Latin, Medieval	bruneus
bufonius	bū-FŌ-nē-us	boo-FŌ-nē-ōōs	Latin	bufo
bulbifera	bul-BI-fe-ra	bōōl-BI-fe-ra	Greek	bolbos
bulbosa	bul-BŌ-sa	bōōl-BŌ-sa	Latin	bolbos
Bupleurum	bū-PLĒŪ-rum	boo-PLĒOO-rōōm	Greek	bous
bursa-pastoris	BUR-sa pas-TŌ-ris	BOOR-sa pas-TŌ-ris	Latin	bursa
bursifolia	bur-si-FŌ-lē-a	bōōr-si-FŌ-lē-a	name, plant	Bursa
Butomaceae	bū-tō-MĀ-sē-ē	boo-tō-MĀ-kā-ī	name, plant	Butomus
Butomus	BŪ-tō-mus	BOO-tō-mōōs	Greek	bous
buxbaumii	buks-BÄ-mē-ī	bōōks-BOW-mē-ē	name, person	Buxbaum, F.
Cabombaceae	ka-bom-BĀ-sē-ē	ka-bom-BÄ-kā-ī	name, plant	Cabomba
Cactaceae	kak-TĀ-sē-ē	kak-TÄ-kā-ī	name, plant	Cactus
caerulea	sē-RŪ-lē-a	kī-ROO-lā-a	Latin	caerulea
caespitosa	sē-spi-TŌ-sa	kī-spi-TŌ-sa	Latin	caespes
caespitosus	sē-spi-TŌ-sus	kī-spi-TŌ-sōōs	Latin	caespes
Calamagrostis	ka-la-ma-GRO-stis	ka-la-ma-GRO-stis	Greek	kalamos
Calamovilfa	ka-la-mō-VIL-fa	ka-la-mō-WIL-fa	Greek + name, plant	kalamos
calceoliformis	kal-sē-ō-li-FŌR-mis	kal-kā-ō-li-FŌR-mis	Latin	calceolus
calcicola	kal-si-KŌ-la	kal-ki-KŌ-la	Latin	calcis
calderi	KĀL-de-rī	KAL-de-rē	name, person	Calder, James Alexander
californica	ka-li-FŌR-ni-ka	ka-li-FŌR-ni-ka	name, place	California
californicus	ka-li-FŌR-ni-kus	ka-li-FŌR-ni-kōōs	name, place	California
Calla	KA-la	KA-la	name, plant	Calla
Callitriche	ka-LI-tri-kē	ka-LI-trē-kā	Greek	kallos
callitrix	KA-li-triks	KA-li-triks	Greek	kallos
Calochortus	ka-lō-KOR-tus	ka-lō-KOR-tōōs	Greek	kallos
Caltha	KAL-tha	KAL-ta	name, plant	Caltha
calycantha	ka-li-KAN-tha	ka-li-KAN-ta	Greek	kalyx

Root 1 Meaning	Root 2	Root 2 Meaning / (referring to)
short, little	stylos	pillar, column, style
1828-1910, Yale prof. of agriculture, first State Botanist in California	i	of, belonging to
1749-1809, Irish physician, amateur botanist in Savannah, Georgia		
Britain	ica	belonging to
ancient name for some grass or grain, (possibly rye) in Macedonia		
ancient name for oats (*Avena* spp.), also meaning 'food'		
brown, tony, dark	escens	in the process of becoming
toad	ium	like or of, diminutive
a swelling, bud or tuber	fera	bearing, carrying
a swelling, bud or tuber	osus	with (the shape of the corm)
ox	pleuron	rib
a purse, bag	pastor	shepherd, herdsman
a plant genus	folia	leaves (with leaves like *Bursa*)
the type genus		
ox, cow	temno	to cut (the sword-like leaves)
1900-1979	ii	of, belonging to
the type genus		
the type genus		
blue, sky blue		
turf, grassy field	osus	with the quality or nature of
turf, grassy field	osus	with the quality or nature of
reed, stalk	agrostis	grass
reed, stalk	Vilfa	name used by Adanson for a genus of grasses
little shoe	forma	shape, form
stone, lime	cola	dweller
Canadian botanist, Dept. of Agric., Ottawa, Flora of Queen Charlotte Is.	i	of, belonging to
state of California, USA	ica	belonging to
state of California, USA	ica	belonging to
ancient name of unknown origin used by Pliny		
beautiful	trichos	hair (the lovely slender stems)
beautiful	trix	maker
beautiful	chortus	grass, fodder
ancient name for a yellow-flowered plant, probably the common marigold		
cup, outer envelope of a flower, calyx	anthos	flower

PRONUNCIATION & DERIVATION

Scientific Name	English Latin Pronunctiaion	Reconstructed Latin Pronunciation	Root Source	Root 1
calycosa	ka-li-KŌ-sa	ka-li-KŌ-sa	Greek	kalyx
calyculata	ka-li-kū-LÄ-ta	ka-li-koo-LÄ-ta	Latin	calyculus
Calypso	ka-LIP-sō	ka-LIP-sō	name, myth	Kalypso
Calystegia	ka-li-STE-jē-a	ka-li-STE-gē-a	Greek	kalyx
Camassia	ka-MA-sē-a	ka-MA-sē-a	Native American	camas
Camelina	ka-ME-li-na	ka-ME-li-na	Greek	chamai
Campanula	kam-PAN-ū-la	kam-PA-noo-la	Latin	campana
Campanulaceae	kam-pa-nū-LÄ-sē-ē	kam-pa-noo-LÄ-kā-ī	name, plant	Campanula
campanularia	kam-pa-nū-LÄ-rē-a	kam-pa-noo-LÄ-rē-a	Latin	campana
campestre	kam-PE-strē	kam-PE-strā	Latin	campester
campestris	kam-PE-stris	kam-PE-stris	Latin	campester
cana	KÄ-na	KÄ-na	Latin	canus
Canadanthus	ka-na-DAN-thus	ka-na-DAN-tõõs	name, place	Canada
canadense	ka-na-DEN-sē	ka-na-DEN-sā	name, place	Canada
canadensis	ka-na-DEN-sis	ka-na-DEN-sis	name, place	Canada
candida	KAN-di-da	KAN-di-da	Latin	candidus
canescens	ka-NE-senz	ka-NE-skens	Latin	canus
Cannabaceae	ka-na-BÄ-sē-ē	ka-na-BÄ-kā-ī	name, plant	Cannabis
cannabinum	ka-NA-bi-num	ka-NA-bi-nõõm	name, plant	Cannabis
Cannabis	KA-na-bis	KA-na-bis	name, plant	Cannabis
capensis	ka-PEN-sis	ka-PEN-sis	name, place	Cape
capillacea	ka-pi-LÄ-sē-a	ka-pi-LÄ-kā-a	Latin	capillus
capillare	ka-pi-LÄ-rē	ka-pi-LÄ-rā	Latin	capillus
capillaris	ka-pi-LÄ-ris	ka-pi-LÄ-ris	Latin	capillus
capitata	ka-pi-TÄ-ta	ka-pi-TÄ-ta	Latin	caput
capitatum	ka-pi-TÄ-tum	ka-pi-TÄ-tõõm	Latin	caput
Capnoides	kap-NOI-dēz	kap-NŌ-ī-dēs	Greek	kapnodis
Caprifoliaceae	kap-ri-fō-li-Ä-s-ē	kap-rē-fō-lē-Ä-kā-ī	name, plant	Caprifolium
Capsella	kap-SE-la	kap-SE-la	Latin	capsa
Caragana	ka-ra-GÄ-na	ka-ra-GÄ-na	name, plant	Caragana
Cardamine	kar-DA-mi-nē	kar-DA-mi-nā	name, plant	Kardamon or Kardamis
cardiaca	kar-DĒ-a-ka	kar-DĒ-a-ka	Latin	cardiacus
cardiophyllus	kar-dē-ō-FI-lus	kar-dē-ō-PI-lõõs	Greek	kardia
Carduus	KAR-dū-us	KAR-doo-õõs	name, plant	Carduus
Carex	KÄ-reks	KÄ-reks	name, plant	Carex

Root 1 Meaning	Root 2	Root 2 Meaning / (referring to)
cup of a flower, calyx	osus	with, like (the full calyx)
cup of a flower, calyx	atus	with, like (calyx-like bracts)
mythical sea nymph who kept Odysseus on her island for 7 years		
cup, outer envelope of a flower, calyx	stege	covering (broad bracts that conceal the calyx)
sweet		
dwarf, on the ground	linon	flax ()
bell	ula	diminutive
the type genus		
little bell	ia	pertaining to
of fields, flat, level		
of fields, flat, level		
grey, ash-colored, hoary		
Canada	anthos	flower
country of Canada	ense	of a place or country
country of Canada	ensis	of a place or country
shiny white, bright, radiant		
grey, ash-colored, hoary	escens	in the process of becoming
the type genus		
hemp, a genus in the Hemp Family		
ancient name for hemp, possibly from the Persian name, Kanab		
Cape Good Hope, South Africa (or any cape)	ensis	of a place or country
hair, capillary	aceus	with, like, pertaining to
hair, capillary	aris	relating to, possessing
hair, capillary	aris	relating to, possessing
head, in a head or dense cluster	atus	with, like
head, in a head or dense cluster	atus	with, like
smoky		(the smoky smell of some species)
the type genus		
box	ella	diminutive (the seedpods)
traditional Mongolian name for this plant		
ancient name for an unknown cress (plant in the Mustard Family)		
suffering from heartburn		
heart	phyllon	leaf
ancient name for plumeless-thistle		
ancient name for sedges		

PRONUNCIATION & DERIVATION

Scientific Name	English Latin Pronunctiaion	Reconstructed Latin Pronunciation	Root Source	Root 1
carolinianum	ka-ro-li-nē-Ā-num	ka-ro-li-nē-Ä-nõõm	name, place	Carolina
carota	ka-RŌ-ta	ka-RŌ-ta	Latin	carota
Carthamus	KAR-tha-mus	KAR-ta-mõõs	Arabic	quartom or qurtom
carthusiana	kar-thū-sē-Ā-na	kar-too-sē-Ä-na	Latin, Medieval	cartusiensis
Carum	KĀ-rum	KÄ-rõõm	name, plant	Careum
carvi	KAR-vī	KAR-wē	name, plant	Karawya, Caria
Caryophyllaceae	ka-rē-o-fi-LĀ-sē-ē	ka-rā-o-pē-LÄ-kā-ī	name, plant	Caryophyllus
Cassiope	ka-SĪ-o-pē	ka-SĒ-o-pā	name, myth	Cassiope
castaneus	kas-TĀ-nē-us	kas-TÄ-nā-õõs	Latin	castanea
Castilleja	ka-sti-LĒ-ya	ka-sti-LÄ-ya	name, person	Castillejo, Domingo
castlegarensis	ka-sel-ga-REN-sis	ka-sel-ga-REN-sis	name, place	Castlegar
Catabrosa	ka-ta-BRŌ-sa	ka-ta-BRŌ-sa	Greek	catabrosis
cataria	ka-TĀ-rē-a	ka-TÄ-rē-a	name, plant	cataria
catenata	ka-te-NĀ-ta	ka-te-NÄ-ta	Latin	catena
cathartica	ka-THAR-ti-ka	ka-TAR-ti-ka	Greek	karthesis
Ceanothus	sē-a-NŌ-thus	kā-a-NŌ-tõõs	name, plant	Keanothus
Celastraceae	se-las-TRĀ-sē-ē	ke-las-TRÄ-kā-ī	name, plant	Celastrus
celosioides	sē-lō-sē-ŌĪ-dēz	kā-lō-sē-ŌĒ-dās	name, plant	Celosia
Centaurea	sen-tä-RĒ-a	ken-tow-RÄ-a	name, myth	Centaurie
Cerastium	se-RA-stē-um	ke-RA-stē-õõm	Greek	keratos
Ceratocephala	se-ra-tō-SE-fa-la	ke-ra-tō-KE-pa-la	Greek	keratos
ceratophorum	se-ra-tō-FŌ-rum	ke-ra-tō-PŌ-rõõm	Greek	kerasos
Ceratophyllaceae	se-ra-tō-fi-LĀ-sē-ē	ke-ra-tō-pē-LÄ-kā-ī	name, plant	Ceratophyllum
Ceratophyllum	se-ra-tō-FI-lum	ke-ra-tō-PI-lõõm	Greek	keratos
cereale	se-rē-Ā-lē	ke-rā-Ä-la	name, myth	Cerealis
cereum	SĒ-rē-um	KÄ-rā-õõm	Latin	cereus
cernua	SER-nū-a	KER-noo-a	Latin	cernuus
cernuum	SER-nū-um	KÄR-noo-õõm	Latin	cernuus
cespitosa	se-spi-TŌ-sa	ke-spi-TŌ-sa	Latin	caespes
cespitosum	se-spi-TŌ-sum	ke-spi-TŌ-sõõm	Latin	caespes
Chaenactis	kē-NAK-tis	kī-NAK-tis	Greek	chaino

Root 1 Meaning	Root 2	Root 2 Meaning / (referring to)
state of Carolina, USA	anus	from or of
ancient name for this plant		
to paint		(the colorful flowers or its use as a dye)
Chartreuse, France, home of the Carthusian order, an ascetic religious order	anus	from or of
ancient name for a plant in the Carrot Family, probably caraway		
ancient Arabic name for these seeds		
the type genus		
wife of King Cepheus, mother of Andromeda, later changed into a constellation		
chestnut colored		
1744-1793, botany professor in Cadiz, Spain		
mountainous region in seBC-swAB	ensis	of a place or country
a devouring, an eating		(the erose/'nibbled' floral bracts (glumes/lemmas)
old generic name for this plant		(originally 'of cats', which are attracted to it)
chain	atus	with, like
cleansing, cathertic		
ancient name for some spiny plant, obscure, probably misspelled		
the type genus		
cock's-comb, an Amaranth Family genus	oides	like, resembling
the Centaur Chiron		(Chiron discovered the medicinal uses of knapweed)
horn		(the slender, curved capsules)
horn	kephale	head (the seed heads covered in tiny horns [pointed achenes])
horn	phoreus	bearer
the type genus		
horn	phyllon	leaf (the stiff, narrow leaf segments)
of Ceres, the goddess of grain and fruits		
waxy		
drooping, leaning forward, nodding		
drooping, leaning forward, nodding		
turf, grassy field	osus	with the quality or nature of
turf, grassy field	osus	with the quality or nature of
to gape, open	actis	ray (the ray-like, outer disk florets with flaring mouths)

PRONUNCIATION & DERIVATION

Scientific Name	English Latin Pronunctiaion	Reconstructed Latin Pronunciation	Root Source	Root 1
Chaenorrhinum	kē-no-RĪ-num	kī-nō-HRĒ-nŏŏm	Greek	chaino
chalcedonica	kal-se-DO-ni-ka	kal-ke-DO-ni-ka	name, place	Chalcedon
chalepense	ka-le-PEN-sē	ka-lā-PEN-sā	name, place	Aleppo
Chamaedaphne	ka-mē-DAF-nē	ka-mī-DAP-nā	Greek	chamai
chamaedrys	ka-MĒ-drēz	ka-MĪ-drās	Greek	chamai
chamaejasme	ka-mē-JAS-mē	ka-mī-YAS-mā	Greek	chamai
chamaemorus	ka-mē-MŌ-rus	ka-mī-MŌ-rŏŏs	Greek	chamai
Chamaenerion	ka-mē-NĒ-rē-on	ka-mī-NĀ-rē-on	Greek	chamai
Chamaerhodos	ka-MĒ-ro-dos	ka-MĪ-hro-dos	Greek	chamai
chamissonis	ka-mi-SŌ-nis	ka-mi-SŌ-nis	name, person	Chamisso, Adelbert von
chamomilla	ka-mō-MI-la	ka-mō-MI-la	name, plant	Chamomilla
cheiranthoides	kī-ran-THŌĪ-dēz	kā-ran-TŌĒ-dās	Latin	Cheiranthus
Chelidonium	ke-li-DŌ-nē-um	ke-li-DŌ-nē-ŏŏm	Greek	chelidon
Chenopodiastrum	kē-nō-pō-dē-A-strum	ke-nō-pō-dē-A-strŏŏm	name, plant	Chenopodium
Chenopodium	kē-nō-PŌ-dē-um	ke-nō-PŌ-dē-ŏŏm	Greek	chen
Cherleria	ker-LE-rē-a	ker-LE-rē-a	name, person	Cherler, John Henry
Chimaphila	ki-MA-fi-la	kē-MA-pi-la	Greek	cheima
chlorantha	klo-RAN-tha	klo-RAN-ta	Greek	chloros
chordorrhiza	kor-dō-RĪ-za	kor-dō-RĒ-za	Greek	chorde
Chorispora	kō-RI-spō-ra	kō-RI-spō-ra	Greek	choris
chrysocarpa	krī-sō-KAR-pa	krē-sō-KAR-pa	Greek	chrysos
Chrysosplenium	kri-sō-SPLĒ-nē-um	kri-sō-SPLĀ-nē-ŏŏm	Greek	chrysos
cicer	SI-ser	KI-ker	name, plant	Cicer
Cichorium	si-KŌ-rē-um	ki-KŌ-rē-ŏŏm	name, plant	Kichore
Cicuta	si-KŪ-ta	kē-KOO-ta	name, plant	Cicuta
cicutarium	si-kū-TĀ-rē-um	ki-koo-TĀ-rē-ŏŏm	name, plant	Cicuta
cilianensis	si-lē-a-NEN-sis	ki-lē-a-NEN-sis	name, place	Ciliani
ciliata	si-lē-Ā-ta	ki-lē-Ä-ta	Latin	cilium
ciliatum	si-lē-Ā-tum	ki-lē-Ä-tŏŏm	Latin	cilium
ciliatus	si-lē-Ā-tus	ki-lē-Ä-tŏŏs	Latin	cilium
ciliolatum	si-lē-ō-LĀ-tum	ki-lē-ō-LÄ-tŏŏm	Latin	cilium
cinereus	si-NE-rē-us	ki-NE-rā-ŏŏs	Latin	cinereus
Cinna	SI-na	KĒ-na	name, plant	Kinna
Circaea	sir-SĒ-a	kir-KĪ-a	name, myth	Circe

Root 1 Meaning	Root 2	Root 2 Meaning / (referring to)
to gape, open	rhinos	snout (the open throat of the corolla)
city of Chalcedon, Turkey	ica	belonging to
a city in northwestern Syria	ense	place of origin
low, dwarf	daphne	laurel tree, after the nymph Daphne became a laurel to escape Apollo
low, dwarf	drys	oak
low, dwarf	jasmin	jasmine-like
low, dwarf	morum	mulberry
low, dwarf	nerion	oleander
low, dwarf	rhodon	rose
1781-1838, French-German-American, on Eschscholtz's 1816 expedition	is	with, like
chamomile, a genus in the Aster Family		
old name for wallflower (Erysimum cheiri)	oides	like, resembling
the swallow		(flowers appeared with the swallows, swallows used it to improve vision)
goosefoot plant	astrum	like, similar to
goose	podos	foot (the shape of some leaves)
botanist who assisted J. Bauhinia in his history of plants		
winter weather	philos	loving (perennially green leaves and the popular name, wintergreen)
green	anthos	flower
twine, rope, gut, musical instrument string	rhiza	root
separate, asunder	spora	seed (the widely spaced seeds)
gold	karpos	fruit
gold	splenios / splynos	a pad or compress/spleen (golden flowers & leaves/medicinal qualities)
chickpea, a genus in the Pea Family		
from the Arabic name for chicory		
ancient name for a poisonous plant in the Carrot Family		
poison-hemlock, a Carrot Family genus	ium	like or of, diminutive
Ciliani estate, Italy	ensis	of a place or country
eyelash	atus	with, like
eyelash	atus	with, like
eyelash	atus	with, like
eyelash	latus	side (the fringed sides)
ash-colored		
ancient name by Dioscorides for a grass		
Greek goddess/enchantress, daughter of Helios, the Sun God, and Perse		

PRONUNCIATION & DERIVATION

Scientific Name	English Latin Pronunctiaion	Reconstructed Latin Pronunciation	Root Source	Root 1
cirrhosa	si-RŌ-sa	ki-HRŌ-sa	Greek	kirrhos
Cirsium	SIR-sē-um	KIR-sē-õõm	Greek	kirsos
Cistaceae	sis-TĀ-sē-ē	kēs-TÄ-kā-ī	name, plant	Cistus
clavatum	klā-VĀ-tum	klā-WÄ-tõõm	Latin	clava
Claytonia	klā-TŌ-nē-a	klä-TŌ-nē-a	name, person	Clayton, John
Clematis	KLE-ma-tis, kle-MA-tis	KLE-ma-tis	Greek	cklema
Cleomaceae	klē-ō-MĀ-sē-ē	klā-ō-MÄ-kā-ī	name, plant	Cleome
Clintonia	klin-TŌ-nē-a	klin-TŌ-nē-a	name, person	Clinton, DeWitt
clintonii	klin-TŌ-nē-ī	klin-TŌ-nē-ē	name, person	Clinton, DeWitt
coarctatum	kō-ark-TĀ-tum	kō-ark-TÄ-tõõm	Latin	coarctatum
coccinea	kok-SI-nē-a	ko-KI-nā-a	Latin	coccineus
Coeloglossum	sē-lo-GLO-sum	koi-lō-GLO-sõõm	Latin + Greek	coelum
collina	ko-LĪ-na	kō-LĒ-na	Latin	collinus
Collinsia	ko-LIN-shē-a	ko-LIN-sē-a	name, person	Collins, Zaccheus
collinsii	ko-LIN-sē-ī	ko-LIN-sē-ē	name, person	Collins, Zaccheus
Collomia	ko-LŌ-mē-a	ko-LŌ-mē-a	Greek	kolla
columbiana	ko-lum-bē-Ā-na	ko-lõõm-bē-Ä-na	name, place	Columbia
columnifera	ko-lum-NI-fe-ra	ko-lõõm-NI-fe-ra	Latin	columna
Comandra	ko-MAN-dra	ko-MAN-dra	Greek	kome
Comarum	KO-ma-rum	KO-ma-rõõm	name, plant	Komaros
comata	ko-MĀ-ta	ko-MÄ-ta	Latin	comatus
Commelinaceae	ko-me-li-NĀ-sē-ē	ko-me-lē-NÄ-kā-ī	name, plant	Commelina
communis	ko-MŪ-nis	ko-MOO-nis	Latin	communis
commutata	ko-mū-TĀ-ta	ko-moo-TÄ-ta	Latin	commutatus
commutatus	ko-mū-TĀ-tus	ko-moo-TÄ-tõõs	Latin	commutatus
compactum	kom-PAK-tum	kom-PAK-tõõm	Latin	compactus
complanatum	kom-pla-NĀ-tum	kom-pla-NÄ-tõõm	Latin	complanatus
compositus	kom-PO-si-tus	kom-PO-si-tõõs	Latin	compositus
compressa	kom-PRE-sa	kom-PRE-sa	Latin	compressus
concinna	kon-SI-na	kon-KI-na	Latin	concinnus
concinnoides	kon-si-NŌĪ-dēz	kon-ki-NŌĒ-däs	Latin	concinnus
condensata	kon-den-SĀ-ta	kon-den-SÄ-ta	Latin	condensus
confertus	kon-FUR-tus	kon-FER-tõõs	Latin	confertus
confusus	kon-FŪ-sus	kon-FOO-sõõs	Latin	confusus
congesta	kon-JES-ta	kon-GES-ta	Latin	congestus

Root 1 Meaning	Root 2	Root 2 Meaning / (referring to)
tendrils	osus	with the quality or nature of
swollen vein or welt		(its use as a remedy for this)
the type genus		
a club	atus	with (the club-shaped strobilus)
1686(1694?)-1773/4, early US botanist, contributed to Gronovius' Flora Virginica		
a shoot, a long lithe branch		
the type genus		
1769-1828, naturalist, governor of NY		
1769-1828, naturalist, governor of NY	ii	of, belonging to
to narrow, hem in or pack together		
scarlet, red like a berry		
heaven, sky	glossa	tongue
hilly		
1764-1831, V.P. Philadelphia Acad. of Natural Sciences, studied lower plants		
V.P. Philadelphia Acad. of Natural Sciences, studied lower plants		
glue (sticky wet seed coats)		
the land discovered by Christopher Columbus (usually western NAm)	anus	from or of
pillar	fera	bearing, carrying
hair	andros	male (the hairy base of the stamens)
ancient name for strawberry tree (*Arbutus unedo*)		(the similar fruits)
with long, shaggy hair	atus	with, like
the type genus		
shared by all or many, public, common		
change, alteration		
change, alteration		
thick, firm, compressed, concentrated		
flattened, leveled		(the flattened banches)
compound, blended, orderly		
compressed, flattened		
beautiful, elegant, symmetrical,		
beautiful, elegant, symmetrical	oides	like, resembling
crowded, packed	atus	with, like
pressed together, crowded, thick		
confused, disorderly		
heap, mass		

PRONUNCIATION & DERIVATION

Scientific Name	English Latin Pronunctiaion	Reconstructed Latin Pronunciation	Root Source	Root 1
Conimitella	ko-ni-mi-TE-la	ko-ni-mē-TE-la	Latin + name, plant	konicos
Conium	ko-NĒ-um	ko-NĒ-ŏŏm	name, plant	Koneion
conjugens	KON-ju-genz	KON-yŏŏ-gens	Latin	con
connectilis	ko-NEK-ti-lis	ko-NEK-ti-lis	Latin	con
conoidea	ko-NÕĒ-dē-a	ko-NÕĒ-dā-a	Greek	konnos
Conringia	kon-RIN-jē-a	kon-RIN-gē-a	name, person	Conring, Hermann
conspicua	kon-SPI-kū-a	kon-SPI-koo-a	Latin	conspicuus
contermina	kon-TUR-mi-na	kon-TÕÕR-mi-na	Latin	conterminus
continentalis	kon-ti-nen-TĀ-lis	kon-ti-nen-TÄ-lis	Latin	continent
contorta	kon-TŌR-ta	kon-TŌR-ta	Latin	contortus
Convallaria	kon-va-LÃ-rē-a	kon-wa-LÄ-rē-a	Latin	convallis
convallarioides	kon-va-la-rē-ŌĪ-dēz	kon-wa-la-rē-ŌĒ-dās	Latin	convallaria
Convolvulaceae	kon-vol-vū-LÃ-sē-ē	kon-wol-woo-LÄ-kā-ī	name, plant	Convolvulus
Convolvulus	kon-VOL-vū-lus	kon-WOL-woo-lŏŏs	Latin	convolvere
convolvulus	kon-VOL-vū-lus	kon-WOL-woo-lŏŏs	Latin	convolvulus
Coptidium	kop-TI-dē-um	kōp-TI-dē-ŏŏm	Greek	koptos
Coptis	KOP-tis	KOP-tis	Greek	koptos
Corallorhiza	ko-ra-lō-RĪ-za	ko-ra-lō-HRĒ-za	Greek	korallion
cordata	kor-DÃ-ta	kor-DÄ-ta	Latin	cordatus
cordifolia	kor-di-FŌ-lē-a	kor-di-FŌ-lē-a	Latin	cordatus
cordillerana	kor-di-le-RÃ-na	kor-di-le-RÄ-na	Spanish	cordillera
Coreopsis	ko-rē-OP-sis	ko-rā-OP-sis	Greek	koris
Corispermum	ko-ri-SPER-mum	ko-ri-SPER-mŏŏm	Greek	koris
Cornaceae	kor-NÃ-sē-ē	kor-NÄ-kā-ī	name, plant	Cornus
corniculatus	kor-ni-kū-LÃ-tus	kor-ni-koo-LÄ-tŏŏs	Latin	corniculum
Cornus	KOR-nus	KOR-nŏŏs	Latin	cornu
cornuta	kor-NŪ-ta	kor-NOO-ta	Latin	cornu
Corydalis	kō-RI-da-lis	ko-RI-da-lis	Greek	korydalos
Corylus	KO-ri-lus	KO-ri-lŏŏs	Greek	korys
corymbosa	ko-rim-BŌ-sa	ko-rim-BŌ-sa	Latin	corymbus
Cota	KŌ-ta	KŌ-ta	name, plant	Cota
Cotoneaster	ko-to-nē-A-ster	ko-to-nē-A-ster	name, plant	Cotonium
cotula	KO-tū-la	KO-too-la	Latin	cotula
cous	KOOS	KOOS	name, place	Cous, Coos
cracca	KRA-ka	KRA-ka	name, plant	Cracca

Root 1 Meaning	Root 2	Root 2 Meaning / (referring to)
cone-shaped (referring to the hypanthium)	mitella	mitrewort, a Saxifrage Family genus
ancient name for poison-hemlock		
with, together	jungatus	join, connect
with, together	necto	tie, bind
cone	oides	like, resembling
1606-1661(1681), professor of phisucs and medicine at Helmstadt, Germany		
visible, remarkable, conspicuous		
neighboring, adjacent		
continuous mass of land		(transcontinental range)
intricate, complex, twisted		
valley		
lily-of-the-valley, a Lily Family genus	oides	like, resembling
the type genus		
twine around		
bindweed, a Morning-Glory Family genus		
cut	idium	small, diminutive (the finely cut leaves)
cut		(the deeply cut leaves)
coral	rhiza	root
heart-shaped		(the shape of the leaves)
heart-shaped	folium	leaf
a chain of mountains		
bug, bedbug	opsis	appearance (the tick-like achenes)
bug, bedbug	sperma	seed (the achenes resembling ticks)
the type genus		
little horn	atus	with, like
horn		(the hardness of the wood)
horn		
crested or tufted lark		(crested hood or to the spur)
helmet		(the protective involucre)
a cluster of fruit or flowers	osus	with the quality of (flowers in corymbs)
possibly from pre-Linnaean generic name later used as a specific epithet		
quince, a genus of Asian plants	aster	a kind of (quince-like leaves, maybe)
a small cup		(the hollow at the base of the leaves)
a small island in the Aegean		
a kind of pulse, a genus in the Pea Family		

PRONUNCIATION & DERIVATION

Scientific Name	English Latin Pronunctiaion	Reconstructed Latin Pronunciation	Root Source	Root 1
crassicarpus	kra-si-KAR-pus	kra-si-KAR-põõs	Latin	crassus
crassifolia	kra-si-FŌ-lē-a	kra-si-FŌ-lē-a	Latin	crassus
Crassulaceae	kra-sū-LÄ-sē-ē	kra-soo-LÄ-kā-ī	name, plant	Crassula
Crataegus	kra-TĒ-gus	kra-TĪ-gõõs	Greek	kratos
crawei	KRÄ-ē-ī	KRÄ-wā-ē	name, person	Crawe, I. B.
crawfordii	KRÄ-fōr-dē-ī	krä-FŌR-dē-ē	name, person	Crawford, E.A.
crenulatum	kre-nū-LÄ-tum	krä-noo-LÄ-tõõm	Latin, Medieval	crena
Crepis	KRE-pis	KRÄ-pis	Greek	krepis
crispa	KRI-spa	KRI-spa	Latin	crispus
crispus	KRI-spus	KRI-spõõs	Latin	crispus
cristata	kris-TÄ-ta	kris-TÄ-ta	Latin	cristatus
cristatum	kris-TÄ-tum	kris-TÄ-tõõm	Latin	cristatus
Crucihimalaya	krū-si-hi-ma-LÄ-a	kroo-ki-hi-ma-LÄ-a	name, plant + name, place	Crucifer
crus-galli	krūs-GA-lē	kroos-GA-lä	Latin	crus
cryptandrus	krip-TAN-drus	krip-TAN-drõõs	Greek	krypto
Cryptantha	krip-TAN-tha	krip-TAN-ta	Greek	krypto
Cryptogramma	krip-to-GRA-ma	krip-to-GRA-ma	Greek	krypto
cserei	SĒ-rē-ī	KSÄ-rä-ē	name, person	Cserei, W. Von
Cucurbitaceae	kū-kur-bi-TÄ-sē-ē	koo-kõõr-bē-TÄ-kā-ī	name, plant	Cucurbita
culinaris	ku-li-NÄ-ris	kõõ-li-NÄ-ris	Latin	culina
cuneata	ku-nē-Ä-ta	kõõ-nā-Ä-ta	Latin	cuneatus
Cupressaceae	kū-pre-SÄ-sē-ē	koo-pre-SÄ-kā-ī	name, plant	Cupressus
cupressocollina	kū-PRE-sō-ko-LĪ-na	koo-PRE-sō-kō-LĒ-na	name, plant	Cupressus
curassavicum	kū-ra-SA-vi-kum	koo-ra-SA-wi-kõõm	name, place	Curacao
curtipendula	kur-ti-PEN-du-la	kõõr-ti-PEN-dõõ-la	Latin	curtus
curtiseta	kur-ti-SĒ-ta	kõõr-ti-SÄ-ta	Latin	curtus
curvatus	kur-VÄ-tus	kõõr-WÄ-tõõs	Latin	curvus
curvipes	KUR-vi-pēz	KOOR-wi-pās	Latin	curvus
Cuscuta	kus-KŪ-ta	kõõs-KOO-ta	name, plant	Cuscuta
cusickii	ku-SI-kē-ī	kõõ-SI-kē-ē	name, person	Cusick, W. C.
cuspidata	kus-pi-DÄ-ta	kõõs-pi-DÄ-ta	Latin	cuspidatus
cyanus	SĪ-a-nus	KĒ-a-nõõs	Greek	kyanos
Cyclachaena	sī-kla-KĒ-na	kē-kla-KĪ-na	Greek	cyclos
cylindrica	si-LIN-dri-ka	ki-LIN-dri-ka	Latin	cylindrus
cymbalaria	sim-ba-LÄ-rē-a	kim-ba-LÄ-rē-a	Latin	cymbalum
Cymopterus	sī-MOP-te-rus	kē-MŌP-te-rõõs	Greek	kuma

Root 1 Meaning	Root 2	Root 2 Meaning / (referring to)
thick, plump, dense	carpo	fruit
thick, plump, dense	folium	leaf
the type genus		
strength		(the unusually strong wood)
1792-1847, its discoverer	ei	of, belonging to
early settler in the White Mountains	ii	of, belonging to
notch	atus	with, like (scalloped edges)
sandal or boot, ancient unknown plant		
curled, wrinkled		
curled, wrinkled		
crested, plumed		
crested, plumed		
a plant in the Mustard Family	Himalaya	Himalayas, where it was were found
leg, shin	gallus	rooster (a cock's spur)
hide, hidden	andros	male
hide, hidden	anthos	flower (tiny, cleistogamous flwrs of some)
hide, hidden	gramma	line (sori under down-rolled leaf edges)
patron of Baumgarten in 1816	i	of, belonging to
the type genus		
kitchen, food		
wedge-shaped		(the shape of the leaves)
the type genus		
Latin name for the Italian cypress tree	collinus	hilly
Curaçao, a Caribbean island in Dutch West Indies (Netherlands Antilles)	ica	belonging to
short	pendulus	hanging
short	seta	bristle, hair
bent	atus	with, like
bent	ipes	stalked
an Arabic name for dodder		
1842-1922, plant collector	ii	of, belonging to
pointed	atus	with, like
dark-blue		
a circle	achaena	achene
cylinder, roller		
cymbal		(the round, cymbal-shaped leaves)
wave (wavy)	pteron	wing

41

PRONUNCIATION & DERIVATION

Scientific Name	English Latin Pronunctiaion	Reconstructed Latin Pronunciation	Root Source	Root 1
Cynoglossum	sī-no-GLO-sum	kē-nō-GLŌ-sõõm	Greek	kynos
Cyperaceae	sī-per-Ā-sē-ē	kē-per-Ä-kā-ī	name, plant	Cyperus
Cyperus	si-PĒ-rus, SĪ-pe-rus	ki-PĀ-rõõs	name, plant	Kypeiros
Cypripedium	si-pri-PĒ-dē-um	ki-pri-PĀ-dē-õõm	name, myth	Kypris
Cystopteridaceae	sis-top-te-ri-DĀ-sē-ē	kēs-top-te-rē-DÄ-kā-ī	name, plant	Cystopteris
Cystopteris	sis-TOP-te-ris	kis-TOP-te-ris	Greek	kystis
Dactylis	DAK-ti-lis	DAK-ti-lis	Greek	daktylos
Dalea	DĀ-lē-a	DÄ-lē-a	name, person	Dale, Samuel
dalmatica	dal-MA-ti-ka	dal-MA-ti-ka	name, place	Dalmatia
Danthonia	dan-THŌ-nē-a	dan-TŌ-nē-a	name, person	Danthione, E.
daphnoides	daf-NŌĪ-dēz	dap-NŌĒ-dās	name, plant	Daphne
Dasiphora	da-SI-fo-ra	da-SI-pō-ra	Greek	dasys
dasycarpum	da-sē-KAR-pum	da-sē-KAR-põõm	Greek	dasys
Datura	da-TŪ-ra	da-TOO-ra	name, plant	Dhatura
Daucus	DÄ-kus	DOW-kõõs	name, plant	Daucus
dawsonensis	dä-so-NEN-sis	dä-so-NEN-sis	name, place	Dawson
dawsonii	dä-SO-nē-ī	dä-SO-nē-ē	name	Dawson
decapetala	de-ka-PE-ta-la	de-ka-PE-ta-la	Greek	dekas
decumbens	dē-KUM-benz	dā-KOOM-bens	Latin	decumbo
deflexa	dē-FLEK-sa	dē-FLEK-sa	Latin	de
delphinifolium	del-fi-ni-FŌ-lē-um	del-pi-ni-FŌ-lē-õõm	name, plant	Delphinium
delphiniifolium	del-fi-nē-i-FŌ-lē-um	del-pi-nē-i-FŌ-lē-õõm	name, plant	Delphinium
Delphinium	del-FI-nē-um	del-PI-nē-õõm	Greek	delphinos
deltoides	del-TŌĪ-dēz	del-TŌĒ-dās	Greek	delta
demersum	de-MER-sum	de-MER-sõõm	Latin	demergo
dendroideum	den-DRŌĪ-dē-um	den-DRŌĒ-dā-õõm	Greek	dendron
Dendrolycopodium	den-drō-lī-kō-PŌ-dē-um	den-drō-lē-kō-PŌ-dē-õõm	Greek + name, plant	dendron
Dennstaedtiaceae	den-stēd-ti-Ā-sē-ē	den-stēd-tē-Ä-kā-ī	name, plant	Dennstaedtia
densa	DEN-sa	DEN-sa	Latin	densus
densiflorum	den-si-FLŌ-rum	den-si-FLŌ-rõõm	Latin	densus
densifolia	den-si-FŌ-lē-a	den-si-FŌ-lē-a	Latin	densus
dentata	den-TÄ-ta	den-TÄ-ta	Latin	dentatus
dentatus	den-TÄ-tus	den-TÄ-tõõs	Latin	dentatus
depauperata	dē-pä-pe-RÄ-ta	dā-pow-pe-RÄ-ta	Latin	de
Deschampsia	dā-SHAMP-sē-a	des-KAMP-sē-a	name, person	Deschamps, Louis Auguste

42

Root 1 Meaning	Root 2	Root 2 Meaning / (referring to)
dog	glossa	tongue (shape and texture of the leaves)
the type genus		
the ancient name for sedge/ cyperus		
Aphrodite/Venus, goddess of love	pedilon	sandal, shoe (flowers like tiny slippers)
the type genus		
bladder or sac	pteris	fern (the hood-like indusium)
finger		(finger-like branches of the panicle)
1659-1739, English doctor, botanist, wrote books on medicinal plants		
Dalmatia region on Adriatic side of Balkan Peninsula, Europe	ica	belonging to
botanist in early 1800s in Marseilles, France		
Arabic name for the shrub mezereum	oides	like, resembling
shaggy, thick-haired	phoreus	bearer (hairy achenes & receptacles)
shaggy, thick-haired	karpos	fruit
Hindustani name for Jimsonweed		
ancient name for a Carrot Family species		
Dawson City or Dawson Range, YT	ensis	of a place or country
Dawson City or Dawson Range, YT	ii	of, belonging to
ten	petalum	petal
to lie down or recline, falling in battle		
down from, out from	flexus	curved, twisted (the down-turned buds or sepals)
larkspur, a genus in the Buttercup Family	folium	leaf
larkspur, a genus in the Buttercup Family	folium	leaf
dolphin		(flower shape likened to that of a dolphin)
the fourth letter of the Greek alphabet	oides	like, resembling
to sink, plunge or dip		(submerged plants)
tree	oides	like, resembling
tree	Lycopodium	clubmoss
the type genus		
thick, close, crowded, dense		
thick, close, crowded, dense	floris	flower
thick, close, crowded, dense	folium	leaf
toothed, serrated		
toothed, serrated		
down from, out from	pauperatus	make poor, deprive
1776-1842(±), surgeon-naturalist on ship to find Jean-François de Galaup		

PRONUNCIATION & DERIVATION

Scientific Name	English Latin Pronunctiaion	Reconstructed Latin Pronunciation	Root Source	Root 1
Descurainia	des-kū-RĀ-nē-a	des-koo-RĀ-nē-a	name, person	Déscourain, F.
desiccatum	de-si-KĀ-tum	de-si-KĀ-tōōm	Latin	dessico
detonsa	dē-TON-sa	dā-TŌN-sa	Latin	de
deweyana	doo-ē-Ā-na	de-wā-Ä-na	name, person	Dewey, C.
diandra	dī-AN-dra	dē-AN-dra	Greek	di
diandrus	dī-AN-drus	dē-AN-drōōs	Greek	di
Dianthus	dī-AN-thus	dē-AN-tōōs	Greek	dios
Dichanthelium	di-kan-THE-lē-um	di-kan-TE-lē-ōōm	Greek	dicha
didymocarpa	di-dē-mō-KAR-pa	di-dē-mō-KAR-pa	Greek	didymos
Dieteria	dī-e-TE-rē-a	dē-e-TE-rē-a	Greek	di
diffusa	di-FŪ-za	di-FOO-sa	Latin	diffusus
Digitaria	di-ji-TĀ-rē-a	di-gi-TÄ-rē-a	Latin	digitus
digyna	DI-ji-na	DI-gi-na	Greek	di
dilatata	dī-lā-TĀ-ta	dē-lā-TÄ-ta	Latin	dilatus
dimorpha	dī-MŌR-fa	dē-MŌR-pa	Greek	di
dioica	dī-Ō-ī-ka	dē-Ō-ē-ka	Greek	di
dioicus	dī-Ō-ī-kus	dē-Ō-ē-kōōs	Greek	di
Diphasiastrum	di-fa-shē-A-strum	di-pa-sē-A-strōōm	name, plant	Diphasium
Diplotaxis	di-plō-TAK-sis	di-plō-TAK-sis	Greek	diplous
discoidea	dis-KŌĪ-dē-a	dis-KŌĒ-dā-a	Latin	discus
discolor	DIS-ko-lor	DIS-ko-lor	Latin	dis
disjunctum	dis-JUNK-tum	dis-YŌŌNK-tōōm	Latin	diiungo
disperma	dīs-PER-ma	dēs-PER-ma	Greek	di
dissectum	di-SEK-tum	di-SEK-tōōm	Latin	dissectus
distans	DIS-tanz	DIS-tans	Latin	distantia
distentifolium	dis-ten-ti-FŌ-lē-um	dis-ten-ti-FŌ-lē-ōōm	Latin	distentus
Distichlis	dis-TIK-lis	dis-TIK-lis	Greek	di
divaricatum	dī-va-ri-KĀ-tum	dē-wa-ri-KÄ-tōōm	Latin	divaricatus
divergens	dī-VER-jenz	dē-WĀR-gens	Latin	divergium
diversifolius	dī-ver-si-FŌ-lē-us	dē-wer-si-FŌ-lē-ōōs	Latin	diversus
dodecandra	dō-de-KAN-dra	dō-de-KAN-dra	Greek	dodeka
Doellingeria	dē-lin-JĒ-rē-a	doi-lin-GÄ-rē-a	name, person	Dollinger, Th.
dortmanna	dort-MA-na	dort-MA-na	name, person	Dortmann
Douglasia	DUG-la-sē-a	dōōg-LÄ-sē-a	name, person	Douglas, David
douglasii	dug-LA-sē-ī	dōōg-LA-sē-ē	name, person	Douglas, David
Downingia	DOW-nin-jē-a	DOO-nin-gē-a	name, person	Downing, Andrew J.

44

Root 1 Meaning	Root 2	Root 2 Meaning / (referring to)
1658-1740, French apothecary & botanist		
dry up, drain	atus	with, like
down from, out from	tonsor	barber (meaning shorn, bare)
1784-1867, US botany prof, studied *Carex*	anus	from or of
two	andros	male
two	andros	male
divine	anthos	flower (flower of Zeus / Jove)
bifid, in two	anthele	tuft or plume of a reed
double, twin, testicle	karpos	fruit
two	etos	year (2-year life cycle)
extensive, spread out, dispersed		
finger		(the finger-like spikes)
two	gyne	female, woman
spread, expanded	atus	with (the wide base of the lip)
two	morphe	form, shape
two	oikos	home, house (male and female flowers on separate plants)
two	oikos	home, house (male and female flowers on separate plants)
early name for a Lycopodiaceae genus	astrum	like, similar to
double	taxis	row (the double row of seeds)
flat, cirsular plate, disc	oides	resembling (fromlack of rays)
twice	color	hue, tint
separated, disjunct		
two	sperma	seed
cut up, dissected		
distance, remoteness (widely-spaced)		
swollen, filled up, distended	folium	leaf
two	stichos	line, row (the 2-ranked leaves)
spread apart		
point of separation		(spreading widely from the centre)
different	folium	leaf
twelve	andros	male ()
botanical explorer		
an early Dutch apothecary	anus	from or of
1798-1834, Scottish botanist, collected in nwNAm, discovered Douglas fir		
1798-1834, Scottish botanist, collected in nwNAm, discovered Douglas fir	ii	of, belonging to
1815-1852, the first great American landscape gardener and horticulturist		

PRONUNCIATION & DERIVATION

Scientific Name	English Latin Pronunctiaion	Reconstructed Latin Pronunciation	Root Source	Root 1
Draba	DRĀ-ba	DRĂ-ba	Greek	drabe
draba	DRĀ-ba	DRĂ-ba	Latin	draba
Dracocephalum	dra-kō-SE-fa-lum	dra-ko-KE-pa-lŏŏm	Greek	drakonis
dracunculus	dra-KUN-kū-lus	dra-KŎŎN-koo-lŏŏs	Greek	drakonis
drepanoloba	dre-pa-nō-LŌ-ba	dre-pa-nō-LŌ-ba	Greek	drepanon
Drosera	DRO-se-ra	DRO-se-ra	Greek	droseros
Droseraceae	dro-se-RĀ-sē-ē	drō-se-RĂ-kā-ī	name, plant	Drosera
drummondiana	DRU-mon-dē-Ā-na	DROO-mon-dē-Ă-na	name, person	Drummond, Thomas D.
drummondii	DRU-mon-dē-ī	drŏŏ-MON-dē-ē	name, person	Drummond, Thomas D.
Dryas	DRĪ-as	DRĒ-as	Latin	dryad
Drymocallis	drī-mo-KA-lis	drē-mo-KA-lis	Greek	drys
Dryopteridaceae	drī-op-te-ri-DĀ-sē-ē	drē-ōp-te-rē-DĂ-kā-ī	name, plant	Dryopteris
Dryopteris	drī-OP-te-ris	drē-OP-te-ris	Greek	drys
dryopteris	drī-OP-te-ris	drē-OP-te-ris	Latin	dryopteris
dubia	DŪ-bē-a	DOO-bē-a	Latin	dubius
dubius	DŪ-bē-us	DOO-bē-ŏŏs	Latin	dubius
dudleyi	DUD-lē-ī	DŎŎD-lē-ē	name, person	Dudley, William R.
dulcamara	dul-ka-MĀ-ra	dŏŏl-ka-MĂ-ra	Latin	dulcis
duriuscula	dū-rē-ŪS-ku-la	doo-rē-OOS-ŏŏ-la	Latin	duriusculus
durum	DŪ-rum	DOO-rŏŏm	Latin	durus
Dyssodia	di-SŌ-dē-a	di-SŌ-dē-a	Greek	dysodia
eatonii	Ē-to-nē-ī	Ē-to-nē-ē	name, person	Eaton, David C.
eburnea	e-BUR-nē-a	e-BOOR-nā-a	Latin	eburneus
echinata	e-kī-NĀ-ta	e-kē-NĂ-ta	Greek	echinos
Echinochloa	e-kī-no-KLŌ-a	e-kē-no-KLŌ-a	Greek	echinos
Echinocystis	e-kī-nō-SIS-tis	e-kē-nō-KIS-tis	Greek	echinos
echinospora	e-kī-nō-SPŌ-ra	e-kē-nō-SPŌ-ra	Greek	echinos
echioides	e-kē-ŌĪ-dēz	e-kē-ŌĒ-dās	name, plant	Echium
Echium	E-kē-um	E-kē-ŏŏm	Greek	echis
edule	e-DŪ-lē	e-DOO-lā	Latin	edulis
effusa	e-FŪ-za	e-FOO-sa	Latin	effusus
egaliksensis	e-ga-lik-SEN-sis	e-ga-lik-SEN-sis	name, place	Egalik
Elaeagnaceae	e-lē-ag-NĀ-sē-ē	e-lī-ag-NĂ-kā-ī	name, plant	Elaeagnus
Elaeagnus	e-lē-AG-nus	e-lī-AG-nŏŏs	Greek + name, plant	elaia

Root 1 Meaning	Root 2	Root 2 Meaning / (referring to)
acrid, sharp		(the burning taste of the leaves)
Draba, a genus in the Mustard Family		
dragon	kephale	head (the gaping flower was likened to a dragon head)
dragon	unculus	diminutive form
sickle	lobus	rounded projection, lobe
dewy		(the tiny drops [glands] on the leaves)
the type genus		
1790-1835, Scottish naturalist, on Franklin's ill-fated Arctic expedition	anus	from or of
1790-1835, Scottish naturalist, on Franklin's ill-fated Arctic expedition	ii	of, belonging to
wood-nymph, tree-nymph		(with leaves like tiny oak leaves, so this was the badge of the Dryads)
tree, thence woodland	kallos	beauty
the type genus		
tree, thence woodland	pteris	fern
woodfern, a Woodfern Family genus		
doubtful, uncertain, wavering		
doubtful, uncertain, wavering		
1849-1911, first botany professor and Botany Dept head at Stanford University	i	of, belonging to
sweet, pleasant	amarus	bitter
rather hard or harsh		
hard, tough, lasting		
disagreeable odour		(the smell of the plants)
1834-1885, an American botanist	ii	of, belonging to
of ivory, white as ivory		
sea urchin, hedgeog	atus	with, like
sea urchin, hedgehog	chloa	grass (spiny spikelets bristling with awns)
sea urchin, hedgehog	cystis	bladder (inflated, spine-covered fruits)
sea urchin, hedgeog	spora	seed
vipersbugloss, a genus in the Borage Family	oides	like, resembling
viper		(nutlets were likened to a viper's head)
eatable		
spread out, extensive		
Egalik Fjord, Greenland	ensis	of a place or country
the type genus		
olive	Agnos	the Greek name for Chaste-tree (leaves like those of a chaste-tree)

PRONUNCIATION & DERIVATION

Scientific Name	English Latin Pronunctiaion	Reconstructed Latin Pronunciation	Root Source	Root 1
elata	ē-LĀ-ta	ā-LÄ-ta	Latin	elatus
Elatinaceae	e-la-ti-NĀ-sē-ē	e-la-tē-NÄ-kā-ī	name, plant	Elatine
Elatine	e-LĀ-ti-nē	e-LÄ-ti-nā	name, plant	Elatine
elatus	ē-LĀ-tus	ā-LÄ-tõõs	Latin	elatus
elegans	E-le-ganz	E-le-gans	Latin	elegans
Eleocharis	e-lē-O-ka-ris	e-lē-O-ka-ris	Greek	helos
elliptica	e-LIP-ti-ka	e-LIP-ti-ka	Latin	ellipticus
ellipticus	e-LIP-ti-kus	e-LIP-ti-kõõs	Latin	ellipticus
Ellisia	e-LI-shē-a	e-LI-sē-a	name, person	Ellis, John
Elodea	e-LŌ-dē-a	e-LŌ-dā-a	Greek	helos
elongata	e-lon-GĀ-ta	e-lon-GÄ-ta	Latin	elongatus
Elyhordeum	e-li-HŌR-dē-um	e-li-HŌR-dē-õõm	name, plant	Elymus
elymoides	e-li-MŌĪ-dēz	e-li-MŌĒ-dās	name, plant	Elymus
Elymus	E-li-mus	E-li-mõõs	name, plant	Elymos
emersum	e-MER-sum	e-MER-sõõm	Latin	emergo
empetriformis	em-pe-tri-FŌR-mis	em-pe-tri-FŌR-mis	name, plant	Empetrum
Empetrum	em-PĒT-rum, EM-pet-rum	EM-pet-rõõm	Greek	en
enanderi	en-AN-de-rī	en-AN-de-rē	name, person	Enander, Sven J.
Endotropis	en-dō-TRŌ-pis	en-dō-TRŌ-pis	Greek	endon
engelmannii	en-gel-MA-nē-ī	en-gel-MA-nē-ē	name, person	Engelmann, George
ensifolius	en-si-FŌ-lē-us	en-si-FŌ-lē-õõs	Latin	ensis
epapillosa	e-pa-pi-LŌ-sa	e-pa-pi-LŌ-sa	Latin	e
epihydrus	e-pi-HĪ-drus	e-pē-HĒ-drõõs	Greek	epi
epigejos	e-pi-JĒ-yos	e-pi-GĒ-yos	Greek	epi
Epilobium	e-pi-LŌ-bē-um	e-pi-LŌ-bē-õõm	Greek	epi
epipsila	e-PIP-si-la	e-PIP-si-la	Greek	epi
Equisetaceae	ek-wi-sē-TĀ-sē-ē	ek-wē-sā-TÄ-kā-ī	name, plant	Equisetum
Equisetum	e-kwi-SĒ-tum	e-kwi-SÄ-tõõm	Latin	equus
Eragrostis	e-ra-GROS-tis	e-ra-GRŌS-tis	Greek	eros
erecta	ē-REK-ta	ā-REK-ta	Latin	erectus
erectum	ē-REK-tum	ā-REK-tõõm	Latin	erectus
Eremogone	e-re-MO-go-nē	e-re-MO-go-nā	Greek	eremo
eremophilus	e-re-MO-fi-lus	e-re-MO-pi-lõõs	Greek	eremo
Eremopyrum	e-re-mō-PĪ-rum	e-re-mō-PĒ-rõõm	Greek	eremo
eriantherus	e-rē-AN-the-rus	e-rē-AN-te-rõõs	Greek	erion
erianthum	e-rē-AN-thum	e-rē-AN-tõõm	Greek	erion
Ericaceae	e-ri-KĀ-sē-ē	e-rē-KÄ-kā-ī	name, plant	Erica

Root 1 Meaning	Root 2	Root 2 Meaning / (referring to)
exalted, elevated, tall	atus	with, like
the type genus		
ancient/classical name of a low, creeping plant with fir-like leaves		
exalted, elevated, tall		
elegant, fine, tasteful		
marsh, low ground, meadow	charis	grace, beauty (graceful plants)
elliptical, about twice as long as wide		
elliptical, about twice as long as wide		
1710?-1776, English botanist		
marsh, low ground		
prolonged		
wildrye	Hordeum	barley
wildrye, a genus in the Grass Family	oides	like, resembling
ancient name for millet		
to rise or emerge	um	from or of
crowberry	forma	shape, form
upon	petros	a stone, rock
1847-1928, Swedish clergyman, studied *Salix*	ii	of, belonging to
within, inner, absorbing or containing	tropis	hull, keel
809-1884, German-US physician and botanist, studied cacti, conifers, oaks	ii	of, belonging to
sword	folium	leaf
out of, from	papilla	nipple, bud (the lack of papillae)
upon	hydrios	of water
upon	geios	earth (the creeping stems/stolons)
upon	lobos	pod, capsule (the inferior ovary)
upon	psilos	bare, smooth
the type genus		
horse	seta	bristle, hair (resembles a horse's tail)
love	agrostis	grass (the common name, love-grass)
upright, erect		
upright, erect		
solitary or deserted	gone	pistil
solitary or deserted	philia	fondness, friendly love
solitary or deserted	pyros	grain, wheat
wool	anthos	flower
wool	anthos	flower
the type genus		

49

PRONUNCIATION & DERIVATION

Scientific Name	English Latin Pronunctiaion	Reconstructed Latin Pronunciation	Root Source	Root 1
Ericameria	e-ri-ka-MĀ-rē-a	e-ri-ka-MÄ-rē-a	Greek	Erica
ericoides	e-ri-KŌĪ-dēz	e-ri-KŌĒ-dās	name, plant	Erica
Erigeron	e-RI-je-ron	e-RI-ge-ron	Greek	eri
Eriocoma	e-rē-O-ko-ma	e-rē-O-kō-ma	Greek	erion
Eriogonum	e-rē-O-go-num	e-rē-O-go-nõõm	Greek	erion
Eriophorum	e-rē-O-fō-rum	e-rē-O-pō-rõõm	Greek	erion
eriopoda	e-rē-O-pō-da	e-rē-O-pō-da	Greek	erion
Erodium	e-RŌ-dē-um	e-RŌ-dē-õõm	Greek	erodios
Eruca	e-RŪ-ka	e-ROO-ka	name, plant	Eruca
Erucastrum	e-rū-KA-strum	e-rõõ-KA-strõõm	name, plant	Eruca
Eryngium	e-RIN-jē-um	e-RIN-gē-õõm	name, plant	Eryngium
Erysimum	e-RI-si-mum	e-RI-si-mõõm	Greek	erysthai
Erythranthe	e-ri-THRAN-thē	e-ri-TRAN-tā	Greek	erythro
Erythronium	e-ri-THRŌ-nē-um	e-ri-TRŌ-nē-õõm	Greek	erythro
erythropoda	e-ri-thrō-PŌ-da	e-ri-trō-PŌ-da	Greek	erythro
erythrospermum	e-ri-thrō-SPER-mum	e-ri-trō-SPER-mõõm	Greek	erythro
Eschscholtzia	e-SHŌL-tzē-a	es-KŌLT-sē-a	name, person	Eschscholtz, J.F.G. von
eschscholtziana	e-SHŌL-tzē-Ā-na	es-KŌLT-sē-Ä-na	name, person	Eschscholtz, JF.G. von
eschscholtzii	e-SHŌL-tzē-ī	es-KŌLT-sē-ē	name, person	Eschscholtz, JF.G. von
Escobaria	es-kō-BĀ-rē-a	es-kō-BÄ-rē-a	name, person	Escobar Zerman
esculentum	es-kū-LEN-tum	es-koo-LEN-tõõm	Latin	esculentus
Eucephalus	ēū-SE-fa-lus	ēoo-KE-pa-lõõs	Greek	eu
eucosmus	ēū-KOS-mus	ēoo-KOS-mõõs	Greek	eu
Euphorbia	ēū-FOR-bē-a	ēoo-POR-bē-a	name, person	Euphorbus
Euphorbiaceae	ēū-for-bi-Ā-sē-ē	ēoo-por-bē-Ä-kā-ī	name, plant	Euphorbia
Euphrasia	ēū-FRĀ-shē-a	ēoo-PRÄ-sē-a	Greek	euphrasia
europaea	ēū-rō-PĒ-a	ēoo-rō-PĪ-a	name, place	Europe
Eurybia	ēū-RI-bē-a	ēoo-RI-bē-a	Greek	eurybia
eurycarpum	ēū-ri-KAR-pum	ēoo-ri-KAR-põõm	Greek	eurys
Euthamia	ēū-THĀ-mē-a	ēoo-TÄ-mē-a	Greek	eu
Eutrema	ēū-TRĒ-ma	ēoo-TRÄ-ma	Greek	eu
Eutrochium	ēū-TRŌ-kē-um	ēoo-TRŌ-kā-õõm	Greek	eu

Root 1 Meaning	Root 2	Root 2 Meaning / (referring to)
heath	meris	division of part (the heath-like leaves)
heath, a genus in the Heath Family	oides	like, resembling
early, spring	geron	old man (flowers change rapidly to hoary seed-heads)
wool	kome	hair of the head, mane (the tuft of silky hair on the lemma)
wool	gonu	knee, joint (woolly plants with swollen joints)
wool	phoros	bearing
wool	podos	foot, stem (the woolly plant base, maybe)
heron		(the long, heron-like beak of the fruit)
classical name for a caterpillar, thus caterpillar plant		
garden-rocket, species of *Eruca*	astrum	like, similar to
ancient name for a prickly plant/thistle		
help or save		(its supposed healing qualities)
red	anthos	flower (red flowers of first species)
red		(reddish flowers or leaves)
red	podos	foot, stem
red	sperma	seed
1793-1831, Estonia botanist/surgeon, on Russian Pacific exped. (1816,1824)		
1793-1831, Estonia botanist/surgeon, on Russian Pacific exped. (1816,1824)	anus	from or of
1793-1831, Estonia botanist/surgeon, on Russian Pacific exped. (1816,1824)	ii	of, belonging to
1874-1949, Mexican Nat'l Agriculture School, Ciudad Juarez Agric. School		
edible		
well or good	kephale	head (the calyx forming a lid over the flower buds)
good, agreeable, well	kosmos	order, ornament, universe
Greek physician of Juba II, King of Mauretania/Numidia		(a strongly laxative plant, named in honour of Juba's rather corpulent pyhsician)
the type genus		
gladness, cheerfulness, delight		(ancient healers used it to preserve eyesight and so bring gladness)
the continent of Europe	ae	of, belonging to
far and wide, wide spreading		
broad, widespread	karpos	fruit
good, normal	thameios	crowded (densely clustered heads)
good, normal	trema	hole, opening
good, normal	trocho	wheel-like (the leaf whorls)

PRONUNCIATION & DERIVATION

Scientific Name	English Latin Pronunctiaion	Reconstructed Latin Pronunciation	Root Source	Root 1
exarata	ek-sa-RÄ-ta	ek-sa-RÄ-ta	Latin	exaratus
exigua	ek-SI-gŭ-a	ek-SI-goo-a	Latin	exiguus
expansa	ek-SPAN-sa	ek-SPAN-sa	Latin	ex
exscapa	ek-SKÄ-pa	ek-SKÄ-pa	Latin	ex
Fabaceae	fa-BÄ-sē-ē	fa-BÄ-kā-ī	name, plant	Faba
Fagopyrum	fa-gō-PĪ-rum	fa-go-PĒ-rōōm	name, plant	Fagus
falcatum	fal-KÄ-tum	fal-KÄ-tōōm	Latin	falcatus
Fallopia	fa-LŌ-pē-a	fa-LŌ-pē-a	name, person	Fallopio, G.
famelica	fa-MĒ-li-ka	fa-MÄ-li-ka	Latin	famelicus
farriae	FA-rē-ē	FA-rē-ī	name, person	Farr, Edith M.
fasciculatum	fa-si-kŭ-LÄ-tum	fas-ki-koo-LÄ-tōōm	Latin	fasciculus
fatua	FA-tŭ-a	FA-too-a	Latin	fatuus
fendleri	FEND-le-rī	FEND-le-rē	name, person	Fendler, Augustus
fendleriana	fend-le-rē-Ä-na	fend-le-rē-Ä-na	name, person	Fendler, Augustus
ferruginea	fe-rŭ-JĪ-nē-a	fe-roo-GĒ-nä-a	Latin	ferrugineus
Festuca	fe-STŪ-ka	fe-STOO-ka	name, plant	Festuca
festucacea	fe-stŭ-KÄ-sē-a	fe-stoo-KÄ-kā-a	name, plant	Festuca
filifolia	fi-li-FŌ-lē-a	fi-li-FŌ-lē-a	Latin	filum
filifolius	fi-li-FŌ-lē-us	fi-li-FŌ-lē-ōōs	Latin	filum
filiformis	fi-li-FOR-mis	fi-li-FOR-mis	Latin	filum
filix-femina	FI-liks FE-mi-na	FI-li-ks FE-mi-na	Latin	filix
filix-mas	FI-liks MAS	FI-liks MAS	Latin	filix
fimbriata	fim-brē-Ä-ta	fim-brē-Ä-ta	Latin	fimbriae
firmum	FIR-mum	FIR-mōōm	Latin	firmus
fistulosa	fis-tu-LŌ-sa	fis-tōō-LŌ-sa	Latin	fistula
flabellaris	fla-be-LÄ-ris	fla-be-LÄ-ris	Latin	flabellum
flabellifolia	fla-be-li-FŌ-lē-a	fla-be-li-FŌ-lē-a	Latin	flabellum
fladnizensis	flad-ni-ZEN-sis	flad-ni-ZEN-sis	name, place	Fladnitz
flagellaris	fla-je-LÄ-ris	fla-ge-LÄ-ris	Latin	flagellum
flammea	FLA-mē-a	FLA-mā-a	Latin	flamma
flammula	FLA-mŭ-la	FLA-moo-la	Latin	flammula
flava	FLÄ-va	FLÄ-wa	Latin	flavus
flavescens	flā-VE-senz	flä-WE-skens	Latin	flavus
flavum	FLÄ-vum	FLÄ-wōōm	Latin	flavus
flexilis	FLEK-si-lis	FLEK-si-lis	Latin	flexilis
flodmanii	flod-MA-nē-ī	flod-MA-nē-ē	name, person	Flodman, J. H.

Root 1 Meaning	Root 2	Root 2 Meaning / (referring to)
to plough up, to raise or produce		
small, slight, short, scanty		
out, off, from, beyond	pansus	spread out (clambering habit)
out, off, from, beyond	scapus	stalk, shaft
the type genus		
beech tree	pyrum	grain, wheat (the beech-nut-like shape of the edible grains)
sickle-shaped		
1532-1562, Italian anatomist		
hungry		
1864-1956, American botanist	iae	belonging to
small bundle	atus	with, like
silly, clumsy, foolish		
1813-1883, German, collected in North and Central America, esp. New Mexico	ii	of, belonging to
1813-1883, German, collected in North and Central America, esp. New Mexico	anus	from or of
rust-colored, dusky, dark		
ancient name for an unknown grass, also means straw or blade of grass		
fescue, a genus in the Grass Family	aceus	with, like, pertaining to
thread	folium	leaf
thread	folium	leaf
thread	forma	shape, form (narrow, thread-like leaves)
fern	feminus	female
fern	mas	male
fringe, thread, border	atus	with, like
strong, stable, firm		
pipe, tube, hollow reed	osus	with the quality or nature of
fan	aris	relating to, possessing
fan	folium	leaf
Mount Fladnitz in Carinthia	ensis	of a place or country
whip, sucker, tentacle	aris	possessing (the whip-like stems)
flame, fire		
little flame		
yellow, blonde, golden		
yellow, blonde, golden	escens	in the process of becoming
yellow, blonde, golden		
flexible, pliant		
1959-1949, US teacher, naturalist, collected in Montana and Nebraska	ii	of, belonging to

PRONUNCIATION & DERIVATION

Scientific Name	English Latin Pronunctiaion	Reconstructed Latin Pronunciation	Root Source	Root 1
floribunda	flō-ri-BUN-da	flō-ri-BOON-da	Latin	flos
fluctuans	FLUK-tū-anz	FLOOK-too-ans	Latin	fluctuo
fluviatile	flu-vē-Ā-ti-lē	flōō-wē-Ä-ti-lā	Latin	fluviatilis
fluviatilis	flu-vē-Ā-ti-lis	flōō-wē-Ä-ti-lis	Latin	fluviatilis
foenea	FĒ-nē-a	FOI-nä-a	Latin	faeneus
foeniculaceum	fē-ni-kū-LĀ-sē-um	foi-ni-koo-LÄ-kä-ōōm	name, plant	foenum
foeniculum	fē-NI-kū-lum	foi-NI-koo-lōōm	Latin	foenum
foliaceum	fo-lē-Ā-sē-um	fo-lē-Ä-kä-ōōm	Latin	folium
foliosum	fo-lē-Ō-sum	fo-lē-Ō-sōōm	Latin	folium
foliosus	fo-lē-Ō-sus	fo-lē-Ō-sōōs	Latin	folium
fontanum	fon-TĀ-num	fon-TÄ-nōōm	Latin	fontanus
formosa	for-MŌ-sa	for-MŌ-sa	Latin	formosus
Fragaria	fra-JĀ-rē-a	fra-GÄ-rē-a	Latin	fragum
fragile	FRA-ji-lē	FRA-gi-lā	Latin	fragilis
fragilis	FRA-ji-lis	FRa-gi-lis	Latin	fragilis
fragrans	FRĀ-granz	FRÄ-grans	Latin	fragum
franklinii	frank-LI-nē-ī	frank-LI-nē-ē	name, person	Franklin, John
fraseri	FRĀ-ze-rī	FRÄ-se-rē	name, person	Fraser, John
Fraxinus	FRAK-si-nus	FRAK-si-nōōs	name, plant	Fraxinus
fremontii	fre-MON-tē-ī	fre-MON-tē-ē	name, person	Fremont, John Charles
friesii	FRĪ-sē-ī	FRĒ-sē-ē	name, person	Fries, Elias Magnus
frigida	FRI-ji-da	FRI-gi-da	Latin	frigidus
frigidus	FRI-ji-dus	FRI-gi-dōōs	Latin	frigidus
Fritillaria	fri-ti-LĀ-rē-a	fri-ti-LÄ-rē-a	Latin	fritillus
frondosa	fron-DŌ-sa	fron-DŌ-sa	Latin	frondosus
frondosus	fron-DŌ-sus	fron-DŌ-sōōs	Latin	frondosus
fueginus	FĒŪ-ji-nus	FĒOO-gi-nōōs	name, place	Tierra del Fuego
fulgens	FUL-jenz	FŌŌL-gens	Latin	fulgeo
fuliginosa	fū-li-ji-NŌ-sa	foo-li-gi-NŌ-sa	Latin	fuligo
Fumaria	fū-MĀ-rē-a	foo-MÄ-rē-a	Latin	fumus
Gaillardia	gā-LAR-dē-a	gä-LAR-dē-a	name, person	Gaillard de Charentoneau
gairdneri	GĀRD-ne-rī	GÄRD-ne-rē	name, person	Gairdner, Meredith
gale	GĀ-lē	GÄ-lā	Anglo Saxon	gagel
Galearis	ga-lē-Ā-ris	ga-lā-Ä-ris	Latin	galea

Root 1 Meaning	Root 2	Root 2 Meaning / (referring to)
flower	abundus	copious, abounding, abundant
undulate, fluctuate		
river, of rivers		
river, of rivers		
made of straw		
hay, due to the sweet smell	aceus	with, like, pertaining to
hay, due to the sweet smell		
leaf	aceus	with, like, pertaining to
leaf	osus	with the quality or nature of
leaf	osus	with the quality or nature of
spring		
well-formed, shapely, beautiful		
fragrant		
easily broken, brittle		
easily broken, brittle		
fragrant		
1786-1847, Arctic explorer	ii	of, belonging to
1750-1811), Scottish, collected in NAm	ii	of, belonging to
ancient name for ash		
1813-1890, US explorer, naturalist, cartographer, collected in western US	ii	of, belonging to
1794-1878, Swedish botany professor who studied Hieracium and fungi	ii	of, belonging to
cold, cool numbed		(of cold regions)
cold, cool numbed		(of cold regions)
dicebox or chessboard		(the shape of the seedpods or the checkered sepals)
leafy, full of leaves		
leafy, full of leaves		
island/archipelago at s tip of South America		
gleam, shine, blaze, flash		
soot, smut		
smoke		(the smoky smell of fresh roots or the pale color of the flowers)
18th century French magristrate, naturalist and patron of botany		
1809-1837, physician and natural historian in western North America	i	of, belonging to
an aromatic marsh plant, sweet gale		
helmet		

PRONUNCIATION & DERIVATION

Scientific Name	English Latin Pronunctiaion	Reconstructed Latin Pronunciation	Root Source	Root 1
Galeopsis	ga-lē-OP-sis	ga-lā-OP-sis	Greek	gale
galericulata	ga-le-ri-kū-LĀ-ta	ga-le-ri-koo-LĀ-ta	Latin	galericulatum
Galinsoga	ga-lin-SŌ-ga	ga-lin-SŌ-ga	name, person	Galinsoga, M.M. de
Galium	GĀ-lē-um	GĀ-lā-ŏŏm	Greek	gala
gallicum	GA-li-kum	GA-li-kŏŏm	name, place	Gallicus
garberi	GAR-be-rī	GAR-be-rē	name, person	Garber, Adam P.
gardneri	GARD-ne-rī	GARD-ne-rē	name, person	Gordon, Alexander
gastonyi	gas-TŌ-nē-ī	gas-TŌ-nē-ē	name, person	Gastony, G. J.
Gaultheria	gäl-THĒ-rē-a	gowl-TĀ-rē-a	name, person	Gaulthier, Jean-François
Gayophytum	gā-ō-FI-tum	gā-ō-PI-tŏŏm	name, person	Gay, Claude
geniculatus	je-ni-ku-LĀ-tus	ge-ni-kŏŏ-LĀ-tŏŏs	Latin	geniculatus
Gentiana	jen-SHĀ-na	gen-tzē-Ä-na	name, person	Gentius
Gentianaceae	jen-sha-NĀ-sē-ē	gen-tzē-a-NĀ-kā-ī	name, plant	Gentiana
Gentianella	jen-sha-NE-la	gen-tzē-a-NE-la	name, plant	Gentiana
Gentianopsis	jen-sha-NOP-sis	gen-tzē-a-NOP-sis	name, plant	Gentiana
genuflexa	je-nū-FLEK-sa	ge-noo-FLEK-sa	Latin	genu
Geocaulon	jē-ō-KĀ-lon	gā-ō-KOW-lon	Latin	geo
Geraniaceae	je-rā-ni-Ā-sē-ē	ge-rä-nē-Ä-kā-ī	name, plant	Geranium
Geranium	je-RĀ-nē-um	ge-RÄ-nā-ŏŏm	Greek	geranos
Geum	JĒ-um	GĒ-ŏŏm	name, plant	Geum
geyeri	GĪ-e-rī	GÄĒ-e-rē	name, person	Geyer, Charles A.
gigantea	ji-gan-TĒ-a	gi-gan-TĀ-a	Latin	giganteus
gilviflorus	gil-vi-FLŌ-ris	gil-wi-FLŌ-ris	Latin	gilvus
githago	gi-THĀ-gō	gi-TÄ-gō	name, plant	Gith
glabella	gla-BE-la	gla-BE-la	Latin	glabellus
glabellus	gla-BE-lus	gla-BE-lŏŏs	Latin	glabellus
glaberrimum	gla-BE-ri-mum	gla-BE-ri-mŏŏm	Latin	glaber
glaberrimus	gla-BE-ri-mus	gla-BE-ri-mŏŏs	Latin	glaber
glabra	GLĀ-bra	GLÄ-bra	Latin	glaber
glabriuscula	gla-brē-US-kū-la	gla-brē-ŎŎS-koo-la	Latin	glaber
glabrum	GLĀ-brum	GLÄ-brŏŏm	Latin	glaber
glacialis	gla-sē-Ā-lis	gla-kē-Ä-lis	Latin	glacialis

Root 1 Meaning	Root 2	Root 2 Meaning / (referring to)
weasel	opsis	appearance (the flower was likened to the head of a weasel)
small leather cap		
1766-1798, Spanish doctor, botanist, Madrid Botanic Grdn superintendent		
milk		(its use to curdle milk)
Gallic, belonging to the priests of Cybele		
1838-1881	i	of, belonging to
1795-?, collected the type specimen, named Gardneri due to misread label	i	of, belonging to
botanist, studies ferns		
1708-1756, French-Canadian naturalist, King's physician for Quebec in 1741		
1800-1873, French botanist, author of Flora of Chile	phyton	plant
knotted, with joints		
King of Illyria, used gentian roots to heal malaria-stricken troops-500 B.C.		
the type genus		
gentian, plants of the genus *Gentiana*	ella	diminutive
gentian, plants of the genus *Gentiana*	opsis	appearance
knee, joint	flexus	curved, twisted
earth	caulis	stem, stalk (long, slightly buried stems)
the type genus		
a crane		(the long beak of the fruit was likened to the beak of a crane)
ancient name for avens used by Pliny		
German botanist who travelled across NAm with missionaries in 1843	ii	of, belonging to
of giants		
pale yellow	floris	flower
an old generic name for a plant of uncertain identity	ago	with the characteristics of
smooth, hairless (diminutive)		
smooth, hairless (diminutive)		
smooth, hairless, bald	imus	utterly, last
smooth, hairless, bald	imus	utterly, last
smooth, hairless, bald		
smooth, hairless, bald	iuscula	with or like, diminutive
smooth, hairless, bald		
icy, frozen		

PRONUNCIATION & DERIVATION

Scientific Name	English Latin Pronunctiaion	Reconstructed Latin Pronunciation	Root Source	Root 1
glandulifera	glan-dū-LI-fe-ra	glan-doo-LI-fe-ra	Old French	glande
glanduliflora	glan-dū-li-FLŌ-ra	glan-doo-li-FLŌ-ra	Old French	glande
glandulosa	glan-dū-LŌ-sa	glan-doo-LŌ-sa	Old French	glande
glandulosum	glan-dū-LŌ-sum	glan-doo-LŌ-sŏŏm	Old French	glande
glauca	GLÄ-ka	GLOW-ka	Latin	glaucus
glaucophylla	glä-ko-FI-lum	glow-ko-PI-lŏŏm	Latin	glaucus
glaucum	GLÄ-kum	GLOW-kŏŏm	Latin	glaucus
glaucus	GLÄ-kus	GLOW-kŏŏs	Latin	glaucus
Glechoma	gle-KŌ-ma	gle-KŌ-ma	name, plant	Glechon
glomerata	glo-me-RÄ-ta	glo-me-RÄ-ta	Latin	glomero
glomeratum	glo-me-RÄ-tum	glo-me-RÄ-tŏŏm	Latin	glomero
glomeratus	glo-me-RÄ-tus	glo-me-RÄ-tŏŏs	Latin	glomero
glutinosa	glū-ti-NŌ-sa	gloo-ti-NŌ-sa	Latin	gluten
Glyceria	gli-SĔ-rē-a	gli-KÄ-rē-a	Greek	glykys
Glycyrrhiza	gli-si-RĪ-za	gli-ki-HRĒ-sa	Greek	glykys
glyptosperma	glip-tō-SPER-ma	glip-tō-SPER-ma	Greek	glyptos
gmelinii	ME-li-nē-ī	me-LI-nē-ē	name, person	Gmelin
Gnaphalium	na-FÄ-lē-um	na-PÄ-lē-ŏŏm	Greek	gnaphalon
Goodyera	good-YĔ-ra	good-YÄ-ra	name, person	Goodyer, John
gracile	GRA-si-lē	GRA-ki-lā	Latin	gracilis
gracilis	GRA-si-lis	GRA-ki-lis	Latin	gracilis
gracillima	gra-SI-li-ma	gra-KI-li-ma	Latin	gracilis
grahamii	GRÄ-ha-mē-ī	GRÄ-ha-mē-ē	name, person	Graham, James D.
gramineum	gra-MI-nē-um	gra-MI-nä-ŏŏm	Latin	gramineus
gramineus	gra-MI-nē-us	gra-MI-nä-ŏŏs	Latin	gramineus
graminifolia	gra-mi-ni-FŌ-lē-a	gra-mē-ni-FŌ-lē-a	Latin	gramineus
grandiflora	gran-di-FLŌ-ra	gran-di-FLŌ-ra	Latin	grandis
grandiflorum	gran-di-FLŌ-rum	gran-di-FLŌ-rŏŏm	Latin	grandis
grandiflorus	gran-di-FLŌ-rus	gran-di-FLŌ-rŏŏs	Latin	grandis
grandis	GRAN-dis	GRAN-dis	Latin	grandis
Gratiola	gra-SHĔ-ō-la	gra-TZĔ-ō-la	Latin	gratia
graveolens	gra-VĔ-ō-lenz	gra-WÄ-ō-lens	Latin	graveolens
grayi	GRÄ-ē-ī	GRÄ-ē-ē	name, person	Gray, Asa
Grindelia	grin-DĒ-lē-a	grin-DÄ-lē-a	name, person	Grindel, David H.
grindelioides	grin-de-lē-ŌĪ-dēs	grin-de-lē-ŌĒ-dās	name, plant	Grindelia

Root 1 Meaning	Root 2	Root 2 Meaning / (referring to)
little gland	ifera	bearing, carrying
little gland	floris	flower
little gland	osus	with the quality or nature of
little gland	osus	with the quality or nature of
bluish-green or grey, sea-colored		
bluish-green or grey, sea-colored	phyllon	leaf
bluish-green or grey, sea-colored		
bluish-green or grey, sea-colored		
ancient name for a mint, possibly pennyroyal (*Mentha pulegium*)		
to form into a ball		
to form into a ball		
to form into a ball		
glue	osus	with the quality or nature of
sweet		(the taste of the edible grain)
sweet	rhiza	root (a source of commercial liquorice)
carved	sperma	seed
a family of German botanists, 1700-1800s	ii	of or belonging to
lock of wool		(the hairy plants)
1592-1664, English botanist, translated Dioscorides' Materia Medica		
slender, thin		
slender, thin		
slender, thin	imus	utterly, last
1799-1865, US topographical engineer and astronomer	ii	of, belonging to
of grass, grassy		
of grass, grassy		
of grass, grassy	folium	leaf
large, full-grown	floris	flower
large, full-grown	floris	flower
large, full-grown	floris	flower
large, full-grown		
favor, grace, loveliness	iola	diminutive
stinking		
1810-1888, Harvard botanist, professor, studied Sierra wildflowers	i	of, belonging to
1776-1836, German physician/botany professor at Riga, Estonia (Russia)		
gumweed, a genus in the Aster Family	oides	like, resembling

PRONUNCIATION & DERIVATION

Scientific Name	English Latin Pronunctiaion	Reconstructed Latin Pronunciation	Root Source	Root 1
groenlandica	grēn-LAN-di-ka	groin-LAN-di-ka	name, place	Greenland
groenlandicum	grēn-LAN-di-kum	groin-LAN-di-kŏŏm	name, place	Greenland
gronovii	gro-NŌ-vē-ī	gro-NŌ-wē-ē	name, person	Gronovius, Johannes F.
Grossulariaceae	gro-sū-la rē-Ā-sē-ē	grō-soo-la-rē-Ä-kā-ī	name, plant	Grossularia
guadalupensis	gwa-da-lū-PEN-sis	gwa-da-loo-PEN-sis	name, place	Guadalupe
Gutierrezia	gū-tē-e-RĒ-zē-a	goo-tzē-e-RÄ-zē-a	name, person	Gutierrez, P. (Rodriguez)
guttatum	gu-TĀ-tum	gŏŏ-TÄ-tŏŏm	Latin	guttus
Gymnocarpium	jim-nō-KAR-pē-um	gim-no-KAR-pā-ŏŏm	Greek	gymnos
gynocrates	jī-nō-KRÄ-tēz	gē-nō-KRÄ-tās	Greek	gyne
Gypsophila	jip-SO-fi-la	gip-SO-pi-la	Greek	gypsos
Hackelia	ha-KĒ-lē-a	ha-KÄ-lē-a	name, person	Hackel, Josef
Halenia	ha-LĒ-nē-a	ha-LÄ-nē-a	name, person	Halen, Jonas
Halerpestes	ha-ler-PE-stēz	ha-ler-PE-stēs	Greek	halo
hallianum	hä-lē-A-num	hä-lē-A-nŏŏm	name, person	Hall, Harvey Monroe
hallii	HÄ-lē-ī	HÄ-lē-ē	name, person	Hall, Harvey Monroe
Haloragaceae	ha-lō-ra-GÄ-sē-ē	ha-lō-ra-GÄ-kā-ī	name, plant	Haloragis
hastata	ha-STĀ-ta	ha-STÄ-ta	Latin	hastatus
haydeniana	hā-de-nē-Ā-na	hä-de-nē-Ä-na	name, person	Hayden, F. V.
Hedeoma	he-dē-Ō-ma	he-dā-Ō-ma	Greek	hedys
hederacea	he-de-RÄ-sē-a	he-de-RÄ-kā-a	name, plant	Hedera
Hedysarum	he-DI-sa-rum	he-DI-sa-rŏŏm	Greek	hedys
Helenium	he-LE-nē-um	he-LE-nē-ŏŏm	name, myth	Helena
heleonastes	he-lē-ō-NAS-tēz	he-lē-ō-NAS-tās	Greek	heleios
Helianthus	hē-lē-AN-thus	he-lē-AN-tŏŏs	Greek	helios
Helictochloa	he-lik-tō-KLŌ-a	he-lik-tō-KLŌ-a	Greek	helicos
helioscopia	he-lē-ō-SKO-pē-a	he-lē-ō-SKO-pē-a	Greek	helios
Heliotropiaceae	hē-lē-ō-trop-ē-Ā-sē-ē	hā-lē-ō-trŏp-ē-Ä-kā-ī	name, plant	Heliotropium
Heliotropium	hē-lē-ō-TRŌ-pē-um	hē-lē-ō-TRŌ-pē-ŏŏm	Greek	helios
Helminthotheca	hel-min-thō-THĒ-ka	hel-min-tō-TÄ-ka	Greek	helmins
Heracleum	he-RA-klē-um, he-ra-KLĒ-um	he-ra-KLĒ-ŏŏm	name, myth	Hercules
hermaphroditica	her-ma-frō-DI-ti-ka	her-ma-prō-DI-ti-ka	Latin	hermaphrodita
Hesperis	HE-spe-ris	HE-spe-ris	Greek	hespera
hesperium	hes-PE-rē-um	hes-PE-rē-ŏŏm	name, place	Hesperia
Hesperostipa	he-spe-rō-STĪ-pa	he-spe-rō-STĒ-pa	Greek + name, plant	hesperos
heterochaetus	he-te-rō-KĒ-ta	he-te-rō-KĪ-ta	Greek	heteros

Root 1 Meaning	Root 2	Root 2 Meaning / (referring to)
island of Greenland	ica	belonging to
island of Greenland	ica	belonging to
1690-1762, Dutch botanist, friend of Linnaeus	ii	of or belonging to
the type genus		
Guadalupe Mountains, TX, USA	ensis	of a place or country
19th century Spanish nobleman, associate of Madrid botanical garden		
spotted, speckled		
naked	karpos	fruit (exposed sporangia, no indusium)
woman, female	kratys	strong
gypsum	philos	loving (prefered habitat of some spp)
1783-1869, Czech botanist		
1727-1810, Swedish botanist		
salt, sea	erpes	creeper
1874-1932, prof., curator, taxonomist at U of California, studied Asteraceae	anus	from or of
1874-1932, prof., curator, taxonomist at U of California, studied Asteraceae	ii	of or belonging to
the type genus		
armed with a spear		
1829-1887, US surgeon, naturalist, explorer	anus	from or of
sweet, pleasant	osme	scent, smell, odour
English-ivy, a Ginseng Family genus	aceus	with, like, pertaining to
sweet, pleasant	saron	broom
Helen of Troy, wife of King Menelaus		
of a marsh	nastes	inhabitant
sun	anthos	flower (the flowers turn to face the sun)
twisted	trichos	hair (twisted awns)
sun	scopos	watcher
the type genus		
sun	tropos	turned (flowers turning to the sun)
worm	theca	case, envelope (the beaked fruits)
the son of Zeus and Alcmene		(Hercules used it 1st for medicine, strong plants used in medicine)
with male and female characteristics		
evening or evening-star		(fragrance is strong in the evening)
land of the evening star, western	ium	like or of, diminutive
evening or western	Stipa	needlegrass, a Grass Family genus
different, other	chaite	long hair

PRONUNCIATION & DERIVATION

Scientific Name	English Latin Pronunctiaion	Reconstructed Latin Pronunciation	Root Source	Root 1
heterophylla	he-te-rō-FI-la	he-te-rō-PI-la	Greek	heteros
heterosperma	he-te-rō-SPER-ma	he-te-rō-SPER-ma	Greek	heteros
Heterotheca	he-te-rō-THĒ-ka	he-te-rō-TĀ-ka	Greek	heteros
Heuchera	HĒŪ-ke-ra	HĒOO-ke-ra	name, person	Heucher, Johann H. von
heucheriformis	heū-ke-ri-FŌR-mis	hēoo-ke-ri-FŌR-mis	name, plant	Heuchera
hians	HĪ-anz	HĒ-ans	Latin	hiare
Hieracium	hī-e-RĀ-sē-um	hē-e-RÄ-kē-ŏŏm	Greek	hierax
hippiana	hi-pē-Ā-na	hi-pē-Ä-na	Greek	hippos
Hippophae	hi-PŌ-fē	hi-PŌ-pī	Greek	hippos
Hippuris	hi-PŪ-ris	hi-POO-ris	Greek	hippos
hirsutula	hir-SŪ-tū-la	hir-SOO-too-la	Latin	hirsutus
hirta	HIR-ta	HIR-ta	Latin	hirtus
hirtellum	hir-TE-lum	hir-TE-lŏŏm	Latin	hirtus
hirtum	HIR-tum	HIR-tŏŏm	Latin	hirtus
hispanica	his-PA-ni-ka	his-PA-ni-ka	name, place	Hispania
hispida	HIS-pi-da	HIS-pi-da	Latin	hispidus
hispidula	his-PI-dū-la	his-PI-doo-la	Latin	hispidus
hitchcockii	hitch-KO-kē-ī	hit-KO-kē-ē	name, person	Hitchcock, Charles Leo
hitchguirei	hitch-GWĪ-rē-ī	hit-GOOĒ-rā-ē	name, person	Hitchguire
hoodii	HŌŌ-dē-ī	HŌŌ-dē-ē	name, person	Hood, Robert
hookeri	HŌŌ-ke-rī	HŌŌ-ke-rē	name, person	Hooker, William J.
hookeriana	hŏŏ-ke-rē-Ā-na	hŏŏ-ke-rē-Ä-na	name, person	Hooker, William J.
hookerianum	hŏŏ-ke-rē-Ā-num	hŏŏ-ke-rē-Ä-nŏŏm	name, person	Hooker, William J.
hookerianus	hŏŏ-ke-rē-Ā-nus	hŏŏ-ke-rē-Ä-nŏŏs	name, person	Hooker, William J.
hordeaceus	hōr-dē-Ā-sē-us	hōr-dā-Ä-kā-ŏŏs	name, plant	Hordeum
Hordeum	HŌR-dē-um	HŌR-dē-ŏŏm	name, plant	Hordeum
horizontalis	ho-ri-zon-TĀ-lis	ho-ri-zon-TÄ-lis	Greek	horizon
hornemannii	horn-MA-nē-ī	horn-MA-nä-ē	name, person	Hornemann, J.
horridus	HOR-i-dus	HOR-i-dŏŏs	Latin	horridus
hortensis	hor-TEN-sis	hor-TEN-sis	Latin	hortus
houghtoniana	how-to-nē-Ā-na	how-to-nē-Ä-na	name, person	Houghton, D.
Houstonia	hū-STŌ-nē-a	hoo-STŌ-nē-a	name, person	Houston, William

Root 1 Meaning	Root 2	Root 2 Meaning / (referring to)
different, other	phyllon	leaf
different, other	sperma	seed
different, other	theca	case, container (2 types of achenes)
1677-1747, professor of medicine and botanist at Wittenberg, Germany		
alumroot, a genus in the Saxifrage Family	forma	shape, form
to yawn, gaping		
hawk		(used in salve for vision like a hawk, hawks said to use it to aid eyesight)
horse	anus	from or of
horse	phaios	to shine (fed to horses for shiny coats)
horse	oura	tail (shoots like a horse's tail)
hairy, bristly, rough		
hairy, shaggy, uncouth, thick growth		
hairy, shaggy, uncouth, thick growth	ellum	diminutive form (few hairs)
hairy, shaggy, uncouth, thick growth		
Hispania, Iberian Peninsula, Spain	ica	belonging to
bristly, rough hairy		
bristly, rough hairy		
1902-1986, published North American Lathyrus & Flora of Pacific Northwest	ii	of or belonging to
unknown		
Admiralty midshipman	ii	of or belonging to
1785-1865, botany prof, floras of New Zealand/Tasmania, India Antarctic Islands	ii	of or belonging to
1785-1865, botany prof, floras of New Zealand/Tasmania, India Antarctic Islands	anus	from or of
1785-1865, botany prof, floras of New Zealand/Tasmania, India Antarctic Islands	anus	from or of
1785-1865, botany prof, floras of New Zealand/Tasmania, India Antarctic Islands		
barley, a genus in the Grass Family	aceus	with, like, pertaining to
ancient name for barley		
the circle where earth and sky meet	alis	of, like ('horizontal)
1770-1841, botany prof. in Copenhagen	ii	of or belonging to
dreadful, terrifying, bristly		
garden	ensis	of a place or country
1809-1845, discoverer of this species	anus	from or of
1695-1733, English botanist, collected in tropical and South America		

PRONUNCIATION & DERIVATION

Scientific Name	English Latin Pronunctiaion	Reconstructed Latin Pronunciation	Root Source	Root 1
howellii	HOW-e-lē-ī	how-E-lē-ē	name, person	Howell, John Thomas
Hudsonia	hud-SŌ-nē-a	hōōd-SŌ-nē-a	name, person	Hudson, William
hudsoniana	hud-so-nē-Ā-na	hōōd-so-nē-Ä-na	name, place	Hudson
hudsonianum	hud-so-nē-Ā-num	hōōd-so-nē-Ä-nōōm	name, place	Hudson
hudsonii	hud-SŌ-nē-ī	hōōd-SŌ-nē-ē	name, place	Hudson
humifusa	hū-mi-FŪ-sa	hoo-mi-FOO-sa	Latin	humifusus
humilis	HŪ-mi-lis	HOO-mi-lis	Latin	humilis
Humulus	HŪ-mū-lus	HOO-moo-lōōs	name, plant	humela
Huperzia	hū-PER-zē-a	hoo-PER-sē-a	name, person	Huperz, J.P.
huronense	hū-ro-NEN-sē	hoo-ro-NEN-sā	name, place	Lake Huron
hybrida	HĪ-bri-da	HĒ-bri-da	Latin	hybrida
hybridum	HĪ-bri-dum	HĒ-bri-dōōm	Latin	hybrida
Hydrangeaceae	hī-dran-jē-Ā-sē-ē	hē-dran-gā-Ä-kā-ī	name, plant	Hydrangea
Hydrilla	hī-DRI-la	hē-DRI-la	Latin	hydra
Hydrocharitaceae	hī-drō-ka-ri-TĀ-sē-ē	hē-drō-ka-rē-TÄ-kā-ī	name, plant	Hydrocharis
hydrophiloides	hī-dro-fi-LŌĪ-dēz	hē-dro-pi-LŌĒ-dās	name, plant	hydrophila
Hydrophyllaceae	hī-drō-fi-LĀ-sē-ē	hē-drō-pē-LÄ-kā-ī	name, plant	Hydrophyllum
Hydrophyllum	hī-drō-FI-lum	hē-drō-PI-lōōm	Greek	hydro
hydropiper	hī-dro-PĪ-per	hē-dro-PĒ-per	Greek	hydropiper
hyemale	hī-e-MĀ-lē	hē-e-MÄ-lā	Latin	hiemalis
hymenoides	hī-me-nō-Ī-dēz	hē-me-nō-Ē-dās	Latin	hymen
Hymenopappus	hī-me-nō-PA-pus	hē-me-nō-PA-pōōs	Greek	hymen
Hymenoxys	hī-me-NOK-sis	hē-me-NOK-sis	Greek	hymen
Hyoscyamus	hī-ō-SĪ-a-mus	hē-ō-SKĒ-a-mōōs	Greek	hyos
hyparctica	hi-PARK-ti-ka	hi-PARK-ti-ka	Greek	hyper
hyperborea	hī-per-BŌ-rē-a	hē-per-BŌ-rā-a	Greek	hyper
hyperboreum	hī-per-BŌ-rē-um	hē-per-BŌ-rā-ōōm	Greek	hyper
hyperboreus	hī-per-BŌ-rē-us	hē-per-BŌ-rā-ōōs	Greek	hyper
Hypericaceae	hī-pe-ri-KĀ-sē-ē	hē-pe-rē-KÄ-kā-ī	name, plant	Hypericum
Hypericum	hī-PE-ri-kum	hē-PE-ri-kōōm	Greek	hyper
Hypopitys	hī-pō-PI-tēz	hē-pō-PI-tēs	Greek	hypo
hyssopifolia	hi-so-pi-FŌ-lē-a	hi-so-pi-FŌ-lē-a	name, plant	Hyssopus
hyssopifolius	hi-so-pi-FŌ-lē-us	hi-so-pi-FŌ-lē-ōōs	name, plant	Hyssopus
hystericina	his-te-ri-SĪ-na	his-te-ri-KĒ-na	Greek	hystrix
idaeus	ī-DĒ-us	ē-DĪ-ōōs	Greek	Idaios
idahoensis	ī-da-hō-EN-sis	ē-da-hō-EN-sis	name, place	Idaho

Root 1 Meaning	Root 2	Root 2 Meaning / (referring to)
1842-1912, collected in Washington and Oregon, wrote Flora of NW America	ii	of or belonging to
1730-1793, English apothecary, botanist, wrote Flora Anglica		
Hudson Bay, Canada	anus	from or of
Hudson Bay, Canada	anus	from or of
Hudson Bay, Canada	ii	of or belonging to
low, procumbent		
low-lying, short, humble, insignificant		
hops, plants of this genus (*Humulus*)		
1771-1816, German physician, botanist		
Lake Huron, Canada/USA	ense	of a place or country
mongrel, half-breed, hybrid		
mongrel, half-breed, hybrid		
the type genus		
a many-headed water-serpent		(its appearance and habitat)
the type genus		
water-loving	oides	like, resembling
the type genus		
water	phyllon	leaf (watery stems and leaves of some)
water-pepper, a Buckwheat Family plant		
of winter		
membrane	oides	resembling (the thin glumes)
membrane (membranous, chaff-like)	pappos	pappus
membrane	oxys	sharp (the sharp, thin pappus scales)
of a hog	kyamos	bean (poisonous to swine)
over, above, beyond	arctos	north
over, above, beyond	boreas	north (north of the Arctic Circle)
over, above, beyond	boreas	north (north of the Arctic Circle)
over, above, beyond	boreas	north (north of the Arctic Circle)
the type genus		
over, above, beyond	eikon	picture (placed above an image to ward off evil at mid-summer festival)
beneath	pitys	pine (its habitat)
hyssop, a genus in the Mint Family	folium	leaf
hyssop, a genus in the Mint Family	folium	leaf
porcupine		
of wooded Mount Ida		
state of Idaho, USA	ensis	of a place or country

PRONUNCIATION & DERIVATION

Scientific Name	English Latin Pronunctiaion	Reconstructed Latin Pronunciation	Root Source	Root 1
Iliamna	i-lē-AM-na	i-lē-AM-na	name, place	Iliamna
illota	i-LŌ-ta	i-LŌ-ta	Latin	illotus
ilvensis	il-VEN-sis	il-WEN-sis	name, place	Ilva
Impatiens	im-PĀ-shenz	im-PÄ-tzē-ens	Latin	impatiens
inamoenus	i-na-MĒ-nus	i-na-MOI-nõõs	Latin	inamoenus
incana	in-KĀ-na	in-KÄ-na	Latin	incanus
incanum	in-KĀ-num	in-KÄ-nõõm	Latin	incanus
incerta	in-SER-ta	in-KER-ta	Latin	incertus
incisa	in-SĪ-za	in-KĒ-sa	Latin	incisus
incisum	in-SĪ-zum	in-KĒ-sõõm	Latin	incisus
inconspicuum	in-kon-SPI-kū-um	in-kon-SPI-koo-õõm	Latin	inconspicuus
incurviformis	in-kur-vi-FŌR-mis	in-kõõr-wi-FŌR-mis	Latin	incurvus
indecora	in-de-KŌ-ra	in-de-KŌ-ra	Latin	indecorus
inerme	i-NER-mē	i-NER-mā	Latin	inermis
inermis	i-NER-mis	i-NER-mis	Latin	inermis
infirminervia	in-fer-mi-NER-vē-a	in-fer-mi-NER-wē-a	Latin	infermus
innovatus	i-nō-VĀ-tus	i-nō-WÄ-tõõs	Latin	innovare
inodorum	i-no-DŌ-rum	i-no-DŌ-rõõm	Latin	inodorus
inops	IN-ops	IN-ops	Latin	inops
integerrimus	in-te-JE-ri-mus	in-te-GE-ri-mõõs	Latin	integer
integrifolia	in-te-gri-FŌ-lē-a	in-te-gri-FŌ-lē-a	Latin	integro
interior	in-TĒ-rē-or	in-TÄ-rē-or	Latin	interior
intermedia	in-ter-MĒ-dē-a	in-ter-MÄ-dē-a	Latin	inter
intermedium	in-ter-MĒ-dē-um	in-ter-MÄ-dē-õõm	Latin	inter
intybus	IN-ti-bus	IN-ti-bõõs	Latin	intybus
inundata	i-nun-DĀ-ta	i-nõõn-DÄ-ta	Latin	inundatus
involucrata	in-vo-lū-KRĀ-ta	in-wo-loo-KRÄ-ta	Latin	involucrum
iowense	ī-ō-WEN-sē	ē-ō-WEN-sā	name, place	Iowa
Iridaceae	ī-ri-DĀ-sē-ē	ē-rē-DÄ-kā-ī	name, plant	Iris
Iris	Ī-ris	Ē-ris	name, myth	Iris
Isatis	Ī-sa-tis	Ē-sa-tis	name, plant	Isatis
ischaemum	is-KĒ-mum	is-KĪ-mõõm	Greek	ischaemia
islandica	is-LAN-di-ka	is-LAN-di-ka	name, place	Iceland
Isoetaceae	ī-sō-ē-TĀ-sē-ē	ē-soy-TÄ-kā-ī	name, plant	Isoetes
Isoetes, Isoëtes	ī-SŌ-ē-tēz, ī-sō-Ē-tēz	ē-SŌ-ā-tēs	Greek	isos
italica	i-TA-li-ka	i-TA-li-ka	name, place	Italy
Iva	Ī-va	Ē-wa	name, plant	Iva

Root 1 Meaning	Root 2	Root 2 Meaning / (referring to)
Lake Iliamna, Alaska		(apparently, Greene heard of Iliamna Lake, Alaska and liked the sound)
unwashed, dirty		
Latin name for the island of Elba, Italy	ensis	of a place or country
desiring immediate action, impatient		(from the explosive pods)
unpleasant		
grown grey		
grown grey		
doubtful, uncertain, obscure		
cut into		
cut into		
not readily visible, not prominent		
bent, crooked	forma	shape, form
unsightly		
unarmed, harmless		
unarmed, harmless		
weak	nervus	sinew, string, vein
to renew	atus	with, like
odourless		
without resources, poor, destitute		
whole, entire	imum	utterly, last (smooth edges)
make whole, renew	folium	leaf (the smooth-edged leaves)
inner, internal		
between, among	medius	middle, centre
between, among	medius	middle, centre
early name for endive or succory		
flooded, inundated		
wrapper, cover, envelope	atus	with, like
state of Iowa, USA	ense	of a place or country
the type genus		
Greek goddess of the rainbow, rainbow		(the many-colored flowers)
ancient name for dyers-woad		(used by ancient Britons to stain their bodies)
styptic		
the country of Iceland	ica	belonging to
the type genus		
ever, equal	etas	green (evergreen)
country of Italy	ica	belonging to
ancient name for the mint *Ajuga iva*		(the similar aroma of these plants)

PRONUNCIATION & DERIVATION

Scientific Name	English Latin Pronunctiaion	Reconstructed Latin Pronunciation	Root Source	Root 1
ixocarpa	ik-sō-KAR-pa	ik-sō-KAR-pa	Greek	ixos
jacea	JĀ-sē-a	YÄ-kā-a	Latin	jacea
jackii ×	JA-kē-ī	YA-kē-ē	name, person	Jack, John George
japonica	ja-PO-ni-kum	ya-PO-ni-kŏŏm	name, place	Japan
japonicus	ja-PO-ni-kus	ya-PO-ni-kŏŏs	name, place	Japan
jeffreyi	JE-frē-ī	YE-frē-ē	name, person	Jeffrey, John
jepsonii	jep-SO-nē-ī	yep-SO-nē-ē	name, person	Jepson, Willis L.
jonesii	JŌN-sē-ī	YŌ-ne-sē-ē	name, person	Jones, Marcus
jubatum	jū-BĀ-tum	yoo-BÄ-tŏŏm	Latin	iubatus
Juncaceae	jun-KĀ-sē-ē	yŏŏn-KÄ-kā-ī	name, plant	Juncus
Juncaginaceae	jun-ka-ji-NĀ-sē-ē	yŏŏn-ka-gē-NÄ-kā-ī	name, plant	Juncago
juncea	JUN-sē-a	YŎŎN-kā-a	Latin	junceus
Juncus	JUN-kus	YOON-kŏŏs	Latin	jungo, jungere
Juniperus	jū-NI-pe-rus	yoo-NI-pe-rŏŏs	name, plant	Juniperus
Kalmia	KAL-mē-a	KAL-mē-a	name, person	Kalm, Pehr (Peter)
kalmii	KAL-mē-ī	KAL-mē-ē	name, person	Kalm, Per
kelloggii	ke-LO-gē-ī	ke-LO-gē-ē	name, person	Kellogg, Albert
kelseyana	kel-sē-Ā-na	kel-sā-Ä-na	name, person	Kelsey, Harlan
kentrophyta	ken-trō-FĪ-ta	ken-trō-PĒ-ta	Greek	kentron
kluanense	kloo-a-NEN-sē	kloo-a-NEN-sā	name, place	Kluane
Knautia	NÄ-sha	NOW-tzē-a	name, person	Knaut, Christian
Koeleria	kē-LĒ-rē-a	koi-LÄ-rē-a	name, person	Koeler, Georg Ludwig
Koenigia	kē-NI-jē-a	koi-NI-gē-a	name, person	Koenig, Carl D. E.
kotzebuei	kot-ze-BOO-ē-ī	kot-se-BOO-ā-ē	name, person	Kotzebue, Otto von
Krascheninnikovia	kras-ke-ni-ni-KŌ-vē-a	kras-ke-ni-ni-KŌ-wē-a	name, person	Krascheninnikov, S.P.
labradorica	la-bra-DŌ-ri-ka	la-bra-DŌ-ri-ka	name, place	Labrador
labradoricum	la-bra-DŌ-ri-kum	la-bra-DŌ-ri-kŏŏm	name, place	Labrador
lacera	LA-se-ra	LA-ke-ra	Latin	lacera
lachenalii	la-ke-NĀ-lē-ī	la-ke-NÄ-lē-ē	name, person	Lachenal, Werner de
lackschewitzii	lak-she-VIT-zē-ī	lak-ske-WIT-zē-ē	name, person	Lackschewitz, K.

Root 1 Meaning	Root 2	Root 2 Meaning / (referring to)
mistletoe, a genus in the Christmas Mistletoe Family	karpos	fruit
hayrack		
1861-1949, Canadian dendrologist & plant collector		
country of Japan	ica	belonging to
country of Japan	ica	belonging to
1826-1854, Edinburgh Botanic Garden gardener, discoverered Jeffrey pine	i	of, belonging to
1867-1946, California botanist	ii	of, belonging to
1852-1934, geologist, botanist, engineer, explored the western US	ii	of, belonging to
crested	atus	with, like
the type genus		
the type genus		
of reeds, slim, slender		
join, unite, bind		(plants used as withes)
ancient name for juniper		
1716-1779, pupil of Linnaeus, collected extensively in Canada		
1716-1779, pupil of Linnaeus, collected extensively in Canada	ii	of, belonging to
1813-1887, US botanist, physician, founded Calif. Academy of Sciences	ii	of, belonging to
American horticulturist nurseryman	anus	from or of
spur	phyton	plant
Kluane region, se YT, Canada	ense	of a place or country
1654-1716, German (Saxon) physician and botanist		
1765-1807, German physician, botany professor, studied grasses		
1774-1851, a German geologist at the British Museum		
1787-1846, a master of the Rurik in its circumnavigation of the world	i	of, belonging to
1713-1755, Russian botanist		
Labrador Peninsula, e Canada	ica	belonging to
Labrador Peninsula, e Canada	ica	belonging to
mangled, lacerated, damaged		
1736-1800, botany professor at Basel, Switzerland	ii	of, belonging to
1911-1995, Montana botanist	ii	of, belonging to

PRONUNCIATION & DERIVATION

Scientific Name	English Latin Pronunctiaion	Reconstructed Latin Pronunciation	Root Source	Root 1
lactiflorum	lak-ti-FLŌ-rum	lak-ti-FLŌ-rõõm	Latin	lact
Lactuca	lak-TŪ-ka	lak-TOO-ka	Latin	lact
lacustre	la-KUS-trē	la-KÕÕS-trā	Latin	lacus
lacustris	la-KUS-tris	la-KÕÕS-tris	Latin	lacus
Ladeania	la-DĒ-nē-a	la-DĪ-nē-a	name, person	LaDean Egan
laeta	LĒ-ta	LĪ-ta	Latin	laetus
laeve	LĒ-vē	LĪ-wā	Latin	laevis
laevigatum	lē-vi-GĀ-tum	lī-wi-GÄ-tõõm	Latin	laevigatus
lagopus	LA-gō-pus	LA-gō-põõs	name, animal	Lagopus
Lamiaceae	LĀ-mi-Ā-sē-ē	LÄ-mē-Ä-kā-ī	name, plant	Lamium
Lamium	LĀ-mē-um	LÄ-mē-õõm	Greek	laimos
lanata	la-NĀ-ta	la-NÄ-ta	Latin	lanatus
lanatum	la-NĀ-tum	la-NÄ-tõõm	Latin	lanatus
lanceolata	lan-sē-ō-LĀ-ta	lan-kā-ō-LÄ-ta	Latin	lanceolatus
lanceolatum	lan-sē-ō-LĀ-tum	lan-kā-ō-LÄ-tõõm	Latin	lanceolatus
lanceolatus	lan-sē-ō-LĀ-tus	lan-kā-ō-LÄ-tõõs	Latin	lanceolatus
langsdorfii	langs-DŌR-fē-ī	langs-DŌR-fē-ē	name, person	Langsdorf, Georg H. von
lanuginosum	la-nū-ji-NŌ-sum	la-noo-gi-NŌ-sõõm	Latin	lanugo
lapathifolia	la-pa-thi-FŌ-lē-a	la-pa-ti-FŌ-lē-a	name, plant	Lapathum
Laportea	la-PŌR-tē-a	la-PŌR-tē-a	name, person	Laporte, F. L. de
lappa	LA-pa	LA-pa	Latin	lappa
lapponica	la-PO-ni-ka	la-PO-ni-ka	name, place	Lapland
lapponicum	la-PO-ni-kum	la-PO-ni-kõõm	name, place	Lapland
lapponicus	la-PO-ni-kus	la-PO-ni-kõõs	name, place	Lapland
Lappula	LAP-ū-la	LAP-poo-la	Latin	lappa
Lapsana	LAP-sa-na	LAP-sa-na	name, plant	Lapsana
laricina	la-ri-SĪ-na	la-ri-KĒ-na	name, plant	Larix
Larix	LA-riks	LA-riks	name, plant	Larix
lasiandra	la-sē-AN-dra	la-sē-AN-dra	Greek	lasios
lasiocarpa	la-sē-ō-KAR-pa	la-sē-ō-KAR-pa	Greek	lasios
lasiodonta	la-sē-ō-DON-ta	la-sē-ō-DON-ta	Greek	lasios
lateriflora	la-te-ri-FLŌ-ra	la-te-ri-FLŌ-ra	Latin	lateris
Lathyrus	LA-thi-rus	LA-ti-rõõs	Greek	la
latifolia	la-ti-FŌ-lē-a	la-ti-FŌ-lē-a	Latin	latus
latifolium	la-ti-FŌ-lē-um	la-ti-FŌ-lē-õõm	Latin	latus
latiglumis	la-ti-GLŪ-mis	la-ti-GLOO-mis	Latin	latus

Root 1 Meaning	Root 2	Root 2 Meaning / (referring to)
milk, milky juice of plants	floris	flower
milk, milky juice of plants		
lake, pool, tank	is	with, like
lake, pool, tank	is	with, like
1949-, mother of the author		
cheerful, glad, pleasant		
smooth, free of hairs or roughness		
smooth, polished, lustrous		
ptarmigan, a genus of grouse-like birds		
the type genus		
throat		(the gaping mouth of the flower)
woolly		
woolly		
spear-like		
spear-like		
spear-like		
Russian consul-general in Rio de Janeiro, on 1803-06 circumnavigation	ii	of, belonging to
down on plants or cheeks	inosus	with the quality or nature of
a kind of sorrel	folium	leaf
Count Castelnau, 1800s entomologist		
bur		
the region, n. of the Arctic Circle in Scandinavia and Kola Pen., Russia	ica	belonging to
the region, n. of the Arctic Circle in Scandinavia and Kola Pen., Russia	ica	belonging to
the region, n. of the Arctic Circle in Scandinavia and Kola Pen., Russia	ica	belonging to
bur	ula	diminutive
old Dioscorides name for an unknown plant		
larch, a genus of trees in the Pine Family		
ancient name for European larch		
hairy	andros	male
hairy	karpos	fruit (the fuzzy seed capsule)
hairy	odontos	tooth
side, flank	floris	flower
very	thuros	passionate (its use as an aphrodisiac)
broad	folium	leaf
broad	folium	leaf
broad	gluma	bract, hull, husk

PRONUNCIATION & DERIVATION

Scientific Name	English Latin Pronunctiaion	Reconstructed Latin Pronunciation	Root Source	Root 1
laxa	LAK-sa	LAK-sa	Latin	laxus
laxiflorum	lak-si-FLŌ-rum	lak-si-FLŌ-rŏŏm	Latin	laxus
laxmannii	laks-MA-nē-ī	aks-MA-nē-ē	name, person	Laxmann, Erik G.
Lechea	LE-kē-a	LE-kē-a	name, person	Leche, Johan
ledinghamii	le-ding-HA-mē-ī	le-ding-HA-mē-ē	name, person	Ledingham, G. F.
leibergii	lī-BUR-gē-ī	lā-BOOR-gē-ē	name, person	Leiberg, John B.
lemmonii	le-MŌ-nē-ī	le-MŌ-nē-ē	name, person	Lemmon, John G.
Lemna	LEM-na	LEM-na	Greek	limnos
Lens	LENZ	LENS	Latin	lens
Lentibulariaceae	len-ti-bū-lā-ri-Ā-sē-ē	len-tē-boo-lä-rē-Ä-kā-ī	name, plant	Lentibularia
lenticularis	len-ti-kū-LĀ-ris	len-ti-koo-LÄ-ris	Latin	lenticula
Leonurus	lē-o-NŪ-rus	lā-ō-NOO-rŏŏs	Greek	leon
lepida	LE-pi-da	LE-pi-da	Latin	lepidus
Lepidium	le-PI-dē-um	le-PI-dē-ŏŏm	Greek	lepis
lepidota	le-pi-DŌ-ta	le-pi-DŌ-ta	Greek	lepidotos
lepidus	LE-pi-dus	LE-pi-dŏŏs	Latin	lepidus
leptalea	lep-TĂ-lē-a	lep-TĂ-lā-a	Greek	leptaleos
Leptarrhena	lep-ta-RĒ-na	lep-ta-HRĀ-na	Greek	lepto
leptocarpum	lep-tō-kar-pum	lep-tō-kar-pŏŏm	Greek	lepto
leptocoma	lep-tō-KŌ-ma	lep-tō-KŌ-ma	Greek	lepto
leptophyllum	lep-tō-FI-lum	lep-tō-PI-lŏŏm	Greek	lepto
leptosepala	lep-tō-SE-pa-la	lep-tō-SE-pa-la	Greek	lepto
Leptosiphon	lep-tō-SĪ-fon	lep-tō-SĔ-pon	Greek	lepto
lettermanii	le-ter-MA-nē-ī	le-ter-MA-nē-ē	name, person	Letterman, G.W.
Leucanthemum	lēū-KAN-the-mum	lēoo-KAN-te-mŏŏm	Greek	leukos
leucocephala	lēū-ko-SE-fa-la	lēoo-ko-KE-pa-la	Greek	leukos
Leucophysalis	lēū-kō-FI-sa-lis	lēoo-kō-PI-sa-lis	Greek + name, plant	leukos
Levisticum	le-VI-sti-kum	le-WI-sti-kŏŏm	name, plant	Ligusticum
Lewisia	LOO-wi-sē-a	loo-WI-sē-a	name, person	Lewis, Meriwether
lewisii	loo-WI-sē-ī	le-WI-sē-ē	name, person	Lewis, Meriwether
Leymus	LĪ-mus	LĒ-mŏŏs	name, plant	Elymus
Liatris	lē-ĀT-ris	lē-ÄT-ris	unknown	unknown
ligulistylis	li-gu-li-STĪ-lis	li-gŏŏ-li-STĒ-lis	Latin + Greek	ligula
ligusticifolia	li-gus-ti-si-FŌ-lē-a	li-gŏŏs-ti-ki-FŌ-lē-a	name, plant	Ligusticum

Root 1 Meaning	Root 2	Root 2 Meaning / (referring to)
loose, slack, roomy		
loose, slack, roomy	floris	flower
1737-1796, Finnish-Swedish clergy & naturalist, known for his work in Siberia	ii	of, belonging to
1704-1764, Swedish botanist		
1911-2006, Saskatchewan botanist and herbarium curator at Univ. of Regina	ii	of, belonging to
1853-1913	ii	of, belonging to
1832-1908, + wife Sara Lemmon, 1836-1923, California forester & collectors	ii	of, belonging to
little lake, marsh, swamp		
ancient name for lentil		(now refers to the shape of a lentil seed)
the type genus		
freckle, lens	aris	relating to, possessing
lion	oura	tail (its similarity to a lion's tail)
charming, agreeable, neat		
scale	ideon	small (small, scale-like seed pods)
scaly		(the small, scurfy scales)
charming, agreeable, neat		
fine, slender		
fine, slender	arrhen	male (the slender filaments)
thin, slender	karpos	fruit
thin, slender	kome	hair of the head, mane
thin, slender	phyllon	leaf
thin, slender	sepalum	leafy division of the calyx, sepal
fine, slender	sipnon	bent tube (fine edges of fruiting scales)
1841-1913, US botanist of St. Louis, MO	ii	of, belonging to
white	anthos	flower
white	kephale	head
white	physalis	ground-cherry, a genus in the Potato Family
said to be a variation of Ligusticum		
1774-1809, explored the US in 1804-06 (with Clark), collecting +80 new species		
1774-1809, explored the US in 1804-06 (with Clark), collecting +80 new species	ii	of, belonging to
anagram of *Elymus*, the genus where species were formerly classified		
little tongue, strap, ladle	stylos	pillar, column, style
lovage, a genus in the Carrot Family	folium	leaf

PRONUNCIATION & DERIVATION

Scientific Name	English Latin Pronunctiaion	Reconstructed Latin Pronunciation	Root Source	Root 1
Liliaceae	li-li-Ā-sē-ē	lē-lē-Ä-kā-ī	name, plant	Lilium
Lilium	LI-lē-um	LI-lē-ōōm	name, plant	Lirion
limosa	li-MŌ-sa	li-MŌ-sa	Latin	limus
Limosella	li-mō-SE-la	li-mō-SE-la	Latin	limus
Linaceae	lī-NĀ-sē-ē	lē-NÄ-kā-ī	name, plant	Linum
Linaria	li-NĀ-rē-a	li-NÄ-rē-a	Greek	linon
lineare	li-nē-Ā-rē	li-nā-Ä-rā	Latin	lineare
linearis	li-nē-Ā-ris	li-nā-Ä-ris	Latin	lineare
linifolium	li-ni-FŌ-lē-um	li-ni-FŌ-lē-ōōm	Latin	linum
Linnaea	li-NĒ-a	li-NĪ-a	name, person	Linnaeus, Carolus
Linum	LĪ-num	LĒ-nōōm	name, plant	Linon
Liparis	LI-pa-ris	LI-pa-ris	Greek	liparos
Lithophragma	li-thō-FRAG-ma	li-tō-PRAG-ma	Greek	lithos
Lithospermum	li-thō-SPER-mum	li-tō-SPER-mōōm	Greek	lithos
litoralis	lī-tō-RĀ-lis	lē-tō-RÄ-lis	Latin	litoralis
livida	LĪ-vi-da	LĒ-wi-da	Latin	lividus
lividum	LĪ-vi-dum	LĒ-wi-dōōm	Latin	lividus
Loasaceae	lō-a-SĀ-sē-ē	lō-a-SÄ-kā-ī	name, plant	Loasa
lobata	lō-BĀ-ta	lō-BÄ-ta	Latin	lobus
Lobelia	lo-BĒ-lē-a	lo-BĀ-lē-a	name, person	L'Obel, Matthias
loeselii	lē-SE-lē-ī	loi-SE-lē-ē	name, person	Loeselius, J.
Logfia	log-FĒ-a	log-FĒ-a	name, plant	Filago
loliacea	lo-lē-Ā-sē-a	lo-lē-Ä-kā-a	name, plant	Lolium
Lolium	LŌ-lē-um	LŌ-lē-ōōm	name, plant	Lolium
Lomatium	lō-MĀ-shum	lō-MÄ-tzē-ōōm	Greek	loma
Lomatogonium	lō-ma-tō-GO-nē-um	lō-ma-tō-GO-nē-ōōm	Greek	loma
lonchitis	lon-KĪ-tis	lon-KĒ-tis	Greek	lonchitis
lonchocarpa	lon-ko-KAR-pa	lon-ko-KAR-pa	Greek	lonche
lonchophylla	lon-ko-FI-la	lon-ko-FI-la	Greek	lonche
lonchophyllus	lon-ko-FI-lus	lon-ko-FI-lōōs	Greek	lonche
longiflora	lon-ji-FLŌ-ra	lon-gi-FLŌ-ra	Latin	longus
longifolia	lon-ji-FŌ-lē-a	lon-gi-FŌ-lē-a	Latin	longus
longifolius	lon-ji-FŌ-lē-us	lon-gi-FŌ-lē-ōōs	Latin	longus
longipedunculata	lon-ji-pe-dun-kū-LĀ-ta	lon-gi-pe-dōōn-koo-LÄ-ta	Latin	longus
longipes	LON-ji-pēz	LON-gi-pās	Latin	longus
longipetala	lon-ji-PE-ta-la	lon-gi-PE-ta-la	Latin	longus
longirostris	lon-ji-RO-stris	lon-gi-RO-stris	Latin	longus

Root 1 Meaning	Root 2	Root 2 Meaning / (referring to)
the type genus		
ancient name for lilies		
mud		(its muddy habitat)
mud	sella	seat (its muddy habitat)
the type genus		
flax		(the flax-like leaves/plants of some species)
narrow with parallel sides, linear		
narrow with parallel sides, linear	aris	possessing (the narrow leaves)
flax, a fenus in the Flax Family	folium	leaf
1707-1778, Swedish botanist, professor, wrote Species Plantarum		(Linnaeus first desribed this plant as a special favorite of his)
ancient name by Theophrastes for flax		
fat, oily, shiny		(the shining, fleshy leaves)
rock, stone	phragma	fence, wall, partition (the habitat)
rock, stone	sperma	seed (the bony, stone-like seeds)
of the seashore		
bluish, blackish and blue		
bluish, blackish and blue		
the type genus		
rounded projection, lobe	atus	with, like
1538-1616, Flemish botanist/herbalist		
1607-1655, German botanist, physician	ii	of, belonging to
an anagram of the earlier genus, *Filago*		
darnel, a genus in the Grass Family	aceus	with, like, pertaining to
ancient name for ryegras/darnel		
bordered, fringed		(the prominent fruit wings)
bordered, fringed	gone	pistil (the fringe at the base of the petals and around the ovary)
a plant with spear-shaped seeds/leaves		
spearhead, lance	karpos	fruit
spearhead, lance	phyllon	leaf
spearhead, lance	phyllon	leaf
long, vast	floris	flower
long, vast	folium	leaf
long, vast	folium	leaf
long, vast	pedunculus	small, slender, stalk
long, vast	stipes	stalk
long, vast	petalum	petal
long, vast	rostrum	beak, nose

PRONUNCIATION & DERIVATION

Scientific Name	English Latin Pronunctiaion	Reconstructed Latin Pronunciation	Root Source	Root 1
longistylis	lon-ji-STĪ-lis	lon-gi-STĒ-lis	Latin	longus
Lonicera	lō-NI-se-ra	lō-NI-ke-ra	name, person	Lonitzer, Adam
Loranthaceae	lō-ran-THĀ-sē-ē	lō-ran-TÄ-kā-ī	name, plant	Loranthhus
lotiflorus	lō-ti-FLŌ-rus	lō-ti-FLŌ-rōōs	name, plant	Lotus
Lotus	LŌ-tus	LŌ-tōōs	name, plant	Lotos
louiseana	loo-wi-sē-Ā-na	loo-wi-sā-Ä-na	name, place	Louisiana
lucida	LOO-si-da	LOO-ki-da	Latin	lucidus
lucidus	LOO-si-dus	LOO-ki-dōōs	Latin	lucidus
ludoviciana	loo-dō-vi-sē-Ā-na	loo-dō-wi-kē-Ä-na	name, place	Louisiana
ludovicianum	loo-dō-vi-sē-Ā-num	loo-dō-wi-kē-Ä-nōōm	name, place	Louisiana
Luetkea	loo-ET-kē-a	loo-ET-kē-a	name, person	Lütke, Fedor Petrovitch
lugens	LOO-jenz	LOO-gens	Latin	lugeo
lunaria	loo-NĀ-rē-a	loo-NÄ-rē-a	Latin	lunaris
Lupinus	loo-PĪ-nus	loo-PĒ-nōōs	Latin	lupus
lupulina	loo-pū-LĪ-na	loo-poo-LĒ-na	name, plant	Lupulus
lupulus	LOO-pū-lus	LOO-poo-lōōs	name, plant	Lupulus
lutea	LOO-tē-a	LOO-tā-a	Latin	luteus
lutescens	loo-TE-senz	loo-TE-skens	Latin	luteus
luteum	LOO-tē-um	LOO-tā-ōōm	Latin	luteus
luteus	LOO-tē-us	LOO-tā-ōōs	Latin	luteus
Luzula	LU-zū-la	LŌŌ-zoo-la	Ital.	lux
luzuloides	lu-zū-LŌĪ-dēz	lōō-zoo-LŌĒ-dās	name, plant	Luzula
lyallii	lī-A-lē-ī	lē-A-lē-ē	name, person	Lyall, David
Lycium	LI-sē-um	LI-kē-ōōm	name, place, name, plant	Lycia / Lykion
Lycopodiaceae	lī-kō-pō-di-Ā-sē-ē	lē-kō-pō-dē-Ä-kā-ī	name, plant	Lycopodium
Lycopodiella	lī-kō-pō-dē-E-la	lē-kō-pō-dē-E-la	name, plant	Lycopodium
Lycopodium	lī-kō-PŌ-dē-um	lē-kō-PŌ-dē-ōōm	Greek	lycos
Lycopus	LI-kō-pus	LI-kō-pōōs	Greek	lycos
Lygodesmia	lī-go-DES-mē-a	lē-gō-DES-mē-a	Greek	lygos
lyrata	lī-RĀ-ta	lē-RÄ-ta	Greek	lyra
Lysimachia	lī-si-MA-kē-a	lē-si-MA-kē-a	Greek	lysis
Lythraceae	lith-RĀ-sē-ē	lēt-RÄ-kā-ī	name, plant	Lythrum
Lythrum	LĪTH-rum	LĒT-rōōm	Greek	lythron

Root 1 Meaning	Root 2	Root 2 Meaning / (referring to)
long, vast	stylos	pillar, column, style
1528-1586, German doctor, botanist, his herbal was popular 1557-1783		
the type genus		
one of several different plants in the Waterlily or Bean Families	floris	flower
ancient name of a plant whose fruit made partakers it forget their homes		
state of Louisiana or former Louisiana Territory (central USA)	anus	from or of
bright, full of light		
bright, full of light		
state of Louisiana or former Louisiana Territory (central USA)	anus	from or of
state of Louisiana or former Louisiana Territory (central USA)	anus	from or of
1797-1882, a Russian explorer, captain of 4th Russian voyage around the world		
mourn, lament		(black flowering heads)
lunar, of the moon		(half-moon shaped leaflets)
wolf		(grew on poor soil, so was believed to destroy the land, as a wolf in the fold)
hops, a genus in the Hemp Family	ina	feminine diminutive
hops, a genus in the Hemp Family		
golden-yellow		
golden-yellow	escens	in the process of becoming
golden-yellow		
golden-yellow		
light		(referring to plants shining with dew)
woodrush, a genus in the Rush Family	oides	like, resembling
1817-1895, physician, botanist, collector	ii	of, belonging to
an ancient district/Roman Province in sw Asia Minor / a prickly shrub		
the type genus		
clubmoss	ella	diminutive
wolf	podos	foot (a fanciful reference to the shoot tips)
wolf	podos	foot (a fanciful reference to the shoot tips)
pliant twig	desme	bundle (many-branched, twiggy stems)
a stringed instrument, lyre	atus	with, like (the lyrate leaves)
end, dissolve, release	mache	strife (its supposed soothing quality)
the type genus		
blood, gore		(red flowers or used to stop bleeding)

PRONUNCIATION & DERIVATION

Scientific Name	English Latin Pronunctiaion	Reconstructed Latin Pronunciation	Root Source	Root 1
maccalliana	ma-ka-lē-Ā-na	ma-ka-lē-Ä-na	name, person	McCalla, William C.
Machaeranthera	ma-kē-ran-THE-ra	ma-kī-ran-TÄ-ra	Greek	machaira
mackenzieana	ma-ken-zē-Ā-na	ma-ken-zē-Ä-na	name, person	Mackenzie, Alexander
macloskeyi	ma-KLO-skē-ī	ma-KLO-skē-ē	name, person	Macloskie, George
macloviana	ma-klō-vē-Ā-na	ma-klō-wē-Ä-na	name, place	Maclovius
macounii	ma-KOW-nē-ī	ma-KOW-nē-ē	name, person	Macoun, John
macracantha	ma-kra-KAN-tha	ma-kra-KAN-ta	Greek	makros
macrantha	ma-KRAN-tha	ma-KRAN-ta	Greek	makros
macrocarpa	ma-kro-KAR-pa	ma-kro-KAR-pa	Greek	makros
macrocarpum	ma-kro-KAR-pum	ma-kro-KAR-pōōm	Greek	makros
macrocephala	ma-kro-SE-fa-la	ma-kro-KE-pa-la	Greek	makros
macrophyllum	mak-ro-FI-lum	mak-ro-PI-lōōm	Greek	makros
macrostachya	mak-ro-STA-kē-a	mak-ro-STA-kē-a	Greek	makros
maculata	ma-ku-LĀ-ta	ma-kōō-LÄ-ta	Latin	macula
maculatum	ma-ku-LĀ-tum	ma-kōō-LÄ-tōōm	Latin	macula
maculosa	ma-ku-LŌ-sa	ma-kōō-LŌ-sa	Latin	macula
Madia	MĀ-dē-a	MÄ-dē-a	name, plant	Madi
magellanica	ma-je-LĀ-ni-ka	ma-ge-LÄ-ni-ka	name, place	Magellan
magellanicus	ma-je-LĀ-ni-kus	ma-ge-LÄ-ni-kōōs	name, place	Magellan
Mahonia	ma-HŌ-nē-a	ma-HŌ-nē-a	name, person	McMahon, Bernard
Maianthemum	mā-AN-the-mum	mä-AN-tē-mōōm	Greek	maios
majalis	ma-JĀ-lis	ma-YÄ-lis	Latin	majalis
major	MĀ-jor	MÄ-yor	Latin	major
majus	MĀ-jus	MÄ-yōōs	Latin	majus
Malaxis	ma-LAK-sis	ma-LAK-sis	Greek	malakos
Malus	MĀ-lus	MÄ-lōōs	name, plant	Malus
Malva	MAL-va	MAL-wa	Greek	malakos
Malvaceae	mal-VĀ-sē-ē	mal-WÄ-kā-ī	name, plant	Malva
malvaceus	mal-VĀ-sē-us	mal-WÄ-kā-ōōs	name, plant	Malva
mamillata	ma-mi-LĀ-ta	ma-mi-LÄ-ta	Latin	mammus
margaritacea	mar-ga-ri-TĀ-sē-a	mar-ga-ri-TÄ-kā-a	Latin	margarita
mariana	ma-rē-Ā-na	ma-rē-Ä-na	name, place	Maryland
marianum	ma-rē-Ā-num	ma-rē-Ä-nōōm	name, person	Mary
marilandica	mä-ri-LAN-di-ka	mä-ri-LAN-di-ka	name, place	Maryland
maritima	ma-RI-ti-ma	ma-RI-ti-ma	Latin	maritimus

Root 1 Meaning	Root 2	Root 2 Meaning / (referring to)
1872-1962, botanical collector and photographer in Alberta	anus	from or of
sword, sickle	anthera	anther (the anther appendages
1764-1820, explorer in northwestern America	anus	from or of
1834-1920, Irish naturalist & educator	i	of, belonging to
an early name for the Falkland Islands	anus	from or of
1831-1920, Canadian gov't botanist	ii	of, belonging to
large, long	acanthus	a thorny, ornamental plant
large, long	anthos	flower
large, long	karpos	fruit
large, long	karpos	fruit
large, long	kephale	head
large, long	phyllon	leaf
large, long	stachys	spike, ear of grain
spot, stain	atus	with, like
spot, stain	atus	with, like
spot, stain	osus	with the quality or nature of
name for Chilean tarweed (*Madia sativa*)		
Strait of Magellan, s tip of South America	ica	belonging to
Strait of Magellan, s tip of South America	ica	belonging to
1775-1816, Irish-US horticulturist, botanist, seedsman and nurseryman		
May	anthos	flower
gelded boar, eunuch		
greater		
bigger, larger		
soft		(the tender leaves or frail plants)
ancient name for apple		
soft		(the use of its leaves to sooth skin)
the type genus		
mallow, a genus in the Mallow Family	aceus	with, like, pertaining to
breast, nipple	atus	with, like
pearl	aceus	with, like, pertaining to
state of Maryland, USA, once+G1228 applied to all of NorthAmerica	anus	from or of
Mary, mother of Christ	anus	from or of (white marks on the leaves were likened to drops of milk)
state of Maryland, USA	ica	belonging to
of the sea, maritime		

PRONUNCIATION & DERIVATION

Scientific Name	English Latin Pronunctiaion	Reconstructed Latin Pronunciation	Root Source	Root 1
maritimus	ma-RI-ti-mus	ma-RI-ti-mõõs	Latin	maritimus
maroccana	ma-ro-KĀ-na	ma-ro-KÄ-na	name, place	Morocco
Marsilea	mar-SI-lē-a	mar-SI-lē-a	name, person	Marsigli, L.F.C.
Marsileaceae	mar-si-lē-Ā-sē-ē	mar-sē-lā-Ä-kā-ī	name, plant	Marsilea
Matricaria	ma-tri-KĀ-rē-a	ma-tri-KÄ-rē-a	Greek	matrix
matricariifolium	ma-tri-kā-rē-i-FŌ-lē-um	ma-tri-kä-rē-i-FŌ-lē-õõm	name, plant	Matricaria
matronalis	mā-trō-NĀ-lis	mä-trō-NÄ-lis	Latin	matronalis
Matteuccia	ma-TOO-shē-a	ma-TÊOO-kē-a	name, person	Matteucci, C.
Matthiola	ma-tē-Ō-la	ma-tē-Ō-la	name, person	Mattioli, P.A.G.
maxima	MAK-si-ma	MAK-si-ma	Latin	maximus
maximiliani	mak-si-mi-lē-Ā-nē	mak-si-mi-lē-Ä-nē	name, person	Maximilian A.P. von W-N
maximum	MAK-si-mum	MAK-si-mõõm	Latin	maximus
media	MĒ-dē-a	MÄ-dē-a	Latin	medius
Medicago	me-di-KĀ-go	me-di-KÄ-go	Greek	Medike
megacephalus	me-ga-SE-fa-lus	me-ga-KE-pa-lõõs	Greek	megas
megarhiza	me-ga-RĪ-za	me-ga-RĒ-za	Greek	megas
Melampyrum	me-lam-PĪ-rum	me-lam-PĒ-rõõm	Greek	melas
melanopsis	me-la-NOP-sis	me-la-NOP-sis	Greek	melas
Melanthiaceae	me-lan-thi-Ā-sē-ē	me-lan-tē-Ä-kā-ī	name, plant	Melanthium
Melica	ME-li-ka	ME-li-ka	name, plant	Melike
Melilotus	me-li-LŌ-tus	me-li-LŌ-tõõs	Greek + name, plant	meli
membranaceum	mem-bra-NĀ-sē-um	mem-bra-NÄ-kā-õõm	Latin	membrana
Mentha	MEN-tha	MEN-ta	name, myth	Minthe
Mentzelia	ment-ZĒ-lē-a	ment-ZÄ-lē-a	name, person	Mentzel, Christian
Menyanthaceae	me-nē-an-THĀ-sē-ē	me-nē-an-TÄ-kā-ī	name, plant	Menyanthes
Menyanthes	me-nē-AN-thez	me-nē-AN-tēs	Greek	menyein
Menziesia	men-ZĒ-shē-a	men-zē-ES-a	name, person	Menzies, Archibald
menziesii	men-ZĒ-sē-ī	men-ZĒ-e-sē-ē	name, person	Menzies, Archibald
Mertensia	mer-TEN-shē-a	mer-TEN-sē-a	name, person	Mertens, Franz Carl
mertensiana	mer-ten-sē-Ā-na	mer-ten-sē-Ä-na	name, person	Mertens, Franz K.
mertensianus	mer-ten-sē-Ā-nus	mer-ten-sē-Ä-nõõs	name, person	Mertens, Franz K.

Root 1 Meaning	Root 2	Root 2 Meaning / (referring to)
of the sea, maritime		
country of Morocco, n. Africa	anus	from or of
1656 or 1658-1730, Italian naturalist		
the type genus		
womb, mother		(use for treating female disorders)
chamomile, a genus in the Aster Family	folium	leaf
of a married woman, Mar 1st, Roman festival of married ladies/matrons		
Italian professor of physics		
1500-1577, Italian physician, naturalist		
largest, greatest		
1782-1867, German explorer, ethnologist and naturalist	i	of, belonging to
largest, greatest		
central, middle		
alfalfa		(its origin in Medea, Persia)
large, great	kephale	head
large, great	rhiza	root
black	pyros	grain, wheat (black seeds of some spp)
black	opsis	appearance
the type genus		
ancient name for the grass sorghum		
honey	Lotos	clover-like plant (nectar-rich flowers)
skin or parchment		
a mythical Greek nymph who was turned into a mint plant by Proserpine		
1622-1701, 17th century German botanist, author and physician		
the type genus		
disclosing	anthos	flower (flowers open progressively)
1754-1842, Scottish, first botanist to the NAm Pacific, surgeon on Discovery		
1754-1842, Scottish, first botanist to the NAm Pacific, surgeon on Discovery	ii	of, belonging to
1764-1831, German botanist on the Senjavin, 1st collector at Sitka, AK		
1764-1831, German botanist	anus	from or of
1764-1831, German botanist	anus	from or of

PRONUNCIATION & DERIVATION

Scientific Name	English Latin Pronunctiaion	Reconstructed Latin Pronunciation	Root Source	Root 1
mertensii	mer-TEN-sē-ī	mer-TEN-sē-ē	name, person	Mertens, Franz K.
michauxiana	mi-shō-ē-Ā-na	mi-kowk-sē-Ä-na	name, person	Michaux, André
michauxianus	mi-shō-ē-Ā-nus	mi-kowk-sē-Ä-nōōs	name, person	Michaux, André
michiganense	mi-shi-ga-NEN-sē	mi-ki-ga-NEN-sā	name, place	Michigan
micrantha	mī-KRAN-tha	mē-KRAN-ta	Greek	mikros
Micranthes	mī-KRAN-thēz	mē-KRAN-tēs	Greek	mikros
micranthus	mī-KRAN-thus	mē-KRAN-tōōs	Greek	mikros
microcarpa	mī-krō-KAR-pa	mē-krō-KAR-pa	Greek	mikros
microcarpum	mī-krō-KAR-pum	mē-krō-KAR-pōōm	Greek	mikros
microcarpus	mī-krō-KAR-pus	mē-krō-KAR-pōōs	Greek	mikros
microglochin	mī-krō-GLO-kin	mē-krō-GLO-kin	Greek	mikros
microphylla	mī-krō-FI-la	mē-krō-FI-la	Greek	mikros
micropoda	mī-krō-PO-da	mē-krō-PO-da	Greek	mikros
microptera	mī-KROP-te-ra	mē-KROP-te-ra	Greek	mikros
Microseris	mī-krō-SE-ris	mē-krō-SE-ris	Greek + name, plant	mikros
Microsteris	mī-krō-STĒ-ris	mē-krō-STÄ-ris	Greek	mikros
miliaceum	mi-lē-Ā-sē-um	mi-lē-Ä-kā-ōōm	name, plant	Milium
Mimulus	MI-mū-lus	MI-moo-lōōs	Greek	mimo
minganense	min-ga-NEN-sē	min-ga-NEN-sā	name, place	Mingan
miniata	mi-nē-Ā-ta	mi-nē-Ä-ta	Latin	miniatus
minima	MI-ni-ma	MI-ni-ma	Latin	minimus
minimum	MI-ni-mum	MI-ni-mōōm	Latin	minimus
minimus	MI-ni-mus	MI-ni-mōōs	Latin	minimus
minor	MĪ-nor	MĒ-nor	Latin	minor
minus	MĪ-nus	MĒ-nōōs	Latin	minus
minutiflora	mi-nū-ti-FLŌ-ra	mi-noo-ti-FLŌ-ra	Latin	minutus
minutum	mi-NŪ-tum	mi-NOO-tōōm	Latin	minutus
mirabile	mi-RA-bi-lē	mi-RA-bi-lā	Latin	mirabilis
Mirabilis	mi-RA-bi-lis	mi-RA-bi-lis	Latin	mirabilis
miser	MĪ-ser	MĒ-ser	Latin	miser
missouriensis	mi-soo-rē-EN-sis	mi-soo-rē-EN-sis	name, place	Missouri
mistassinica	mis-ta-SI-ni-ka	mis-ta-SI-ni-ka	name, place	Mistassini
Mitella	mi-TE-la	mi-TE-la	Latin	mitra
modestus	mo-DES-tus	mo-DES-tōōs	Latin	modestus

Root 1 Meaning	Root 2	Root 2 Meaning / (referring to)
1764-1831, German botanist	ii	of, belonging to
1746-1803, French botanist, wrote Flora Boreali Americana	anus	from or of
1746-1803, French botanist, wrote Flora Boreali Americana	anus	from or of
state Michigan, USA		
small, little	anthos	flower
small, little	anthos	flower
small, little	anthos	flower
small, little	karpos	fruit
small, little	karpos	fruit
small, little	karpos	fruit
small, little	glochin	point of an arrow
small, little	phyllon	leaf
small, little	podos	foot
small, little	pteron	wing, feather
small, little	seris	chicory, a lettuce-like plant in the Aster Family
small, little	aster	star
millet, various annual forage or cereal grasses but usually *Panicum milaceum*	aceus	with, like, pertaining to
ape		(markings on the seeds were thought to resemble the face of a monkey)
Mingan region, Quebec, Canada	ense	of a place or country
bright red, vermillion		
smallest, least		
smallest, least		
smallest, least		
less, smaller		
less, not		
little, small, minute	floris	flower
little, small, minute		
wonderful, miraculous		
wonderful, miraculous		
pitiful, wretched, poor		
state of Missouri, USA	ensis	of a place or country
Mistassini region, Quebec, Canada	ica	belonging to
cap, bishop's cap	ella	diminutive (the shape of the capsules)
moderate, gentle, discreet		

PRONUNCIATION & DERIVATION

Scientific Name	English Latin Pronunctiaion	Reconstructed Latin Pronunciation	Root Source	Root 1
Moehringia	mē-RIN-jē-a	moi-RIN-gē-a	name, person	Moehring, Paul H.G.
mollis	MO-lis	MO-lis	Latin	mollis
Molluginaceae	mo-lū-ji-NĀ-sē-ē	mō-loo-gē-NÄ-kā-ī	name, plant	Molluga
Mollugo	mo-LŪ-gō	mo-LOO-gō	name, plant	Mollugo
Monarda	mō-NAR-da	mō-NAR-da	name, person	Monardes, Nicholás B.
Moneses	mō-NĒ-sēz	mō-NĀ-sēs	Greek	mono
monocephala	mo-nō-SE-fa-la	mo-nō-KE-pa-la	Greek	mono
monophyllos	mo-nō-FI-los	mo-nō-PI-los	Greek	mono
Monotropa	mo-NO-tro-pa, mo-no-TRŌ-pa	mo-NO-trō-pa	Greek	mono
monotropa	mo-nō-TRŌ-pa	mo-nō-TRŌ-pa	name, plant	Monotropa
monspeliense	mon-spe-lē-EN-sē	mon-spe-lā-EN-sā	name, place	Montpellier
monspeliensis	mon-spe-lē-EN-sis	mon-spe-lē-EN-sis	name, place	Montpellier
montana	mon-TĀ-na	mon-TÄ-na	Latin	montanus
montanensis	mon-ta-NEN-sis	mon-ta-NEN-sis	name, place	Montana
montanum	mon-TĀ-num	mon-TÄ-nōōm	Latin	montanus
Montia	MON-tē-a	MON-tē-a	name, person	Monti, G.
Montiaceae	mon-tē-Ā-sē-ē	mon-tē-Ä-kā-ī	name, plant	Montia
monticola	mon-TI-ko-la	mon-TI-ko-la	Latin	montanus
moschatellina	mo-ska-TE-li-na	mo-ska-TE-li-na	Latin	moschatus
Muhlenbergia	mū-len-BER-jē-a	moo-len-BER-gē-a	name, person	Muhlenberg, G.H.E.
Mulgedium	mul-JĒ-dē-um	mōōl-GĀ-dē-ōōm	Latin	mulgere
multifida	mul-TI-fi-da	mōōl-TI-fi-da	Latin	multus
multifidum	mul-TI-fi-dum	mōōl-TI-fi-dōōm	Latin	multus
multiflora	mul-ti-FLŌ-ra	mōōl-ti-FLŌ-ra	Latin	multus
multiflorum	mul-ti-FLŌ-rum	mōōl-ti-FLŌ-rōōm	Latin	multus
multiradiata	mul-ti-ra-dē-Ā-ta	mōōl-ti-ra-dē-Ä-ta	Latin	multus
multisecta	mul-ti-SEK-ta	mōōl-ti-SEK-ta	Latin	multus
Munroa	mun-RŌ-a	MŌŌN-rō-a	name, person	Munro, william
muralis	mū-RĀ-lis	moo-RÄ-lis	Latin	muralis
muricata	mū-ri-KĀ-ta	moo-ri-KÄ-ta	Latin	muricatus
murinum	mū-RĪ-num	moo-RĒ-nōōm	Latin	murinus
murorum	mū-RŌ-rum	moo-RŌ-rōōm	Latin	murus
Musineon	mū-SI-nē-on	moo-SI-nā-on	name, plant	Musineon
Myosotis	mī-o-SŌ-tis	mē-ō-SŌ-tis	Greek	myos

Root 1 Meaning	Root 2	Root 2 Meaning / (referring to)
1710-1791/1792, a physician, botanist, ornithologist of Oldenburg, Germany		
soft, flexible, calm, gentle		
the type genus		
ancient name for bedstraw, originally from mollis, soft		
1493-1588, Spanish physician and botanist		
single, one, alone	hesis	delight (the beautiful single flower)
single, one, alone	kephale	head
single, one, alone	phyllon	leaf
single, one, alone	tropos	turned (the flowers turned to one side)
Indianpipe genus		
city of Montpellier, s. France	ense	of a place or country
city of Montpellier, s. France	ensis	of a place or country
of mountains, mountainous		
state of Montana, USA	ensis	of a place or country
of mountains, mountainous		
1682-1760, botany prof., Bologna, Italy		
the type genus		
of mountains, mountainous	cola	dweller
perfumed with musk	ellina	feminine diminutive
1753-1815, US minister, grass study, Cataloge Plantarum Americae Septentrionalis		
to milk		(the milky sap)
many, much, abundant	fid	divided into many parts
many, much, abundant	fid	divided into many parts
many, much, abundant	floris	flower
many, much, abundant	floris	flower
many, much, abundant	radius	ray
many, much, abundant	sectus	cut, divided
1818-1880, English agrostologist		
of a wall		
rough with short, hard points		
of mice		
of walls		
ancient name for fennel (Foeniculum) or some other member of the Carrot Family		
of a mouse	ous	ear (the short, soft-hairy leaves)

PRONUNCIATION & DERIVATION

Scientific Name	English Latin Pronunctiaion	Reconstructed Latin Pronunciation	Root Source	Root 1
Myosurus	mī-o-SŪ-rus	mē-ō-SOO-rōōs	Greek	myos
myosuroides	mī-o-sū-RŌĪ-dēz	mē-ō-soo-RŌĒ-dās	name, plant	Myosurus
Myrica	mi-RĪ-ka	mi-RĒ-ka	name, plant	Myrike
Myricaceae	mē-ri-KĀ-sē-ē	mē-rē-KĀ-kā-ī	name, plant	Myrica
Myriophyllum	mi-rē-o-FI-lum	mi-rē-o-PI-lōōm	Greek	myrios
Myriopteris	mi-rē-OP-te-ris	mi-rē-OP-te-ris	Greek	myrios
myrsinites	mir-si-NĪ-tēz	mir-si-NĒ-tās	name, plant	Myrsine
myrtillifolia	mir-ti-li-FŌ-lē-a	mõõr-ti-li-FŌ-lē-a	Latin	Myrtus
myrtilloides	mir-ti-LŌĪ-dēz	mir-ti-LŌĒ-dās	Latin	Myrtus
myrtillus	MIR-ti-lus	MIR-ti-lõõs	Latin	Myrtus
Nabalus	NA-ba-lus	NA-ba-lõõs	Arabic/Indian	nabalus
Najas	NĀ-yas	NÄ-yas	Greek	naias
nana	NĀ-na	NÄ-na	Greek	nanos
napus	NĀ-pus	NÄ-põõs	Latin	napus
nardina	nar-DĪ-na	nar-DĒ-na	Latin	nardus
Nassella	na-SE-la	na-SE-la	Latin	nassa
Nasturtium	na-STUR-shum	na-STŌÕR-tzē-õõm	Latin	nasus
natans	NĀ-tans	NÄ-tans	Latin	natans
nauseosa	nä-sē-Ō-sa	now-sā-Ō-sa	Latin	nausea
Navarretia	na-va-RĒ-sha	na-wa-RÄ-tzē-a	name, person	Navarrete, Francisco F.
nebrascensis	ne-bras-KEN-sis	ne-bras-KEN-sis	name, place	Nebraska
neglecta	ne-GLEK-ta	ne-GLEK-ta	Latin	neglectus
neglectus	ne-GLEK-tus	ne-GLEK-tõõs	Latin	neglectus
negundo	ne-GUN-dō	ne-GÕÕN-dō	name, plant	negundo
nelsoniana	nel-so-nē-Ā-na	nel-so-nē-Ä-na	name, person	Nelson, James Carlton
nelsonii	nel-SO-nē-ī	nel-SO-nē-ē	name, person	Nelson, Aven
Nemophila	ne-MO-fi-la	ne-MŌ-pi-la	Greek	nemos
nemoralis	ne-mo-RĀ-lis	ne-mo-RÄ-lis	Latin	nemoralis
nemorosa	ne-mo-RŌ-sa	ne-mo-RŌ-sa	Latin	nemorosus
neoalaskana	nē-ō-a-las-KĀ-na	nā-ō-a-las-KÄ-na	Greek	neo
neoglandulosum	nē-ō-glan-dū-LŌ-sum	nā-ō-glan-doo-LŌ-sõõm	Greek + French, Old	neo
Neoholmgrenia	nē-ō-hōlm-GRE-nē-a	nā-ō-hōlm-GRE-nē-a	Greek + name, plant	neo
neolunaria	nē-ō-loo-NĀ-rē-a	nā-ō-loo-NÄ-rē-a	Greek + Latin	neo
Neottia	nē-Ō-tē-a	nā-Ō-tē-a	Greek	neossia

Root 1 Meaning	Root 2	Root 2 Meaning / (referring to)
of a mouse	oura	tail (long, spike-like fruit cluster)
mousetail genus in the Buttercup Family	oides	like, resembling
ancient name for tamarisk (*Tamarix*) or some other fragrant shrub		(like tamarisk, whose aromatic, waxy covering was also used in candles)
the type genus		
myriad, numberless	phyllon	leaf (the much divided leaves)
myriad, numberless	pteris	fern (much divided leaves)
myrtle shrub in the Mrytle Family	ites	of, like
myrtle shrub in the Mrytle Family	folium	leaf
myrtle shrub in the Mrytle Family	oides	like, resembling
myrtle shrub in the Mrytle Family		
rattlesnakeroot, an Aster Family genus		
water-nymph		
dwarf		
turnip		
doormat grass, a Grass Family genus	ina	feminine diminutive
narrow-necked wicker basket, fish basket	ella	diminutive
nose	tortus	twisted (the pungent smell)
swimming, floating		
vomiting, nausea	osus	with the quality or nature of
?-1742, anatomist, naturalist, physician to Felipe V of Spain		
state of Nebrasca, USA	ensis	of a place or country
disregarded, slighted, neglected		
disregarded, slighted, neglected		
chastetree (*Vitex negundo*), a tree in the Vervain Family		(the similar leaves)
1867-1944, US teacher, amateur botanist, collected widely in Oregon	anus	from or of
1859-1952, author, taxonomist, founded Rocky Mountain Herbarium	ii	of, belonging to
glade	philos	loving
woody, sylvan		
well-wooded	osus	with the quality or nature of
new, young, recent	Alaska	the state of Alaska, USA
new, young, recent	glande	little gland
new, young, recent	Holmgrenia	earlier genus name for these plants
new, young, recent	lunaris	lunar, of the moon
bird's nest		(the fibrous roots)

PRONUNCIATION & DERIVATION

Scientific Name	English Latin Pronunctiaion	Reconstructed Latin Pronunciation	Root Source	Root 1
Nepeta	NE-pe-ta	NE-pe-ta	name, plant	Nepeta
nephrophylla	ne-frō-FĪ-la	ne-prō-PĒ-la	Greek	nephros
Neslia	NE-slē-a	NE-slē-a	name, person	Nesle, J.A. de
nevadensis	ne-va-DEN-sis	ne-wa-DEN-sis	name, place	Nevada
niger	NĪ-jer	NĒ-ger	Latin	niger
nigra	NĪ-gra	NĒ-gra	Latin	niger
nigricans	NĪ-gri-kanz	NĒ-gri-kans	Latin	niger
nigrum	NĪ-grum	NĒ-grōōm	Latin	niger
nitens	NĪ-tenz	NĒ-tens	Latin	nitens
nitidibaccatum	ni-ti-di-ba-KÄ-tum	ni-ti-di-ba-KÄ-tōōm	Latin	nitidus
nitidus	ni-TI-dus	ni-TI-dōōs	Latin	nitidus
nivalis	ni-VÄ-lis	ni-WÄ-lis	Latin	nivalis
nivea	NI-vē-a	NI-wā-a	Latin	niveus
noctiflora	nok-ti-FLŌ-ra	nok-ti-FLŌ-ra	Latin	nocti
nodosa	nō-DŌ-sa	nō-DŌ-sa	Latin	nodosus
nodosus	nō-DŌ-sus	nō-DŌ-sōōs	Latin	nodosus
noli-tangere	NŌ-li-TAN-je-rē	NŌ-li-TAN-ge-rā	Latin	noli
Nonea	NŌ-nē-a	NŌ-nā-a	name, person	Nonne, J.P.
nootkatensis	noot-ka-TEN-sis	noot-ka-TEN-sis	name, place	Nootka
norvegica	nor-VĒ-ji-ka	nor-WÄ-gi-ka	name, place	Norway
Nothocalais	nō-thō-KA-lā	nō-tō-KA-līs	Greek + name, myth	nothos
novolympica	no-vō-LIM-pi-ka	no-wō-LIM-pi-ka	Lat. + name, place	novus
nuda	NŪ-da	NOO-da	Latin	nudus
nudicaule	nū-di-KÄ-lē	noo-di-KOW-lā	Latin	nudus
nudicaulis	nū-di-KÄ-lis	noo-di-KOW-lis	Latin	nudus
Nuphar	NŪ-far	NOO-par	name, plant	Nufar
nutans	NŪ-tanz	NOO-tans	Latin	nuto
Nuttallanthus	nu-ta-LAN-thus	nōō-ta-LAN-tōōs	name, person	Nuttall, Thomas
nuttalliana	NU-ta-lē-Ä-na	NŌŌ-ta-lē-Ä-na	name, person	Nuttall, Thomas
nuttallianum	NU-ta-lē-Ä-num	NŌŌ-ta-lē-Ä-nōōm	name, person	Nuttall, Thomas
nuttallii	nu-TA-lē-ī	nōō-TA-lē-ē	name, person	Nuttall, Thomas
Nyctaginaceae	nik-ta-ji-NÄ-sē-ē	nēk-ta-gē-NÄ-kā-ī	name, plant	Nyctago
nyctaginea	nik-ta-JI-nē-a	nik-ta-GI-nā-a	Greek	nyktos
nyctelea	nik-TE-lē-a	nik-TE-lā-a	Greek	nyktos

Root 1 Meaning	Root 2	Root 2 Meaning / (referring to)
ancient name for catnip		
kidney	phyllon	leaf
botanist of Poitiers, France		
state of Nevada, USA	ensis	of a place or country
black, dark, dusky		
black, dark, dusky		
black, dark, dusky		
black, dark, dusky		(the color of the berries)
bright, brilliant, sparkling		
shining, bright, glowing	bacca	berry
shining, bright, glowing		
snowy, covered in snow		
snowy, covered in snow		
night	floris	flower
knotty		
knotty		
do not	tangere	touch
1729-1772, physician of Erfurt		
Nootka Island, w. of Vancouver Is., BC	ensis	of a place or country
country of Norway	ica	belonging to
false, spurious	Calais	a figure of Greek mythology who had scales on his back
new, young, recent	Olympos	Greek island said to be the seat of the gods
bare, naked		
bare, naked	caulis	stem, stalk
bare, naked	caulis	stem, stalk
ancient Arabic name for an unknown waterlily and a geographic location		
nod, droop, sway		
1786-1859, US botanist, wrote Genera of North American Plants		
1786-1859, US botanist, wrote Genera of North American Plants	anus	from or of
1786-1859, US botanist, wrote Genera of North American Plants	anus	from or of
1786-1859, US botanist, wrote Genera of North American Plants	ii	of, belonging to
the type genus		
night		blooming
night	lea	of

PRONUNCIATION & DERIVATION

Scientific Name	English Latin Pronunctiaion	Reconstructed Latin Pronunciation	Root Source	Root 1
Nymphaea	nim-FĒ-a	nim-PĪ-a	Greek	nymphaia
Nymphaeaceae	nim-fē-Ā-sē-ē	nēm-pē-Ä-kā-ī	name, plant	Nymphaea
oblongifolia	ob-lon-ji-FŌ-lē-a	ob-lon-gi-FŌ-lē-a	Latin	oblongus
obtusa	ob-TŪ-sa	ob-TOO-sa	Latin	obtusus
obtusata	ob-tū-SĀ-ta	ob-too-SÄ-ta	Latin	obtusus
obtusifolius	ob-tū-si-FŌ-lē-us	ob-too-si-FŌ-lē-ōōs	Latin	obtusus
obtusiloba	ob-tū-si-LŌ-ba	ob-too-si-LŌ-ba	Latin	obtusus
occidentale	ok-si-den-TĀ-lē	o-ki-den-TÄ-lā	Latin	occidentalis
occidentalis	ok-si-den-TĀ-lis	o-ki-den-TÄ-lis	Latin	occidentalis
ochroleuca	ōk-ro-LĒŪ-ka	ōk-ro-LĒOO-ka	Greek	ochros
octoflora	ok-tō-FLŌ-ra	ok-tō-FLŌ-ra	Latin	octo
Odontarrhena	o-don-ta-RĒ-na	o-dōn-ta-HRÄ-na	Greek	odontos
Odontites	ō-don-TĪ-tēz	o-don-TĒ-tēs	Greek	odontos
odontoloma	ō-don-to-LŌ-ma	ō-don-to-LŌ-ma	Greek	odontos
oederi	Ē-de-rī	OI-de-rē	name, person	Oeder, Georg, C.E Oldenburg
Oenothera	ē-no-THĒ-ra	oi-no-TÄ-ra	Greek	oinos
officinale	o-fi-si-NÄ-lē	o-fi-ki-NÄ-lā	Latin	officina
officinalis	o-fi-si-NÄ-lis	o-fi-ki-NÄ-lis	Latin	officina
oleracea	ō-le-RÄ-sē-a	ō-le-RÄ-kā-a	Latin	oleraceus
oligosanthes	o-li-gō-SAN-thēz	o-li-gō-SAN-tās	Greek	oligos
oligosperma	o-li-gō-SPER-ma	o-li-gō-SPER-ma	Greek	oligos
Onagraceae	o-na-GRÄ-sē-ē	ō-na-GRÄ-kā-ī	name, plant	Onagra
oneidense	o-nī-DEN-sē	o-nā-DEN-sa	Native American	Oneida
Onobrychis	o-no-BRĪ-kis	o-NO-bri-kis	Greek	onos
Onocleaceae	o-nō-klē-Ā-sē-ē	ō-nō-klā-Ä-kā-ī	name, plant	Onoclea
Ononis	ō-NŌ-nis	ō-NŌ-nis	name, plant	Ononis
Ophioglossaceae	o-fi-ō-glo-SĀ-sē-ē	ō-pē-ō-glō-SÄ-kā-ī	name, plant	Ophioglossum
Oplopanax	o-plo-PA-naks	o-PLO-pa-naks	Greek + name, plant	hoplon
oppositifolia	o-po-si-ti-FŌ-lē-a	o-po-si-ti-FŌ-lē-a	Latin	oppositus
opulus	O-pū-lus	O-poo-lōōs	name, plant	Opulus
Opuntia	ō-PUN-sha	ō-PŌŌN-tzē-a	name, plant	Opuntia
orbiculata	ōr-bi-kū-LÄ-ta	ōr-bi-koo-LÄ-ta	Latin	orbiculatus
Orchidaceae	or-ki-DÄ-sē-ē	or-kē-DÄ-kā-ī	name, plant	Orchis
oregana	ō-re-GÄ-na	ō-re-GÄ-na	name, place	Oregon

Root 1 Meaning	Root 2	Root 2 Meaning / (referring to)
water nymphs, mythical beings of seas, streams and woods		(beautiful flowers in aquatic habitats)
the type genus		
oblong, longer than wide	folium	leaf
blunt, dull		
blunt, dull	atus	like (the blunt tip of the leaf)
blunt, dull	folium	leaf
blunt, dull	lobus	rounded projection, lobe
of the west		
of the west		
pale yellow	leukos	white
eight	floris	flower
tooth	arrhen	male
tooth		(use for treating toothaches)
tooth	loma	fringe, hem, margin
1728-1791, Copenhagen botany professor, first editor of Flora Danica	i	of, belonging to
wine	theras	seeker (said to induce a taste for wine)
workshop, factory		(use in apothecary shops)
workshop, factory		(use in apothecary shops)
herbaceus, vegetable		
few, scanty	anthos	flower
few, scanty	sperma	seed
the type genus, due to confusion of Oenothera and Onagra		
American aboriginal group of the New York region		
an ass	brychis	eat greedily (value as forage)
the type genus		
classic name for rest-harrow, a shrub with pink flowers and trifoliate leaves		
the type genus		
weapon	Panax	ginseng
opposite	folium	leaf
a kind of maple		
ancient name for another plant from around the town of Opus, Greece		
circular		
the type genus		
state of Oregon, USA or old Hudson's Bay Territory of Oregon (now OR/WA)	anus	from or of

PRONUNCIATION & DERIVATION

Scientific Name	English Latin Pronunctiaion	Reconstructed Latin Pronunciation	Root Source	Root 1
orientalis	ō-rē-en-TĂ-lis	ō-rē-en-TĂ-lis	name, place	orient
Orobanchaceae	o-rō-ban-KĀ-sē-ē	o-rō-ban-KĂ-kā-ī	name, plant	Orobanche
Orthilia	ōr-THI-lē-a	ōr-TI-lē-a	Greek	orthilia
Orthocarpus	ōr-thō-KAR-pus	ōr-tō-KAR-pŏŏs	Greek	orthos
orthoceras	or-thō-SĒ-ras	or-tō-KĀ-ras	Greek	orthos
Oryzopsis	ō-ri-ZOP-sis	ō-ri-ZOP-sis	Latin	oryza
Osmorhiza	os-mō-RĪ-za	os-mō-HRĒ-za	Greek	osme
ovalifolia	ō-va-li-FŌ-lē-a	ō-wa-li-FŌ-lē-a	Latin	ovatus
ovalifolium	ō-va-li-FŌ-lē-um	ō-wa-li-FŌ-lē-ŏŏm	Latin	ovatus
ovata	ō-VĀ-ta	ō-WĂ-ta	Latin	ovatus
ovatum	ō-VĀ-tum	ō-WĂ-tŏŏm	Latin	ovatus
ovina	ō-VĪ-na	ō-WĒ-na	Latin	ovus
Oxalidaceae	ok-sa-li-DĀ-sē-ē	ok-sa-lē-DĂ-kā-ī	name, plant	Oxalis
Oxalis	OK-sa-lis	OK-sa-lis	Greek	oxys
oxyacanthoides	ok-sē-a-kan-THŌĪ-dēz	ok-sē-a-kan-TŌĒ-dās	Greek	oxys
Oxybasis	ok-si-BĀ-sis	ok-si-BĂ-sis	Greek	oxys
oxycoccos	ok-si-KO-kus	ok-si-KO-kŏŏs	Greek	oxys
Oxyria	ok-SI-rē-a	ōk-SI-rē-a	Greek	oxys
Oxytropis	ok-SI-trō-pis	ok-SI-trō-pis	Greek	oxys
pachystachya	pa-ki-STA-kē-a	pa-ki-STA-kē-a	Greek	pachys
Packera	PA-ke-ra	PA-ke-ra	name, person	Packer, John G.
pallasii	pa-LĀ-sē-ī	pa-LĂ-sē-ē	name, person	Pallas, Peter Simon
pallens	PA-lenz	PA-lens	Latin	pallens
pallida	PA-li-da	PA-li-da	Latin	pallidus
pallidum	PA-li-dum	PA-li-dŏŏm	Latin	pallidus
pallidus	PA-li-dus	PA-li-dŏŏs	Latin	pallidus
paludosa	pa-lū-DŌ-sa	pa-loo-DŌ-sa	Latin	paludosus
palustre	pa-LUS-trē	pa-LOOS-trā	Latin	paluster
palustris	pa-LUS-tris	pa-LOOS-tris	Latin	paluster
paniculata	pa-ni-kū-LĀ-ta	pa-ni-koo-LĂ-ta	Latin	paniculus
Panicum	PA-ni-kum	PA-ni-kŏŏm	name, plant	Panicum
Papaver	pa-PA-ver	pa-PĂ-wer	name, plant	Papaver
Papaveraceae	pa-pa-ver-Ā-sē-ē	pa-pa-wer-Ă-kā-ī	name, plant	Papaver
papposa	pa-PŌ-sa	pa-PŌ-sa	Greek	pappos
papyrifera	pa-pī-RI-fe-ra	pa-pē-RI-fe-ra	Greek	papyrodes
paradoxum	pa-ra-DOK-sum	pa-ra-DOK-sŏŏm	Greek	paradoxos
Parietaria	pa-rē-e-TĂ-rē-a	pa-rē-e-TĂ-rē-a	Latin	parietarius

Root 1 Meaning	Root 2	Root 2 Meaning / (referring to)
land of the rising sun, East/Orient (e Asia)	alis	of, like
the type genus		
straight spiral		(the one-sided flower cluster)
upright, straight	carpos	fruit
straight, correct	keras	horn (the straight pods)
rice	opsis	appearance (the rice-like grains)
scent, odour	rhiza	root (the fragrant crushed root)
egg-shaped, ovate	folium	leaf
egg-shaped, ovate	folium	leaf
egg-shaped, ovate		
egg-shaped, ovate		
sheep	ina	feminine diminutive
the type genus		
sharp, pointed, sour		(the sour taste of the plants)
sharp, pointed, sour	akanthos	a thorny plant
sharp, pointed, sour	basis	foundation, base
sharp, pointed, sour	kokkos	grain, seed
sharp, pointed, sour		(the sour taste of the plants)
sharp, pointed, sour	tropis	hull, keel (sharply pointed keel petal)
thick	stachys	spike, ear of grain
1929-, UofAlberta botanist, studied arctic/alpine flora, revised Flora of AB		
1741-1811, German student of the Siberian flora and eminent zoologist	ii	of, belonging to
pale, sick-looking, pallid		
pale, ashen, pallid, grey-green		
pale, ashen, pallid, grey-green		
pale, ashen, pallid, grey-green		
marshy, swampy		
marshy, swampy		
marshy, swampy		
small ear of millet	atus	like (the branched flower clusters)
classical name for millet		
ancient name for poppy		
the type genus		
the hairs or teeth at the tip of achenes in the Aster Family	osus	with the quality or nature of
like payprus or paper	fera	bearing, carrying
strange, contrary to expectations		
of walls		

PRONUNCIATION & DERIVATION

Scientific Name	English Latin Pronunctiaion	Reconstructed Latin Pronunciation	Root Source	Root 1
Parnassia	par-NA-shē-a	par-NA-sē-a	name, place	Parnassus
Paronychia	pa-ro-NI-kē-a	pa-ro-NI-kē-a	Greek	paronychia
parryana	pa-rē-Ā-na	pa-rē-Ä-na	name, person	Parry, Charles Christopher
parryi	PA-rē-ī	PA-rē-ē	name, person	Parry, Charles Christopher
parviflora	par-vi-FLŌ-ra	par-wi-FLŌ-ra	Latin	parvus
parviflorum	par-vi-FLŌ-rum	par-wi-FLŌ-rōōm	Latin	parvus
parviflorus	par-vi-FLŌ-rus	par-wi-FLŌ-rōōs	Latin	parvus
parvifolia	par-vi-FŌ-lē-a	par-wi-FŌ-lē-a	Latin	parvus
Pascopyrum	pas-kō-PĪ-rum	pas-kō-PĒ-rōōm	Latin + Greek	pasco
passerinum	pa-se-RĪ-num	pa-se-RĒ-nōōm	Latin	passerinus
Pastinaca	pa-sti-NĀ-ka	pa-sti-NÄ-ka	Latin	pastinare
patagonica	pa-ta-GŌ-ni-ka	pa-ta-GŌ-ni-ka	name, place	Patagonia
patula	PA-tū-la	PA-too-la	Latin	patulus
pauciflora	pä-si-FLŌ-ra	pow-ki-FLŌ-ra	Latin	pauci
pauciflorum	pä-si-FLŌ-rum	pow-ki-FLŌ-rōōm	Latin	pauci
pauciflorus	pä-si-FLŌ-rus	pow-ki-FLŌ-rōōs	Latin	pauci
paucifolia	pä-si-FŌ-lē-a	pow-ki-FŌ-lē-a	Latin	pauci
paucifolius	pä-si-FŌ-lē-is	pow-ki-FŌ-lē-ōōs	Latin	pauci
paucispicula	pä-si-SPĪ-kū-la	pow-ki-SPĒ-koo-la	Latin	pauci
paupercula	pä-PER-kū-la	pow-PER-koo-la	Latin	pauperculus
Paxistima	pa-KIS-ti-ma	pa-KIS-ti-ma	Greek	pachys
paysonii	pā-SŌ-nē-ī	pä-SŌ-nē-ē	name, person	Payson, Edwin Blake
peckii	PE-kē-ī	PE-kē-ē	name, person	Peck, Charles
pectinata	pek-ti-NĀ-ta	pek-ti-NÄ-ta	Latin	pecten
pectinatus	pek-ti-NĀ-tus	pek-ti-NÄ-tōōs	Latin	pecten
pedatifida	pe-da-TI-fi-da	pe-da-TI-fi-da	Latin + Greek	pedis
pedatus	pe-DĀ-tus	pe-DÄ-tōōs	Latin	pedis
pedicellaris	pe-di-se-LĀ-ris	pe-di-ke-LÄ-ris	Latin, New	pedicellis
Pedicularis	pe-di-kū-LĀ-ris	pe-di-koo-LÄ-ris	Latin	pediculus
Pediomelum	pe-dē-ō-ME-lum	pe-dē-ō-ME-lōōm	Greek	pedion
pedunculata	pe-dun-kū-LĀ-ta	pe-dōōn-koo-LÄ-ta	Latin	pedunculus
pedunculosum	pe-dun-kū-LŌ-sum	pe-dōōn-koo-LŌ-sōōm	Latin	pedunculus
Pellaea	PE-lē-a	pe-LĪ-a	Greek	pellos
pellita	pe-LĪ-ta	pe-LĒ-ta	Latin	pellitus

Root 1 Meaning	Root 2	Root 2 Meaning / (referring to)
the Greek mountain where the Delphic Oracle was situated		(the source of the plant)
a painful infection of the finger, especially under the nail, a whitlow		(its use to cure this disease)
1823-1890, English-US botanist, discovered many species in the sw US	anus	from or of
1823-1890, English-US botanist, discovered many species in the sw US	i	of, belonging to
small, little	floris	flower
small, little	floris	flower
small, little	floris	flower
small, little	folium	leaf
to feed, pasture	pyros	grain, wheat
a sparrow	inus	pertaining to (flower like a sparrow's egg)
to prepare the ground for planting		
region of Patagonia, s. Argentina-s. Chile	ica	belonging to
open, spreading, broad		
few, little	floris	flower
few, little	floris	flower
few, little	floris	flower
few, little	folium	leaf
few, little	folium	leaf
few, little	spiculum	point, dart, sting
poor, little		
thick	stigma	stigma
1893-1927, Wyoming botany prof., studied Brassicaceae and *Cryptantha*	ii	of, belonging to
1833-1917, American botanist	ii	of, belonging to
comb	atus	with, like (comb-like)
comb	atus	with, like (comb-like)
foot	findo	split, divide
foot	atus	like (radiating toes, like a bird's foot)
flower/fruit stalk, pedicel (little foot)	aris	relating to, possessing
a louse		(its use as a remedy for this)
plain	melon	apple-shaped fruit
small, slender, stalk	atus	with, like
small, slender, stalk	osus	with the quality or nature of
dusky, dark		(the dark stalks of some spp)
clothed in skins, wearing a leather coat		

PRONUNCIATION & DERIVATION

Scientific Name	English Latin Pronunctiaion	Reconstructed Latin Pronunciation	Root Source	Root 1
pendulocarpa	pen-du-lō-KAR-pa	pen-dŏŏ-lō-KAR-pa	Latin + Greek	pendulus
pennsylvanica	pen-sil-VĀ-ni-ka	pen-sil-WĀ-ni-ka	name, place	Pennsylvania
Penstemon	pen-STĒ-mon	pen-STĀ-mon	Greek	pente
pensylvanica	pen-sil-VĀ-ni-ka	pen-sil-WĀ-ni-ka	name, place	Pennsylvania
pentandra	pen-TAN-dra	pen-TAN-dra	Greek	pente
peplus	PEP-lus	PEP-lŏŏs	Latin	peplus
peregrina	pe-re-GRĪ-na	pe-re-GRĒ-na	Latin	peregrinus
perenne	pe-RE-nē	pe-RE-nā	Latin	perennis
perfoliatum	per-fo-lē-Ā-tum	per-fo-lē-Ā-tŏŏm	Latin	perfo
perforatum	per-for-Ā-tum	per-for-Ā-tŏŏm	Latin	perfo
Perideridia	pe-ri-de-RI-dē-a	pe-ri-de-RI-dē-a	Greek	peri
Peritoma	pe-RI-to-ma	pe-RI-to-ma	Greek	peri
persica	PER-si-ka	PER-si-ka	name, place	Persia
Persicaria	per-si-KĀ-rē-a	per-si-KĀ-rē-a	Latin	persica
persicum	PER-si-kum	PER-si-kŏŏm	name, place	Persia
petasata	pe-ta-SĀ-ta	pe-ta-SĀ-ta	Latin	petasatus
Petasites	pe-ta-SĪ-tēz	pe-ta-SĒ-tēs	Greek	petasos
petiolaris	pe-tē-ō-LĀ-ris	pe-tē-ō-LĀ-ris	Latin	petiolus
petiolata	pe-tē-ō-LĀ-ta	pe-tē-ō-LĀ-ta	Latin	petiolus
petricosa	pe-tri-KŌ-sa	pe-tri-KŌ-sa	Greek	petra
petrophila	pe-trō-FI-la	pe-trō-PI-la	Greek	petra
Phacelia	fa-SĒ-lē-a	pa-KĀ-lē-a	Greek	phakelos
phaeocephala	fē-ō-SE-fa-la	pī-ō-KE-pa-la	Greek	phaios
Phalaris	FA-la-ris	PA-la-ris	Greek	phalos
Phegopteris	fe-GOP-te-ris	pe-GOP-te-ris	Greek	phegos
philadelphicum	fi-la-DEL-fi-kum	pi-la-DEL-pi-kŏŏm	name, place	Philadelphia
philadelphicus	fi-la-DEL-fi-kus	pi-la-DEL-pi-kŏŏs	name, place	Philadelphia
Philadelphus	fi-la-DEL-fus	pi-la-DEL-pŏŏs	name, person	Philadelphus, Ptolemy
Phleum	FLĒ-um	PLĒ-ŏŏm	name, plant	Phleos
phlomoides	flō-MŌĪ-dēz	plō-MŌĒ-dās	name, plant + Latin	Phlomis
Phlox	FLOKS	PLOKS	Greek	phlox
Phragmites	frag-MĪ-tēz	prag-MĒ-tēs	Greek	phragma
Phrymaceae	fri-MĀ-sē-ē	prē-MĀ-kā-ī	name, plant	Phryma
Phyllodoce	fi-LO-do-sē	pi-LO-do-kā	name, myth	Phyllodoce
Physalis	FI-sa-lis	PI-sa-lis	Greek	physalis
Physaria	fī-SĀ-rē-a	pē-SĀ-rē-a	Greek	physa

Root 1 Meaning	Root 2	Root 2 Meaning / (referring to)
hanging	karpos	fruit
state of Pennsylvania, USA	ica	belonging to
five	stemon	thread, stamen (the sterile 5th stamen)
state of Pennsylvania, USA	ica	belonging to
five	andros	male
robe, tunic, robe for the statue of Athena		
foreign, strange, exotic		
perennial, lasting through the years		
to pierce, to bore through	folium	leaf
to pierce, to bore through	atus	with, like
around	derris	a leather coat (tough seed pods)
around	tomos	division, section, slice (the lid-like [circumscissile] calyx base)
country of Persia (now Iran)	ica	belonging to
peach		(the shape of the leaves)
country of Persia (now Iran)	ica	belonging to
wearing a hat	atus	with, like
a flat, wide-brimmed hat like that of Hermes		(the large basal leaves)
little foot, stalk, stem	aris	relating to, possessing
little foot, stalk, stem	atus	with, like
rock	osus	with the quality or nature of
rock	philia	fondness, friendly love
a bundle, fascicle, cluster		(the tight clusters of flowers)
dusky, dark brown	kephale	head
having a patch of white, crested		
beech	pteris	fern
city of Philadelphia, PA, USA	ica	belonging to
city of Philadelphia, PA, USA	ica	belonging to
Greek King of Egypt, 283(309)-247 B.C.		
ancient name of some kind of swamp-growing grass/reed		
Jerusalem-sage, an Old World genus in the Mint Family	oides	like, resembling
a flame		(the brilliant flowers of some spp)
fence, screen, hedge		(its hedge-like growth along ditches)
the type genus		
a sea-nymph of early Greek mythology, mentioned by Virgil		
bladder, bubble		(the inflated calyx)
bladder, bellows		(the inflated fruit)

PRONUNCIATION & DERIVATION

Scientific Name	English Latin Pronunctiaion	Reconstructed Latin Pronunciation	Root Source	Root 1
Physocarpus	fī-sō-KAR-pus	pē-sōō-KAR-põõs	Greek	physa
Physostegia	fī-so-STE-jē-a	pē-sō-STE-gē-a	Greek	physa
Picea	PĪ-sē-a	PĒ-kē-a	name, plant	Picis
Picradeniopsis	pi-kra-de-nē-OP-sis	pi-kra-de-nē-OP-sis	name, plant	Picradenia
picta	PIK-ta	PIK-ta	Latin	pictus
pilosa	pi-LŌ-sa	pi-LŌ-sa	Latin	pilosus
Pilosella	pī-lō-SE-la	pē-lō-SE-la	Greek	pilos
piloselloides	pi-lō-se-LŌĪ-dēz	pi-lō-se-LŌĒ-dās	Latin	pilosus
Pimpinella	pim-pi-NE-la	pim-pi-NE-la	Latin	bipinnula
Pinaceae	pi-NÄ-sē-ē	pē-NÄ-kā-ī	name, plant	Pinus
Pinguicula	pin-GWI-kū-la	pin-GOOĒ-koo-la	Latin	pinguis
pinnata	pi-NÄ-ta	pi-NÄ-ta	Latin	pinnatus
pinnatum	pi-NÄ-tum	pi-NÄ-tõõm	Latin	pinnatus
Pinus	PĪ-nus	PĒ-nõõs	name, plant	Pinus
piperi	PĪ-pe-rī	PĒ-pe-rē	name, person	Piper, Charles Vancouver
Piptatheropsis	pip-ta-the-ROP-sis	pip-ta-te-ROP-sis	Greek	pipto
Plagiobothrys	pla-jē-ō-BŌTH-rēz	pla-gē-ō-BŌT-rēs	Greek	plagios
planifolia	pla-ni-FŌ-lē-a	pla-ni-FŌ-lē-a	Latin	planus
Plantaginaceae	plan-ta-ji-NÄ-sē-ē	plan-ta-gē-NÄ-kā-ī	name, plant	Plantago
Plantago	plan-TÄ-go	plan-TÄ-go	Latin	planta
planum	PLÄ-num	PLÄ-nõõm	Latin	planus
Platanthera	pla-TAN-the-ra	pla-TAN-te-ra	Greek	platanon
plattensis	pla-TEN-sis	pla-TEN-sis	name, place	Platte
plicata	pli-KÄ-ta	pli-KÄ-ta	Latin	plicatus
plumarius	plū-MÄ-rē-us	ploo-MÄ-rē-õõs	Latin	pluma
Poa	PŌ-a	PŌ-a	name, plant	Poa
Poaceae	pō-Á-sē-ē	pō-Á-kā-ī	name, plant	Poa
Podagrostis	pō-da-GRO-stis	pō-da-GRO-stis	Greek	podos
podocarpa	pō-dō-kar-pa	pō-dō-kar-pa	Greek	podos
Polanisia	po-la-NI-shē-a	pō-la-NI-sē-a	Greek	poly
Polemoniaceae	pō-le-mō-ni-Á-sē-ē	pō-le-mō-nē-Ä-kā-ī	name, plant	Polemonium
Polemonium	po-le-MŌ-nē-um	po-le-MŌ-nē-õõm	name, person	Polemon
polemonoides	po-le-mō-NŌĪ-dēz	po-le-mō-NŌĒ-dās	name, plant	Polemonium
polifolia	po-li-FŌ-lē-a	po-li-FŌ-lē-a	Latin	polia
polyacantha	po-li-a-KAN-tha	po-lē-a-KAN-ta	Greek	poly
Polygala	po-LI-ga-la	po-LI-ga-la	Greek	poly
Polygalaceae	pō-li-ga-LÄ-sē-ē	pō-lē-ga-LÄ-kā-ī	name, plant	Polygala

Root 1 Meaning	Root 2	Root 2 Meaning / (referring to)
bladder, bellows	karpos	fruit (the inflated fruit)
bladder	stege	covering (the inflated calyx)
ancient name for some pine, pitch		
ancient name for the genus *Hymenoxys*	opsis	resembling
painted, colored		
hairy	osus	with the quality or nature of
hair	ella	diminutive (small, hairy habit)
hairy	ella	diminutive form
twice divided leaflets		
the type genus		
fat		(the greasy feel/look of the leaves)
feathered, winged	atus	with, like
feathered, winged		
ancient/classical name		
1867-1926, U.S.D.A. agronomist, expert on Pacific Northwest flora	i	of, belonging to
to fall		awn
oblique, slanting	bothros	a pit, scar (scar or pits on the nutlet)
flat, even, level	folium	leaf
the type genus		
footprint		(the shape of the leaves)
flat, even, level		
anything broad and flat		flower
Platte River region, KA-NB, USA	ensis	of a place or country
folded		
down, soft feather	arium	place where
ancient name for grass/turf, from the Indo-European "poi", rich & luxuriant		
the type genus		
foot	agrostis	grass
foot	karpos	fruit (stalked fruits)
many, much	anisos	unequal (the unequal stamens)
the type genus		
Greek herbalist and healer		(another medicinal plant)
the Jacob's-ladder genus		
grey-colored precious stone	folium	leaf
many, much	akanthos	a prickly, thorny plant
many, much	gala	milk (its use to increase lactation)
the type genus		

PRONUNCIATION & DERIVATION

Scientific Name	English Latin Pronunctiaion	Reconstructed Latin Pronunciation	Root Source	Root 1
Polygaloides	po-li-ga-LOI-dēz	po-li-ga-LOI-dēs	name, plant	Polygala
polygaloides	po-li-ga-LŌĪ-dēz	po-lē-ga-LŌĪ-dās	name, plant	Polygala
Polygonaceae	po-li-gō-NĀ-sē-ē	pō-lē-gō-NĀ-kā-ī	name, plant	Polygonum
Polygonum	po-LI-go-num	po-LI-go-nŏŏm	Greek	poly
polyphyllus	po-li-FI-lus	po-li-FI-lŏŏs	Greek	poly
Polypodiaceae	po-li-pō-di-Ā-sē-ē	pō-lē-pō-dē-Ä-kā-ī	name, plant	Polypodium
Polypodium	po-li-PŌ-dē-um	po-li-PŌ-dē-ŏŏm	Greek	poly
Polypogon	po-li-PŌ-gon	po-li-PŌ-gon	Greek	poly
polyrhiza	po-li-RĪ-za	po-li-RĒ-se	Greek	poly
Polystichum	po-LI-sti-kum	po-LI-stē-kŏŏm	Greek	poly
ponderosa	pon-de-RŌ-sa	pon-de-RŌ-sa	Latin	ponderosus
ponticum	PON-ti-kum	PON-ti-kŏŏm	name, place	Pontus
Populus	PO-pū-lus	PO-poo-lŏŏs	Latin	populus
porrifolius	por-i-FŌ-lē-us	por-i-FŌ-lē-ŏŏs	Latin	porrum
porsildii	por-SIL-dē-ī	por-SIL-dē-ē	name, person	Porsild, A.E. or Porsild, M. P.
porteri	POR-te-rī	POR-te-rē	name, person	Porter, Thomas C.
Portulaca	por-tū-LA-ka	por-too-LA-ka	Latin	porto
Portulacaceae	por-tū-la-KĀ-sē-ē	por-too-la-KÄ-kā-ī	name, plant	Portulaca
Potamogeton	po-ta-mo-JĒ-ton	pō-ta-mō-GÄ-ton	Greek	potamos
Potamogetonaceae	po-ta-mō-jē-to-NĀ-sē-ē	po-ta-mō-gā-to-NĀ-kā-ī	name, plant	Potamogeton
Potentilla	pō-ten-TI-la	pō-ten-TI-la	Latin	potens
powellii	POW-lē-ī	pow-E-lē-ē	name, person	Powell, John Wesley
praealta	prē-AL-ta	prī-AL-ta	Latin	praealtus
praegracilis	prē-GRA-si-lis	prī-GRA-ki-lis	Latin	praegracilis
praelongus	prē-LON-gus	prī-LON-gŏŏs	Latin	praelongus
praemorsa	prē-MOR-sa	prī-MOR-sa	Latin	praemorsum
prairea	PRĀ-rē-a	PRÄ-rā-a	French, Old	praierie
pratense	prā-TEN-sē	prä-TEN-sā	Latin	pratum
pratensis	prā-TEN-sis	prä-TEN-sis	Latin	pratum
pratericola	prā-te-RI-kō-la	prä-te-RI-kō-la	Latin	pratum
praticola	prā-TI-kō-la	prä-TI-kō-la	Latin	pratum
preslii	PRES-lē-ī	PRES-lē-ē	name, person	Presl, Carl Bořiwog
Primula	PRI-mū-la	PRI-moo-la	Latin	primus
Primulaceae	pri-mū-LĀ-sē-ē	prē-moo-LÄ-kā-ī	name, plant	Primula
procerus	PRŌ-sē-rus	PRŌ-kā-rŏŏs	Latin	procerus

Root 1 Meaning	Root 2	Root 2 Meaning / (referring to)
plant genus	oides	resembling
milkwort, a Milkwort Family genus	oides	like, resembling
the type genus		
many, much	gonu	knee, joint (the many, swollen joints)
many, much	phyllon	leaf
the type genus		
many, much	pous	foot (many branches/knobs on rhizomes)
many, much	pogon	beard (long awns or bristly panicles)
many, much	rhiza	root
many, much	stichos	line, row (the many rows of sori)
heavy, weighty, massive		
an ancient country/Roman province in ne Asia Minor (now Turkey)		
people, the tree of the public		(leaves blowing in a breeze were likened to a moving populace)
leek, chive	folium	leaf
1901-1977, arctic flora CAN Herbarium curator, 1872-1956 Danish botanist	ii	of, belonging to
1822-1901, Pennsylvania botany professor, studied Colorado flora	i	of, belonging to
small gate or door	ula	diminutive (the tiny capsule lid)
the type genus		
river	geiton	neighbor
the type genus		
powerful	illa	diminutive (the reputed medicinal value)
1834-1902, Colorado R. explorer, prof, Bureau of Ethnology, Geological Survey	ii	of, belonging to
very high, very deep		
lanky, very slender		
very long, very tall		
die prematurely, die too soon		
meadow, indirectly from Latin *pratum*	eus	of or like
meadow	ense	of a place or country
meadow	ensis	of a place or country
meadow	cola	dweller
meadow	cola	dweller
1794-1852, botanist in Prague, wrote Reliquiae Haenkeanae	ii	of, belonging to
the first		(its early flowering)
the type genus		
tall, slender, long		

PRONUNCIATION & DERIVATION

Scientific Name	English Latin Pronunctiaion	Reconstructed Latin Pronunciation	Root Source	Root 1
procumbens	prō-KUM-benz	prō-KŎŎM-bens	Latin	procumbens
prolixa	prō-LIK-sa	prō-LIK-sa	Latin	prolixus
propinqua	pro-PIN-kwa	pro-PIN-kwa	Latin	propinquus
Prosartes	prō-SAR-tēz	prō-SAR-tēs	Greek	prosartes
prostrata	prō-STRĀ-ta	prō-STRÄ-ta	Latin	prosterno
Prunella	pru-NE-la	prŏŏ-NE-la	name, plant	Brunella
Prunus	PRŪ-nus	PROO-nŏŏs	name, plant	Prunus
Psathyrostachys	sa-thi-rō-STA-kēz	sa-ti-rō-STA-kēs	Greek	psathurotes
pseudacorus	sēū-DA-kō-rus	sēoo-DA-kō-rŏŏs	Greek + name, plant	pseudos
pseudaurea	sēū-DÄ-rē-a	sēoo-DOW-rā-a	Greek	pseudos
pseudocyperus	sēū-do-si-PĒ-rus	sēoo-dō-ki-PĀ-rŏŏs	Greek + name, plant	pseudos
Pseudognaphalium	sēū-dō-na-FĀ-lē-um	sēoo-dō-na-FĀ-lē-ŏŏm	Greek	pseudos
pseudomonticola	sēū-dō-mon-TI-ko-la	sēoo-dō-mon-TI-ko-la	Greek	pseudos
pseudomyrsinites	sēū-dō-mir-si-NĪ-tēz	sēoo-dō-mir-si-NĒ-tās	Greek + name, plant	pseudos
pseudonatronatus	sēū-dō-nā-tro-NĀ-tus	sēoo-dō-nä-tro-NÄ-tŏŏs	Greek + Arabic	pseudos
Pseudoroegneria	sēū-dō-rēg-NE-rē-a	sēoo-do-roig-NE-rē-a	Greek + name, plant	pseudos
pseudorupestris	sēū-dō-rū-PES-tris	sēoo-dō-roo-PES-tris	Greek + Latin	pseudos
Pseudotsuga	sēū-dō-SŪ-ga	sēoo-dō-TSOO-ga	Greek + name, plant	pseudos
Psilocarphus	sī-lo-KAR-fus	sē-lo-KAR-pŏŏs	Greek	psilos
psilostachya	sī-lō-STA-kē-a	psē-lō-STA-kē-a	Greek	psilos
ptarmica	TAR-mi-ka	PTAR-mi-ka	Greek	ptarmikos
Pteridaceae	tē-ri-di-Ā-sē-ē	tā-rē-dē-Ä-kā-ī	name, plant	Pteridium
Pteridium	te-RI-dē-um	te-RI-dē-ŏŏm	name, plant	Pteris
Pterospora	te-ROS-pō-ra	te-ROS-pō-ra	Greek	pteros
pubescens	pū-BE-senz	poo-BE-skens	Latin	pubes
Puccinellia	poo-chē-NĒ-lē-a, puk-si-NE-lē-a	pŏŏ-ki-NE-lē-a	name, person	Puccinelli, Benedetto
pudica	pu-DĪ-kus	pŏŏ-DĒ-kŏŏs	Latin	pudicus
pulchella	pul-KE-la	pŏŏl-KE-la	Latin	pulchellus
pulchellum	pul-KE-lum	pŏŏl-KE-lŏŏm	Latin	pulchellus
pulcherrima	pul-KE-ri-ma	pŏŏl-KE-ri-ma	Latin	pulcher
pulcherrimum	pul-KE-ri-mum	pŏŏl-KE-ri-mŏŏm	Latin	pulcher
Pulsatilla	pul-sa-TI-la	pŏŏl-sa-TI-la	Latin	pulsare
pumila	PŪ-mi-la	POO-mi-la	Latin	pumilus
pumilum	PŪ-mi-lum	POO-mi-lŏŏm	Latin	pumilus

Root 1 Meaning	Root 2	Root 2 Meaning / (referring to)
bent forward, face downward, prostrate		
long, stretched out, freely growing		
near, neighboring, allied, related		
attached		
throw in front, prostrate	atus	with, like
the pre-Linnaean name for these plants		
ancient name of the plum		
brittleness		
false, lie	Acorus	sweetflag genus in the Calamus Family
false, lie	aureus	gold, golden
false, lie	cyperus	Cyperus genus in the Sedge Family
false	Gnaphalium	cudweed genus in the Asteraceae
false, lie	montanus	of mountains, mountainous
false, lie	myrsine	myrtle, a European shrub in the Mrytle Family
false, lie	natron	sodium carbonate, containing sodium
false, lie	Roegneria	genus in the Poaceae
false, lie	rupestris	of rocks
false, lie	Tsuga	hemlock genus in the Pinaceae
naked, bare	karphos	splinter, twig, chaff, straw (the lack of scales at the base of disk flowers)
naked, bare	stachys	spike, ear of grain
causing to sneeze		
the type genus		
a genus in the Polypodiaceae	ium	like or of, diminutive
a wing	spora	seed (the seeds with one wing)
covered in down, with soft, downy hair	escens	in the process of becoming
1808-1850, an Italian botanist professor, Director of Botanical Gardens in Lucca		
chaste, pure, modest		
cute little		
cute little		
beautiful, handsome	imum	utterly, last
beautiful, handsome	imum	utterly, last
to beat		diminutive (the downy seedheads are beaten about by the wind)
dwarf, of short stature		
dwarf, of short stature		

PRONUNCIATION & DERIVATION

Scientific Name	English Latin Pronunctiaion	Reconstructed Latin Pronunciation	Root Source	Root 1
pumilus	PŪ-mi-lus	POO-mi-lŏŏs	Latin	pumilus
pumpellianus	pum-pe-lē-Ā-nus	pŏŏm-pe-lē-Ä-nŏŏs	name, person	Pumpelly (probably)
punctata	punk-TĀ-ta	pŏŏnk-TĀ-ta	Latin	punctum
pungens	PUN-jenz	POON-gens	Latin	pungens
puniceum	pū-NI-sē-um	poo-NI-kā-ŏŏm	Latin	puniceus
purpurascens	pur-pū-RA-senz	pŏŏr-poo-RA-skens	Latin	purpureus
purpurea	pur-PŪR-rē-a	pŏŏr-POOR-ā-a	Latin	purpureus
purpureum	pur-PŪ-rē-um	pŏŏr-POO-rā-oom	Latin	purpureus
purshii	PUR-shē-ī	PŎŎR-sē-ē	name, person	Pursh, Frederick T.
pusilla	pu-SI-la	pŏŏ-SI-la	Latin	pusillus
pusillum	pu-SI-lum	pŏŏ-SI-lŏŏm	Latin	pusillus
pusillus	pu-SI-lus	pŏŏ-SI-lŏŏs	Latin	pusillus
pycnocarpa	pik-no-KAR-pa	pik-no-KAR-pa	Greek	pycnos
pygmaea	pig-MĒ-a	pig-MĪ-a	Greek	pygmaios
pygmaeum	pig-MĒ-um	pig-MĪ-ŏŏm	Greek	pygmaios
pygmaeus	pig-MĒ-us	pig-MĪ-ŏŏs	Greek	pygmaios
pyrifolia	pi-ri-FŌ-ē-a	pi-ri-FŌ-ē-a	Latin	pyrus
Pyrola	pi-RŌ-la, PI-ro-la	PI-ro-la	name, plant	Pyrus
pyrolifolia	pi-rō-li-FŌ-lē-a	pi-rō-li-FŌ-lē-a	Latin	pyrola
Pyrrocoma	pi-rō-KŌ-ma	pi-rō-KŌ-ma	Greek	pyrros
quadriradiata	kwad-ri-ra-dē-A-ta	kwad-ri-ra-dē-A-ta	Latin	quadri
quamash	KWA-mash	KWA-mas	Native American	quamash
Quercus	KWER-kus	KWER-kŏŏs	Celtic	quer
quinqueflora	kwin-kwe-FLŌ-ra	kwin-kwe-FLŌ-ra	Latin	quinque
quinquefolia	kwin-kwe-FŌ-lē-a	kwin-kwe-FŌ-lē-a	Latin	quinque
racemosa	ra-sē-MŌ-sa	ra-kā-MŌ-sa	Latin	raceme
racemosum	ra-sē-MŌ-sum	ra-kā-MŌ-sŏŏm	Latin	raceme
racemosus	ra-sē-MŌ-sus	ra-kā-MŌ-sŏŏs	Latin	raceme
radicans	rā-DĪ-kanz	rä-DĒ-kans	Latin	radicis
radicatus	rā-di-KĀ-tus	rä-di-KĀ-tŏŏs	Latin	radicis
ramosissimum	rā-mō-SI-si-mum	rä-mō-SI-si-mŏŏm	Latin	ramosus
ramosum	rā-MŌ-sum	rä-MŌ-sŏŏm	Latin	ramosus
Ranunculaceae	ra-nun-kū-LĀ-sē-ē	ra-nŏŏn-koo-LÄ-kā-ī	name, plant	Ranunculus
ranunculifolia	ra-nun-kū-li-FŌ-lē-a	ra-nŏŏn-koo-li-FŌ-lē-a	name, plant	Ranunculus
Ranunculus	ra-NUN-kū-lus	ra-NŎŎN-koo-lŏŏs	Greek	rana
rapa	RĀ-pa	RÄ-pa	Latin	rapum

Root 1 Meaning	Root 2	Root 2 Meaning / (referring to)
dwarf, of short stature		
a person not identified in the original description of this species	anus	from or of
point, dot, prick, puncture	atus	with, like
sharp, acrid, biting		
reddish, purplish-red		
purple	ascens	becoming
purple		
purple		
1774-1820, German-US botanist, wrote Flora Americae Septentrionalis	ii	of, belonging to
petty, puny, a trifle		
petty, puny, a trifle		
petty, puny, a trifle		
dense, thick	karpos	fruit
dwarf, pygmy		
dwarf, pygmy		
dwarf, pygmy		
pear, a genus in the Rose Family	folium	leaf
pear tree	ola	diminutive (leaves like pear)
genus in the Wintergreen Family	folium	leaf
flame-colored	coma	hair (pappus)
with or of four of the things named	radiatus	with rays or spokes
sweet		
fine	cuez	tree
five	floris	flower
five	folium	leaf
a racemose flower cluster	osus	with the quality or nature of
a racemose flower cluster	osus	with the quality or nature of
a racemose flower cluster	osus	with the quality or nature of
a root (rooting stems)		
a root	atus	with (conspicuous roots)
having many branches, branch-like	issimus	superlative, very
having many branches, branch-like		
the type genus		
genus in the Buttercup Family	folium	leaf
frog		diminutive (small plants of places where frogs abound)
turnip, bulb		

105

PRONUNCIATION & DERIVATION

Scientific Name	English Latin Pronunctiaion	Reconstructed Latin Pronunciation	Root Source	Root 1
raphanistrum	ra-fa-NI-strum	ra-pa-NI-strōōm	name, plant	Raphanastrum
Raphanus	RA-fa-nus	RA-pa-nōōs	Greek	raphanos
rapunculoides	ra-pun-kū-LŌĪ-dēz	ra-pōōn-koo-LŌĒ-dās	Latin	rapum
Ratibida	ra-TI-bi-da	ra-TI-bi-da	unknown	unknown
raupii	RÄ-pē-ī	ROW-pē-ē	name, person	Raup, Hugh Miller
raynoldsii	RÄ-nold-sē-ī	RÄ-nold-sē-ē	name, person	Raynolds, William F.
recta	REK-ta	REK-ta	Latin	rectus
rediviva	re-di-VĪ-va	re-di-WĒ-wa	Latin	redivivus
regelii	re-GE-lē-ī	re-GE-lē-ē	name, person	Regel, Eduard August von
renifolia	rē-ni-FŌ-lē-a	rē-ni-FŌ-lē-a	Latin	renes
repens	RĒ-penz	RĀ-pens	Latin	repens
reticulata	rē-ti-kū-LÄ-ta	rā-ti-koo-LÄ-ta	Latin	reticulatus
retroflexus	re-trō-FLEK-sus	re-trō-FLEK-sōōs	Latin	retro
retrofracta	re-trō-FRAK-ta	re-trō-FRAK-ta	Latin	retro
retrorsa	re-TROR-sa	re-TROR-sa	Latin	retrorsus
Reynoutria	rā-NOO-trē-a	rā-NOO-trē-a	name, person	van Reynoutre
rhabarbarum	ra-BAR-bum	ra-BAR-bōōm	name, plant	Rhabarbum
Rhamnaceae	ram-NÄ-sē-ē	ram-NÄ-kā-ī	name, plant	Rhamnus
rhamnoides	ram-NŌĪ-dēz	ram-NŌĒ-dās	name, plant	Rhamnus
Rhamnus	RAM-nus	HRAM-nōōs	name, plant	Rhamnus
Rhaponticum	ra-PON-ti-cum	hra-PŌN-ti-kōōm	name, plant	Rha
Rheum	RĒ-um	HRĒ-ōōm	name, plant	Rheon
rhexiifolia	rek-sē-i-FŌ-lē-a	rek-sā-i-FŌ-lē-a	name, plant	Rhexia
Rhinanthus	rī-NAN-thus	hrē-NAN-tōōs	Greek	rhis
Rhodiola	rō-dē-Ō-la	hrō-DĒ-ola	Greek	rhodon
Rhododendron	rō-dō-DEN-dron	hrō-dō-DEN-dron	Latin	rhodon
rhoeas	RĒ-as	ROI-as	Greek	rhoias
rhombifolia	rom-bi-FŌ-lē-a	rom-bi-FŌ-lē-a	Latin	rhombus
rhomboideus	rom-BŌĪ-dē-us	rom-BŌĒ-dā-ôôs	Latin	rhombus
Rhus	RŪS	HROOS	name, plant	Rhous
Rhynchospora	rin-KO-spo-ra	hrin-KO-spo-ra	Greek	rhynchos
Ribes	RĪ-bēz	RĒ-bēs	Arabic	ribas
richardsonii	ri-chard-SŌ-nē-ī	ri-kard-SŌ-nē-ē	name, person	Richardson,R., Richardson,J.
richardsonis	ri-chard-SŌ-nis	ri-kard-SŌ-nis	name, person	Richardson,R., Richardson,J.

Root 1 Meaning	Root 2	Root 2 Meaning / (referring to)
generic name used by Tournefort		
appearing quickly		(the rapid germination of the seeds)
turnip, bulb	unculus	diminutive, like, resembling
unknown		
1901-1995, Harvard prof., forester, studied Salix, collected in nw Canada	ii	of, belonging to
1820-1894, US explorer, map maker, engineer and Army officer	ii	of, belonging to
straight, upright, proper		
restored, brought back to life		
1815-1892, St. Petersburg Botanical Museum, studied Birches	ii	of, belonging to
kidney	folium	leaf
creeping		
netted, net-like, from reticula, cord		
backward, back	flexus	curved, twisted
backward, back	fractus	broken, interrupted
backwards, in reverse		
Dutch/French botanist		
rhubarb, literally barbarian rhubarb		
the type genus		
buckthorn, a Buckthorn Family genus	oides	like, resembling
ancient name for buckthorn		
ancient name for Volga River, where the radix pontica (rhubarb) grew		
name from Dioscorides for unknown plant		
meadow-beauty, a Melastome Family genus	folium	leaf
snout	anthos	flower (projecting beak on the corolla)
a rose		diminutive (rose-scented roots)
a rose	dendron	tree
a kind of wild poppy		
diamond-shaped	folium	leaf
diamond-shaped	oides	like, resembling
ancient name for sumac		
snout, horn, beak	spora	seed (the beaked achenes)
an acid-tasting berry		
1663-1741, English doctor/botanist or 1787-1865, Scot on Franklin Arctic trip	ii	of, belonging to
1663-1741, English doctor/botanist or 1787-1865, Scot on Franklin Arctic trip	is	with, like

PRONUNCIATION & DERIVATION

Scientific Name	English Latin Pronunctiaion	Reconstructed Latin Pronunciation	Root Source	Root 1
rigida	RI-ji-da	RI-gi-da	Latin	rigidus
rigidum	RI-ji-dum	RI-gi-dŏŏm	Latin	rigidus
rigidus	RI-ji-dus	RI-gi-dŏŏs	Latin	rigidus
ringens	RIN-jenz	RIN-gens	Latin	ringens
riparius	rī-PĀ-rē-us	rē-PÄ-rā-ŏŏs	Latin	ripa
rivale	rī-VĀ-lē	rē-WÄ-lā	Latin	rivus
rivalis	rī-VĀ-lis	rē-WÄ-lis	Latin	rivus
rivularis	rī-vū-LĀ-ris	rē-woo-LÄ-ris	Latin	rivulus
rivuloadamensis	rī-vū-lō-a-da-MEN-sis	rē-woo-lō-a-da-MEN-sis	Latin + name, person	rivulus
rivulopugnensis	rī-vū-lō-pug-NEN-sis	rē-woo-lō-pŏŏg-NEN-sis	Latin	rivulus
robbinsii	RO-bin-sē-ī	ro-BIN-sē-ē	name, person	Robbins, James W.
Romanzoffia	rō-man-ZO-fē-a	rō-man-ZO-fē-a	name, person	Romanzoff, Ct. Nikolay P.
romanzoffiana	rō-man-zo-fē-Ā-na	rō-man-zo-fē-Ä-na	name, person	Romanzoff, Ct. Nikolay P.
Rorippa	rō-RI-pa	rō-RI-pa	name, plant	Rorippen
Rosa	RŌ-sa	RŌ-sa	name, plant	Rosa
Rosaceae	rō-SĀ-sē-ē	rō-SÄ-kā-ī	name, plant	Rosa
rosea	RŌ-se-a	RŌ-sā-a	Latin	roseus
rossica	RO-si-ka	RO-si-ka	name, person	Ross, Sir J. C.
rossii	RO-sē-ī	RO-sē-ē	name, person	Ross, Sir J. C.
rostrata	ro-STRĀ-ta	ro-STRÄ-ta	Latin	rostratum
rostratum	ro-STRĀ-tum	ro-STRÄ-tŏŏm	Latin	rostratum
rotatum	ro-TĀ-tum	ro-TÄ-tŏŏm	Latin	rota
rotundifolia	ro-tun-di-FŌ-le-a	ro-tŏŏn-di-FŌ-le-a	Latin	rotunda
ruaxes	roo-AK-sēz	roo-AK-sās	unknown	unknown
rubella	roo-BE-la	roo-BE-la	Latin	ruber
rubescens	roo-BE-senz	roo-BE-skens	Latin	ruber
Rubiaceae	roo-bi-Ā-sē-ē	roo-bē-Ä-kā-ī	name, plant	Ruber
rubra	ROO-bra	ROO-bra	Latin	ruber
rubribracteolata	roo-bri-brak-tē-ō-LĀ-ta	roo-bri-brak-tā-ō-LÄ-ta	Latin	ruber
rubricaulis	roo-bri-KĀ-lis	roo-bri-KOW-lis	Latin	ruber
Rubus	RŪ-bus	ROO-bŏŏs	name, plant	Rubus
Rudbeckia	rud-BE-kē-a	rŏŏd-BE-kē-a	name, person	Rudbeck, O.J. and Olaus O.
ruderale	roo-de-RĀ-lē	roo-de-RÄ-lā	Latin	ruderis
rufa	ROO-fa	ROO-fa	latin	rufus
rufescens	roo-FE-senz	roo-FE-skens	Latin	rufus

Root 1 Meaning	Root 2	Root 2 Meaning / (referring to)
stiff, inflexible, hard, rigid		
stiff, inflexible, hard, rigid		
stiff, inflexible, hard, rigid		
gaping		
river bank, shore	ium	like or of, diminutive
stream, brook	alis	of, like
stream, brook	alis	of, like
small stream or brook	aris	relating to, possessing
small stream or brook	Adams	Adams Creek, where this plant was found
small stream or brook	pugno	fight, dispute
1801-1879, Massachusetts botanist, pioneer student of Potamogeton	ii	of, belonging to
1754-1826, Russian Chancellor, sponsored 2nd Pacific expedition		
1754-1826, Russian Chancellor, sponsored 2nd Pacific expedition	anus	from or of
ancient Saxon vernacular name mentioned by Euricus Cordus		
ancient name for roses		
the type genus		
rose-colored, made of roses		
1800-1862, British Arctic/Antarctic explorer	ica	belonging to
1800-1862, British Arctic/Antarctic explorer	ii	of, belonging to
beak, snout	atus	with, like
beak, snout	atus	with, like
wheel	atus	with, like (wheel-shaped)
round, circular, spherical	folium	leaf
unknown		
red	ella	diminutive form
red	escens	in the process of becoming
the type genus		
red		
red	bractea	scale, small leaf (literally, gold leaf)
red	caulis	stem, stalk
ancient Roman name for blackberry		
1630-1702 and 1660-1740, Swedish father and son botany professors		
rubbish, debris, crushed stone		(its usual habitat)
red, reddish		
red, reddish	escens	in the process of becoming

PRONUNCIATION & DERIVATION

Scientific Name	English Latin Pronunctiaion	Reconstructed Latin Pronunciation	Root Source	Root 1
Rumex	RŪ-meks	ROO-meks	name, plant	Rumex
runcinata	run-si-NĀ-ta	rōōn-ki-NÄ-ta	Latin	runcinatus
rupestris	roo-PES-tris	roo-PES-tris	Latin	rupestris
Ruppia	RU-pē-a	RÕÕ-pē-a	name, person	Ruppius, H.B.
Ruppiaceae	ru-pi-Ā-sē-ē	rōō-pē-Ä-kā-ī	name, plant	Ruppia
russeolum	ru-SĒ-ō-lum	rōō-SÄ-ō-lōōm	Latin	russeolus
rusticana	ru-sti-KĀ-na	rōō-sti-KÄ-na	Latin	rusticanus
rydbergii	RĪD-ber-gē-ī	rēd-BER-gē-ē	name, person	Rydberg, Per Axel
Sabulina	sa-bū-LĪ-na	sa-boo-LĒ-na	Latin	sabulum
Sagina	sa-JĪ-na	sa-GĒ-na	Latin	sagina
saginoides	sa-jē-NŌĪ-dēz	sa-gē-NÕĒ-dās	name, plant	Sagina
Sagittaria	sa-ji-TĀ-rē-a	sa-gi-TÄ-rē-a	Latin	sagitta
sagittata	sa-ji-TĀ-ta	sa-gi-TÄ-ta	Latin	sagitta
sagittatus	sa-ji-TĀ-tus	sa-gi-TÄ-tōōs	Latin	sagitta
Salicaceae	sa-li-KĀ-sē-ē	sa-lē-KÄ-kā-ī	name, plant	Salix
salicaria	sa-li-KĀ-rē-a	sa-li-KÄ-rā-a	name, plant	Salix
Salicornia	sa-li-KOR-nē-a	sa-li-KOR-nē-a	Latin	sal
salina	sa-LĪ-na	sa-LĒ-na	Latin	sal
Salix	SĀ-liks	SÄ-liks	name, plant	Salix
Salsola	SAL-so-la	SAL-so-la	Latin	salsus
salsuginea	sal-su-JĪ-nē-a	sal-sōō-GĒ-nā-a	Latin	salsuginis
Salvia	SAL-vē-a	SAL-wē-a	name, plant	Salvia
Sambucus	sam-BŪ-kus	sam-BOO-kōōs	Greek	sambuce
sandbergii	sand-BER-gē-ī	sand-BER-gē-ē	name, person	Sandberg, John Herman
sanguinalis	san-ji-NĀ-lis	san-gooē-NÄ-lis	Latin	sanguinalis
Sanicula	sa-NI-kū-la	sa-NI-koo-la	Latin	sanare
Santalaceae	san-ta-LĀ-sē-ē	san-ta-LÄ-kā-ī	name, plant	Santalum
Sapindaceae	sa-pin-DĀ-sē-ē	sa-pēn-DÄ-kā-ī	name, plant	Sapindus
Saponaria	sa-pō-NĀ-rē-a	sa-po-NÄ-rē-a	Latin	sapo
Sarcobatus	sar-KO-ba-tus	sar-KO-ba-tōōs	Greek	sarco
sarothrae	sa-RŌ-thrē	sa-RÕ-trī	Greek	sarotron
Sarracenia	sa-ra-SĒ-nē-a	sa-ra-KÄ-nē-a	name, person	Sarracenus de l'Étang, M.
Sarraceniaceae	sa-ra-sē-ni-Ā-sē-ē	sa-ra-kā-nē-Ä-kā-ī	name, plant	Sarracenia
sartwellii	sart-WE-lē-ī	sart-WE-lē-ē	name, person	Sartwell, Henry Parker
sativa	sa-TĪ-va	sa-TĒ-wa	Latin	sativus
sativum	sa-TĪ-vum	sa-TĒ-wōōm	Latin	sativus

Root 1 Meaning	Root 2	Root 2 Meaning / (referring to)
ancient name for sorrel and dock		
planed off, smooth		
of rocks		
1688, 1689-1719, German botanist		
the type genus		
somewhat reddish		
rustic, country, rural		
1860-1931, New York Bot. Gardens, wrote Flora of the Rockies and others	ii	of, belonging to
sand, gravel		
fattening, stuffing		(the fattening quality on sheep)
Pearlwort, a genus in the Pink Family	oides	like, resembling
arrow		(the shape of the leaves)
arrow		(the shape of the leaves)
arrow		(the shape of the leaves)
the type genus		
willow, a genus in the Willow Family	aria	feminine suffix
salt	cornu	horn (saline plants with horn-like branches)
salt	inus	belonging to
ancient name meaning leap or spring		
salty		
saltiness, brackishness		
early Latin name of sage		(its similarity to sage)
an ancient musical instrument made from elderwood		(use in flutes and whistles)
1848-1917, botanist	ii	of, belonging to
of blood, bloody		
to heal		
the type genus		
the type genus		
soap		(juice forms a lather with water)
flesh	batos	thorn (fleshy leaves with spiny stems)
broom		
1659-1734, physician at the Court of Quebec, naturalist and plant collector		
the type genus		
1792-1867, US surgeon and botanist	ii	of, belonging to
planted, sown		
planted, sown		

PRONUNCIATION & DERIVATION

Scientific Name	English Latin Pronunctiaion	Reconstructed Latin Pronunciation	Root Source	Root 1
Saussurea	sä-SŪ-rē-a	sow-SOO-rē-a	name, person	Saussure, H.B. and N.T.
sawatchense	sa-wat-CHEN-sē	sa-wat-KEN-sā	name, place	Sawatch
saxatilis	sak-SĀ-ti-lis	sak-SĀ-ti-lis	Latin	saxatilis
Saxifraga	sak-si-FRA-ga, sak-SI-fra-ga	sak-SI-fra-ga	Latin	saxum
saxifraga	sak-si-FRA-ga	sak-SI-fra-ga	name, plant	Saxifraga
Saxifragaceae	sak-si-fru-GĀ-sē-ē	sak-sē-frōō-GĀ-kā-ī	name, plant	Saxifraga
saximontana	sak-si-mon-TĀ-na	sak-si-mon-TĀ-na	Latin	saxum
saximontanum	sak-si-mon-TĀ-num	sak-si-mon-TĀ-nōōm	Latin	saxum
saximontanus	sak-si-mon-TĀ-nus	sak-si-mon-TĀ-nōōs	Latin	saxum
scabra	SKĀ-bra	SKĀ-bra	Latin	scaber
scandens	SKAN-denz	SKAN-dens	Latin	scando
scariosum	ska-rē-Ō-sum	ska-rē-Ō-sōōm	Latin, New	scariosus
sceleratus	ske-le-RĀ-tus	ske-le-RĀ-tōōs	Greek	skleros
Sceptridium	sep-TRI-dē-um	skep-TRI-dē-ōōm	Greek	scepter
scheuchzeri	SHOO-ze-rī	SKĒOOK-ze-rē	name, person	Scheuchzer, J.J.
Scheuchzeria	SHŪK-zē-rē-a, skēūk-ZĒ-rē-a	skēook-ZĀ-rē-a	name, person	Scheuchzer, J.J. and Johann
Scheuchzeriaceae	shēūk-zē-ri-Ā-sē-ē	shēook-zā-rē-Ä-kā-ī	name, plant	Scheuchzeria
Schizachne	ski-ZAK-nē	ski-ZAK-nā	Greek	schizo
Schizachyrium	ski-za-KĒ-rē-um	ski-za-KĀ-rē-ōōm	Greek	schizo
Schoenoplectus	skē-nō-PLEK-tus	skoi-no-PLEK-tōōs	Greek	schoinos
schoenoprasum	skē-NO-pra-sum	skoi-NO-pra-sōōm	Greek	schoinos
schreberi	SHRĒ-be-rī	SKRE-be-rē	name, person	Schreber, J.C.D
schweinitzii	shwī-NIT-zē-ī	swā-NIT-zē-ē	name, person	Schweinitz, L.D. von
scilloides	ski-LŌĪ-dēs	ski-LŌĒ-dās	Latin	scilla
scirpoidea	skir-PŌĪ-dē-a	skir-PŌĒ-dā-a	Latin	scirpus
scirpoides	skir-PŌĪ-dēz	skir-PŌĒ-dās	Latin	scirpus
Scirpus	SKIR-pus	SKIR-pōōs	name, plant	Scirpus
Scleranthus	skle-RAN-thus	skle-RAN-tōōs	Greek	scleros
Scolochloa	sko-LO-klō-a	sko-LO-klo-a	Greek	scolops
scoparia	skō-PĀ-rē-a	skō-PĀ-rē-a	Latin	scoparius
scoparium	skō-PĀ-rē-um	skō-PĀ-rē-ōōm	Latin	scoparius
scopulina	skō-pū-LĪ-na	skō-poo-LĒ-na	Latin	scopulus
scopulinum	skō-pū-LĪ-num	skō-poo-LĒ-nōōm	Latin	scopulus
scorzonerifolia	skor-zo-ne-ri-FŌ-lē-a	skor-zo-ne-ri-FŌ-lē-a	name, plant	Scorzonera
scouleri	SKOO-le-rī	SKOO-le-rē	name, person	Scouler, John

Root 1 Meaning	Root 2	Root 2 Meaning / (referring to)
1740-1799, a Swiss botanist, geologist and son Theodore, naturalist		
Sawatch Mts., CO, USA		
living among rocks		
rock, stone	frangere	to break (bulblets were used to treat bladder stones)
saxifrage, genus in the Saxifrage Family		
the type genus		
rock, stone	montanus	of mountains, mountainous
rock, stone	montanus	of mountains, mountainous
rock, stone	montanus	of mountains, mountainous
rough, itchy		
to climb or scale		
thin, papery, scarious		
hard, tough	atus	with, like
staff		(the tall, upright spore-bearing leaf)
1672-1733, a professor at Zurich	i	of, belonging to
1672-1733 and 1684-1738, Swiss botanists in Zurich		
the type genus		
to split, divide	achne	down, chaff (split tip of the lemma)
to split, divide	achyron	chaff, husk (split flowering scales)
a rush	plektos	twisted, plaited
a rush	prasinos	leek
1739-1810, professor at Erlangen	i	of, belonging to
1780-1834, German botanist who worked in Bethlehem, PA	ii	of, belonging to
squill, a genus in the Lily Family	oides	like, resembling
bulrush	oides	like, resembling
bulrush	oides	like, resembling
ancient name of Pliny for a rush/bulrush		
hard	anthos	flower (tough calyx tube or receptacle)
prickle	chloa	grass
sweeper, broom-like		
sweeper, broom-like		
cliff, crag, projecting rock		
cliff, crag, projecting rock		
black-salsify, a genus in the Aster Family	folium	leaf
1804-1871, surgeon, naturalist, collector in the Columbia River region	i	of, belonging to

PRONUNCIATION & DERIVATION

Scientific Name	English Latin Pronunctiaion	Reconstructed Latin Pronunciation	Root Source	Root 1
scouleriana	skoo-le-rē-Ā-na	skoo-le-rē-Ä-na	name, person	Scouler, John
scribneri	SKRIB-ne-rī	SKRIB-ne-rē	name, person	Scribner, Frank L.
Scrophularia	skro-fū-LĀ-rē-a	skro-poo-LÄ-rē-a	Latin	scrofulae
Scrophulariaceae	skro-fū-lā-ri-Ā-sē-ē	skro-poo-lä-rē-Ä-kā-ī	name, plant	Scrophularia
Scutellaria	skū-te-LĀ-rē-a	skoo-te-LÄ-rē-a	Latin	scutella
scutellata	skū-te-LĀ-ta	skoo-te-LÄ-ta	Latin	scutella
Secale	se-KĀ-lē	se-KÄ-lā	name, plant	Secale
secalinus	se-ka-LĪ-nus	se-ka-LĒ-nōōs	name, plant	Secale
secunda	se-KUN-da	se-KOON-da	Latin	secundus
Securigera	se-kū-RI-je-ra	se-koo-RI-ge-ra	Latin	securiger
Sedum	SĒ-dum	SÄ-dōōm	Latin	sedo
seguieri	SE-gē-ā-rē, se-gooē-Ā-rē	se-gooē-Ä-rē	name, person	Séguier, J.
Selaginella	se-la-ji-NE-la	se-la-gi-NE-la	Latin	selago
Selaginellaceae	sē-la-ji-ne-LĀ-sē-ē	se-la-gē-ne-LÄ-kā-ī	name, plant	Selaginella
selaginoides	se-la-ji-NŌĪ-dēz	se-la-gi-NŌĒ-dās	Latin	selago
selago	se-LĀ-gō	se-LÄ-gō	Latin, New	savin
selkirkii	sel-KIR-kē-ī	sel-KIR-kē-ē	name, person	Selkirk, Thomas D.
sempervirens	sem-per-VĪ-renz	sem-per-WĒ-rens	Latin	semper
Senecio	se-NĒ-shē-ō, se-NĒ-shō	se-NÄ-kē-ō	Latin	senex
senega	SE-ne-ga	SE-ne-ga	Native American	Seneca
sepium	SĒ-pē-um	SE-pē-ōōm	Latin	sepes
septentrionale	sep-ten-trē-ō-NĀ-lē	sep-ten-trē-ō-NÄ-lā	Latin	septentrionalis
septentrionalis	sep-ten-trē-ō-NĀ-lis	sep-ten-trē-ō-NÄ-lis	Latin	septentrionalis
sericea	sē-RI-sē-a	sā-RI-kā-a	Latin	serica
sericeus	sē-RI-sē-us	sā-RI-kā-ōōs	Latin	serica
serissima	sē-RI-si-ma	sā-RI-si-ma	Latin	serica
serpillifolia	ser-pi-li-FŌ-lē-a	ser-pi-li-FŌ-lē-a	name, plant	Serpyllum
serriola	se-rē-Ō-la	se-rē-Ō-la	name, plant	Serriola
serrulata	ser-ū-LĀ-ta	ser-oo-LÄ-ta	Latin	serra
sessiliflora	se-si-li-FLŌ-ra	se-si-li-FLŌ-ra	Latin	sessilis
Setaria	se-TĀ-rē-a	se-TÄ-rē-a	Latin	seta
Shepherdia	she-PUR-dē-a	se-PŌŌR-dē-a	name, person	Shepherd, John
sheridana	she-ri-DĀ-na	se-ri-DÄ-na	name, place	Sheridan

Root 1 Meaning	Root 2	Root 2 Meaning / (referring to)
1804-1871, surgeon, naturalist, collector in the Columbia River region	anus	from or of
1851-1938, botanist in USDA, Washington, D.C., studied grasses	i	of, belonging to
swellings of the neck glands		(fleshy knobs on rhizomes were used to heal swollen neck glands [scrophula])
the type genus		
a little dish or tray		(bell-shaped 'lid' of the fruiting calyx)
saucer, shallow bowl	atus	with, like (the saucer-like shape)
ancient name for rye		
rye, a kind of grain	inus	pertaining to
following, behind, ranking below		(flowers on one side only)
axe-bearing		
to sit		(many spp grow on rocks and walls)
1733 – 1784, French botanist (SE-gē-ā)		
a kind of clubmoss	ella	diminutive
the type genus		
a kind of clubmoss	oides	like, resembling
a low European shrub	ago	with the characteristics of
1771-1820, Scottish philanthropist funded the Red River settlement, MB	ii	of, belonging to
always, ever	vireo	to be green
an old man		(the downy seed heads look like white hair and then a bald head)
aboriginal tribe from Great Lakes region		
hedge, fence, partition	ium	like or of, diminutive (used in hedges)
northern, literally, the 7 plowing oxen, the 7 stars of Ursa Major	alis	of, like
northern, literally, the 7 plowing oxen, the 7 stars of Ursa Major	alis	of, like
silk		(silky hairs)
silk		(silky hairs)
silk	issimus	superlative, very (silky hairs)
an early name for wild thyme	folium	leaf (leaves like wild thyme)
an old name for chicory		
saw, hence saw-toothed	atula	with, diminutive
low growing, short stalked	floris	flower
bristle, hair	i	(the bristly spikelets)
1764-1836, an English botanist, curator of Liverpool botanical garden		
town in n Wyoming, USA		

115

PRONUNCIATION & DERIVATION

Scientific Name	English Latin Pronunctiaion	Reconstructed Latin Pronunciation	Root Source	Root 1
Shinnersoseris	shi-ner-so-SE-ris	si-ner-so-SE-ris	name, person	Shinners, Lloyd H.
Sibbaldia	si-BAL-dē-a	si-BAL-dē-a	name, person	Sibbald, Sir Robert
sibirica	sī-BI-ri-ka	sē-BI-ri-ka	name, place	Siberia
sibiricum	sī-BI-ri-kum	sē-BI-ri-kõõm	name, place	Siberia
siccata	si-KÃ-ta	si-KÄ-ta	Latin	siccata
Silene	sī-LĒ-nē	sē-LÃ-nā	Greek	sialon
Silybum	SI-li-bum	SI-li-bõõm	name, plant	Silybum
simplex	SIM-pleks	SIM-pleks	Latin	simplex
simpliciuscula	sim-pli-SĒ-ū-skū-la	sim-pli-KĒ-oo-skoo-la	Latin	simplex
simulata	si-mū-LÃ-ta	si-moo-LÄ-ta	Latin	simulo
Sinapis	si-NÃ-pis	si-NÃ-pis	name, plant	Sinapi
sinuata	si-nū-Ã-ta	si-noo-Ä-ta	Latin	sinuo
Sisymbrium	si-SIM-brē-um	si-SIM-brē-õõm	name, plant	Sisymbrium
Sisyrinchium	si-si-RIN-kē-um	si-si-RIN-kē-õõm	name, plant	Sisyrinchium
sitchense	sit-KEN-sē	sit-KEN-sā	name, place	Sitka
sitchensis	sit-KEN-sis	sit-KEN-sis	name, place	Sitka
Sium	SĪ-um	SĒ-õõm	name, plant	sion
Smelowskia	sme-LOW-skē-a	sme-LOW-skē-a	name, person	Smielowski, Timofei A.
smithii	SMI-thē-ī	SMI-tē-ē	name, person	Smith, J.E. or Smith, ?
Solanaceae	so-la-NÃ-sē-ē	so-la-NÄ-kā-ī	name, plant	Solanum
Solanum	so-LÃ-num	so-LÄ-nõõm	name, plant	Solanum
Solidago	so-li-DÃ-go	so-li-DÃ-go	Latin	solido
solstitialis	sol-sti-shē-Ã-lis	sol-sti-tzē-Ä-lis	Latin	solstitium
somniferum	som-NI-fe-rum	som-NI-fe-rõõm	Latin	somnus
Sonchus	SON-kus	SON-kõõs	name, plant	Sonchus
sophia	SÕ-fē-a	SÕ-pē-a	name, plant	Sophia
sophioides	sō-fē-ō-Ī-dēz	sō-pē-ō-Ē-dās	Greek	sophia
Sorbaria	sor-BÃ-rē-a	sor-BÄ-rē-a	name, plant	Sorbus
sorbifolia	sor-bi-FŌ-lē-a	sor-bi-FŌ-lē-a	name, plant	Sorbus
Sorbus	SOR-bus	SOR-bõõs	name, plant	Sorbus
sororia	so-RÕ-rē-a	so-RÕ-rē-a	Latin	sororius
Sparganium	spar-GÃ-nē-um	spar-GÄ-nē-õõm	Greek	sparganion
sparsiflorum	spar-si-FLŌ-rum	spar-si-FLŌ-rõõm	Latin	sparsus
spartea	SPAR-tē-a	SPAR-tā-a	Latin	sparteus
spathulatum	spa-thū-LÃ-tum	spa-too-LÃ-tõõm	Greek	spathe
spatulata	spa-tū-LÃ-ta	spa-too-LÃ-ta	Greek	spathe

Root 1 Meaning	Root 2	Root 2 Meaning / (referring to)
1918-1971, American botanist		
1641-1722, first professor of medicine at Edinburgh		
Siberia region, nc Russia	ica	belonging to
Siberia region, nc Russia	ica	belonging to
dried up		
saliva		(the sticky secretions on the stems)
ancient name of a thistle used for food		
single, simple		
single, simple	iuscula	with or like, diminutive
imitate, copy	atus	with, like
ancient Celtic name for mustard, ultimately of Egyptian origin		(the mustard flavor of the seeds)
bend, curve	atus	with, like (the wavy edges)
ancient name of a Mustard Family plant		
name from Theophrastus, plant unknown		
town in the Alaska Panhandle, AK, USA	ense	of a place or country
town in the Alaska Panhandle, AK, USA	ensis	of a place or country
old Celtic/Greek name of a marsh plant		
1769/1770-1815, a Russian botanist, wrote *Hortus petropolitanus*		
1759-1828, English, founded Linnaean Society or one of many Smiths	ii	of, belonging to
the type genus		
New Latin name for nightshade		
to unite, make whole or heal		(its supposed healing qualities)
summer solstice, longest day of the year	alis	of, like
sleep	fera	bearing, carrying
ancient Greek name for sowthistle		
an earlier name for tansymustard		
an earlier name for tansymustard	oides	like, resembling
the mountain-ash genus	aria	of, like
mountain-ash, a genus in Rosaceae	folium	leaf
ancient name of pear or service-tree		
of a sister, sisterly		
swaddling-band, diaper, ribbon		(the ribbon-like leaves)
scattered, few, sprinkled	floris	flower
broom		(shaped like or used to make brooms)
broad flat tool for mixing, broad-sword	atus	with, like
broad flat tool for mixing, broad-sword	atus	with, like

PRONUNCIATION & DERIVATION

Scientific Name	English Latin Pronunctiaion	Reconstructed Latin Pronunciation	Root Source	Root 1
spatulatus	spa-tū-LÄ-tus	spa-too-LÄ-tōōs	Greek	spathe
speciosa	spe-sē-Ō-sa	spe-kē-Ō-sa	Latin	speciosus
spectabilis	spek-TÄ-bi-lis	spek-TÄ-bi-lis	Latin	spectabilis
Spergula	SPER-gū-la	SPER-goo-la	Latin	spargere
Spergularia	sper-gū-LÄ-rē-a	sper-goo-LÄ-rē-a	name, plant	Spergula
Sphaeralcea	sfē-RAL-sē-a	spī-RAL-kā-a	Greek	sphaira
Sphenopholis	sfe-NO-fo-lis	spe-NO-po-lis	Greek	sphen
spicata	spī-KÄ-ta	spē-KÄ-ta	Latin	spica
spicatum	spī-KÄ-tum	spē-KÄ-tōōm	Latin	spica
Spinacia	spi-NÄ-shē-a	spi-NÄ-kē-a	name, plant	Spinaca
spinosa	spī-NŌ-sa	spē-NŌ-sa	Latin	spinosus
spinosum	spī-NŌ-sum	spē-NŌ-sōōm	Latin	spinosus
Spiraea	spī-RĒ-a	spē-RĪ-a	Greek	speira
Spiranthes	spī-RAN-thēz	spē-RAN-tēs	Greek	speira
Spirodela	spī-ro-DĒ-la	spē-ro-DÄ-la	Greek	speira
splendens	SPLEN-denz	SPLEN-dens	Latin	splendor
Sporobolus	spo-RO-bo-lus	spo-RO-bo-lōōs	Greek	sporos
sprengelii	spren-GE-lē-ī	spren-GE-lē-ē	name, person	Sprengel, C.P.J.
spurium	SPŪ-rē-um	SPOO-rē-ōōm	Latin	spurius
squarrosa	skwa-RŌ-sa	skwa-RŌ-sa	Latin	squarrosus
squarrosus	skwa-RŌ-sus	skwa-RŌ-sōōs	Latin	squarrosus
Stachys	STÄ-kis	STÄ-kis	Greek	stachus
standleyi	STAND-lē-ī	stand-LĒ-ē	name, person	Standley, Paul Carpenter
Stellaria	ste-LÄ-rē-a	ste-LÄ-rē-a	Latin	stella
stellatum	ste-LÄ-tum	ste-LÄ-tōōm	Latin	stella
stelleri	STE-le-rī	STE-le-rē	name, person	Steller, Georg Wilhelm
stenantha	ste-NAN-tha	ste-NAN-ta	Greek	stenos
stenoloba	ste-nō-LŌ-ba	ste-nō-LŌ-ba	Greek	stenos
stenopetalum	ste-nō-PE-ta-lum	ste-nō-PE-ta-lōōm	Greek	stenos
stenophyllus	ste-nō-FI-lus	ste-nō-PI-lōōs	Greek	stenos
stenoptera	ste-nō-TE-ra	ste-nō-TE-ra	Greek	stenos
Stephanomeria	ste-fa-no-ME-rē-a	ste-pa-no-ME-rē-a	Greek	stephane
stipata	stī-PÄ-ta	stē-PÄ-ta	Latin	stipatus
stoebe	STĒ-bē	STOI-bā	Greek	stoibe
stolonifera	stō-lo-NĪ-fe-ra	stō-lo-NĒ-fe-ra	Latin	stolo
stramonium	stra-MŌ-nē-um	stra-MŌ-nē-ōōm	name, plant	Stramonium

Root 1 Meaning	Root 2	Root 2 Meaning / (referring to)
broad flat tool for mixing, broad-sword	atus	with, like
beautiful, splendid		
notably showy [from spectus, behold!]		
to scatter		(the sowing of seeds for forage)
spurrey, a related genus	aria	of, like
globe, sphere	alcea	a mallow (its spherical fruit + the common name globe mallow)
a wedge	pholis	scale (the broad upper glume)
spike, ear of grain	atus	with, like
spike, ear of grain	atus	with, like
ancient Spanish name for this plant		
thorny, difficult		
thorny, difficult		
a coil, spiral or wreath		(the use of flowering stems in garlands)
a coil, spiral or wreath	anthos	flower (the spirally twisted inflorescence)
a coil, spiral or wreath	delos	evident (cord-like roots)
brightness, brilliance, splendor		
seed, spore	ballein	to cast forth (throwing of seeds)
1766-1833, Halle prof. of botany/medicine	ii	of, belonging to
false, illegitimate		
rough with stiff leave or scales		
rough with stiff leave or scales		
ear of grain or a spike		(the spike-like flower cluster)
1884-1963, curator US Nat'l Herbarium, studied Alaska, Mex., Central Am flora	i	of, belonging to
a star	aria	of, like (the star-like flowers)
a star	atus	with, like (star-like flowers)
1709-1746, a German naturalist on Bering's expedition to Siberia	i	of, belonging to
narrow	anthos	flower
narrow	lobus	rounded projection, lobe
narrow	petalum	petal
narrow	phyllon	leaf
narrow	pteron	wing, feather
wreath or crown	meris	division of part
crowded, packed together		(use in brooms and bedding)
stuffing, padding or heap		
shoot, runner, branch	fera	bearing, carrying
Theophrastes name for jimsonweed		

PRONUNCIATION & DERIVATION

Scientific Name	English Latin Pronunctiaion	Reconstructed Latin Pronunciation	Root Source	Root 1
streptanthifolia	strep-tan-thi-FŌ-lē-a	strep-tan-ti-FŌ-lē-a	name, plant	Streptanthus
streptopoides	strep-tō-PŌĪ-dēz	strep-tō-PŌĒ-dās	name, plant	Streptopus
Streptopus	STREP-to-pus	STREP-to-pŏŏs	Greek	streptos
striata	strī-Ā-ta	strē-Ä-ta	Latin	striatus
stricta	STRIK-ta	STRIK-ta	Latin	strictus
strictifolius	strik-ti-FŌ-lē-us	strik-ti-FŌ-lē-ŏŏs	Latin	strictus
strigosus	stri-GŌ-sus	stri-GŌ-sŏŏs	Latin	strigosus
strumarium	strū-MĀ-rē-um	stroo-MÄ-rē-ŏŏm	Latin	struma
struthiopteris	stru-thē-OP-te-ris	strŏŏ-tē-OP-te-ris	Greek	strouthion
Stuckenia	SHTOO-ke-nē-a, stu-KE-nē-a	stŏŏ-KE-nē-a	name, person	Stucken, Wilhelm A.
stygius	STI-jē-us	STĒ-gē-ŏŏs	Latin	stygius
Suaeda	SWĀ-da	SWĪ-da	name, plant	Suaeda
suave	sū-Ā-vē	soo-Ä-wā	Latin	suavis
subarctica	sub-ARK-ti-ka	sŏŏb-ARK-ti-ka	Latin	sub
subglabrum	sub-GLĀB-rum	sŏŏb-GLÄB-rŏŏm	Latin	sub
subgorodkovii	sub-gō-rod-KŌ-vē-ī	sŏŏb-gō-rod-KŌ-wē-ē	Latin + name, person	sub
subjuga	sub-JŪ-ga	sŏŏb-YOO-ga	Latin	sub
subnuda	sub-NŪ-da	sŏŏb-NOO-da	Latin	sub
subnudum	sub-NŪ-dum	sŏŏb-NOO-dŏŏm	Latin	sub
subspicatum	sub-spī-KĀ-tum	sŏŏb-spē-KÄ-tŏŏm	Latin	sub
subulata	su-bū-LĀ-ta	sŏŏ-boo-LÄ-ta	Latin	subula
subvaliana	sub-vä-lē-Ā-na	sŏŏb-wä-lē-Ä-na	name, person	Vahl, Jens L.M.
Suckleya	SUK-lē-ya	SŎŎK-lā-ya	name, person	Suckley, George
suckleyana	suk-lē-Ā-na	sŏŏk-lā-Ä-na	name, person	Suckley, George
suckleyi	SUK-lē-ī	SOOK-lē-ē	name, person	Suckley, George
sudetica	sū-DĀ-ti-ka	soo-DE-ti-ka	name, place	Sudeten
suffrutescens	suf-ru-TE-senz	sŏŏf-rŏŏ-TE-skens	Latin	suf
Suksdorfia	suks-DŌR-fē-a	sŏŏks-DŌR-fē-a	name, person	Suksdorf, Wilhelm N.
suksdorfiana	suks-dor-fē-Ā-na	sooks-dor-fē-Ä-na	name, person	Suksdorf, Wilhelm N.
sulphurescens	sul-fū-RE-senz	sŏŏl-poo-RE-skens	Latin	sulphureus
supina	su-PĪ-na	sŏŏ-PĒ-na	Latin	supinus
sychnocephala	sik-nō-SE-fa-la	sik-nō-KE-pa-la	Greek	sychnos
sylvaticum	sil-VĀ-ti-kum	sil-WÄ-ti-kŏŏm	Latin	sylva
sylvestris	sil-VES-tris	sil-WES-tris	Latin	sylva

Root 1 Meaning	Root 2	Root 2 Meaning / (referring to)
jewel flower, a genus of mustard plants	folium	leaf
twistedstalk, a genus in the Lily Family	oides	like, resembling
twisted	pous	foot (the abruptly bent flower stalks)
grooved, furrowed, fluted		
straight, narrow (the erect plants)		
close, straight, narrow	folium	leaf
thin, meagre, shriveled		
swollen gland, tumour	ium	like or of, diminutive
ostrich	pteron	wing, feather
1860-1901, German botanist, collected in Australia and America		
stygian, dismal, hellish, deadly	ium	like or of, diminutive
ancient Arabic name for these plants		
sweet		
under, less than, somewhat	arctos	north
under, less than, somewhat	glaber	smooth, hairless, bald
under, less than, somewhat	Gorodkov, Boris N.	1890-1953, Russian Arctic geobotanist and explorer
under, less than, somewhat	jugum	yoke, pair
under, less than, somewhat	nudus	bare, naked
under, less than, somewhat	nudus	bare, naked
under, less than, somewhat	spica	spike, ear of grain
awl	atus	with, like
1796-1854, Danish botanist, son of botanist Martin Vahl	sub	under, less than
1830-1869, physician and naturalist		
1830-1869, physician and naturalist	anus	from or of
1830-1869, physician and naturalist	i	of, belonging to
mountain region in Czech Republic-Poland	ica	belonging to
under, less than, somewhat	fruticosus	shrubby (the woody base)
1850-1932, German-US botanist, studied flora of the Pacific Northwest		
1850-1932, German/US botanist, studied flora of the Pacific Northwest		
of sulfur, sulfury	escens	in the process of becoming
lying flat on the back and turned upwards		
many, great, large, long	kephale	head
forest	ica	belonging to
forest	estris	living in, growing in

PRONUNCIATION & DERIVATION

Scientific Name	English Latin Pronunctiaion	Reconstructed Latin Pronunciation	Root Source	Root 1
Symphoricarpos	sim-fo-ri-KAR-pos	sim-po-ri-KAR-pos	Greek	symphysis
Symphyotrichum	sim-fē-o-TRI-kum	sim-pē-o-TRI-kŏŏm	Greek	symphysis
Symphytum	SIM-fi-tum	SIM-pi-tŏŏm	Greek	symphysis
Syringa	si-RIN-ga	si-RIN-ga	Greek	syrinx
syzigachne	si-zi-GAK-nē	si-zi-GAK-na	Greek	syzygos
tabernaemontani	ta-ber-nē-mon-TÄ-nī	ta-ber-nī-mon-TÄ-nē	Latin	taberna
tahoensis	ta-hō-EN-sis	ta-hō-EN-sis	name, place	Tahoe
tanacetifolia	ta-na-sē-ti-FŌ-lē-a	ta-na-kā-ti-FŌ-lē-a	name, plant	Tanacetum
Tanacetum	ta-na-SĒ-tum	ta-na-KÄ-tŏŏm	name, plant	Tanazita
tangutica	tan-GŪ-ti-ka	tan-GOO-ti-ka	Greek	tangos
Taraxacum	ta-RAK-sa-kum	ta-RAK-sa-kŏŏm	Arabic, Greek	taraxos+akos, taraxia+keomai
Taraxia	ta-RAK-sē-a	ta-RAK-sē-a	name, plant	taraxacoides
tatarica	ta-TA-ri-ka	ta-TA-ri-ka	name, place	Tatary
tataricum	ta-TA-ri-kum	ta-TA-ri-kŏŏm	name, place	Tatary
Taxaceae	tak-SÄ-sē-ē	tak-SÄ-kā-ī	name, plant	Taxus
Taxus	TAK-sus	TAK-sŏŏs	name, plant	Taxus
tectorum	tek-TŌ-rum	tek-TŌ-rŏŏm	Latin	tectum
Telesonix	te-le-SO-niks	te-le-SO-niks	Greek	teleos
Tellima	te-LĪ-ma	te-LĒ-ma	name, plant	Mitella
temulentum	tē-mu-LEN-tum	tā-mŏŏ-LEN-tŏŏm	Latin	temulentus
tenax	TE-naks	TE-naks	Latin	tenax
tenella	te-NE-la	te-NE-la	Latin	tenellus
tenellus	te-NE-lus	te-NE-lŏŏs	Latin	tenellus
tenera	TE-ne-ra	TE-ne-ra	Latin	tener
tenerrima	te-NE-ri-ma	te-NE-ri-ma	Latin	tenerrimus
tenuiflora	te-nī-FLŌ-ra	te-nooē-FLŌ-ra	Latin	tenuis
tenuis	TE-nū-is	TE-noo-is	Latin	tenuis
Tephroseris	te-FRŌ-se-ris	te-PRŌ-se-ris	Greek	tephros
testiculata	tes-ti-kū-LÄ-ta	tes-ti-koo-LÄ-ta	Latin	testiculus
tetragona	te-tra-GŌ-na	te-tra-GŌ-na	Greek	tetra
tetrahit	TE-tra-hit	TE-tra-hit	Latin	tetrait
tetrandrum	te-TRAN-drum	te-TRAN-drŏŏm	Greek	tetra
Tetraneuris	tet-ra-NĒŪ-ris	te-tra-NĒOO-ris	Greek	tetra
texanus	tek-SA-nus	tek-SA-nŏŏs	name, place	Texas
textile	TEK-sti-lē	TEK-sti-lā	Latin	textilis
Thalictrum	tha-LIK-trum	ta-LIK-trŏŏm	name, plant	Thaliktron

Root 1 Meaning	Root 2	Root 2 Meaning / (referring to)
borne/growing together, coalescing	carpos	fruit
borne/growing together, coalescing	trichos	hair
borne/growing together, coalescing	phyton	plant (its use to heal wounds)
a pipe		(branches of related shrubs used for pipes)
yoked together, paired, joined	achne	down, chaff
hut, shop	montanus	of mountains, mountainous
lake region in CA-NV, USA	ensis	of a place or country
tansy, a genus in the Aster Family	folium	leaf
ancient name for this plant		
rancid	ica	belonging to
a bitter herb, disorder + remedy, eye disorder + to cure		(reputed healing qualities)
with leaves similar to Leontodon taraxacoides		
ancient region between the Sea of Japan and Dnieper (n of the Black Sea)	ica	belonging to
ancient region between the Sea of Japan and Dnieper (n of the Black Sea)	ica	belonging to
the type genus		
ancient name for the yew tree		
roof		
complete	onxy	claw
anagram of this related genus		
intoxicated, drunken		
holding fast, clinging, obstinate		
delicate and dainty		
delicate and dainty		
tender, soft, slender		
very slender		
slender, fine, delicate	floris	flower
slender, fine, delicate		
ash-colored or hoary		
male genital gland, testicle	atus	with, like
four	gonia	an angle
an old generic name meaning 4-parted		
four	andros	male (the 4 anthers)
four	neuron	nerve
state of Texas, USA	anus	from or of
woven		
name by Dioscorides for an unknown plant		

PRONUNCIATION & DERIVATION

Scientific Name	English Latin Pronunctiaion	Reconstructed Latin Pronunciation	Root Source	Root 1
thapsus	THAP-sus	TAP-sŏŏs	name, plant	Thapsos
Thelesperma	the-le-SPER-ma	te-le-SPER-ma	Greek	thele
Thelypteridaceae	thē-lip-te-ri-DĀ-sē-ē	te-lēp-te-rē-DĀ-kā-ī	name, plant	Thelypteris
theophrasti	thē-ō-FRAS-tī	tā-ō-PRAS-tē	Greek	Theophrastos
thermale	ther-MĀ-lē	ter-MÄ-lā	Latin	thermae
Thermopsis	ther-MOP-sis	ter-MOP-sis	name, plant	Thermos
Thesium	THĒ-sē-um	TĀ-sē-ŏŏm	Greek	thes
Thinopyrum	thi-no-PĪ-rum	ti-no-PĒ-rŏŏm	Greek	thinos
Thlaspi	THLA-spī	TLA-spē	Greek	thlaein
Thuja	THOO-ya	TOO-ya	name, plant	Thuia
thymiflorum	tī-mi-FLŌ-rum	tē-mi-FLŌ-rŏŏm	name, plant	Thymus
thyrsiflora	thir-si-FLŌ-ra	tir-si-FLŌ-ra	Greek	thyrsos
Tiarella	tē-a-RE-la	tē-a-RE-la	Latin	tiara
tilesii	ti-LE-sē-ī	ti-LE-sē-ē	name, person	Tileseus von Tilenau, W.
tilingii	ti-LIN-gē-ī	ti-LIN-gē-ē	name, person	Tiling, Heinrich S.T.
tincta	TINK-ta	TINK-ta	Latin	tinctus
tinctoria	tink-TŌ-rē-a	tink-TŌ-rē-a	Latin	tinctorius
tinctorius	tink-TŌ-rē-us	tink-TŌ-rē-ŏŏs	Latin	tinctorius
Tofieldia	tō-FĒL-dē-a	tō-FĀL-dē-a	name, person	Tofield, T.
Tofieldiaceae	tō-FĒL-di-Ā-sē-ē	tō-fēl-dē-Ä-kā-ī	name, plant	Tofieldia
tomentosa	tō-men-TŌ-sa	tō-men-TŌ-sa	Latin	tomentum
tomentosum	tō-men-TŌ-sum	tō-men-TŌ-sŏŏm	Latin	tomentum
Tomostima	to-MO-sti-ma	to-MO-si-ma	Greek	tomos
Tonestus	to-NE-stus	to-NE-stŏŏs	name, plant	Stenotus
tonsa	TON-sa	TON-sa	Latin	tonsus
torreyi	TŌ-rē-ī	TŌ-rē-ē	name, person	Torrey, John
Torreyochloa	tō-rē-o-KLŌ-a	tō-rē-o-KLŌ-a	name, person	Torrey, John
Townsendia	town-SEN-dē-a	town-SEN-dē-a	name, person	Townsend, D.
Toxicodendron	tok-si-kō-DEN-dron	tōk-si-kō-DEN-dron	Greek	toxikon
Toxicoscordion	tok-si-kō-SKOR-dē-on	tok-si-kō-SKOR-dē-on	Greek	toxikon
trachycarpa	tra-ki-KAR-pa	tra-ki-KAR-pa	Greek	trachys
trachycaulus	tra-ki-KÄ-lus	tra-ki-KOW-lŏŏs	Greek	trachys
trachyphylla	tra-ki-FI-la	tra-ki-PI-la	Greek	trachys
Tradescantia	tra-des-KAN-sha	tra-des-KAN-tzē-a	name, person	Tradescant, J.
Tragopogon	tra-go-PŌ-gon	tra-go-PŌ-gon	Greek	tragos
tragus	TRA-gus	TRA-gŏŏs	Greek	tragos

Root 1 Meaning	Root 2	Root 2 Meaning / (referring to)
a plant of Thapsos in Sicily		
a nipple	sperma	seed (the papillose achenes)
the type genus		
renowned botanist and philosopher		
hot springs, public baths	alis	of, like
lupine	opsis	appearance (lupine-like flower clusters)
laboring servant		(its simple appearance)
beach	pyros	grain, wheat
to crush (the flattened pod)		
ancient name of a resinous evergreen		
thyme, a genus in the Mint Family	floris	flower
densely branched cluster	floris	flower
turban (the shape of the pistil)	ella	diminutive
1769-1857, with Krusenstern on first Russian circumnavigation (1802-1806)	ii	of, belonging to
1818-1871, Baltic physician/botanist, collected in Alaska, Calif., Nevada	ii	of, belonging to
to dye or color		
used in dyeing		
used in dyeing		
1730-1779, an English botanist		
the type genus		
woolly hairs	osus	with the quality or nature of
woolly hairs	osus	with the quality or nature of
section	tima	time
anagram of *Stenotus*		
haircut, hairdo, oar		
1796-1873, chemistry/botany prof., co-authored Flora of North America	i	of, belonging to
1796-1873, US chemistry/botany prof, studied 100s of plants from explorers	chloa	grass
1787-1858, Philadelphia botanist		
poison	dendron	tree
poison	scordion	garlic
rough	karpos	fruit
rough	caulis	stem, stalk
rough	phyllon	leaf
1608-1662, gardener to Charles I of England		
goat	pogon	beard (feathery seed heads)
goat		

PRONUNCIATION & DERIVATION

Scientific Name	English Latin Pronunctiaion	Reconstructed Latin Pronunciation	Root Source	Root 1
tremuloides	tre-mu-LŌĪ-dēz	tre-mõõ-LŌĔ-dās	name, plant	Tremula
triandra	trī-AN-dra	trē-AN-dra	Greek	treis
triangularis	trī-an-gū-LĀ-ris	trē-an-goo-LĀ-ris	Latin	triangulus
triangulivalvis	trī-an-gū-li-VAL-vis	trē-an-goo-li-WAL-wis	Latin	triangulus
Triantha	trī-AN-tha	trē-AN-ta	Greek	treis
trichocarpa	trī-kō-KAR-pa	trē-kō-KAR-pa	Greek	trichos
Trichophorum	tri-kō-FŌ-rum	tri-kō-PŌ-rõõm	Greek	trichos
trichophyllus	trī-kō-FI-lus	trē-kō-PI-lõõs	Greek	trichos
tricolor	TRĪ-ko-lor	TRĔ-ko-lor	Latin	trias
tricuspidata	trī-kus-pi-DĀ-ta	trē-kõõs-pi-DÄ-ta	Latin	trias
tridentata	trī-den-TĀ-ta	trē-den-TÄ-ta	Latin	trias
trifida	TRI-fi-da	TRI-fi-da	Latin	trias
trifidum	TRI-fi-dum	TRI-fi-dõõm	Latin	trias
trifidus	TRI-fi-dus	TRI-fi-dõõs	Latin	trias
triflorum	trī-FLŌ-rum	trē-FLŌ-rõõm	Latin	trias
trifolia	trī-FŌ-lē-a	trē-FŌ-lē-a	Latin	trias
trifoliata	trī-fō-lē-Ā-ta	trē-fō-lē-Ä-ta	Latin	trias
Trifolium	trī-FŌ-lē-um	trē-FŌ-lē-õõm	Latin	trias
trifolium	trī-FŌ-lē-um	trē-FŌ-lē-õõm	Latin	trias
Triglochin	trī-GLŌ-kin	trē-GLŌ-kin	Greek	treis
triglumis	trī-GLŪ-mis	trē-GLOO-mis	Latin	trias
Trigonella	tri-go-NE-la	tri-go-NE-la	Latin	trigonum
Trillium	TRI-lē-um	TRI-lē-õõm	Greek	treis
tripartita	trī-par-TĪ-ta	trē-par-TĔ-ta	Latin	trias
Tripleurospermum	tri-plēū-rō-SPER-mum	tri-plēoo-rō-SPER-mõõm	Greek	treis + pleuron
Tripterocalyx	trip-te-rō-KĀ-liks	trip-te-rō-KĀ-liks	Greek	tri + pteros
Trisetum	trī-SĒ-tum	trē-SÄ-tõõm	Greek	treis
trisperma	trī-SPER-ma	trē-SPER-ma	Latin	trias
triste	TRIS-tē	TRIS-tā	Latin	tristis
trisulca	trī-SUL-ka	trē-SOOL-ka	Latin	trias
triternatum	trī-ter-NĀ-tum	trē-ter-NÄ-tõõm	Latin	trias
triticeum	trī-TI-sē-um	trē-TI-kā-õõm	name, plant	Triticum
Triticum	TRI-ti-kum	TRI-ti-kõõm	name, plant	Triticum
triviale	tri-vē-Ā-lē	tri-wē-Ä-lā	Latin	trivialis
trivialis	tri-vē-Ā-lis	tri-wē-Ä-lis	Latin	trivialis
Trollius	TRŌ-lē-us	TRŌ-lē-õõs	German	troll
truncata	trun-KĀ-ta	trõõn-KÄ-ta	Latin	truncus
Tsuga	SOO-ga	TSOO-ga	name, plant	Tsuga

Root 1 Meaning	Root 2	Root 2 Meaning / (referring to)
quivering poplar, *Populus tremula*	oides	resembling (leaves quiver in the wind)
three	andros	male
triangular		
triangular	valva	valve
three	anthos	flower (flowers in 3s)
hair	karpos	fruit
hair	phoros	bearing
hair	phyllon	leaf
three	color	tint, hue
three	cuspidatus	pointed
three	dentatus	toothed, serrated
three	findo	split, divide
three	findo	split, divide
three	findo	split, divide
three	floris	flower
three	folium	leaf
three	folium	leaf
three	folium	leaf
three	folium	leaf
three	glochis	point (3-pointed capsules)
three	gluma	bract, hull, husk
triangle (the corolla of one species)	ella	diminutive
three (all parts in 3s)		
three	partitio	division, distribution
three + ribbed	sperma	seed
three + winged	kalyx	calyx
three	seta	bristle, hair
three	sperma	seed
sad, weeping		
three	sulcus	furrow, groove
three	ternatus	consisting of three
wheat, a genus in the Grass Family		
ancient/classical Latin name		
common, vulgare		
common, vulgare		
a globe		
lopped, trimmed	atus	with, like
Japanese name of a native hemlock		

PRONUNCIATION & DERIVATION

Scientific Name	English Latin Pronunctiaion	Reconstructed Latin Pronunciation	Root Source	Root 1
tunux	TOO-nooks	TOO-nooks	name, person	Tunux
turionifera	tū-rē-o-NI-fe-ra	too-rē-o-NI-fe-ra	Latin	turionis
turkestanicum	tur-kes-TAN-i-kum	tōōr-kes-TAN-i-kōōm	name, place	Turkestan
Turritis	TU-ri-tis	TŌŌ-ri-tis	Latin	turris
Typha	TĪ-fa	TĒ-pa	name, plant	Typhe
Typhaceae	tī-FÄ-sē-ē	tē-PÄ-kā-ī	name, plant	Typha
tyrellii	TĪ-re-lē-ī	tē-RE-lē-ē	name, person	Tyrrell, Joseph Bull
uliginosa	ū-lī-ji-NŌ-sa	oo-lē-gi-NŌ-sa	Latin	uligo
uliginosum	ū-lī-ji-NŌ-sum	oo-lē-gi-NŌ-sōōm	Latin	uligo
Ulmaceae	ul-MÄ-sē-ē	ōōl-MÄ-kā-ī	name, plant	Ulmus
Ulmus	UL-mus	ŌŌL-mōōs	name, plant	Ulmus
umbellata	um-be-LÄ-ta	ōōm-be-LÄ-ta	Latin	umbella
umbellatum	um-be-LÄ-tum	ōōm-be-LÄ-tōōm	Latin	umbella
umbellatus	um-be-LÄ-tus	ōōm-be-LÄ-tōōs	Latin	umbella
umbrinella	um-bri-NE-la	ōōm-bri-NE-la	Latin	umbrinus
umbrosa	um-BRŌ-sa	ōōm-BRŌ-sa	Latin	umbrosa
unalascencis	u-na-las-KEN-sis	ōō-na-las-KEN-sis	name, place	Unalaska
unalaschkensis	u-na-las-KEN-sis	ōō-na-las-KEN-sis	name, place	Unalaska
uncinatus	un-sī-NÄ-tus	ōōn-kē-NÄ-tōōs	Latin	uncinatus
undulatum	un-dū-LÄ-tum	ōōn-doo-LÄ-tōōm	Latin	undulatus
uniflora	ū-ni-FLŌ-ra	oo-ni-FLŌ-ra	Latin	unus
uniflorus	ū-ni-FLŌ-rus	oo-ni-FLŌ-rōōs	Latin	unus
uniglumis	ū-ni-GLŪ-mis	oo-ni-GLOO-mis	Latin	unus
unispicata	ū-ni-spi-KÄ-ta	oo-ni-spi-KÄ-ta	Latin	unus
uralensis	ū-ra-LEN-sis	oo-ra-LEN-sis	name, place	Ural
urens	Ū-renz	OO-rens	Latin	urens
ursopedensis	ur-sō-pe-DEN-sis	ōōr-sō-pe-DEN-sis	Latin	ursus
Urtica	UR-ti-ka	ŌŌR-ti-ka	Latin	uro
Urticaceae	ur-ti-KÄ-sē-ē	ōōr-tē-KÄ-kā-ī	name, plant	Urtica
usitatissimum	ū-si-ta-TI-si-mum	oo-si-ta-TI-si-mōōm	Latin	usitatus
utahensis	ū-ta-HEN-sis	oo-ta-HEN-sis	name, place	Utah
Utricularia	ū-tri-kū-LÄ-rē-a	oo-tri-koo-LÄ-rē-a	Latin	utriculus
utriculata	ū-tri-kū-LÄ-ta	oo-tri-koo-LÄ-ta	Latin	utriculus
uva-ursi	Ū-va-UR-sī	oo-wa-OOR-sē	Latin	uva
Vaccaria	va-KÄ-rē-a	wa-KÄ-rē-a	Latin	vacca
Vaccinium	vak-SI-nē-um	wa-KI-nē-ōōm	name, plant	Vaccinium
vaginata	va-ji-NÄ-ta	wa-gi-NÄ-ta	Latin	vagina

Root 1 Meaning	Root 2	Root 2 Meaning / (referring to)
a Tlingit warrior who led the 1805 attack on Russian fort near Yakutat		
shoot, sprout, turion	fera	bearing, carrying
region between Iran and Siberia, Asia		
tower (from tower mustard)		
ancient Greek name for cattail		
the type genus		
mining engineer who collected in the Yukon around 1898	ii	of, belonging to
moisture, marshiness	osus	with the quality or nature of
moisture, marshiness	osus	with the quality or nature of
the type genus		
ancient Latin name for elm		
a parasol (flower cluster shape)	atus	with, like
a parasol (flower cluster shape)	atus	with, like
a parasol (flower cluster shape)	atus	with, like
darkened, shady	ella	diminutive (slightly darkened)
shade-loving		
island in the Aleutians, AK, USA	ensis	of a place or country
island in the Aleutians, AK, USA	ensis	of a place or country
hooked, barbed		
wavy, undulating (wavy leaves)		
one	floris	flower
one	floris	flower
one	gluma	bract, hull, husk
one	spica	spike, ear of grain
Ural Mountains, c. Russia	ensis	of a place or country
burning, stinging		
bear	pedis	foot
I burn (burning sensation on contact)		
the type genus		
usual, customary, common	issimus	superlative, very
state of Utah, USA	ensis	of a place or country
little bag, bladder or bottle (leaves)		
little bag, bladder or bottle (leaves)	atus	with, like
a grape	ursus	bear
a cow (used as fodder)		
ancient Latin name for blueberry		
sheath, scabbard	atus	with, like

PRONUNCIATION & DERIVATION

Scientific Name	English Latin Pronunctiaion	Reconstructed Latin Pronunciation	Root Source	Root 1
vaginatum	va-ji-NÄ-tum	wa-gi-NÄ-tõõm	Latin	vagina
Vahlodea	va-LŌ-dē-a	wa-LŌ-dā-a	name, person	Vahl, Jens Laurentius M.
Valeriana	va-le-rē-Ā-na	wa-le-rē-Ä-na	name, person	Valerianus, Valeria
valesiaca	va-lē-sē-Ā-ka	wa-lā-sē-Ä-ka	name, place	Valesia
vallicola	va-LI-kō-la	wa-LI-kō-la	Latin	vallum
varia	VĀ-rē-a	WÄ-rē-a	Latin	varius
variabilis	va-rē-A-bi-lis	wa-rē-A-bi-lis	Latin	varius
variegata	va-rē-e-GĀ-ta	wa-rē-e-GÄ-ta	Latin	varius
variegatum	va-rī-e-GĀ-tum	wa-rē-ā-GÄ-tõõm	Latin	varius
vaseyi	VĀ-sē-ī	WÄ-sā-ē	name, person	Vasey, George Richard
velutinus	vel-Ū-ti-nus	we-LOO-ti-nõõs	Latin, New	velutinus
venenosum	ve-nē-NŌ-sum	we-nā-NŌ-sõõm	Latin	venenum
venosus	ve-NŌ-sus	we-NŌ-sõõs	Latin	venosus
Ventenata	ven-te-NÄ-ta	wen-te-NÄ-ta	name, person	Ventenat, Étienne P.
ventosa	ven-TŌ-sa	wen-TŌ-sa	Latin	ventosus
venulosum	ven-ū-LŌ-sum	wen-oo-LŌ-sõõm	Latin	venosus
Veratrum	ve-RĀ-trum	we-RÄ-trõõm	name, plant	Veratrum
Verbascum	ver-BAS-kum	wer-BAS-kõõm	name, plant	Barbascum
Verbena	ver-BĒ-na	wer-BÄ-na	name, plant	Verbena
Verbenaceae	ver-bē-NÄ-sē-ē	wer-bā-NÄ-kā-ī	name, plant	Verbena
vermiculatus	ver-mi-kū-LÄ-tus	wer-mi-koo-LÄ-tõõs	Latin	vermiculatus
verna	VER-na	WER-na	Latin	vernus
Veronica	ve-RO-ni-ka	we-RŌ-ni-ka	name, person	St. Veronica
verticillata	ver-ti-si-LÄ-ta	wer-ti-ki-LÄ-ta	Latin	verticillus
verticillatum	ver-ti-si-LÄ-tum	wer-ti-ki-LÄ-tõõm	Latin	verticillus
verum	VĒ-rum	WÄ-rõõm	Latin	verum
vesca	VES-ka	WES-ka	Latin	vescus
vesicaria	ve-si-KÄ-rē-a	we-si-KÄ-rē-a	Latin	vesica
vestita	ves-TĪ-ta	wes-TĒ-ta	Latin	vestitus
vexilliflexus	vek-si-li-FLEK-sus	wek-si-li-FLEK-sõõs	Latin	vexillum
Viburnum	vī-BUR-num	wē-BŌŌR-nõõm	name, plant	Viburnum
Vicia	VI-shē-a	WI-kē-a	Latin	vinco
viciifolia	vi-sē-i-FŌ-lē-a	wi-kē-i-FŌ-lē-a	name, plant	Vicia
villosa	vi-LŌ-sa	wi-LŌ-sa	Latin	villosus

Root 1 Meaning	Root 2	Root 2 Meaning / (referring to)
sheath, scabbard	atus	with, like
Danish botanist 1796-1854, the son of botanist Martin Vahl		
Roman emperor 253-260, province in Pannonia		
province in Switzerland	iaca	belonging to
wall	cola	dweller
changing, of different sorts/colors		
changing, of different sorts/colors	abilis	tending to be, capable of
changing, of different sorts/colors		
changing, of different sorts/colors		
1853, son of George Vasey (a USDA botanist) who collected in California	i	of, belonging to
velvety		
poison	osus	with the quality or nature of
veiny		
1757-1808, French botanist, librarian, clergyman and author		
windy, shift as the wind		
veiny	ulus	diminutive
Modern Latin name of the hellebore		
ancient name for this plant, spelling corrupted to *Verbascum*		
ancient name for common European vervain or any sacred herb		
the type genus		
wormy, worm-like (with wavy lines)		
Spring, of Spring		
the maiden who gave her handkerchief to Christ on his way to Calvary		
little whirlwind, whorl (flowers)	atus	with, like
little whirlwind, whorl	atus	with, like
truly, yes, genuine		
weak, feeble, poor, nibbled off		
bladder, blister	aria	feminine suffix
clothing, apparel		
banner, flag	flexus	curved, twisted
Modern Latin name for wayfaring-tree		
to bind, twining		
vetch, a genus in the Pea Family	folium	leaf
hair		

131

PRONUNCIATION & DERIVATION

Scientific Name	English Latin Pronunctiaion	Reconstructed Latin Pronunciation	Root Source	Root 1
villosula	vi-LO-sū-la	wi-LO-soo-la	Latin	villosus
villosum	vi-LŌ-sum	wi-LŌ-sōōm	Latin	villosus
Viola	vī-Ō-la, VĪ-ō-la	WĒ-ō-la	name, plant	Viola
violacea	vī-ō-LÄ-sē-a	wē-ō-LÄ-kā-a	Latin	viola
Violaceae	vī-ō-LÄ-sē-ē	wē-ō-LÄ-kā-ī	name, plant	Viola
violaceus	vī-ō-LÄ-sē-us	wē-ō-LÅ-kā-ōōs	Latin	viola
virgata	vir-GÄ-ta	wir-GÄ-ta	Latin	virgatus
virgatum	vir-GÄ-tum	wir-GÅ-tōōm	Latin	virgatus
virginiana	vir-ji-nē-Ā-na	wir-gi-nē-Ä-na	name, place	Virginia
virginianum	vir-ji-nē-Ā-num	wir-gi-nē-Ä-nōōm	name, place	Virginia
virginianus	vir-ji-nē-Ā-nus	wir-gi-nē-Ä-nōōs	name, place	Virginia
virginicus	vir-JI-ni-kus	wir-GI-ni-kōōs	name, place	Virginia
viride	VI-ri-dē	WI-ri-dā	Latin	viridis
viridicarinatum	VI-ri-di-ka-ri-NÄ-tum	WI-ri-di-ka-ri-NÄ-tōōm	Latin	viridis
viridiflora	VI-ri-di-FLŌ-ra	VI-ri-di-FLŌ-ra	Latin	viridis
viridis	VI-ri-dis	WI-ri-dis	Latin	viridis
viridula	vi-RI-dū-la	wi-RI-doo-la	Latin	viridis
virosa	vi-RŌ-sa	wi-RŌ-sa	Latin	virosus
viscosissimum	vis-kō-SI-si-mum	wis-kō-SI-si-mōōm	Latin	viscosus
viscosum	vis-KŌ-sum	wis-KŌ-sōōm	Latin	viscosus
viscosus	vis-KŌ-sus	wis-KŌ-sōōs	Latin	viscosus
vitis-idaea	VĪ-tis ī-DĒ-a	WĒ-tis ē-DĪ-a	Latin	vitis
vivipara	vi-VI-pa-ra	wi-WI-pa-ra	Latin	viviparus
viviparoidea	vi-vi-pa-RŌĪ-dē-a	wi-wi-pa-RŌĒ-dā-a	Latin	viviparus
vulgare	vul-GÄ-rē	wōōl-GÄ-rā	Latin	vulgaris
vulgaris	vul-GÄ-ris	wōōl-GÄ-ris	Latin	vulgaris
vulgata	vul-GÄ-ta	wōōl-GÄ-ta	Latin	vulgatus
vulneraria	vul-ne-RÄ-rē-a	wōōl-ne-RÄ-rē-a	Latin	vulnerno
Vulpia	VUL-pē-a	WŌŌL-pē-a	name, person	Vulpius, Johann S.
vulpinoidea	vul-pi-NŌĪ-dē-a	wōōl-pi-NŌĒ-dā-a	name, animal	Vulpes
wallacei	WA-la-sē-ī	WA-la-kē-ē	name, person	Wallace, W.A.
watertonense ×	wa-ter-to-NEN-sē	wa-ter-to-NEN-sā	name, place	Waterton
watsonianum	wat-so-nē-Ā-num	wat-so-nē-Ä-nōōm	name, person	Watson, Wm. or Watson, S.
watsonii	wat-SŌ-nē-ī	wat-SŌ-nē-ē	name, person	Watson, Wm. or Watson, S.
wheeleri	WĒ-le-rī	WĀ-le-rē	name, person	Wheeler, George M.
wilcoxianum	wil-kok-sē-Ā-num	wil-kok-sā-Ä-nōōm	name, person	Wilcox, E.N.

Root 1 Meaning	Root 2	Root 2 Meaning / (referring to)
hair	ula	diminutive
hair		
ancient/classical Latin name		
violet color	aceus	with, like, pertaining to
the type genus		
violet color	aceus	with, like, pertaining to
made of twigs or osiers		
made of twigs or osiers		
state of Virginia, USA	anus	from or of
state of Virginia, USA	anus	from or of
state of Virginia, USA	anus	from or of
state of Virginia, USA	ica	belonging to
green		
green	carina	keel
green	floris	flower
green		
green	ula	diminutive
fond of men, longing after men		
sticky, clammy	issimus	superlative, very
sticky, clammy		
sticky, clammy		
vine, grape vine	idaeus	Mount Ida (now Mt. Psiloriti) in Crete
bearing active, living young		
bearing active, living young	oides	like, resembling
common, usual, everyday		
common, usual, everyday		
common, usual, everyday		
wound, hurt (used for healing)		
1760-1846, German pharmacist and botanist, studied the flora of Baden		
fox	oides	like, resembling
Los Angeles area collector, circa 1854	i	of, belonging to
town/park in sw AB, Canada		
1715-1787, English botanist-doctor or 1826-1892, Gray Herbarium Curator	anus	from or of
1715-1787, English botanist-doctor or 1826-1892, Gray Herbarium Curator	ii	of, belonging to
1842-1905, explored & mapped Great Basin from the 40th parallel to Mexico	i	of, belonging to
1869-1961, Illinois agrostologist/collector	anus	from or of

PRONUNCIATION & DERIVATION

Scientific Name	English Latin Pronunctiaion	Reconstructed Latin Pronunciation	Root Source	Root 1
williamsii	wi-lē-AM-sē-ī	wi-lē-AM-sē-ē	name, person	Williams, R.S.
Wolffia	WOL-fē-a	WOL-fē-a	name, person	Wolff, Johann Friedrich
wolfii	WOL-fē-ī	WOL-fē-ē	name, person	Wolf, Carl Brandt
Woodsia	WOOD-sē-a	WOOD-sē-a	name, person	Woods, Joseph
Woodsiaceae	wood-si-Ā-sē-ē	wood-sē-Ä-kā-ī	name, plant	Woodsia
woodsii	WOOD-sē-ī	WOOD-sē-ē	name, person	Woods, Joseph
wormskjoldii	worm-skī-OL-dē-ī	worm-skē-ŌL-dē-ē	name, person	Wormskjold, Morten
wyethii	wī-E-thē-ī	wē-E-tē-ē	name, person	Wyeth, Nathaniel J.
wyomingensis	wī-ō-ming-EN-sis	wē-ō-min-GEN-sis	name, place	Wyoming
xanthiifolia	zan-thē-i-FŌ-lē-a	ksan-tē-i-FŌ-lā-a	name, plant	Xanthium
Xanthisma	zan-THIZ-ma	zan-TIS-ma	Greek	xanthos
Xanthium	ZAN-thē-um	ZAN-tē-ŏŏm	Greek	xanthos
xerantica	ze-RAN-ti-ka	kse-RAN-ti-ka	Greek	xeros
Xerophyllum	ze-ro-FI-lum	ze-ro-PI-lŏŏm	Greek	xeros
Yucca	YU-ka	YŎŎ-ka	name, plant	Yucca
Zannichellia	za-ni-KE-lē-a	za-ni-KE-lē-a	name, person	Zannichelli, G.G.
Zizania	zi-ZĀ-nē-a	zi-ZÄ-nē-a	name, plant	Zizanion
Zizia	ZI-zē-a	ZI-zē-a	name, person	Ziz, Johann B.
zosteriformis	zo-ste-ri-FŌR-mis	zo-ste-ri-FŌR-mis	name, plant	Zostera

Root 1 Meaning	Root 2	Root 2 Meaning / (referring to)
1859-1945, NY Botanical Garden bryologist	ii	of, belonging to
1788-1806, German botanist and physician, wrote on *Lemna* in 1801		
1905-1974, botanist, Santa Ana Bot. Garden, studied oaks, cypresses	ii	of, belonging to
1776-1864, an English architect and botanist, studied *Rosa*		
the type genus		
1776-1864, English architect and botanical author, studied *Rosa*	ii	of, belonging to
1783-1845, Danish, on Kotzebue's first expeditn, collected at Kodiak & Sitka	ii	of, belonging to
1802-1856, Oregon botanist, pioneer, blazed much of the Oregon Trail	ii	of, belonging to
state of Wyoming, USA	ensis	of a place or country
cocklebur, a genus in the Aster Family	folium	leaf
yellow (flowers)	ismos	condition or quality
yellow (for dying hair)		
dry	ica	belonging to
dry	phyllon	leaf
traditional Haitian/Caribbean name for yucca, manihot and/or cassava		
1662-1729, Venetian botanist, physician		
ancient name for a wild, weedy grain that grew in wheat fields		
1779-1829, Rhenish botanist		
little bag, bladder or bottle (leaves)	forma	shape, form

ALPHABETICAL SCIENTIFIC NAMES

Scientific Name	Suggested Common Name	VASCAN and/or ACIMS Common Name(s)	Rank
Abies	fir	fir	genus
Abies balsamea	balsam fir	balsam fir	species
Abies bifolia	subalpine fir	Rocky Mountain alpine fir, subalpine fir	species
Abutilon	velvetleaf	velvetleaf	genus
Abutilon theophrasti	velvetleaf	velvetleaf	species
Acer	maple	maple	genus
Acer glabrum	mountain maple	Rocky Mountain maple, mountain maple	species
Acer negundo	Manitoba maple	Manitoba maple	species
Achillea	yarrow	yarrow	genus
Achillea alpina	manyflower yarrow	Siberian yarrow, many-flowered yarrow	species
Achillea borealis	common yarrow	common yarrow	species
Achillea ptarmica	sneezewort yarrow	sneezeweed yarrow, sneezewort yarrow	species
Achnatherum	needlegrass	needlegrass	genus
Achnatherum nelsonii	Nelson needlegrass	Nelson's needlegrass	species
Achnatherum richardsonii	Richardson needlegrass	Richardson's needlegrass, Richardson needle grass	species
Aconitum	monkshood	monkshood	genus
Aconitum delphiniifolium	mountain monkshood	mountain monkshood, monkshood	species
Acoraceae	sweetflag family	sweetflag family	family
Acorus	sweetflag	sweetflag	genus
Acorus americanus	American sweetflag	American sweetflag, sweet flag	species
Actaea	baneberry	baneberry	genus
Actaea rubra	red baneberry	red baneberry, red and white baneberry	species
Adenocaulon	pathfinder	pathfinder	genus
Adenocaulon bicolor	pathfinder	pathfinder	species
Adiantum	maidenhair	maidenhair	genus
Adiantum aleuticum	Aleutian maidenhair	Aleutian maidenhair fern, western maidenhair fern	species
Adoxa	muskroot	muskroot	genus
Adoxa moschatellina	muskroot	muskroot, moschatel	species
Adoxaceae	moschatel family	moschatel family	family
Agastache	giant-hyssop	giant-hyssop	genus
Agastache foeniculum	blue giant-hyssop	blue giant hyssop, giant hyssop	species
Agoseris	false-dandelion	false-dandelion	genus
Agoseris aurantiaca	orange false-dandelion	orange agoseris, orange false dandelion	species
Agoseris glauca	yellow false-dandelion	pale agoseris, yellow false dandelion	species

ALPHABETICAL SCIENTIFIC NAMES

Scientific Name	Suggested Common Name	VASCAN and/or ACIMS Common Name(s)	Rank
Agrimonia	agrimony	agrimony	genus
Agrimonia striata	woodland agrimony	woodland agrimony, agrimony	species
Agropyron	wheatgrass	wheatgrass	genus
Agropyron cristatum	crested wheatgrass	crested wheatgrass	species
Agropyron fragile	Siberian wheatgrass	Siberian wheatgrass	species
Agrostemma	corncockle	corncockle	genus
Agrostemma githago	common corncockle	common corncockle	species
Agrostis	bentgrass	bentgrass	genus
Agrostis exarata	spike bentgrass	spike bentgrass, spike redtop	species
Agrostis gigantea	giant bentgrass	redtop, giant bentgrass	species
Agrostis mertensii	northern bentgrass	northern bentgrass, northern bent grass	species
Agrostis scabra	rough bentgrass	rough bentgrass, rough hair grass	species
Agrostis stolonifera	creeping bentgrass	creeping bentgrass, redtop	species
Agrostis variabilis	mountain bentgrass	mountain bentgrass, alpine redtop	species
Alisma	waterplantain	waterplantain	genus
Alisma gramineum	narrowleaf water-plantain	grass-leaved water-plantain, narrow-leaved water-plantain	species
Alisma triviale	broadleaf water-plantain	northern water-plantain, broad-leaved water-plantain	species
Alismataceae	waterplantain family	water-plantain family	family
Alliaria	garlic-mustard	garlic-mustard	genus
Alliaria petiolata	garlic-mustard	garlic mustard	species
Allium	onion	onion	genus
Allium cernuum	nodding onion	nodding onion	species
Allium geyeri	Geyer onion	Geyer's onion	species
Allium schoenoprasum	wild chives	wild chives	species
Allium textile	prairie onion	prairie onion	species
Almutaster	marsh-aster	marsh-aster	genus
Almutaster pauciflorus	fewflower marsh-aster	marsh alkali aster, few-flowered aster	species
Alnus	alder	alder	genus
Alnus incana	grey alder	grey alder, alder	species
Alnus alnobetula/viridis	green alder	green alder	species
Alopecurus	foxtail	foxtail	genus
Alopecurus aequalis	shortawn foxtail	short-awned foxtail	species
Alopecurus arundinaceus	creeping foxtail	creeping foxtail	species
Alopecurus carolinianus	Carolina foxtail	tufted foxtail, Carolina foxtail	species
Alopecurus geniculatus	water foxtail	water foxtail	species
Alopecurus magellanicus	alpine foxtail	alpine foxtail	species
Alopecurus pratensis	meadow foxtail	meadow foxtail	species
Alyssum	alyssum	alyssum	genus

ALPHABETICAL SCIENTIFIC NAMES

Scientific Name	Suggested Common Name	VASCAN and/or ACIMS Common Name(s)	Rank
Alyssum alyssoides	small alyssum	small alyssum	species
Alyssum desertorum	desert alyssum	desert alyssum	species
Alyssum turkestanicum	desert alyssum	desert alyssum	species
Amaranthaceae	amaranth family	amaranth family	family
Amaranthus	amaranth	amaranth	genus
Amaranthus albus	white amaranth	white amaranth	species
Amaranthus blitoides	prostrate amaranth	prostrate amaranth	species
Amaranthus californicus	California amaranth	California amaranth, Californian amaranth	species
Amaranthus powellii	Powell amaranth	Powell's amaranth	species
Amaranthus retroflexus	redroot amaranth	redroot amaranth, red-root pigweed	species
Amaryllidaceae	amaryllis family	amaryllis family	family
Ambrosia	ragweed	ragweed	genus
Ambrosia acanthicarpa	bur ragweed	burr ragweed, bur ragweed	species
Ambrosia artemisiifolia	common ragweed	common ragweed	species
Ambrosia psilostachya	perennial ragweed	perennial ragweed	species
Ambrosia trifida	great ragweed	great ragweed	species
Amelanchier	saskatoon, serviceberry	saskatoon, serviceberry	genus
Amelanchier alnifolia	saskatoon	saskatoon	species
Amphiscirpus	bulrush	bulrush	genus
Amphiscirpus nevadensis	Nevada bulrush	Nevada bulrush	species
Amsinckia	fiddleneck	fiddleneck	genus
Amsinckia menziesii	Menzies fiddleneck	Menzies' fiddleneck, fiddle-neck	species
Anacardiaceae	sumac family	sumac family	family
Anaphalis	everlasting	everlasting	genus
Anaphalis margaritacea	pearly everlasting	pearly everlasting	species
Andersonglossum	wild-comfrey	wild-comfrey	genus
Andersonglossum virginianum	northern wild-comfrey	northern wild comfrey, wild comfrey	genus
Andromeda	bog-rosemary	bog-rosemary	genus
Andromeda polifolia	bog-rosemary	bog rosemary	species
Androsace	fairy-candelabra	fairy-candelabra	genus
Androsace chamaejasme	sweetflower fairy-candelabra	sweet-flowered fairy-candelabra, sweet-flowered androsace	species
Androsace occidentalis	western fairy-candelabra	western fairy-candelabra, western fairy candelabra	species
Androsace septentrionalis	northern fairy-candelabra	northern fairy-candelabra, northern fairy candelabra	species
Anemonastrum	anemone	anemone	genus
Anemonastrum canadense	Canada anemone	Canada anemone	species
Anemonastrum richardsonii	yellow anemone	Richardson's anemone, yellow anemone	species

ALPHABETICAL SCIENTIFIC NAMES

Scientific Name	Suggested Common Name	VASCAN and/or ACIMS Common Name(s)	Rank
Anemonastrum sibiricum	narcissus anemone	one-flowered anemone, narcissus anemone	species
Anemone	anemone	anemone	genus
Anemone canadensis	Canada anemone	Canada anemone	species
Anemone cylindrica	candle anemone	long-headed anemone, candle anemone, long-fruited anemone	species
Anemone drummondii	Drummond anemone	Drummond's anemone	species
Anemone multifida	cutleaf anemone	cut-leaved anemone	species
Anemone narcissiflora	narcissus anemone	one-flowered anemone, narcissus anemone	species
Anemone parviflora	smallflower anemone	small-flowered anemone, small wood anemone	species
Anemone quinquefolia	wood anemone	wood anemone	species
Anemone richardsonii	yellow anemone	Richardson's anemone, yellow anemone	species
Anemone virginiana	tall anemone	tall anemone, Virginia anemone	species
Anethum	dill	dill	genus
Anethum graveolens	dill	dill	species
Angelica	angelica	angelica	genus
Angelica arguta	white angelica	sharp-toothed angelica, white angelica	species
Angelica dawsonii	Dawson angelica	Dawson's angelica, yellow angelica	species
Angelica genuflexa	kneeling angelica	kneeling angelica	species
Antennaria	pussytoes	pussytoes	genus
Antennaria alpina	alpine pussytoes	alpine pussytoes, alpine everlasting	species
Antennaria anaphaloides	pearly pussytoes	pearly pussytoes, tall everlasting	species
Antennaria aromatica	scented pussytoes	scented pussytoes	species
Antennaria corymbosa	flat-top pussytoes	flat-top pussytoes, corymbose everlasting	species
Antennaria dimorpha	cushion pussytoes	low pussytoes, cushion everlasting	species
Antennaria howellii	Howell pussytoes	Howell's pussytoes, small pussytoes	species
Antennaria lanata	woolly pussytoes	woolly pussytoes, woolly everlasting	species
Antennaria luzuloides	woodrush pussytoes	woodrush pussytoes, silvery everlasting	species
Antennaria media	Rocky-Mountain pussytoes	Rocky Mountain pussytoes	species
Antennaria microphylla	littleleaf pussytoes	little-leaved pussytoes, littleleaf pussytoes	species

ALPHABETICAL SCIENTIFIC NAMES

Scientific Name	Suggested Common Name	VASCAN and/or ACIMS Common Name(s)	Rank
Antennaria monocephala	onehead pussytoes	pygmy pussytoes, one-headed everlasting	species
Antennaria neglecta	broadleaf pussytoes	field pussytoes, broad-leaved everlasting	species
Antennaria parvifolia	small-leaf pussytoes	small-leaved pussytoes, small-leaved everlasting	species
Antennaria pulcherrima	showy pussytoes	showy pussytoes, showy everlasting	species
Antennaria racemosa	racemose pussytoes	racemose pussytoes, racemose everlasting	species
Antennaria rosea	rosy pussytoes	rosy pussytoes, rosy everlasting	species
Antennaria umbrinella	umber pussytoes	umber pussytoes, brown-bracted mountain everlasting	species
Anthemis	stinking-chamomile	stinking-chamomile	genus
Anthemis cotula	stinking-chamomile	stinking chamomile, mayweed	species
Anthoxanthum	sweetgrass	sweetgrass	genus
Anthoxanthum hirtum	common sweetgrass	hairy sweetgrass, sweet grass	species
Anthoxanthum monticola	alpine sweetgrass	alpine sweetgrass	species
Anthyllis	kidney-vetch	kidney-vetch	genus
Anthyllis vulneraria	common kidney-vetch	common kidney-vetch	species
Anticlea	death-camas, bronzebells	death-camas, bronzebells	genus
Anticlea elegans	white death-camas	mountain death camas, white camas	species
Anticlea occidentalis	western bronzebells	western mountain-bells, bronzebells	species
Aphyllon	broomrape	broomrape	genus
Aphyllon fasciculatum	clustered broomrape	clustered broomrape, clustered broom-rape	species
Aphyllon ludovicianum	Louisiana broomrape	Louisiana broomrape, Louisiana broom-rape	species
Aphyllon purpureum	western oneflower broomrape	western one-flowered broomrape, one-flowered cancer-root	species
Apiaceae	carrot family	carrot family	family
Apocynaceae	milkweed family	milkweed family, dogbane family	family
Apocynum	dogbane	dogbane	genus
Apocynum androsaemifolium	spreading dogbane	spreading dogbane	species
Apocynum cannabinum	hemp dogbane	hemp dogbane, Indian hemp	species
Aquilegia	columbine	columbine	genus
Aquilegia brevistyla	blue columbine	blue columbine	species
Aquilegia flavescens	yellow columbine	yellow columbine	species
Aquilegia formosa	western columbine	western columbine, Sitka columbine	species
Aquilegia jonesii	Jones columbine	Jones' columbine	species
Arabidopsis	rockcress	rockcress	genus

ALPHABETICAL SCIENTIFIC NAMES

Scientific Name	Suggested Common Name	VASCAN and/or ACIMS Common Name(s)	Rank
Arabidopsis lyrata	lyreleaf rockcress	lyre-leaved rockcress, lyreleaf rockcress	species
Arabis	rockcress	rockcress	genus
Arabis eschscholtziana	Eschscholtz rockcress	Eschscholtz's rockcress	species
Arabis nuttallii	Nuttall rockcress	Nuttall's rockcress, Nuttall's rock cress	species
Arabis pycnocarpa	hairy rockcress	cream-flowered rockcress, hairy rockcress	species
Araceae	arum family	arum family	family
Aralia	sarsaparilla	sarsaparilla	genus
Aralia nudicaulis	wild sarsaparilla	wild sarsaparilla	species
Araliaceae	ginseng family	ginseng family	family
Arceuthobium	dwarf-mistletoe	dwarf-mistletoe	genus
Arceuthobium americanum	America dwarf-mistletoe	lodgepole pine dwarf mistletoe, dwarf mistletoe	species
Arctagrostis	polargrass	polargrass	genus
Arctagrostis latifolia	wideleaf polargrass	wide-leaved polargrass	species
Arctium	burdock	burdock	genus
Arctium lappa	great burdock	great burdock	species
Arctium minus	common burdock	common burdock	species
Arctium tomentosum	woolly burdock	woolly burdock	species
Arctostaphylos	bearberry	bearberry	genus
Arctostaphylos uva-ursi	common bearberry	common bearberry	species
Arctous	alpine-bearberry	alpine-bearberry	genus
Arctous rubra	alpine-bearberry	red bearberry, alpine bearberry	species
Arenaria	sandwort	sandwort	genus
Arenaria longipedunculata	longstem sandwort	long-stemmed sandwort, sandwort	species
Arenaria serpyllifolia	thymeleaf sandwort	thyme-leaved sandwort	species
Arethusa	dragon's-mouth	dragon's-mouth	genus
Arethusa bulbosa	dragon's-mouth	dragon's-mouth, dragon's mouth	species
Aristida	three-awn	three-awn	genus
Aristida purpurea	purple three-awn	purple threeawn grass, red three-awn	species
Aristolochiaceae	Dutchman's-pipe family	Dutchman's-pipe family	family
Armoracia	horseradish	horseradish	genus
Armoracia rusticana	horseradish	horseradish, horse-radish	species
Arnica	arnica	arnica	genus
Arnica angustifolia	alpine arnica	narrow-leaved arnica, alpine arnica	species
Arnica chamissonis	Chamisso arnica	Chamisso's arnica, leafy arnica	species
Arnica cordifolia	heartleaf arnica	heart-leaved arnica	species
Arnica fulgens	shining arnica	hillside arnica, shining arnica	species

ALPHABETICAL SCIENTIFIC NAMES

Scientific Name	Suggested Common Name	VASCAN and/or ACIMS Common Name(s)	Rank
Arnica gracilis	graceful arnica	slender arnica, graceful arnica	species
Arnica lanceolata	lanceleaf arnica	lance-leaved arnica, lanceleaf arnica	species
Arnica latifolia	broadleaf arnica	broad-leaved arnica	species
Arnica lonchophylla	spearleaf arnica	spear-leaved arnica	species
Arnica longifolia	longleaf arnica	long-leaved arnica	species
Arnica louiseana	Lake Louise arnica	Lake Louise arnica	species
Arnica mollis	hairy arnica	hairy arnica, cordilleran arnica	species
Arnica ovata	sticky arnica	sticky arnica, lawless arnica	species
Arnica parryi	Parry arnica	Parry's arnica, nodding arnica	species
Arnica rydbergii	Rydberg arnica	Rydberg's arnica, narrow-leaved arnica	species
Arnica sororia	twin arnica	twin arnica	species
Artemisia	wormwood, sagebrush	wormwood, sagebrush	genus
Artemisia abrotanum	southern wormwood	southern wormwood, southernwood	species
Artemisia absinthium	absinthe wormwood	absinthe wormwood	species
Artemisia biennis	biennial wormwood	biennial wormwood, biennial sagewort	species
Artemisia borealis	northern wormwood	boreal wormwood, northern wormwood	species
Artemisia campestris	plains wormwood	field wormwood, plains wormwood	species
Artemisia cana	silver sagebrush	silver wormwood, silver sagebrush	species
Artemisia dracunculus	dragon wormwood	dragon wormwood, dragonwort	species
Artemisia frigida	pasture wormwood	prairie sagebrush, pasture sagewort	species
Artemisia hyperborea	forked wormwood	forked wormwood	species
Artemisia longifolia	longleaf wormwood	long-leaved wormwood, long-leaved sagewort	species
Artemisia ludoviciana	silver wormwood	silver wormwood, prairie sagewort	species
Artemisia michauxiana	Michaux wormwood	Michaux's wormwood, Michaux's sagewort	species
Artemisia norvegica	alpine wormwood	alpine wormwood, mountain sagewort	species
Artemisia tilesii	Tilesius wormwood	Tilesius wormwood, Herriot's sagewort	species
Artemisia tridentata	big sagebrush	big sagebrush	species
Artemisia vulgaris	common wormwood	common wormwood	species
Aruncus	goatsbeard	goatsbeard	genus
Aruncus dioicus	common goatsbeard	common goatsbeard	species
Asarum	wild-ginger	wild-ginger	genus
Asarum canadense	Canada wild-ginger	Canada wild ginger	species

ALPHABETICAL SCIENTIFIC NAMES

Scientific Name	Suggested Common Name	VASCAN and/or ACIMS Common Name(s)	Rank
Asclepias	milkweed	milkweed	genus
Asclepias ovalifolia	ovalleaf milkweed	oval-leaved milkweed, low milkweed	species
Asclepias speciosa	showy milkweed	showy milkweed	species
Asclepias viridiflora	green milkweed	green comet milkweed, green milkweed	species
Askellia	delicate-hawksbeard	hawksbeard	genus
Askellia elegans	elegant hawksbeard	elegant hawksbeard	species
Askellia pygmaea	dwarf hawksbeard	dwarf hawksbeard, dwarf hawk's-beard	species
Asparagaceae	asparagus family	asparagus family	family
Asparagus	asparagus	asparagus	genus
Asparagus officinalis	garden asparagus	garden asparagus, asparagus	species
Asperugo	madwort	madwort	genus
Asperugo procumbens	German madwort	German madwort, madwort	species
Asperula	woodruff	woodruff	genus
Asperula arvensis	blue woodruff	blue woodruff, quinsywort	species
Aspleniaceae	spleenwort family	spleenwort family	family
Asplenium	spleenwort	spleenwort	genus
Asplenium viride	green spleenwort	green spleenwort	species
Aster	aster	aster	genus
Aster alpinus	alpine aster	alpine aster	species
Asteraceae	aster family	aster family	family
Astragalus	milkvetch	milkvetch	genus
Astragalus agrestis	purple milkvetch	field milk-vetch, purple milk vetch	species
Astragalus alpinus	alpine milkvetch	alpine milk-vetch, alpine milkvetch	species
Astragalus americanus	American milkvetch	American milk-vetch, American milk vetch	species
Astragalus australis	southern milkvetch	southern milk-vetch, Indian milkvetch	species
Astragalus bisulcatus	twogroove milkvetch	two-grooved milk-vetch, two-grooved milkvetch	species
Astragalus bodinii	Bodin milkvetch	Bodin's milk-vetch, Bodin's milk vetch	species
Astragalus bourgovii	Bourgov milkvetch	Bourgov's milk-vetch, Bourgov's milk vetch	species
Astragalus canadensis	Canada milkvetch	Canada milk-vetch, Canadian milkvetch	species
Astragalus cicer	chickpea milkvetch	chickpea milk-vetch, cicer milk vetch	species
Astragalus crassicarpus	ground-plum milkvetch	ground plum milk-vetch, ground-plum	species
Astragalus drummondii	Drummond milkvetch	Drummond's milk-vetch, Drummond's milk vetch	species

ALPHABETICAL SCIENTIFIC NAMES

Scientific Name	Suggested Common Name	VASCAN and/or ACIMS Common Name(s)	Rank
Astragalus eucosmus	elegant milkvetch	elegant milk-vetch	species
Astragalus flexuosus	flexible milkvetch	flexible milk-vetch, slender milkvetch	species
Astragalus gilviflorus	plains milkvetch	plains milk-vetch, cushion milkvetch	species
Astragalus kentrophyta	spiny milkvetch	spiny milk-vetch, prickly milk vetch	species
Astragalus laxmannii	Laxmann milkvetch	Laxmann's milk-vetch, ascending purple milk-vetch	species
Astragalus lotiflorus	lotus milkvetch	lotus milk-vetch, low milk vetch	species
Astragalus miser	timber milkvetch	timber milk-vetch, timber milkvetch	species
Astragalus missouriensis	Missouri milkvetch	Missouri milk-vetch, Missouri milkvetch	species
Astragalus pectinatus	narrowleaf milkvetch	narrow-leaved milk-vetch, narrow-leaved milk vetch	species
Astragalus purshii	Pursh milkvetch	Pursh's milk-vetch, Pursh's milkvetch	species
Astragalus robbinsii	Robbins milkvetch	Robbins' milk-vetch, Robbins' milk vetch	species
Astragalus spatulatus	tufted milkvetch	tufted milk-vetch, tufted milk vetch	species
Astragalus tenellus	looseflower milkvetch	loose-flowered milk-vetch, loose-flowered milk vetch	species
Astragalus vexilliflexus	bentflower milkvetch	bent-flowered milk-vetch, few-flowered milkvetch	species
Athyriaceae	ladyfern family	ladyfern family	family
Athyrium	ladyfern	ladyfern	genus
Athyrium distentifolium	alpine ladyfern	alpine lady fern	species
Athyrium filix-femina	common ladyfern	common lady fern, lady fern	species
Atocion	sweet-William	sweet-William	genus
Atocion armeria	sweet-William	sweet William catchfly	species
Atriplex	saltbush	saltbush	genus
Atriplex argentea	silver saltbush	silver saltbush	species
Atriplex canescens	fourwing saltbush	four-wing saltbush	species
Atriplex dioica	saline saltbush	saline saltbush	species
Atriplex gardneri	Gardner saltbush	Gardner's saltbush	species
Atriplex glabriuscula	glabrous saltbush	glabrous saltbush, glabrous orach	species
Atriplex heterosperma	Russian saltbush	Russian saltbush, Russian atriplex	species
Atriplex hortensis	garden saltbush	garden saltbush, garden orache	species
Atriplex oblongifolia	oblongleaf saltbush	oblong-leaved saltbush, saltbush	species
Atriplex patula	spear saltbush	spear saltbush, spear orach	species

ALPHABETICAL SCIENTIFIC NAMES

Scientific Name	Suggested Common Name	VASCAN and/or ACIMS Common Name(s)	Rank
Atriplex powellii	Powell saltbush	Powell's saltbush	species
Atriplex prostrata	creeping saltbush	creeping saltbush, prostrate saltbush	species
Atriplex rosea	redscale saltbush	redscale saltbush, red scale saltbush	species
Atriplex suckleyi	Suckley saltbush	Suckley's saltbush, endolepis	species
Atriplex truncata	wedgescale saltbush	wedgescale saltbush, saltbush	species
Avena	oat	oat	genus
Avena fatua	wild oat	common wild oats, wild oat	species
Avena sativa	cultivated oat	cultivated oats, cultivated oat	species
Axyris	Russian-pigweed	Russian-pigweed	genus
Axyris amaranthoides	Russian-pigweed	Russian pigweed	species
Bacopa	water-hyssop	water-hyssop	genus
Bacopa rotundifolia	disc water-hyssop	round-leaved water hyssop, water hyssop	species
Balsaminaceae	balsam family	balsam family	family
Balsamorhiza	balsamroot	balsamroot	genus
Balsamorhiza sagittata	arrowleaf balsamroot	arrow-leaved balsamroot, balsamroot	species
Barbarea	wintercress	wintercress	genus
Barbarea orthoceras	American wintercress	erect-fruit wintercress, American winter cress	species
Barbarea vulgaris	bitter wintercress	bitter wintercress, yellow rocket	species
Bassia	bassia, summer-cypress	bassia, summer-cypress	genus
Bassia hyssopifolia	fivehook bassia	five-hooked bassia, five-hook bassia	species
Bassia scoparia	summer-cypress	common kochia, summer-cypress	species
Beckmannia	sloughgrass	sloughgrass	genus
Beckmannia syzigachne	American sloughgrass	American sloughgrass, slough grass	species
Berberidaceae	barberry family	barberry family	family
Berberis	barberry	barberry	genus
Berberis vulgaris	common barberry	common barberry	species
Berteroa	hoary-alyssum	hoary-alyssum	genus
Berteroa incana	hoary-alyssum	hoary alyssum	species
Besseya	kittentails	kittentails	genus
Betula	birch	birch	genus
Betula glandulosa	glandular birch	glandular birch, bog birch	species
Betula nana	arctic dwarf birch	arctic dwarf birch	species
Betula neoalaskana	Alaska paper birch	Alaska paper birch, Alaska birch	species
Betula occidentalis	water birch	water birch	species
Betula papyrifera	paper birch	paper birch, white birch	species
Betula pumila	dwarf birch	bog birch, dwarf birch	species

ALPHABETICAL SCIENTIFIC NAMES

Scientific Name	Suggested Common Name	VASCAN and/or ACIMS Common Name(s)	Rank
Betulaceae	birch family	birch family	family
Bidens	beggarticks	beggarticks	genus
Bidens cernua	nodding beggarticks	nodding beggarticks	species
Bidens frondosa	devil beggarticks	devil's beggarticks, common beggarticks	species
Bidens tripartita	threepart beggarticks	three-parted beggarticks, tall beggarticks	species
Bidens vulgata	tall beggarticks	tall beggarticks	species
Bistorta	bistort	bistort	genus
Bistorta bistortoides	western bistort	western bistort	species
Bistorta vivipara	alpine bistort	alpine bistort	species
Blitum	strawberry-blite, goosefoot	strawberry-blite, goosefoot	genus
Blitum capitatum	strawberry-blite	strawberry-blite, strawberry blite	species
Blitum nuttallianum	Nuttall povertyweed	Nuttall's povertyweed, spear-leaved goosefoot	species
Blysmopsis	red-bulrush	red-bulrush	genus
Blysmopsis rufa	red-bulrush	red bulrush	species
Boechera	rockcress	rockcress	genus
Boechera calderi	Calder rockcress	Calder's rockcress	species
Boechera collinsii	Collins rockcress	Collins' rockcress	species
Boechera drepanoloba	soldier rockcress	soldier rockcress	species
Boechera grahamii	Graham rockcress	Graham's rockcress, limestone rockcress	species
Boechera lemmonii	Lemmon rockcress	Lemmon's rockcress	species
Boechera lyallii	Lyall rockcress	Lyall's rockcress	species
Boechera pendulocarpa	danglepod rockcress	dangle-pod rockcress	species
Boechera retrofracta	reflexed rockcress	reflexed rockcress	species
Boechera stricta	Drummond rockcress	Drummond's rockcress, Drummond's rock cress	species
Bolboschoenus	tuber-bulrush	tuberous bulrush	genus
Bolboschoenus fluviatilis	river tuber-bulrush	river bulrush	species
Bolboschoenus maritimus	alkali tuber-bulrush	saltmarsh bulrush, alkali bulrush	species
Boraginaceae	borage family	borage family	family
Borago	borage	borage	genus
Borago officinalis	common borage	common borage, oxtongue	species
Boschniakia	groundcone	groundcone	genus
Boschniakia rossica	northern groundcone	northern groundcone, ground-cone	species
Botrychium	moonwort	moonwort	genus
Botrychium ×watertonense	Waterton moonwort	Waterton moonwort, Waterton grapefern	Hybrid
Botrychium ascendens	ascending moonwort	upswept moonwort, ascending grape fern	species
Botrychium campestre	field moonwort	prairie moonwort, field grape fern	species

ALPHABETICAL SCIENTIFIC NAMES

Scientific Name	Suggested Common Name	VASCAN and/or ACIMS Common Name(s)	Rank
Botrychium crenulatum	scalloped moonwort	dainty moonwort, scalloped grapefern	species
Botrychium hesperium	western moonwort	western moonwort, western grape fern	species
Botrychium lanceolatum	triangle moonwort	triangle moonwort	species
Botrychium lineare	slender moonwort	slender moonwort, straight-leaf moonwort	species
Botrychium lunaria	common moonwort	common moonwort, moonwort	species
Botrychium matricariifolium	chamomile moonwort	daisy-leaved moonwort, chamomile grape-fern	species
Botrychium michiganense	Michigan moonwort	Michigan moonwort, Michigan grapefern	species
Botrychium minganense	Mingan moonwort	Mingan moonwort, Mingan grape fern	species
Botrychium neolunaria	North America moonwort	North American moonwort	species
Botrychium pallidum	pale moonwort	pale moonwort	species
Botrychium paradoxum	paradox moonwort	paradox moonwort, paradoxical grape fern	species
Botrychium pedunculosum	stalked moonwort	stalked moonwort, stalked grape fern	species
Botrychium pinnatum	northwestern moonwort	northwestern moonwort, northwestern grapefern	species
Botrychium simplex	least moonwort	least moonwort, dwarf grape fern	species
Botrychium spathulatum	spatula moonwort	spatulate moonwort, spatulate grape fern	species
Botrychium tunux	Tunux moonwort	Tunux' moonwort, moosewort	species
Botrypus	rattlesnake-fern	rattlesnake-fern	genus
Botrypus virginianus	rattlesnake-fern	rattlesnake fern, Virginia grape fern	species
Bouteloua	grama	grama	genus
Bouteloua curtipendula	side-oats grama	side-oats grama	species
Bouteloua gracilis	blue grama	blue grama	species
Brasenia	watershield	watershield	genus
Brasenia schreberi	watershield	watershield	species
Brassica	mustard	mustard	genus
Brassica juncea	Chinese mustard	Chinese mustard, Indian mustard	species
Brassica napus	rapeseed mustard	rapeseed, rutabaga	species
Brassica nigra	black mustard	black mustard	species
Brassica rapa	field mustard	field mustard, Bird's rape	species
Brassicaceae	mustard family	mustard family	family
Braya	braya	braya	genus
Braya glabella	smooth braya	smooth braya	species
Braya humilis	low braya	low braya	species
Braya purpurascens	purple braya	purple braya	species
Brickellia	brickellia	brickellia	genus

ALPHABETICAL SCIENTIFIC NAMES

Scientific Name	Suggested Common Name	VASCAN and/or ACIMS Common Name(s)	Rank
Brickellia grandiflora	largeflower brickellia	large-flowered brickellia	species
Briza	quaking-grass	quaking-grass	genus
Briza maxima	big quaking-grass	big quaking grass	species
Bromus	brome	brome	genus
Bromus ciliatus	fringed brome	fringed brome	species
Bromus commutatus	hairy brome	hairy brome, hairy chess	species
Bromus diandrus	great brome	great brome	species
Bromus hordeaceus	soft brome	soft brome, soft chess	species
Bromus inermis	smooth brome	smooth brome	species
Bromus japonicus	Japanese brome	Japanese brome, Japanese chess	species
Bromus latiglumis	broadglume brome	broad-glumed brome, Canada brome	species
Bromus porteri	Porter brome	Porter's brome	species
Bromus pumpellianus	Pumpelly brome	Pumpelly's brome, Pumpelly brome	species
Bromus richardsonii	Richardson brome	Richardson's brome	species
Bromus riparius	meadow brome	Asian meadow brome	species
Bromus secalinus	rye brome	rye brome, rye chess	species
Bromus sitchensis	Sitka brome	Sitka brome, Alaska brome, keeled brome, mountain brome	species
Bromus squarrosus	corn brome	corn brome, field brome	species
Bromus tectorum	downy brome	downy brome	species
Bromus vulgaris	Columbia brome	Columbia brome, woodland brome	species
Bupleurum	thoroughwax	thoroughwax	genus
Bupleurum americanum	American thoroughwax	American thoroughwax, thorough-wax	species
Butomaceae	flowering-rush family	flowering-rush family	family
Butomus	flowering-rush	flowering-rush	genus
Butomus umbellatus	flowering-rush	flowering-rush	species
Cabombaceae	watershield family	watershield family	family
Cactaceae	cactus family	cactus family	family
Calamagrostis	reedgrass	reedgrass	genus
Calamagrostis canadensis	bluejoint reedgrass	bluejoint reedgrass, bluejoint	species
Calamagrostis epigeios	chee reedgrass	chee reedgrass	species
Calamagrostis lapponica	Lapland reedgrass	Lapland reedgrass, Lapland reed grass	species
Calamagrostis montanensis	plains reedgrass	plains reedgrass, plains reed grass	species
Calamagrostis purpurascens	purple reedgrass	purple reedgrass, purple reed grass	species

ALPHABETICAL SCIENTIFIC NAMES

Scientific Name	Suggested Common Name	VASCAN and/or ACIMS Common Name(s)	Rank
Calamagrostis rubescens	pine reedgrass	pine reedgrass, pine reed grass	species
Calamagrostis stricta	slimstem reedgrass	slim-stemmed reedgrass, narrow reed grass	species
Calamovilfa	sandgrass	sandgrass	genus
Calla	calla	calla	genus
Calla palustris	wild calla	wild calla, water arum	species
Callitriche	water-starwort	water-starwort	genus
Callitriche hermaphroditica	northern water-starwort	northern water-starwort	species
Callitriche palustris	spring water-starwort	spring water-starwort	species
Callitriche stenoptera	narrowwing water-starwort	narrow-winged water-starwort	species
Calochortus	mariposa-lily	mariposa-lily	genus
Calochortus apiculatus	three-spot mariposa-lily	three-spot mariposa lily, mariposa lily	species
Caltha	marshmarigold	marshmarigold	genus
Caltha leptosepala	white marshmarigold	white marsh marigold, mountain marsh-marigold	species
Caltha natans	floating marshmarigold	floating marsh marigold, floating marsh-marigold	species
Caltha palustris	yellow marshmarigold	yellow marsh marigold, marsh-marigold	species
Calypso	calypso	calypso	genus
Calypso bulbosa	calypso	calypso, Venus'-slipper	species
Calystegia	false-bindweed	false-bindweed	genus
Calystegia macounii	Macoun false-bindweed	Macoun's false bindweed	species
Calystegia sepium	hedge false-bindweed	hedge false bindweed, wild morning-glory	species
Camassia	camas	camas	genus
Camassia quamash	blue camas	common camas, blue camas	species
Camelina	falseflax	falseflax	genus
Camelina alyssum	flatseed falseflax	flat-seed false-flax	species
Camelina microcarpa	smallseed falseflax	small-seeded false flax	species
Camelina sativa	largeseed falseflax	large-seeded false flax	species
Campanula	bellflower	bellflower	genus
Campanula alaskana	Alaska bellflower	Alaska bellflower, harebell	species
Campanula aparinoides	marsh bellflower	marsh bellflower	species
Campanula glomerata	clustered bellflower	clustered bellflower	species
Campanula lasiocarpa	mountain bellflower	mountain bellflower, Alaska harebell	species
Campanula rapunculoides	creeping bellflower	creeping bellflower	species
Campanula uniflora	alpine harebell	arctic bellflower, alpine harebell	species
Campanulaceae	bellflower family	bellflower family	family
Canadanthus	northern-aster	northern-aster	genus
Canadanthus modestus	large northern-aster	great northern aster, large northern aster	species

ALPHABETICAL SCIENTIFIC NAMES

Scientific Name	Suggested Common Name	VASCAN and/or ACIMS Common Name(s)	Rank
Cannabaceae	hemp family	hemp family	family
Cannabis	hemp	hemp	genus
Cannabis sativa	hemp	hemp	species
Capnoides	rock-harlequin	rock-harlequin	genus
Capnoides sempervirens	rock-harlequin	rock harlequin, pink corydalis	species
Caprifoliaceae	honeysuckle family	honeysuckle family	family
Capsella	shepherd's-purse	shepherd's-purse	genus
Capsella bursa-pastoris	shepherd's-purse	common shepherd's purse	species
Caragana	caragana	caragana	genus
Caragana arborescens	common caragana	Siberian pea shrub, common caragana	species
Cardamine	bittercress	bittercress	genus
Cardamine bellidifolia	alpine bittercress	alpine bittercress, alpine bitter cress	species
Cardamine dentata	toothed bittercress	toothed bittercress	species
Cardamine parviflora	smallflower bittercress	small-flowered bittercress, small bittercress	species
Cardamine pensylvanica	Pennsylvania bittercress	Pennsylvania bittercress	species
Cardamine polemonoides	northern field bittercress	Nyman's bittercress, northern field bittercress	species
Cardamine umbellata	umbel bittercress	umbel bittercress, mountain cress	species
Carduus	plumeless-thistle	plumeless-thistle	genus
Carduus acanthoides	spiny plumeless-thistle	spiny plumeless thistle, plumeless thistle	species
Carduus nutans	nodding thistle	nodding thistle	species
Carex	sedge	sedge	genus
Carex adusta	lesser brown sedge	lesser brown sedge, browned sedge	species
Carex albonigra	black-and-white sedge	black-and-white-scale sedge, black-and-white sedge	species
Carex aperta	open sedge	open sedge	species
Carex aquatilis	water sedge	water sedge	species
Carex arcta	northern cluster sedge	northern clustered sedge, narrow sedge	species
Carex arctogena	northern capitate sedge		species
Carex atherodes	wheat sedge	wheat sedge, awned sedge	species
Carex athrostachya	slenderbeak sedge	slender-beaked sedge, long-bracted sedge	species
Carex atratiformis	scabrous black sedge	scabrous black sedge	species
Carex atrosquama	lesser blackscale sedge	lesser black-scale sedge, dark-scaled sedge	species
Carex aurea	golden sedge	golden sedge	species
Carex backii	Back sedge	Back's sedge	species
Carex bebbii	Bebb sedge	Bebb's sedge	species

ALPHABETICAL SCIENTIFIC NAMES

Scientific Name	Suggested Common Name	VASCAN and/or ACIMS Common Name(s)	Rank
Carex bicolor	two-color sedge	two-coloured sedge, two-color sedge	species
Carex brevior	shortbeak sedge	short-beaked sedge, slender-beaked sedge	species
Carex brunnescens	brownish sedge	brownish sedge	species
Carex buxbaumii	Buxbaum sedge	Buxbaum's sedge, brown sedge	species
Carex canescens	hoary sedge	hoary sedge	species
Carex capillaris	hair sedge	hair-like sedge	species
Carex capitata	capitate sedge	capitate sedge	species
Carex chordorrhiza	creeping sedge	creeping sedge, prostrate sedge	species
Carex concinna	northern elegant sedge	northern elegant sedge, beautiful sedge	species
Carex concinnoides	northwest sedge	northwestern sedge, low northern sedge	species
Carex cordillerana	cordillera sedge	cordilleran sedge	species
Carex crawei	Crawe sedge	Crawe's sedge	species
Carex crawfordii	Crawford sedge	Crawford's sedge	species
Carex deflexa	bent northern sedge	bent northern sedge, bent sedge	species
Carex deweyana	Dewey sedge	Dewey's sedge	species
Carex diandra	twostamen sedge	lesser panicled sedge, two-stamened sedge	species
Carex disperma	twoseed sedge	two-seeded sedge	species
Carex douglasii	Douglas sedge	Douglas' sedge, Douglas sedge	species
Carex duriuscula	needleleaf sedge	needle-leaved sedge, low sedge	species
Carex eburnea	bristleleaf sedge	bristle-leaved sedge	species
Carex echinata	star sedge	star sedge, little prickly sedge	species
Carex enanderi	Enander sedge	Enander's sedge	species
Carex epapillosa	blackened sedge	blackened sedge	species
Carex filifolia	threadleaf sedge	thread-leaved sedge	species
Carex flava	yellow sedge	yellow sedge	species
Carex foenea	bronze sedge	bronze sedge, silvery-flowered sedge	species
Carex fuliginosa	shortleaf sedge	short-leaved sedge, nodding sedge	species
Carex garberi	Garber sedge	Garber's sedge, elk sedge	species
Carex geyeri	Geyer sedge	Geyer's sedge	species
Carex glacialis	glacier sedge	glacier sedge	species
Carex gynocrates	northern bog sedge	northern bog sedge	species
Carex haydeniana	Hayden sedge	cloud sedge, Hayden's sedge	species
Carex heleonastes	Hudson Bay sedge	Hudson Bay sedge	species
Carex hoodii	Hood sedge	Hood's sedge	species

ALPHABETICAL SCIENTIFIC NAMES

Scientific Name	Suggested Common Name	VASCAN and/or ACIMS Common Name(s)	Rank
Carex hookeriana	Hooker sedge	Hooker's sedge	species
Carex houghtoniana	Houghton sedge	Houghton's sedge, sand sedge	species
Carex hystericina	porcupine sedge	porcupine sedge	species
Carex illota	sheep sedge	sheep sedge, small-headed sedge	species
Carex incurviformis	curved-spike sedge	curved-spike sedge	species
Carex infirminervia	weaknerve sedge	weak-nerved sedge	species
Carex inops	long-stolon sedge	long-stolon sedge	species
Carex interior	inland sedge	inland sedge	species
Carex kelloggii	Kellogg sedge	Kellogg's sedge	species
Carex lachenalii	Lachenal sedge	Lachenal's sedge, two-parted sedge	species
Carex lacustris	lake sedge	lake sedge, lakeshore sedge	species
Carex lapponica	Lapland sedge	Lapland sedge	species
Carex lasiocarpa	woollyfruit sedge	woolly-fruit sedge, hairy-fruited sedge	species
Carex lenticularis	lakeshore sedge	lenticular sedge, shore sedge	species
Carex leptalea	bristlestalk sedge	bristle-stalked sedge	species
Carex limosa	mud sedge	mud sedge	species
Carex livida	livid sedge	livid sedge	species
Carex loliacea	ryegrass sedge	ryegrass sedge, rye-grass sedge	species
Carex mackenziei	Mackenzie sedge		species
Carex macloviana	thickspike sedge	Falkland Island sedge, thick-spike sedge	species
Carex magellanica	boreal bog sedge	boreal bog sedge, bog sedge	species
Carex maritima	seaside sedge	seaside sedge	species
Carex media	intermediate sedge	intermediate sedge	species
Carex mertensii	Mertens sedge	Mertens' sedge, purple sedge	species
Carex microglochin	fewseed fen sedge	few-seeded fen sedge, short-awned sedge	species
Carex micropoda	smallroot sedge	small-rooted sedge, spiked sedge	species
Carex microptera	smallwing sedge	small-winged sedge	species
Carex myosuroides	mousetail bogsedge	mouse-tail bog sedge, bog-sedge	species
Carex nardina	spikenard sedge	nard sedge, fragrant sedge	species
Carex nebrascensis	Nebraska sedge	Nebraska sedge	species
Carex nigricans	black alpine sedge	black alpine sedge	species
Carex obtusata	blunt sedge	blunt sedge	species
Carex oligosperma	fewseed sedge	few-seeded sedge, few-fruited sedge	species
Carex pachystachya	thickhead sedge	thick-headed sedge, sedge	species
Carex parryana	Parry sedge	Parry's sedge	species
Carex pauciflora	fewflower sedge	few-flowered sedge	species
Carex paysonis	Payson sedge	Payson's sedge	species
Carex peckii	Peck sedge	Peck's sedge	species
Carex pedunculata	longstalk sedge	long-stalked sedge, stalked sedge	species

ALPHABETICAL SCIENTIFIC NAMES

Scientific Name	Suggested Common Name	VASCAN and/or ACIMS Common Name(s)	Rank
Carex pellita	woolly sedge	woolly sedge	species
Carex petasata	pasture sedge	pasture sedge	species
Carex petricosa	stone sedge	rock-dwelling sedge, stone sedge	species
Carex phaeocephala	dunhead sedge	dunhead sedge, head-like sedge	species
Carex podocarpa	shortstalk sedge	graceful mountain sedge, alpine sedge	species
Carex praegracilis	clustered field sedge	clustered field sedge, graceful sedge	species
Carex prairea	prairie sedge	prairie sedge	species
Carex praticola	meadow sedge	northern meadow sedge, meadow sedge	species
Carex preslii	Presl sedge	Presl's sedge, Presl sedge	species
Carex pseudocyperus	cyperus sedge	cyperus-like sedge	species
Carex raynoldsii	Raynolds sedge	Raynolds' sedge, Raynold's sedge	species
Carex retrorsa	turned sedge	retrorse sedge, turned sedge	species
Carex richardsonii	Richardson sedge	Richardson's sedge	species
Carex rossii	Ross sedge	Ross' sedge	species
Carex rostrata	beaked sedge	swollen beaked sedge, beaked sedge	species
Carex rupestris	rock sedge	rock sedge	species
Carex sartwellii	Sartwell sedge	Sartwell's sedge	species
Carex saxatilis	rock sedge	russet sedge, rocky-ground sedge	species
Carex saximontana	Rocky Mountain sedge	Rocky Mountain sedge	species
Carex scirpoidea	singlespike sedge	single-spike sedge, rush-like sedge	species
Carex scoparia	broom sedge	pointed broom sedge, broom sedge	species
Carex scopulorum	mountain sedge	Holm's Rocky Mountain sedge	species
Carex siccata	dryspike sedge	dry-spike sedge, hay sedge	species
Carex simpliciuscula	simple bog-sedge	simple bog sedge, simple bog-sedge	species
Carex simulata	mimic sedge	mimic sedge	species
Carex spectabilis	showy sedge	showy sedge	species
Carex sprengelii	Sprengel sedge	Sprengel's sedge	species
Carex stipata	awlfruit sedge	awl-fruited sedge	species
Carex supina	weak arctic sedge	weak arctic sedge, weak sedge	species
Carex sychnocephala	manyhead sedge	many-headed sedge, long-beaked sedge	species
Carex tahoensis	Lake Tahoe sedge	Lake Tahoe sedge	species
Carex tenera	tender sedge	tender sedge, broad-fruited sedge	species
Carex tenuiflora	sparseflower sedge	sparse-flowered sedge, thin-flowered sedge	species
Carex tincta	tinged sedge	tinged sedge	species
Carex tonsa	bald sedge	deep-green sedge, bald sedge	species
Carex torreyi	Torrey sedge	Torrey's sedge	species

ALPHABETICAL SCIENTIFIC NAMES

Scientific Name	Suggested Common Name	VASCAN and/or ACIMS Common Name(s)	Rank
Carex trisperma	threeseed sedge	three-seeded sedge	species
Carex umbellata	umbellate sedge	umbellate sedge	species
Carex utriculata	bottle sedge	northern beaked sedge, small bottle sedge	species
Carex vaginata	sheathed sedge	sheathed sedge	species
Carex vesicaria	blister sedge	inflated sedge, blister sedge	species
Carex viridula	green sedge	greenish sedge, green sedge	species
Carex vulpinoidea	fox sedge	fox sedge	species
Carex xerantica	whitescale sedge	dryland sedge, white-scaled sedge	species
Carthamus	safflower	safflower	genus
Carthamus tinctorius	safflower	safflower	species
Carum	caraway	caraway	genus
Carum carvi	wild caraway	wild caraway, caraway	species
Caryophyllaceae	pink family	pink family	family
Cassiope	mountain-heather	mountain-heather	genus
Cassiope mertensiana	western mountain-heather	white mountain heather, western mountain-heather	species
Cassiope tetragona	fourangle mountain-heather	four-angled mountain heather, white mountain-heather	species
Castilleja	paintbrush	paintbrush	genus
Castilleja cusickii	Cusick paintbrush	Cusick's paintbrush, yellow paintbrush	species
Castilleja elegans	elegant paintbrush	elegant paintbrush	species
Castilleja hispida	harsh paintbrush	harsh paintbrush, hispid paintbrush	species
Castilleja lutescens	stiff yellow paintbrush	stiff yellow paintbrush	species
Castilleja miniata	great red paintbrush	great red paintbrush, common red paintbrush	species
Castilleja occidentalis	western paintbrush	western paintbrush, lance-leaved paintbrush	species
Castilleja parviflora	smallflower paintbrush	small-flowered paintbrush, small-flowered Indian paintbrush	species
Castilleja purpurascens	purple paintbrush	purple paintbrush	species
Castilleja raupii	Raup paintbrush	Raup's paintbrush, purple paintbrush	species
Castilleja rhexiifolia	splitleaf paintbrush	rhexia-leaved paintbrush, alpine red paintbrush	species
Castilleja septentrionalis	northeastern paintbrush	northeastern paintbrush	species
Castilleja sessiliflora	downy paintbrush	downy paintbrush	species
Catabrosa	whorlgrass	whorlgrass	genus
Catabrosa aquatica	water whorlgrass	water whorlgrass, brook grass	species
Ceanothus	ceanothus	ceanothus	genus
Ceanothus velutinus	snowbrush ceanothus	snowbrush ceanothus	species
Celastraceae	bittersweet family	bittersweet family	family
Centaurea	knapweed	knapweed, cornflower, starflower	genus

ALPHABETICAL SCIENTIFIC NAMES

Scientific Name	Suggested Common Name	VASCAN and/or ACIMS Common Name(s)	Rank
Centaurea cyanus	garden cornflower	bachelor's button, cornflower	species
Centaurea diffusa	diffuse knapweed	diffuse knapweed	species
Centaurea jacea	brown knapweed	brown knapweed	species
Centaurea macrocephala	bighead knapweed	globe knapweed, bighead knapweed	species
Centaurea montana	mountain cornflower	mountain cornflower, mountain star-thistle	species
Centaurea solstitialis	yellow starthistle	yellow starthistle, yellow star-thistle	species
Centaurea stoebe	spotted knapweed	spotted knapweed	species
Cerastium	chickweed	chickweed	genus
Cerastium arvense	field chickweed	field chickweed, field mouse-ear chickweed	species
Cerastium beeringianum	Bering chickweed	Bering Sea chickweed, alpine mouse-ear chickweed	species
Cerastium brachypodum	shortstalk chickweed	short-stalked chickweed, short-stalk mouse-ear chickweed	species
Cerastium fontanum	common chickweed	common mouse-ear chickweed	species
Cerastium nutans	nodding chickweed	nodding chickweed, long-stalked mouse-ear chickweed	species
Ceratocephala	butterwort	butterwort	genus
Ceratocephala testiculata	curveseed butterwort	horn-seed buttercup, curveseed butterwort	species
Ceratophyllaceae	hornwort family	hornwort family	family
Ceratophyllum	hornwort	hornwort	genus
Ceratophyllum demersum	common hornwort	common hornwort, hornwort	species
Chaenactis	pincushion	pincushion	genus
Chaenactis douglasii	hoary pincushion	hoary pincushion	species
Chaenorhinum minus	dwarf-snapdragon	dwarf snapdragon	species
Chaenorrhinum	dwarf-snapdragon	dwarf-snapdragon	genus
Chamaedaphne	leatherleaf	leatherleaf	genus
Chamaedaphne calyculata	leatherleaf	leatherleaf	species
Chamaenerion	fireweed	fireweed	genus
Chamaenerion angustifolium	common fireweed	fireweed, common fireweed	species
Chamaenerion latifolium	broadleaf fireweed	river beauty, broad-leaved fireweed	species
Chamaerhodos	little-rose	little-rose	genus
Chamaerhodos erecta	little-rose	rose chamaerhodos, chamaerhodos	species
Chelidonium	celandine	celandine	genus
Chelidonium majus	celandine	rose chamaerhodos, greater celandine	species
Chenopodiastrum	goosefoot	goosefoot	genus
Chenopodiastrum simplex	mapleleaf goosefoot	maple-leaved goosefoot	species

ALPHABETICAL SCIENTIFIC NAMES

Scientific Name	Suggested Common Name	VASCAN and/or ACIMS Common Name(s)	Rank
Chenopodium	goosefoot	goosefoot, lamb's-quarters	genus
Chenopodium album	lamb's-quarters	common lamb's-quarters, lamb's-quarters	species
Chenopodium atrovirens	darkgreen goosefoot	dark-green goosefoot	species
Chenopodium berlandieri	Berlandier goosefoot	Berlandier's goosefoot, Berlandier goosefoot	species
Chenopodium desiccatum	aridland goosefoot	aridland goosefoot	species
Chenopodium fremontii	Fremont goosefoot	Fremont's goosefoot	species
Chenopodium hians	gaping goosefoot	gaping goosefoot	species
Chenopodium incanum	mealy goosefoot	mealy goosefoot	species
Chenopodium leptophyllum	slimleaf goosefoot	slim-leaved goosefoot, narrow-leaved goosefoot	species
Chenopodium pratericola	meadow goosefoot	meadow goosefoot	species
Chenopodium subglabrum	smooth goosefoot	smooth goosefoot	species
Chenopodium watsonii	Watson goosefoot	Watson's goosefoot	species
Cherleria	stitchwort	stitchwort	genus
Cherleria biflora	mountain stitchwort	mountain stitchwort, dwarf alpine sandwort	species
Cherleria obtusiloba	alpine stitchwort	alpine stitchwort, Arctic sandwort	species
Chimaphila	pipsissewa	pipsissewa	genus
Chimaphila umbellata	pipsissewa	common pipsissewa, prince's-pine	species
Chorispora	blue-mustard	blue-mustard	genus
Chorispora tenella	blue-mustard	blue mustard	species
Chrysosplenium	golden-saxifrage	golden-saxifrage	genus
Chrysosplenium iowense	Iowa golden-saxifrage	Iowa golden-saxifrage, golden saxifrage	species
Chrysosplenium tetrandrum	northern golden-saxifrage	northern golden-saxifrage, green saxifrage	species
Cichorium	chicory	chicory	genus
Cichorium intybus	wild chicory	wild chicory, chicory	species
Cicuta	water-hemlock	water-hemlock	genus
Cicuta bulbifera	bulbous water-hemlock	bulbous water-hemlock, bulb-bearing water-hemlock	species
Cicuta maculata	spotted water-hemlock	spotted water-hemlock, water-hemlock	species
Cicuta virosa	narrowleaf water-hemlock	northern water-hemlock, narrow-leaved water-hemlock	species
Cinna	woodreed	woodreed	genus
Cinna latifolia	drooping woodreed	drooping woodreed, drooping wood-reed	species
Circaea	enchanters-nightshade	enchanters-nightshade	genus
Circaea alpina	small enchanter's-nightshade	small enchanter's nightshade	species
Cirsium	thistle	thistle	genus
Cirsium arvense	creeping thistle	creeping thistle, Canada thistle	species

ALPHABETICAL SCIENTIFIC NAMES

Scientific Name	Suggested Common Name	VASCAN and/or ACIMS Common Name(s)	Rank
Cirsium drummondii	Drummond thistle	Drummond's thistle	species
Cirsium flodmanii	Flodman thistle	Flodman's thistle	species
Cirsium foliosum	leafy thistle	leafy thistle	species
Cirsium hookerianum	Hooker thistle	Hooker's thistle, white thistle	species
Cirsium palustre	marsh thistle	marsh thistle	species
Cirsium scariosum	meadow thistle	meadow thistle	species
Cirsium undulatum	wavyleaf thistle	wavy-leaved thistle	species
Cirsium vulgare	bull thistle	bull thistle	species
Cistaceae	rockrose family	rockrose family	family
Claytonia	springbeauty	springbeauty	genus
Claytonia lanceolata	western springbeauty	western spring beauty	species
Claytonia megarhiza	alpine springbeauty	alpine spring beauty	species
Clematis	clematis	clematis	genus
Clematis ligusticifolia	western white clematis	western white clematis, western clematis	species
Clematis occidentalis	purple clematis	purple clematis	species
Clematis tangutica	golden clematis	golden clematis, yellow clematis	species
Cleomaceae	spiderflower family	spiderflower family	family
Clintonia	clintonia	clintonia	genus
Clintonia uniflora	singleflower clintonia	single-flowered clintonia, corn lily	species
Coeloglossum	frog-orchid	frog-orchid	genus
Coeloglossum viride	frog-orchid	frog orchid, bracted bog orchid	species
Collinsia	blue-eyed-Mary	blue-eyed-Mary	genus
Collinsia parviflora	smallflower blue-eyed-Mary	small-flowered blue-eyed Mary, blue-eyed Mary	species
Collomia	collomia	collomia	genus
Collomia linearis	narrowleaf collomia	narrow-leaved collomia	species
Comandra	bastard-toadflax	bastard-toadflax	genus
Comandra umbellata	bastard-toadflax	bastard toadflax, common comandra	species
Comarum	marsh-cinquefoil	marsh-cinquefoil	genus
Comarum palustre	marsh-cinquefoil	marsh cinquefoil	species
Commelinaceae	spiderwort family	spiderwort family	family
Conimitella	mitrewort	mitrewort	genus
Conimitella williamsii	Williams mitrewort	Williams' mitrewort, conimitella	species
Conium	poison-hemlock	poison-hemlock	genus
Conium maculatum	poison-hemlock	poison-hemlock, poison hemlock	species
Conringia	hare's-ear-mustard	hare's-ear-mustard	genus
Conringia orientalis	hare's-ear-mustard	hare's-ear mustard	species
Convallaria	lily-of-the-valley	lily-of-the-valley	genus
Convallaria majalis	European lily-of-the-valley	European lily-of-the-valley	species
Convolvulaceae	bindweed family	bindweed family	family
Convolvulus	bindweed	bindweed	genus
Convolvulus arvensis	field bindweed	field bindweed	species

ALPHABETICAL SCIENTIFIC NAMES

Scientific Name	Suggested Common Name	VASCAN and/or ACIMS Common Name(s)	Rank
Conyza	fleabane	horseweed	species
Coptidium	Lapland-buttercup	Lapland-buttercup	genus
Coptidium lapponicum	Lapland-buttercup	Lapland buttercup	species
Coptis	goldthread	goldthread	genus
Coptis trifolia	goldthread	goldthread	species
Corallorhiza	coralroot	coralroot	genus
Corallorhiza maculata	spotted coralroot	spotted coralroot	species
Corallorhiza mertensiana	Merten coralroot	Pacific coralroot, Merten coralroot	species
Corallorhiza striata	striped coralroot	striped coralroot	species
Corallorhiza trifida	pale coralroot	early coralroot, pale coralroot	species
Coreopsis	tickseed	tickseed	genus
Coreopsis tinctoria	golden tickseed	golden tickseed, common tickseed	species
Corispermum	bugseed	bugseed	genus
Corispermum americanum	American bugseed	American bugseed	species
Corispermum hookeri	Hooker bugseed	Hooker's bugseed	species
Corispermum pallasii	Pallas bugseed	Pallas' bugseed	species
Corispermum villosum	hairy bugseed	hairy bugseed	species
Cornaceae	dogwood family	dogwood family	family
Cornus	dogwood, bunchberry	dogwood, bunchberry	genus
Cornus canadensis	Canada bunchberry	bunchberry	species
Cornus sericea	red-osier dogwood	red-osier dogwood	species
Cornus unalaschkensis	Alaska bunchberry	Alaska bunchberry, western bunchberry	species
Corydalis	corydalis	corydalis	genus
Corydalis aurea	golden corydalis	golden corydalis	species
Corylus	hazelnut	hazelnut	genus
Corylus cornuta	beaked hazelnut	beaked hazelnut	species
Cota	yellow-chamomile	yellow-chamomile	genus
Cota tinctoria	yellow-chamomile	yellow chamomile	species
Cotoneaster	cotoneaster	cotoneaster	genus
Cotoneaster lucidus	shiny cotoneaster	shiny cotoneaster, Peking cotoneaster	species
Crassulaceae	stonecrop family	stonecrop family	family
Crataegus	hawthorn	hawthorn	genus
Crataegus aquacervensis	Elkwater hawthorn	Elkwater hawthorn	species
Crataegus castlegarensis	Castlegar hawthorn	Castlegar hawthorn, Castlegar hawthorn	species
Crataegus chrysocarpa	fireberry hawthorn	fireberry hawthorn, round-leaved hawthorn	species
Crataegus cupressocollina	Cypress Hills hawthorn	Cypress Hills hawthorn	species
Crataegus douglasii	Douglas hawthorn	Douglas' hawthorn, Douglas hawthorn	species
Crataegus macracantha	largethorn hawthorn	large-thorned hawthorn, western hawthorn	species

ALPHABETICAL SCIENTIFIC NAMES

Scientific Name	Suggested Common Name	VASCAN and/or ACIMS Common Name(s)	Rank
Crataegus rivuloadamensis	Adams Creek hawthorn	Adams Creek hawthorn	species
Crataegus rivulopugnensis	Battle Creek hawthorn	Battle Creek hawthorn	species
Crataegus rubribracteolata	redbract hawthorn	red bracteole hawthorn	species
Crataegus sheridana	Great Plains hawthorn	Great Plains hawthorn	species
Crataegus ursopedensis	bearpaw hawthorn	bear's paw hawthorn	species
Crepis	hawksbeard	hawksbeard	genus
Crepis atribarba	slender hawksbeard	slender hawksbeard, slender hawk's-beard	species
Crepis capillaris	smooth hawksbeard	smooth hawksbeard, green hawk's-beard	species
Crepis intermedia	intermediate hawksbeard	limestone hawksbeard, intermediate hawk's-beard	species
Crepis occidentalis	western hawksbeard	western hawksbeard, small-flowered hawk's-beard	species
Crepis runcinata	dandelion hawksbeard	dandelion hawksbeard, scapose hawk's-beard	species
Crepis tectorum	narrowleaf hawksbeard	narrow-leaved hawksbeard, annual hawk's-beard	species
Crucihimalaya	fissurewort	fissurewort	genus
Crucihimalaya virgata	twiggy fissurewort	twiggy fissurewort, slender mouse-ear-cress	species
Cryptantha	cryptantha	cryptantha	genus
Cryptantha celosioides	cock's-comb cryptantha	cock's-comb cryptantha	species
Cryptantha fendleri	Fendler cryptantha	Fendler's cryptantha, Fendler's cryptanthe	species
Cryptantha kelseyana	Kelsey cryptantha	Kelsey's cryptantha, Kelsey's cat's eye	species
Cryptantha minima	tiny cryptantha	tiny cryptantha	species
Cryptogramma	rockbrake	rockbrake	genus
Cryptogramma acrostichoides	American rockbrake	American rockbrake, parsley fern	species
Cryptogramma stelleri	Steller rockbrake	Steller's rockbrake, Steller's rock brake	species
Cucurbitaceae	gourd family	gourd family	family
Cupressaceae	cypress family	cypress family	family
Cuscuta	dodder	dodder	genus
Cuscuta gronovii	swamp dodder	swamp dodder	species
Cuscuta umbrosa	bigfruit dodder	large-fruit dodder, big-fruit dodder	species
Cyclachaena	false-ragweed	false-ragweed	genus
Cyclachaena xanthiifolia	false-ragweed	false ragweed	species
Cymopterus	spring-parsley	spring-parsley	genus
Cymopterus glomeratus	plains spring-parsley	plains spring parsley	species
Cynoglossum	hound's-tongue	hound's-tongue	genus
Cynoglossum officinale	common hound's-tongue	common hound's-tongue, hound's-tongue	species
Cynoglossum virginianum	northern wild-comfrey	northern wild comfrey, wild comfrey	species

ALPHABETICAL SCIENTIFIC NAMES

Scientific Name	Suggested Common Name	VASCAN and/or ACIMS Common Name(s)	Rank
Cyperaceae	sedge family	sedge family	family
Cyperus	flatsedge	flatsedge	genus
Cyperus schweinitzii	Schweinitz flatsedge	Schweinitz's flatsedge, sand nut-grass	species
Cyperus squarrosus	awned flatsedge	awned flatsedge, awned nut-grass	species
Cypripedium	ladyslipper	ladyslipper	genus
Cypripedium acaule	pink ladyslipper	pink lady's-slipper, stemless lady's-slipper	species
Cypripedium montanum	mountain ladyslipper	mountain lady's-slipper	species
Cypripedium parviflorum	yellow ladyslipper	yellow lady's-slipper	species
Cypripedium passerinum	sparrowegg ladyslipper	sparrow's-egg lady's-slipper	species
Cystopteridaceae	bladderfern family	bladderfern family	family
Cystopteris	bladderfern	bladderfern	genus
Cystopteris fragilis	fragile bladderfern	fragile fern, fragile bladder fern	species
Cystopteris montana	mountain bladderfern	mountain bladder fern	species
Dactylis	orchardgrass	orchardgrass	genus
Dactylis glomerata	orchardgrass	orchard grass	species
Dactylorhiza	frog-orchid	frog orchid, bracted bog orchid	species
Dalea	prairieclover	prairieclover	genus
Dalea candida	white prairieclover	white prairie-clover	species
Dalea purpurea	purple prairieclover	purple prairie-clover	species
Danthonia	oatgrass	oatgrass	genus
Danthonia californica	California oatgrass	California oatgrass, California oat grass	species
Danthonia intermedia	timber oatgrass	timber oatgrass, intermediate oat grass	species
Danthonia parryi	Parry oatgrass	Parry's oatgrass, Parry oat grass	species
Danthonia spicata	poverty oatgrass	poverty oatgrass, poverty oat grass	species
Danthonia unispicata	onespike oatgrass	one-spike oatgrass, one-spike oat grass	species
Dasiphora	shrubby-cinquefoil	shrubby-cinquefoil	genus
Dasiphora fruticosa	shrubby-cinquefoil	shrubby cinquefoil	species
Datura	jimsonweed	jimsonweed	genus
Datura stramonium	jimsonweed	jimsonweed	species
Daucus	carrot	carrot	genus
Daucus carota	wild carrot	wild carrot	species
Delphinium	larkspur	larkspur	genus
Delphinium bicolor	little larkspur	flathead larkspur, low larkspur	species
Delphinium glaucum	tall larkspur	tall larkspur	species
Delphinium nuttallianum	Nuttall larkspur	upland larkspur, Nuttall's larkspur	species
Dendrolycopodium	groundpine	groundpine	genus
Dendrolycopodium dendroideum	groundpine	round-branched tree-clubmoss, ground-pine	species

ALPHABETICAL SCIENTIFIC NAMES

Scientific Name	Suggested Common Name	VASCAN and/or ACIMS Common Name(s)	Rank
Dennstaedtiaceae	brackenfern family	brackenfern family	family
Deschampsia	hairgrass	hairgrass	genus
Deschampsia cespitosa	tufted hairgrass	tufted hairgrass, tufted hair grass	species
Deschampsia elongata	slender hairgrass	slender hairgrass, slender hair grass	species
Descurainia	tansymustard	tansymustard	genus
Descurainia incana	grey tansymustard	grey tansy mustard	species
Descurainia incisa	mountain tansymustard	mountain tansy mustard	species
Descurainia pinnata	green tansymustard	green tansy mustard	species
Descurainia sophia	flixweed tansymustard	flixweed	species
Descurainia sophioides	northern tansymustard	northern tansy mustard, northern tansy-mustard	species
Dianthus	pink	pink	genus
Dianthus armeria	grass pink	Deptford pink, grass pink	species
Dianthus barbatus	sweet William	sweet William	species
Dianthus deltoides	maiden pink	maiden pink	species
Dianthus plumarius	garden pink	garden pink	species
Dianthus seguieri	ragged pink	ragged pink, European pink	species
Dichanthelium	panicgrass	panicgrass	genus
Dichanthelium lanuginosum	woolly panicgrass	woolly panicgrass, hairy panicgrass	species
Dichanthelium leibergii	Leiberg panicgrass	Leiberg's panicgrass, Leiberg's millet	species
Dichanthelium oligosanthes	fewflower panicgrass	few-flowered panicgrass, sand millet	species
Dichanthelium thermale	Geyser panicgrass	Geyser panicgrass	species
Dichanthelium wilcoxianum	Wilcox panicgrass	Wilcox's panicgrass	species
Dieteria	hoary-aster	hoary-aster	genus
Dieteria canescens	hoary-aster	hoary aster	species
Digitaria	crabgrass	crabgrass	genus
Digitaria ischaemum	smooth crabgrass	smooth crabgrass	species
Digitaria sanguinalis	hairy crabgrass	hairy crabgrass, crabgrass	species
Diphasiastrum	groundcedar	groundcedar	genus
Diphasiastrum alpinum	alpine groundcedar	alpine clubmoss, alpine club-moss	species
Diphasiastrum complanatum	northern groundcedar	northern ground-cedar, ground-cedar	species
Diphasiastrum sitchense	Sitka groundcedar	Sitka ground-cedar, ground-fir	species
Diplotaxis	wallrocket	wallrocket	genus
Diplotaxis muralis	annual wallrocket	annual wall rocket, sand rocket	species
Distichlis	saltgrass	saltgrass	genus
Distichlis spicata	saltgrass	saltgrass	species
Dodecatheon	shootingstar	shootingstar, shooting star	species
Doellingeria	white-aster	white-aster	genus

ALPHABETICAL SCIENTIFIC NAMES

Scientific Name	Suggested Common Name	VASCAN and/or ACIMS Common Name(s)	Rank
Doellingeria umbellata	flattop white-aster	flat-top white aster, flat-topped white aster	species
Douglasia	dwarf-primrose	dwarf-primrose	genus
Douglasia montana	mountain dwarf-primrose	Rocky Mountain dwarf primrose, mountain dwarf-primula	species
Downingia	calicoflower	calicoflower	genus
Downingia laeta	Great Basin calicoflower	Great Basin downingia, downingia	species
Draba	draba	draba	genus
Draba albertina	slender draba	slender draba	species
Draba aurea	golden draba	golden draba	species
Draba borealis	boreal draba	boreal draba	species
Draba cana	hoary draba	hoary draba	species
Draba crassifolia	snowbed draba	snowbed draba	species
Draba densifolia	denseleaf draba	dense-leaved draba	species
Draba fladnizensis	Austrian draba	Austrian draba	species
Draba glabella	smooth draba	smooth draba	species
Draba incerta	Yellowstone draba	Yellowstone draba	species
Draba juvenilis	longstalk draba	long-stalked draba	species
Draba lonchocarpa	lancepod draba	lance-pod draba	species
Draba macounii	Macoun draba	Macoun's draba	species
Draba nemorosa	woodland draba	woodland draba	species
Draba nivalis	snow draba	snow draba	species
Draba novolympica	Mt. Olympic draba	Mt. Olympic draba	species
Draba oligosperma	fewseed draba	few-seed draba	species
Draba paysonii	Payson draba	Payson's draba	species
Draba porsildii	Porsild draba	Porsild's draba	species
Draba praealta	tall draba	tall draba	species
Draba ruaxes	coast mountain draba	coast mountain draba	species
Draba stenoloba	Alaska draba	Alaska draba	species
Draba ventosa	Wind River draba	Wind River draba	species
Draba verna	spring draba	spring draba	species
Dracocephalum	dragonhead	dragonhead	genus
Dracocephalum parviflorum	American dragonhead	American dragonhead	species
Dracocephalum thymiflorum	thymeflower dragonhead	thyme-flowered dragonhead, thyme-leaved dragonhead	species
Drosera	sundew	sundew	genus
Drosera anglica	English sundew	English sundew, oblong-leaved sundew	species
Drosera linearis	slenderleaf sundew	slender-leaved sundew	species
Drosera rotundifolia	roundleaf sundew	round-leaved sundew	species
Droseraceae	sundew family	sundew family	family
Dryas	mountain-avens	mountain-avens	genus
Dryas drummondii	Drummond mountain-avens	Drummond's mountain avens, yellow mountain avens	species

ALPHABETICAL SCIENTIFIC NAMES

Scientific Name	Suggested Common Name	VASCAN and/or ACIMS Common Name(s)	Rank
Dryas hookeriana	Hooker mountain-avens	Hooker's mountain avens, white mountain avens	species
Dryas integrifolia	entireleaf mountain-avens	entire-leaved mountain avens, northern white mountain avens	species
Drymocallis	woodbeauty	woodbeauty	genus
Drymocallis arguta	tall woodbeauty	tall wood beauty, white cinquefoil	species
Drymocallis pseudorupestris	sticky woodbeauty	false rock-loving cinquefoil, sticky cinquefoil	species
Dryopteridaceae	shieldfern family	shieldfern family, woodfern family	family
Dryopteris	shieldfern	woodfern	genus
Dryopteris carthusiana	spinulose shieldfern	spinulose wood fern, narrow spinulose shield fern	species
Dryopteris cristata	crested shieldfern	crested wood fern, crested shield fern	species
Dryopteris expansa	spreading shieldfern	spreading wood fern, broad spinulose shield fern	species
Dryopteris filix-mas	male shieldfern	male fern	species
Dryopteris fragrans	fragrant shieldfern	fragrant wood fern, fragrant shield fern	species
Dyssodia	fetid-dogweed	fetid-dogweed	genus
Dyssodia papposa	fetid-dogweed	fetid dogweed	species
Echinochloa	barnyardgrass	barnyardgrass	genus
Echinochloa crus-galli	large barnyardgrass	large barnyard grass, barnyard grass	species
Echinochloa muricata	rough barnyardgrass	rough barnyard grass, rough barnyard grass	species
Echinocystis	wild-cucumber	wild-cucumber	genus
Echinocystis lobata	wild-cucumber	wild cucumber	species
Echium	viper's-bugloss	viper's-bugloss	genus
Echium vulgare	common viper's-bugloss	common viper's bugloss, blueweed	species
Elaeagnaceae	oleaster family	oleaster family	family
Elaeagnus	wolfwillow, Russian-olive	wolfwillow, Russian-olive	genus
Elaeagnus angustifolia	Russian-olive	Russian olive	species
Elaeagnus commutata	wolfwillow	wolf-willow, silverberry	species
Elatinaceae	waterwort family	waterwort family	family
Elatine	waterwort	waterwort	genus
Elatine triandra	threestamen waterwort	three-stamened waterwort, waterwort	species
Eleocharis	spikerush	spikerush	genus
Eleocharis acicularis	needle spikerush	needle spikerush, needle spike-rush	species
Eleocharis compressa	flatstem spikerush	flat-stemmed spikerush, flat-stem spikerush	species

ALPHABETICAL SCIENTIFIC NAMES

Scientific Name	Suggested Common Name	VASCAN and/or ACIMS Common Name(s)	Rank
Eleocharis elliptica	elliptic spikerush	elliptic spikerush, slender spikerush	species
Eleocharis engelmannii	Engelmann spikerush	Engelmann's spikerush, Engelmann's spike-rush	species
Eleocharis erythropoda	bald spikerush	red-stemmed spikerush, bald spikerush	species
Eleocharis macrostachya	longhead spikerush	long-headed spikerush, creeping spikerush	species
Eleocharis mamillata	softstem spikerush	soft-stemmed spikerush, spike-rush	species
Eleocharis ovata	ovate spikerush	ovate spikerush	species
Eleocharis palustris	common spikerush	common spikerush, creeping spike-rush	species
Eleocharis quinqueflora	fewflower spikerush	few-flowered spikerush, few-flowered spike-rush	species
Eleocharis suksdorfiana	Suksdorf spikerush	Suksdorf's spikerush	species
Eleocharis uniglumis	oneglume spikerush	single-glumed spikerush, creeping spikerush	species
Ellisia	waterpod	waterpod	genus
Ellisia nyctelea	waterpod	waterpod	species
Elodea	waterweed	waterweed	genus
Elodea bifoliata	twoleaf waterweed	two-leaved waterweed	species
Elodea canadensis	Canada waterweed	Canada waterweed	species
Elodea nuttallii	Nuttall waterweed	Nuttall's waterweed	species
Elyhordeum ×macounii	Macoun wildrye	Macoun's wildrye, Macoun's wild rye	Hybrid
Elyhordeum	wildrye	wildrye	genus
Elymus	wildrye	wildrye	genus
Elymus albicans	northern wildrye	Montana wildrye, awned northern wheat grass	species
Elymus canadensis	Canada wildrye	Canada wildrye	species
Elymus curvatus	awnless wildrye	awnless wildrye	species
Elymus elymoides	squirreltail wildrye	long-bristled wildrye, squirreltail	species
Elymus glaucus	blue wildrye	blue wildrye, smooth wild rye	species
Elymus lanceolatus	thickspike wildrye	thick-spike wildrye, northern wheat grass	species
Elymus repens	quackgrass	quackgrass	species
Elymus scribneri	Scribner wildrye	Scribner's wildrye, Scribner's wheat grass	species
Elymus trachycaulus	slender wildrye	slender wildrye, slender wheatgrass	species
Elymus violaceus	high wildrye	high wildrye	species
Elymus virginicus	Virginia wildrye	Virginia wildrye	species
Empetrum	crowberry	crowberry	genus

ALPHABETICAL SCIENTIFIC NAMES

Scientific Name	Suggested Common Name	VASCAN and/or ACIMS Common Name(s)	Rank
Empetrum nigrum	crowberry	black crowberry, crowberry	species
Endotropis	alderleaf-buckthorn	alderleaf-buckthorn	genus
Endotropis alnifolia	alderleaf-buckthorn	alderleaf-buckthorn	species
Epilobium	willowherb	willowherb	genus
Epilobium anagallidifolium	alpine willowherb	alpine willowherb	species
Epilobium brachycarpum	annual willowherb	tall annual willowherb, annual willowherb	species
Epilobium campestre	smooth willowherb	smooth willowherb, smooth boisduvalia	species
Epilobium ciliatum	northern willowherb	northern willowherb	species
Epilobium clavatum	club willowherb	club-fruited willowherb, club willowherb	species
Epilobium glaberrimum	glaucous willowherb	glaucous willowherb	species
Epilobium hallianum	Hall willowherb	Hall's willowherb	species
Epilobium hornemannii	Hornemann willowherb	Hornemann's willowherb	species
Epilobium lactiflorum	whiteflower willowherb	white-flowered willowherb	species
Epilobium leptocarpum	slenderfruit willowherb	slender-fruited willowherb, slender-fruit willowherb	species
Epilobium leptophyllum	narrowleaf willowherb	narrow-leaved willowherb	species
Epilobium luteum	yellow willowherb	yellow willowherb	species
Epilobium minutum	little willowherb	little willowherb	species
Epilobium mirabile	hairystem willowherb	hairy-stemmed willowherb	species
Epilobium palustre	marsh willowherb	marsh willowherb	species
Epilobium saximontanum	Rocky Mountain willowherb	Rocky Mountain willowherb	species
Equisetaceae	horsetail family	horsetail family	family
Equisetum	horsetail, scouringrush	horsetail, scouringrush	genus
Equisetum arvense	field horsetail	field horsetail, common horsetail	species
Equisetum fluviatile	water horsetail	water horsetail, swamp horsetail	species
Equisetum hyemale	common scouringrush	common scouring-rush	species
Equisetum laevigatum	smooth scouringrush	smooth scouring-rush	species
Equisetum palustre	marsh horsetail	marsh horsetail	species
Equisetum pratense	meadow horsetail	meadow horsetail	species
Equisetum scirpoides	dwarf scouringrush	dwarf scouring-rush	species
Equisetum sylvaticum	woodland horsetail	woodland horsetail	species
Equisetum variegatum	variegated scouringrush	variegated scouring-rush, variegated horsetail	species
Eragrostis	stinkgrass	stinkgrass	genus
Eragrostis cilianensis	stinkgrass	stinkgrass, skunk-grass	species
Eremogone	sandwort	sandwort	genus
Eremogone capillaris	threadleaf sandwort	thread-leaved sandwort, linear-leaved sandwort	species
Eremogone congesta	ballhead sandwort	ballhead sandwort, rocky-ground sandwort	species
Eremopyrum	false-wheatgrass	false-wheatgrass	genus

ALPHABETICAL SCIENTIFIC NAMES

Scientific Name	Suggested Common Name	VASCAN and/or ACIMS Common Name(s)	Rank
Eremopyrum triticeum	annual false-wheatgrass	annual false wheatgrass, annual wheat grass	species
Ericaceae	heath family	heath family	family
Ericameria	rabbitbush	rabbitbush	genus
Ericameria nauseosa	rubber rabbitbrush	rubber rabbitbrush, rabbitbrush	species
Erigeron	fleabane	fleabane	genus
Erigeron acris	bitter fleabane	bitter fleabane, northern daisy fleabane	species
Erigeron annuus	annual fleabane	annual fleabane, whitetop	species
Erigeron aureus	golden fleabane	golden fleabane	species
Erigeron caespitosus	tufted fleabane	tufted fleabane	species
Erigeron canadensis	horseweed fleabane	Canada horseweed, horseweed	species
Erigeron compositus	cutleaf fleabane	cut-leaved fleabane	species
Erigeron divergens	diffuse fleabane	diffuse fleabane	species
Erigeron elatus	tall fleabane	swamp fleabane, tall fleabane	species
Erigeron flagellaris	creeping fleabane	trailing fleabane, creeping fleabane	species
Erigeron glabellus	smooth fleabane	streamside fleabane, smooth fleabane	species
Erigeron glacialis	subalpine fleabane	subalpine fleabane	species
Erigeron grandiflorus	largeflower fleabane	large-flowered fleabane	species
Erigeron humilis	low fleabane	low fleabane, purple fleabane	species
Erigeron hyssopifolius	hyssopleaf fleabane	hyssop-leaved fleabane, wild daisy fleabane	species
Erigeron lackschewitzii	Lackschewitz fleabane	Lackschewitz's fleabane, front-range fleabane	species
Erigeron lanatus	woolly fleabane	woolly fleabane	species
Erigeron lonchophyllus	shortray fleabane	short-rayed fleabane	species
Erigeron nivalis	snow fleabane	snow fleabane	species
Erigeron ochroleucus	buff fleabane	buff fleabane	species
Erigeron pallens	pale alpine fleabane	pale fleabane, pale alpine fleabane	species
Erigeron peregrinus	wandering fleabane	wandering fleabane, wandering daisy	species
Erigeron philadelphicus	Philadelphia fleabane	Philadelphia fleabane	species
Erigeron pumilus	shaggy fleabane	shaggy fleabane, hairy fleabane	species
Erigeron radicatus	taproot fleabane	taproot fleabane, dwarf fleabane	species
Erigeron speciosus	showy fleabane	showy fleabane	species
Erigeron strigosus	rough fleabane	rough fleabane	species
Erigeron trifidus	threelobe fleabane	three-lobed fleabane, trifid-leaved fleabane	species
Eriocoma	ricegrass	ricegrass	genus
Eriocoma hymenoides	Indian ricegrass	Indian ricegrass, Indian rice grass	species
Eriogonum	umbrella-plant	buckwheat	genus
Eriogonum androsaceum	rockjasmine umbrella-plant	androsace buckwheat, cushion umbrella-plant	species

ALPHABETICAL SCIENTIFIC NAMES

Scientific Name	Suggested Common Name	VASCAN and/or ACIMS Common Name(s)	Rank
Eriogonum cernuum	nodding umbrella-plant	nodding buckwheat, nodding umbrella-plant	species
Eriogonum flavum	yellow umbrella-plant	yellow buckwheat, yellow umbrella-plant	species
Eriogonum ovalifolium	cushion umbrella-plant	cushion buckwheat, silver-plant	species
Eriogonum pauciflorum	fewflower umbrella-plant	few-flowered buckwheat, few-flower buckwheat	species
Eriogonum umbellatum	sulphur umbrella-plant	sulphur-flowered buckwheat, subalpine umbrellaplant	species
Eriophorum	cottongrass	cottongrass	genus
Eriophorum angustifolium	narrowleaf cottongrass	narrow-leaved cottongrass, narrowleaf cotton-grass	species
Eriophorum brachyantherum	closed-sheath cottongrass	closed-sheathed cottongrass, close-sheathed cotton grass	species
Eriophorum callitrix	beautiful cottongrass	beautiful cottongrass, russett cotton grass	species
Eriophorum gracile	slender cottongrass	slender cottongrass, beautiful cotton grass	species
Eriophorum russeolum	russet cottongrass	russet cottongrass, slender cotton grass	species
Eriophorum scheuchzeri	Scheuchzer cottongrass	Scheuchzer's cottongrass, one-spike cotton grass	species
Eriophorum vaginatum	tussock cottongrass	tussock cottongrass, sheathed cotton grass	species
Eriophorum viridicarinatum	greenkeel cottongrass	green-keeled cottongrass, thin-leaved cotton grass	species
Erodium	storksbill	storksbill	genus
Erodium cicutarium	common storksbill	common storksbill	species
Eruca	gardenrocket	gardenrocket	genus
Eruca vesicaria	gardenrocket	garden rocket	species
Erucastrum	dogmustard	dogmustard	genus
Erucastrum gallicum	common dogmustard	common dog mustard, dog mustard	species
Eryngium	cross-thistle	cross-thistle	genus
Eryngium planum	cross-thistle	plains eryngo, cross-thistle	species
Erysimum	wallflower	wallflower	genus
Erysimum asperum	prairie wallflower	prairie rocket	species
Erysimum cheiranthoides	wormseed wallflower	wormseed wallflower, wormseed mustard	species
Erysimum coarctatum	crowded wallflower	crowded wormseed mustard	species
Erysimum inconspicuum	smallflower wallflower	small-flowered wallflower, small-flowered rocket	species
Erysimum pallasii	Pallas wallflower	Pallas' wallflower, purple alpine rocket	species
Erythranthe	monkeyflower	monkeyflower	genus
Erythranthe breweri	Brewer monkeyflower	Brewer's monkeyflower	species

ALPHABETICAL SCIENTIFIC NAMES

Scientific Name	Suggested Common Name	VASCAN and/or ACIMS Common Name(s)	Rank
Erythranthe floribunda	small yellow monkeyflower	purple-stemmed monkeyflower, small yellow monkeyflower	species
Erythranthe geyeri	Geyer monkeyflower	Geyer's yellow monkeyflower, smooth monkeyflower	species
Erythranthe guttata	seep monkeyflower	seep monkeyflower, yellow monkeyflower	species
Erythranthe lewisii	Lewis monkeyflower	Lewis' monkeyflower, red monkeyflower	species
Erythranthe moschatus	musk monkeyflower	musk monkeyflower	species
Erythranthe patula	stalkleaf monkeyflower	stalk-leaved monkeyflower	species
Erythranthe tilingii	Tiling monkeyflower	Tiling's monkeyflower, large mountain monkeyflower	species
Erythronium	glacier-lily	glacier-lily	genus
Erythronium grandiflorum	yellow glacier-lily	yellow glacier lily, glacier lily	species
Eschscholtzia	California-poppy	California-poppy	genus
Eschscholzia californica	California-poppy	California poppy	species
Escobaria	cushion-cactus	cushion-cactus	genus
Escobaria vivipara	cushion-cactus	pincushion cactus, cushion cactus	species
Eucephalus	aster	aster	genus
Eucephalus engelmannii	Engelmann aster	Engelmann's aster, elegant aster	species
Euphorbia	spurge	spurge	genus
Euphorbia agraria	field spurge	field spurge	species
Euphorbia glyptosperma	ridgeseed spurge	ridge-seeded spurge	species
Euphorbia helioscopia	sun spurge	sun spurge, wartweed	species
Euphorbia peplus	petty spurge	petty spurge	species
Euphorbia serpillifolia	thymeleaf spurge	thyme-leaved spurge	species
Euphorbia virgata	leafy spurge	leafy spurge	species
Euphorbiaceae	spurge family	spurge family	family
Euphrasia	eyebright	eyebright	genus
Euphrasia hudsoniana	Hudson Bay eyebright	Hudson Bay eyebright, eyebright	species
Euphrasia nemorosa	common eyebright	common eyebright	species
Euphrasia subarctica	subarctic eyebright	subarctic eyebright	species
Eurybia	wood-aster	aster	genus
Eurybia conspicua	showy wood-aster	western showy aster, showy aster	species
Eurybia sibirica	Siberian wood-aster	Siberian aster, Arctic aster	species
Euthamia	goldentop	goldentop	genus
Euthamia graminifolia	common goldentop	grass-leaved goldenrod, flat-topped goldenrod	species
Eutrema	saltwater-cress	saltwater-cress	genus
Eutrema salsugineum	saltwater-cress	saltwater-cress, mouse-ear cress	species
Eutrochium	Joe-Pye-weed	Joe-Pye-weed	genus
Eutrochium maculatum	spotted Joe-Pye-weed	spotted Joe Pye weed, spotted Joe-pye weed	species
Fabaceae	legume family	legume family	family

ALPHABETICAL SCIENTIFIC NAMES

Scientific Name	Suggested Common Name	VASCAN and/or ACIMS Common Name(s)	Rank
Fagopyrum	buckwheat	buckwheat	genus
Fagopyrum esculentum	common buckwheat	common buckwheat	species
Fagopyrum tataricum	Tartary buckwheat	Tartarian buckwheat, tartary buckwheat	species
Fallopia	false-buckwheat	falsle-buckwheat	genus
Fallopia convolvulus	black false-buckwheat	Eurasian black bindweed, wild buckwheat	species
Fallopia scandens	climbing false-buckwheat	climbing false buckwheat	species
Festuca	fescue	fescue	genus
Festuca altaica	northern rough-fescue	northern rough fescue	species
Festuca baffinensis	Baffin fescue	Baffin Island fescue, Arctic fescue	species
Festuca brachyphylla	alpine fescue	short-leaved fescue, alpine fescue	species
Festuca campestris	mountain rough-fescue	mountain rough fescue	species
Festuca hallii	plains rough-fescue	plains rough fescue	species
Festuca idahoensis	Idaho fescue	Idaho fescue, bluebunch fescue	species
Festuca minutiflora	smallflower fescue	small-flowered fescue, tiny-flowered fescue	species
Festuca occidentalis	western fescue	western fescue	species
Festuca ovina	sheep fescue	sheep fescue	species
Festuca rubra	red fescue	red fescue	species
Festuca saximontana	Rocky Mountain fescue	Rocky Mountain fescue	species
Festuca subulata	bearded fescue	bearded fescue	species
Festuca trachyphylla	hard fescue	hard fescue	species
Festuca valesiaca	steppe fescue	steppe fescue	species
Festuca viviparoidea	viviparous fescue	viviparous fescue	species
Fragaria	strawberry	strawberry	genus
Fragaria vesca	woodland strawberry	woodland strawberry	species
Fragaria virginiana	wild strawberry	wild strawberry	species
Fraxinus	ash	ash	genus
Fraxinus pennsylvanica	green ash	red ash, green ash	species
Fritillaria	fritillary	fritillary	genus
Fritillaria pudica	yellow fritillary	yellow fritillary, yellowbell	species
Fumaria	fumitory	fumitory	genus
Fumaria officinalis	common fumitory	common fumitory, fumitory	species
Gaillardia	blanketflower	blanketflower	genus
Gaillardia aristata	great blanketflower	great blanketflower, gaillardia	species
Galearis	roundleaf-orchid	roundleaf-orchid	genus
Galearis rotundifolia	roundleaf-orchid	small round-leaved orchid, round-leaved orchid	species
Galeopsis	hempnettle	hempnettle	genus
Galeopsis speciosa	largeflower hempnettle	large-flowered hemp-nettle, yellow hemp-nettle	species
Galeopsis tetrahit	common hempnettle	common hemp-nettle, hemp-nettle	species

ALPHABETICAL SCIENTIFIC NAMES

Scientific Name	Suggested Common Name	VASCAN and/or ACIMS Common Name(s)	Rank
Galinsoga	galinsoga	galinsoga	genus
Galinsoga quadriradiata	hairy galinsoga	hairy galinsoga, galinsoga	species
Galium	bedstraw	bedstraw	genus
Galium aparine	cleavers bedstraw	common bedstraw, cleavers	species
Galium bifolium	twinleaf bedstraw	thin-leaved bedstraw, two-leaved bedstraw	species
Galium boreale	northern bedstraw	northern bedstraw	species
Galium labradoricum	Labrador bedstraw	Labrador bedstraw	species
Galium spurium	false cleavers	false cleavers	species
Galium trifidum	threepetal bedstraw	three-petalled bedstraw, small bedstraw	species
Galium triflorum	sweetscented bedstraw	three-flowered bedstraw, sweet-scented bedstraw	species
Galium verum	yellow bedstraw	yellow bedstraw	species
Gaultheria	wintergreen	wintergreen	genus
Gaultheria hispidula	creeping snowberry	creeping snowberry	species
Gaultheria humifusa	alpine wintergreen	alpine wintergreen	species
Gayophytum	groundsmoke	groundsmoke	genus
Gayophytum racemosum	racemose groundsmoke	racemose groundsmoke	species
Gentiana	gentian	gentian	genus
Gentiana affinis	pleated gentian	pleated gentian, prairie gentian	species
Gentiana calycosa	mountain gentian	mountain bog gentian, mountain gentian	species
Gentiana fremontii	lowly gentian	lowly gentian, marsh gentian	species
Gentiana glauca	pale gentian	pale gentian, alpine gentian	species
Gentiana lutea	yellow gentian	yellow gentian	species
Gentiana prostrata	moss gentian	moss gentian	species
Gentianaceae	gentian family	gentian family	family
Gentianella	dwarf-gentiana	dwarf-gentiana	genus
Gentianella amarella	autumn dwarf-gentian	autumn dwarf gentian, felwort	species
Gentianella propinqua	four-part dwarf-gentian	four-parted gentian	species
Gentianopsis	fringed-gentian	fringed-gentian	genus
Gentianopsis detonsa	northern fringed-gentian	sheared gentian, northern fringed gentian	species
Gentianopsis virgata	Macoun fringed-gentian	lesser fringed gentian, Macoun's gentian	species
Geocaulon	false-toadflax	false-toadflax	genus
Geocaulon lividum	false-toadflax	northern comandra, northern bastard toadflax	species
Geraniaceae	geranium family	geranium family	family
Geranium	geranium	geranium	genus
Geranium bicknellii	Bicknell geranium	Bicknell's geranium	species
Geranium carolinianum	Carolina geranium	Carolina geranium, Carolina wild geranium	species
Geranium erianthum	woolly geranium	woolly geranium	species

ALPHABETICAL SCIENTIFIC NAMES

Scientific Name	Suggested Common Name	VASCAN and/or ACIMS Common Name(s)	Rank
Geranium pratense	meadow geranium	meadow geranium, meadow crane's-bill	species
Geranium richardsonii	white geranium	white geranium, wild white geranium	species
Geranium viscosissimum	sticky purple geranium	sticky purple geranium	species
Geum	avens	avens	genus
Geum aleppicum	yellow avens	yellow avens	species
Geum macrophyllum	largeleaf avens	large-leaved avens, large-leaved yellow avens	species
Geum rivale	purple avens	water avens, purple avens	species
Geum triflorum	threeflower avens	three-flowered avens	species
Glechoma	ground-ivy	ground-ivy	genus
Glechoma hederacea	ground-ivy	ground-ivy, ground ivy	species
Glyceria	mannagrass	mannagrass	genus
Glyceria borealis	northern mannagrass	boreal mannagrass, northern manna grass	species
Glyceria elata	tufted tall mannagrass	tufted tall mannagrass, tufted tall manna grass	species
Glyceria grandis	tall mannagrass	tall mannagrass, common tall manna grass	species
Glyceria pulchella	graceful mannagrass	graceful mannagrass, graceful manna grass	species
Glyceria striata	fowl mannagrass	fowl mannagrass, fowl manna grass	species
Glycyrrhiza	wild-licorice	wild-licorice	genus
Glycyrrhiza lepidota	wild-licorice	wild licorice	species
Gnaphalium	cudweed	cudweed	genus
Gnaphalium palustre	marsh cudweed	western marsh cudweed, marsh cudweed	species
Gnaphalium uliginosum	low cudweed	low cudweed	species
Goodyera	rattlesnake-plantain	rattlesnake-plantain	genus
Goodyera oblongifolia	Menzies rattlesnake-plantain	Menzies' rattlesnake-plantain, rattlesnake plantain	species
Goodyera repens	dwarf rattlesnake-plantain	dwarf rattlesnake-plantain, lesser rattlesnake plantain	species
Gratiola	hedge-hyssop	hedge-hyssop	genus
Gratiola neglecta	clammy hedge-hyssop	clammy hedge-hyssop	species
Grindelia	gumweed	gumweed	genus
Grindelia hirsutula	hairy gumweed	hairy gumweed	species
Grindelia squarrosa	curlycup gumweed	curly-cup gumweed	species
Grossulariaceae	currant family	currant family	family
Gutierrezia	snakeweed	snakeweed	genus
Gutierrezia sarothrae	broom snakeweed	broom snakeweed, broomweed	species
Gymnocarpium	oakfern	oakfern	genus

ALPHABETICAL SCIENTIFIC NAMES

Scientific Name	Suggested Common Name	VASCAN and/or ACIMS Common Name(s)	Rank
Gymnocarpium continentale	Nahanni oakfern	Nahanni oak fern, northern oak fern	species
Gymnocarpium disjunctum	Pacific oakfern	Pacific oak fern, western oak fern	species
Gymnocarpium dryopteris	common oakfern	common oak fern, oak fern	species
Gypsophila	baby's-breath	baby's-breath	genus
Gypsophila elegans	annual baby's-breath	showy baby's-breath, annual baby's-breath	species
Gypsophila paniculata	tall baby's-breath	tall baby's-breath, common baby's-breath	species
Gypsophila scorzonerifolia	glandular baby's-breath	glandular baby's-breath, pink baby's-breath	species
Hackelia	stickseed	stickseed	genus
Hackelia deflexa	nodding stickseed	nodding stickseed, northern stickseed	species
Hackelia floribunda	manyflower stickseed	many-flowered stickseed, large-flowered stickseed	species
Hackelia micrantha	Jessica stickseed	blue stickseed, Jessica's stickseed	species
Halenia	spurred-gentian	spurred-gentian	genus
Halenia deflexa	American spurred-gentian	American spurred-gentian, spurred gentian	species
Halerpestes	seaside-buttercup	seaside-buttercup	genus
Halerpestes cymbalaria	seaside-buttercup	seaside buttercup	species
Haloragaceae	watermilfoil family	watermilfoil family	family
Hedeoma	false-pennyroyal	false-pennyroyal	genus
Hedeoma hispida	rough false-pennyroyal	rough false-pennyroyal, pennyroyal	species
Hedysarum	hedysarum	hedysarum	genus
Hedysarum americanum	alpine hedysarum	alpine hedysarum	species
Hedysarum boreale	northern hedysarum	northern hedysarum	species
Hedysarum sulphurescens	yellow hedysarum	yellow hedysarum	species
Helenium	sneezeweed	sneezeweed	genus
Helenium autumnale	sneezeweed	common sneezeweed, sneezeweed	species
Helianthus	sunflower	sunflower	genus
Helianthus annuus	common sunflower	common sunflower, common annual sunflower	species
Helianthus maximilianii	Maximilian sunflower	Maximilian sunflower, narrow-leaved sunflower	species
Helianthus nuttallii	Nuttall sunflower	Nuttall's sunflower, common tall sunflower	species
Helianthus pauciflorus	stiff sunflower	stiff sunflower	species
Helianthus petiolaris	prairie sunflower	prairie sunflower	species
Helictochloa	oatgrass	oatgrass	genus
Helictochloa hookeri	Hooker oatgrass	Hooker's oatgrass, Hooker's oat grass	species

ALPHABETICAL SCIENTIFIC NAMES

Scientific Name	Suggested Common Name	VASCAN and/or ACIMS Common Name(s)	Rank
Heliotropiaceae	heliotrope family	heliotrope family	family
Heliotropium	heliotrope	heliotrope	genus
Heliotropium curassavicum	salt heliotrope	salt heliotrope, spatulate-leaved heliotrope	species
Helminthotheca	oxtongue	oxtongue	genus
Helminthotheca echioides	bristly oxtongue	bristly oxtongue	species
Heracleum	cowparsnip	cowparsnip	genus
Heracleum maximum	American cowparsnip	American cow parsnip, cow parsnip	species
Hesperis	dame's-rocket	dame's-rocket	genus
Hesperis matronalis	dame's-rocket	dame's rocket	species
Hesperostipa	needle-and-thread	needle-and-thread, porcupinegrass	genus
Hesperostipa comata	needle-and-thread	needle-and-thread grass, needle-and-thread	species
Hesperostipa curtiseta	northern porcupinegrass	northern porcupine grass, western porcupine grass	species
Hesperostipa spartea	plains porcupinegrass	plains porcupine grass, porcupine grass	species
Heterotheca	golden-aster	golden-aster	genus
Heterotheca villosa	hairy golden-aster	hairy goldenaster, golden aster	species
Heuchera	alumroot	alumroot	genus
Heuchera cylindrica	roundleaf alumroot	round-leaved alumroot, sticky alumroot	species
Heuchera glabra	alpine alumroot	smooth alumroot, alpine alumroot	species
Heuchera parvifolia	littleleaf alumroot	little-leaved alumroot, small-leaved alumroot	species
Heuchera richardsonii	Richardson alumroot	Richardson's alumroot	species
Hieracium	hawkweed	hawkweed	genus
Hieracium albiflorum	white hawkweed	white hawkweed	species
Hieracium scouleri	Scouler hawkweed	Scouler's hawkweed, woolly hawkweed	species
Hieracium triste	slender hawkweed	woolly hawkweed, slender hawkweed	species
Hieracium umbellatum	umbellate hawkweed	umbellate hawkweed, narrow-leaved hawkweed	species
Hippophae	sea-buckthorn	sea-buckthorn	genus
Hippophae rhamnoides	sea-buckthorn	sea buckthorn	species
Hippuris	mare's-tail	mare's-tail	genus
Hippuris montana	mountain mare's-tail	mountain mare's-tail	species
Hippuris vulgaris	common mare's-tail	common mare's-tail	species
Hordeum	barley	barley	genus
Hordeum brachyantherum	meadow barley	meadow barley	species
Hordeum jubatum	foxtail barley	foxtail barley	species
Hordeum murinum	mouse barley	mouse barley	species
Hordeum pusillum	little barley	little barley	species

ALPHABETICAL SCIENTIFIC NAMES

Scientific Name	Suggested Common Name	VASCAN and/or ACIMS Common Name(s)	Rank
Hordeum vulgare	common barley	common barley, cultivated barley	species
Houstonia	bluets	bluets	genus
Houstonia longifolia	longleaf bluets	long-leaved bluets	species
Hudsonia	sandheather	sandheather	genus
Hudsonia tomentosa	woolly sandheather	woolly beach-heather, sand heather	species
Humulus	hop	hop	genus
Humulus lupulus	common hop	common hop	species
Huperzia	firmoss	firmoss	genus
Huperzia continentalis	continental firmoss	continental firmoss, alpine firmoss	species
Huperzia occidentalis	western firmoss	western firmoss	species
Huperzia selago	northern firmoss	northern firmoss, mountain club-moss	species
Hydrangeaceae	hydrangea family	hydrangea family	family
Hydrilla	waterthyme	waterthyme	genus
Hydrilla verticillata	waterthyme	waterthyme	species
Hydrocharitaceae	frogbit family	frog-bit family	family
Hydrophyllaceae	waterleaf family	waterleaf family	family
Hydrophyllum	waterleaf	waterleaf	genus
Hydrophyllum capitatum	ballhead waterleaf	ballhead waterleaf, woollen-breeches	species
Hymenopappus	hymenopappus	hymenopappus	genus
Hymenopappus filifolius	fineleaf hymenopappus	fine-leaved hymenopappus, tufted hymenopappus	species
Hymenoxys	bitterweed	bitterweed	genus
Hymenoxys richardsonii	Richardson bitterweed	Richardson's bitterweed, Colorado rubber-plant	species
Hyoscyamus	henbane	henbane	genus
Hyoscyamus niger	black henbane	black henbane	species
Hypericaceae	St. John's-wort family	St. John's-wort family	family
Hypericum	St. John's-wort	St. John's-wort	genus
Hypericum fraseri	Fraser St. John's-wort	Fraser's St. John's-wort, Fraser's Marsh-St. John's-wort	species
Hypericum majus	large St. John's-wort	large St. John's-wort, large Canada St. John's-wort	species
Hypericum perforatum	common St. John's-wort	common St. John's-wort, St. John's-wort	species
Hypericum scouleri	Scouler St. John's-wort	Scouler's St. John's-wort, western St. John's-wort	species
Hypopitys	pinesap	pinesap	genus
Hypopitys monotropa	pinesap	pinesap	species
Iliamna	wild-hollyhock	wild-hollyhock	genus
Iliamna rivularis	streambank wild-hollyhock	streambank globe-mallow, mountain hollyhock	species
Impatiens	jewelweed	jewelweed	genus

ALPHABETICAL SCIENTIFIC NAMES

Scientific Name	Suggested Common Name	VASCAN and/or ACIMS Common Name(s)	Rank
Impatiens capensis	spotted jewelweed	spotted jewelweed, spotted touch-me-not	species
Impatiens glandulifera	purple jewelweed	purple jewelweed, Himalayan balsam	species
Impatiens noli-tangere	western jewelweed	western jewelweed	species
Iridaceae	iris family	iris family	family
Iris	iris	iris	genus
Iris missouriensis	western blue iris	western blue iris, western blue flag	species
Iris pseudacorus	yellow iris	yellow iris	species
Isatis	woad	woad	genus
Isatis tinctoria	dyer woad	dyer's woad	species
Isoetaceae	quillwort family	quillwort family	family
Isoetes bolanderi	Bolander quillwort	Bolander's quillwort	species
Isoetes echinospora	spinyspore quillwort	spiny-spored quillwort, northern quillwort	species
Isoetes maritima	coastal quillwort	coastal quillwort	species
Isoetes occidentalis	western quillwort	western quillwort	species
Isoetes, Isoëtes	quillwort	quillwort	genus
Iva	povertyweed	povertyweed	genus
Iva axillaris	povertyweed	povertyweed	species
Juncaceae	rush family	rush family	family
Juncaginaceae	arrowgrass family	arrowgrass family	family
Juncus	rush	rush	genus
Juncus alpinoarticulatus	alpine rush	alpine rush	species
Juncus balticus	wire rush	Baltic rush, wire rush	species
Juncus biglumis	twoglume rush	two-glumed rush	species
Juncus brevicaudatus	shorttail rush	short-tailed rush, short-tail rush	species
Juncus bufonius	toad rush	toad rush	species
Juncus castaneus	chestnut rush	chestnut rush	species
Juncus confusus	fewflower rush	Colorado rush, few-flowered rush	species
Juncus drummondii	Drummond rush	Drummond's rush	species
Juncus dudleyi	Dudley rush	Dudley's rush	species
Juncus ensifolius	swordleaf rush	dagger-leaved rush, equitant-leaved rush	species
Juncus filiformis	thread rush	thread rush	species
Juncus longistylis	longstyle rush	long-styled rush	species
Juncus mertensianus	Merten rush	Merten's rush, slender-stemmed rush	species
Juncus nevadensis	Nevada rush	Sierra rush, Nevada rush	species
Juncus nodosus	knotted rush	knotted rush	species
Juncus parryi	Parry rush	Parry's rush	species
Juncus regelii	Regel rush	Regel's rush	species
Juncus saximontanus	Rocky Mountain rush	Rocky Mountain rush	species
Juncus stygius	moor rush	moor rush	species

ALPHABETICAL SCIENTIFIC NAMES

Scientific Name	Suggested Common Name	VASCAN and/or ACIMS Common Name(s)	Rank
Juncus tenuis	path rush	path rush, slender rush	species
Juncus torreyi	Torrey rush	Torrey's rush	species
Juncus triglumis	threeflower rush	three-flowered rush, white rush	species
Juncus vaseyi	Vasey rush	Vasey's rush, big-head rush	species
Juniperus	juniper	juniper	genus
Juniperus communis	common juniper	common juniper, ground juniper	species
Juniperus horizontalis	creeping juniper	creeping juniper	species
Juniperus scopulorum	Rocky Mountain juniper	Rocky Mountain juniper	species
Kalmia	laurel	laurel	genus
Kalmia microphylla	western laurel	western bog laurel, mountain laurel	species
Kalmia polifolia	pale laurel	pale bog laurel, northern laurel	species
Kalmia procumbens	alpine laurel	alpine azalea	species
Knautia	scabious	scabious	genus
Knautia arvensis	field scabious	field scabious	species
Koeleria	junegrass	junegrass	genus
Koeleria macrantha	prairie junegrass	prairie junegrass, June grass	species
Koenigia	koenigia	koenigia	genus
Koenigia islandica	island koenigia	Iceland purslane, koenigia	species
Krascheninnikovia	winterfat	winterfat	genus
Krascheninnikovia lanata	winterfat	winterfat, winter-fat	species
Lactuca	lettuce	lettuce	genus
Lactuca biennis	tall blue lettuce	tall blue lettuce	species
Lactuca serriola	prickly lettuce	prickly lettuce	species
Ladeania	scurfpea	scurfpea	genus
Ladeania lanceolata	lanceleaf scurfpea	lance-leaved scurf-pea, scurf pea	species
Lamiaceae	mint family	mint family	family
Lamium	deadnettle	deadnettle	genus
Lamium amplexicaule	henbit deadnettle	common dead-nettle, henbit	species
Laportea	woodnettle	woodnettle	genus
Laportea canadensis	Canada woodnettle	Canada wood nettle, Canada wood-nettle	species
Lappula	stickseed	stickseed	genus
Lappula occidentalis	western stickseed	western stickseed, western bluebur	species
Lappula squarrosa	bristly stickseed	bristly stickseed, bluebur	species
Lapsana	nipplewort	nipplewort	genus
Lapsana communis	nipplewort	common nipplewort, nipplewort	species
Larix	larch	larch	genus
Larix laricina	tamarack	tamarack	species
Larix lyallii	subalpine larch	subalpine larch	species
Larix occidentalis	western larch	western larch	species
Lathyrus	vetchling	vetchling	genus

ALPHABETICAL SCIENTIFIC NAMES

Scientific Name	Suggested Common Name	VASCAN and/or ACIMS Common Name(s)	Rank
Lathyrus ochroleucus	creamy vetchling	cream-colored vetchling	species
Lathyrus palustris	marsh vetchling	marsh vetchling	species
Lathyrus venosus	veiny vetchling	veiny vetchling, purple peavine	species
Lechea	pinweed	pinweed	genus
Lechea intermedia	largepod pinweed	large-pod pinweed, narrowleaf pinweed	species
Lemna	duckweed	duckweed	genus
Lemna trisulca	star duckweed	star duckweed, ivy-leaved duckweed	species
Lemna turionifera	common duckweed	turion duckweed	species
Lens	lentil	lentil	genus
Lens culinaris	lentil	lentil	species
Lentibulariaceae	bladderwort family	bladderwort family	family
Leonurus	motherwort	motherwort	genus
Leonurus cardiaca	motherwort	common motherwort, motherwort	species
Lepidium	peppergrass	peppergrass, hoarycress	genus
Lepidium appelianum	globepod hoarycress	globe-pod hoarycress, globe-podded hoary cress	species
Lepidium campestre	field peppergrass	field peppergrass, cow cress	species
Lepidium chalepense	lenspod hoarycress	lens-pod hoarycress	species
Lepidium densiflorum	common peppergrass	common peppergrass, common pepper-grass	species
Lepidium draba	heartpod hoarycress	heart-pod hoarycress, heart-podded hoary cress	species
Lepidium latifolium	broadleaf peppergrass	broad-leaved peppergrass, broad-leaved pepper-grass	species
Lepidium perfoliatum	claspingleaf peppergrass	clasping-leaved peppergrass, perfoliate pepper-grass	species
Lepidium ramosissimum	branched peppergrass	branched peppergrass, branched pepper-grass	species
Lepidium ruderale	roadside peppergrass	roadside peppergrass	species
Lepidium sativum	garden peppergrass	garden peppergrass, garden cress	species
Leptarrhena	leatherleaf-saxifrage	leatherleaf-saxifrage	genus
Leptarrhena pyrolifolia	leatherleaf-saxifrage	leather-leaved saxifrage	species
Leptosiphon	linanthus	linanthus	genus
Leptosiphon septentrionalis	northern linanthus	northern linanthus	species
Leucanthemum	daisy	daisy	genus
Leucanthemum vulgare	oxeye daisy	oxeye daisy, ox-eye daisy	species
Leucophysalis	false-groundcherry	false-groundcherry	genus
Leucophysalis grandiflora	large false-groundcherry	large false ground-cherry, large white ground-cherry	species
Levisticum	lovage	lovage	genus
Levisticum officinale	garden lovage	garden lovage, lovage	species

ALPHABETICAL SCIENTIFIC NAMES

Scientific Name	Suggested Common Name	VASCAN and/or ACIMS Common Name(s)	Rank
Lewisia	lewisia	lewisia	genus
Lewisia pygmaea	alpine lewisia	alpine lewisia	species
Lewisia rediviva	bitterroot lewisia	Oregon bitterroot, bitter-root	species
Leymus	lymegrass	lymegrass, dunegrass	genus
Leymus cinereus	Great Basin lymegrass	Great Basin lymegrass, giant wild rye	species
Leymus innovatus	downy lymegrass	downy lymegrass, hairy wild rye	species
Leymus mollis	American dunegrass	sea lymegrass, American dunegrass	species
Liatris	blazingstar	blazingstar	genus
Liatris ligulistylis	meadow blazingstar	meadow blazing-star, meadow blazingstar	species
Liatris punctata	dotted blazingstar	dotted blazing-star, dotted blazingstar	species
Lilaea	flowering-quillwort	flowering-quillwort	species
Liliaceae	lily family	lily family	family
Lilium	lily	lily	genus
Lilium philadelphicum	wood lily	wood lily, western wood lily	species
Limosella	mudwort	mudwort	genus
Limosella aquatica	water mudwort	water mudwort, mudwort	species
Linaceae	flax family	flax family	family
Linaria	toadflax	toadflax	genus
Linaria dalmatica	Dalmatian toadflax	Dalmatian toadflax	species
Linaria maroccana	Morocco toadflax	Moroccan toadflax, Morocco toadflax	species
Linaria vulgaris	common toadflax	butter-and-eggs, common toadflax	species
Linnaea	twinflower	twinflower	genus
Linnaea borealis	twinflower	twinflower	species
Linum	flax	flax	genus
Linum compactum	compact flax	compact flax	species
Linum lewisii	Lewis blue flax	Lewis' wild blue flax, wild blue flax	species
Linum rigidum	stiff yellow flax	large-flowered yellow flax, yellow flax	species
Linum usitatissimum	common flax	common flax	species
Liparis	twayblade	twayblade	genus
Liparis loeselii	Loesel twayblade	Loesel's twayblade	species
Lithophragma	woodland-star	woodland-star	genus
Lithophragma glabrum	bulbous woodland-star	smooth woodland-star, rockstar	species
Lithophragma parviflorum	smallflower woodland-star	small-flowered woodland-star, small-flowered rockstar	species
Lithospermum	gromwell	gromwell	genus
Lithospermum incisum	narrowleaf gromwell	narrow-leaved puccoon	species
Lithospermum occidentale	western false gromwell	western false gromwell	species

ALPHABETICAL SCIENTIFIC NAMES

Scientific Name	Suggested Common Name	VASCAN and/or ACIMS Common Name(s)	Rank
Lithospermum ruderale	woolly gromwell	western puccoon, woolly gromwell	species
Loasaceae	stickleaf family	stickleaf family	family
Lobelia	lobelia	lobelia	genus
Lobelia dortmanna	water lobelia	water lobelia	species
Lobelia kalmii	Kalm lobelia	Kalm's lobelia	species
Lobelia spicata	spiked lobelia	pale-spike lobelia, spiked lobelia	species
Logfia	fluffweed	fluffweed	genus
Logfia arvensis	field fluffweed	field cottonrose, field fluffweed	species
Lolium	ryegrass	ryegrass	genus
Lolium arundinaceum	tall ryegrass	tall ryegrass, tall fescue	species
Lolium multiflorum	annual ryegrass	annual ryegrass, Italian ryegrass	species
Lolium perenne	perennial ryegrass	perennial ryegrass	species
Lolium persicum	Persian ryegrass	Persian ryegrass, Persian darnel	species
Lolium pratense	meadow ryegrass	meadow ryegrass, meadow fescue	species
Lolium temulentum	darnel ryegrass	bearded ryegrass, darnel	species
Lomatium	desert-parsley	desert-parsley	genus
Lomatium cous	biscuitroot desert-parsley	cous-root desert-parsley, biscuit-root	species
Lomatium dissectum	fernleaf desert-parsley	fern-leaved desert-parsley	species
Lomatium foeniculaceum	hairyfruit desert-parsley	fennel-leaved desert-parsley, hairy-fruited wild parsley	species
Lomatium macrocarpum	largefruit desert-parsley	large-fruited desert-parsley, long-fruited wild parsley	species
Lomatium sandbergii	Sandberg desert-parsley	Sandberg's desert-parsley, Sandberg's wild parsley	species
Lomatium simplex	Great Basin desert-parsley	Great Basin desert-parsley	species
Lomatium triternatum	nineleaf desert-parsley	nine-leaved desert-parsley, western wild parsley	species
Lomatogonium	marsh-felwort	marsh-felwort	genus
Lomatogonium rotatum	marsh-felwort	marsh felwort	species
Lonicera	honeysuckle	honeysuckle	genus
Lonicera dioica	twining honeysuckle	limber honeysuckle, twining honeysuckle	species
Lonicera involucrata	bracted honeysuckle	bracted honeysuckle	species
Lonicera tatarica	tatarian honeysuckle	Tatarian honeysuckle	species
Lonicera utahensis	Utah honeysuckle	Utah honeysuckle, red twinberry	species
Lonicera villosa	mountain fly-honeysuckle	mountain fly-honeysuckle, mountain fly-honeysuckle	species
Loranthaceae	mistletoe family	mistletoe f amily	family
Lotus	birdsfoot-trefoil	birdsfoot-trefoil	genus
Lotus corniculatus	birdsfoot-trefoil	garden bird's-foot trefoil, bird's-foot trefoil	species
Luetkea	partridgefoot	partridgefoot	genus
Luetkea pectinata	partridgefoot	partridgefoot	species

ALPHABETICAL SCIENTIFIC NAMES

Scientific Name	Suggested Common Name	VASCAN and/or ACIMS Common Name(s)	Rank
Lupinus	lupine	lupine	genus
Lupinus argenteus	silvery lupine	silvery lupine, silvery perennial lupine	species
Lupinus lepidus	dwarf lupine	dwarf lupine, alpine lupine	species
Lupinus minimus	least lupine	least lupine	species
Lupinus nootkatensis	Nootka lupine	Nootka lupine	species
Lupinus polyphyllus	largeleaf lupine	large-leaved lupine	species
Lupinus pusillus	low lupine	low lupine, annual lupine	species
Lupinus sericeus	silky lupine	silky lupine, silky perennial lupine	species
Lupinus wyethii	Wyeth lupine	Wyeth's lupine	species
Luzula	woodrush	woodrush	genus
Luzula acuminata	hairy woodrush	hairy woodrush, wood-rush	species
Luzula arcuata	curved woodrush	curved woodrush, curved wood rush	species
Luzula groenlandica	Greenland woodrush	Greenland woodrush, wood-rush	species
Luzula hitchcockii	Hitchcock woodrush	Hitchcock's woodrush, smooth wood-rush	species
Luzula multiflora	manyflower woodrush	many-flowered woodrush, field wood-rush	species
Luzula parviflora	smallflower woodrush	small-flowered woodrush, small-flowered wood-rush	species
Luzula piperi	Piper woodrush	Piper's woodrush, mountain wood-rush	species
Luzula rufescens	rusty woodrush	rusty woodrush, reddish wood-rush	species
Luzula spicata	spiked woodrush	spiked woodrush, spiked wood-rush	species
Lycium	matrimony-vine	matrimony-vine	genus
Lycium barbarum	matrimony-vine	common matrimony vine, matrimony vine	species
Lycopodiaceae	clubmoss family	clubmoss family	family
Lycopodiella	bog-clubmoss	bog-clubmoss	genus
Lycopodiella inundata	inundated bog-clubmoss	northern bog clubmoss, bog club-moss	species
Lycopodium	clubmoss	clubmoss	genus
Lycopodium annotinum	stiff clubmoss	stiff clubmoss, stiff club-moss	species
Lycopodium lagopus	onecone clubmoss	one-cone clubmoss	species
Lycopus	water-horehound	water-horehound	genus
Lycopus americanus	American water-horehound	American water-horehound	species

ALPHABETICAL SCIENTIFIC NAMES

Scientific Name	Suggested Common Name	VASCAN and/or ACIMS Common Name(s)	Rank
Lycopus asper	rough water-horehound	rough water-horehound, western water-horehound	species
Lycopus uniflorus	northern water-horehound	northern water-horehound	species
Lygodesmia	skeletonplant	skeletonplant	genus
Lygodesmia juncea	rush skeletonplant	rush skeletonplant, skeletonweed	species
Lysimachia	loosestrife	loosestrife, starflower	genus
Lysimachia ciliata	fringed loosestrife	fringed yellow loosestrife, fringed loosestrife	species
Lysimachia europaea	Arctic starflower	arctic starflower	species
Lysimachia hybrida	lowland yellow loosestrife	lowland yellow loosestrife, lance-leaved loosestrife	species
Lysimachia latifolia	broadleaf starflower	broad-leaved starflower, northern starflower	species
Lysimachia maritima	sea milkwort	sea milkwort	species
Lysimachia minima	chaffweed	chaffweed	species
Lysimachia thyrsiflora	tufted loosestrife	tufted yellow loosestrife, tufted loosestrife	species
Lythraceae	loosestrife family	loosestrife family	family
Lythrum	loosestrife	loosestrife	genus
Lythrum salicaria	purple loosestrife	purple loosestrife	species
Machaeranthera	tansy-aster	tansy-aster	genus
Machaeranthera tanacetifolia	tansy-aster	Tahoka daisy, tansy aster	species
Madia	tarweed	tarweed	genus
Madia glomerata	clustered tarweed	clustered tarweed, tarweed	species
Mahonia	barberry	barberry	genus
Mahonia repens	creeping barberry	creeping barberry, creeping mahonia	species
Maianthemum	false-Solomon-seal	false-Solomon-seal, lily-of-the-valley	genus
Maianthemum canadense	wild lily-of-the-valley	wild lily-of-the-valley	species
Maianthemum amplexicaule	western false-Solomon-seal	western false Solomon's seal, false Solomon's-seal	species
Maianthemum stellatum	starflower false-Solomon-seal	star-flowered false Solomon's seal, star-flowered Solomon's-seal	species
Maianthemum trifolium	threeleaf false-Solomon-seal	three-leaved false Solomon's seal, three-leaved Solomon's-seal	species
Malaxis	addermouth	adder's-mouth	genus
Malaxis monophyllos	white addermouth	white adder's-mouth	species
Malaxis paludosa	bog addermouth	bog adder's-mouth	species
Malus	crabapple	crabapple	genus
Malus sp.	crabapple	crabapple	species
Malva	mallow	mallow	genus
Malva neglecta	common mallow	common mallow, round-leaved mallow	species
Malva parviflora	smallflower mallow	small-flowered mallow	species

ALPHABETICAL SCIENTIFIC NAMES

Scientific Name	Suggested Common Name	VASCAN and/or ACIMS Common Name(s)	Rank
Malva pusilla	low mallow	small mallow, round-leaved mallow	species
Malva sylvestris	high mallow	high mallow	species
Malva verticillata	whorled mallow	whorled mallow	species
Malvaceae	mallow family	mallow family	family
Marsilea	waterclover	waterclover	genus
Marsilea vestita	hairy waterclover	hairy water-clover, hairy pepperwort	species
Marsileaceae	water-clover family	water-clover family	family
Matricaria	chamomile	chamomile	genus
Matricaria chamomilla	wild chamomile	wild chamomile	species
Matricaria discoidea	pineappleweed	pineappleweed	species
Matteuccia	ostrich-fern	ostrich-fern	genus
Matteuccia struthiopteris	ostrich-fern	ostrich fern	species
Matthiola	stock	stock	genus
Matthiola longipetala	night-scented stock	night-scented stock	species
Medicago	medick, alfalfa	medick, alfalfa	genus
Medicago lupulina	black medick	black medick	species
Medicago sativa	alfalfa	alfalfa	species
Melampyrum	cow-wheat	cow-wheat	genus
Melampyrum lineare	narrowleaf cow-wheat	American cow-wheat, cow-wheat	species
Melanthiaceae	bunchflower family		family
Melica	oniongrass	oniongrass	genus
Melica smithii	Smith oniongrass	Smith's oniongrass	species
Melica spectabilis	purple oniongrass	purple oniongrass, onion grass	species
Melica subulata	Alaska oniongrass	Alaska oniongrass, Alaska onion grass	species
Melilotus	sweetclover	sweetclover	genus
Melilotus albus	white sweetclover	white sweet-clover	species
Melilotus officinalis	yellow sweetclover	yellow sweet-clover	species
Mentha	mint	mint	genus
Mentha canadensis/ Mentha arvensis	wild mint	Canada mint, wild mint	species
Mentha spicata	spearmint	spearmint	species
Mentzelia	blazingstar	blazingstar	genus
Mentzelia decapetala	tenpetal blazingstar	ten-petalled blazing star, sand-lily	species
Menyanthaceae	buckbean family	buckbean family	family
Menyanthes	buckbean	buckbean	genus
Menyanthes trifoliata	buckbean	bog buckbean, buck-bean	species
Menziesia	false-azalea	false-azalea	genus
Menziesia ferruginea	false-azalea	false azalea	species
Mertensia	bluebells	bluebells	genus
Mertensia lanceolata	lanceleaf bluebells	lance-leaved bluebells, lance-leaved lungwort	species

ALPHABETICAL SCIENTIFIC NAMES

Scientific Name	Suggested Common Name	VASCAN and/or ACIMS Common Name(s)	Rank
Mertensia longiflora	longflower bluebells	long-flowered bluebells, large-flowered lungwort	species
Mertensia paniculata	tall bluebells	tall bluebells, tall lungwort	species
Micranthes	slender-saxifrage	saxifrage	genus
Micranthes ferruginea	rusty saxifrage	rusty saxifrage	species
Micranthes lyallii	redstem saxifrage	red-stemmed saxifrage	species
Micranthes nelsoniana	heartleaf saxifrage	Nelson's saxifrage, cordate-leaved saxifrage	species
Micranthes nivalis	alpine saxifrage	snow saxifrage, alpine saxifrage	species
Micranthes occidentalis	western saxifrage	western saxifrage, rhomboid-leaved saxifrage	species
Micranthes odontoloma	brook saxifrage	streambank saxifrage, brook saxifrage	species
Micranthes oregana	Oregon saxifrage	Oregon saxifrage	species
Microseris	microseris	microseris	genus
Microseris nutans	nodding microseris	nodding microseris	species
Microsteris	slender-phlox	slender-phlox	genus
Microsteris gracilis	slender-phlox	slender phlox	species
Mimulus	monkeyflower	monkeyflower	genus
Mimulus ringens	squarestem monkeyflower	square-stemmed monkeyflower, square-stem monkeyflower	species
Minuartia	stitchwort	stitchwort	genus
Mirabilis	four-o'clock	four-o'clock	genus
Mirabilis albida	hairy four-o'clock	hairy four-o'clock, hairy umbrellawort	species
Mirabilis linearis	narrowleaf four-o'clock	narrow-leaved four-o'clock, narrowleaf umbrella-wort	species
Mirabilis nyctaginea	heartleaf four-o'clock	heart-leaved four-o'clock, heart-leaved umbrellawort	species
Mitella	mitrewort	mitrewort	genus
Mitella breweri	Brewer mitrewort	Brewer's mitrewort, Brewer's bishop's-cap	species
Mitella nuda	naked mitrewort	naked mitrewort, bishop's-cap	species
Mitella pentandra	fivestamen mitrewort	five-stamen mitrewort, bishop's-cap	species
Mitella trifida	Pacific mitrewort	Pacific mitrewort, bishop's-cap	species
Moehringia	sandwort	sandwort	genus
Moehringia lateriflora	bluntleaf sandwort	grove sandwort, blunt-leaved sandwort	species
Molluginaceae	carpetweed family	carpetweed family	family
Mollugo	carpetweed	carpetweed	genus
Mollugo verticillata	green carpetweed	green carpetweed	species
Monarda	bergamot	bergamot	genus
Monarda fistulosa	wild bergamot	wild bergamot	species
Moneses	oneflower-wintergreen	oneflower-wintergreen	genus

ALPHABETICAL SCIENTIFIC NAMES

Scientific Name	Suggested Common Name	VASCAN and/or ACIMS Common Name(s)	Rank
Moneses uniflora	oneflower-wintergreen	one-flowered wintergreen	species
Monotropa	Indianpipe	Indianpipe	genus
Monotropa uniflora	Indianpipe	Indian pipe, Indian-pipe	species
Montia	montia	montia	genus
Montia linearis	narrowleaf montia	narrow-leaved montia, linear-leaved montia	species
Montia parvifolia	littleleaf montia	small-leaved montia	species
Montiaceae	water-chickweed family	water chickweed family	family
Muhlenbergia	muhly	muhly	genus
Muhlenbergia asperifolia	alkali muhly	alkali muhly, scratch grass	species
Muhlenbergia cuspidata	plains muhly	plains muhly	species
Muhlenbergia glomerata	spike muhly	spike muhly, bog muhly	species
Muhlenbergia paniculata	tumblegrass muhly	prairie tumblegrass, tumble grass	species
Muhlenbergia racemosa	marsh muhly	marsh muhly	species
Muhlenbergia richardsonis	mat muhly	mat muhly	species
Mulgedium	blue-lettuce	blue-lettuce	genus
Mulgedium pulchellum	blue-lettuce	blue lettuce, common blue lettuce	species
Munroa	buffalograss	buffalograss	genus
Munroa squarrosa	false buffalograss	false buffalograss, false buffalo grass	species
Musineon	wild-parsley	wild-parsley	genus
Musineon divaricatum	leafy wild-parsley	leafy wild parsley, leafy musineon	species
Myosotis	forget-me-not	forget-me-not	genus
Myosotis arvensis	field forget-me-not	field forget-me-not	species
Myosotis asiatica	alpine forget-me-not	Asian forget-me-not, alpine forget-me-not	species
Myosotis laxa	small forget-me-not	small forget-me-not	species
Myosotis stricta	upright forget-me-not	upright forget-me-not, forget-me-not	species
Myosurus	mousetail	mousetail	genus
Myosurus apetalus	bristly mousetail	bristly mousetail	species
Myosurus minimus	tiny mousetail	tiny mousetail, least mousetail	species
Myrica	sweetgale	sweetgale	genus
Myrica gale	sweetgale	sweet gale	species
Myricaceae	wax-myrtle family	wax-myrtle family	family
Myriophyllum	watermilfoil	watermilfoil	genus
Myriophyllum sibiricum	Siberian watermilfoil	Siberian water-milfoil, spiked water-milfoil	species
Myriophyllum spicatum	Eurasian watermilfoil	Eurasian water-milfoil	species
Myriophyllum verticillatum	whorled watermilfoil	whorled water-milfoil, water-milfoil	species
Myriopteris	lipfern	lipfern	genus
Myriopteris gracilis	slender lipfern	slender lip fern	species
Myriopteris gracillima	lace lipfern	lace lip fern, lace fern	species

ALPHABETICAL SCIENTIFIC NAMES

Scientific Name	Suggested Common Name	VASCAN and/or ACIMS Common Name(s)	Rank
Nabalus	rattlesnakeroot	rattlesnakeroot	genus
Nabalus alatus	western rattlesnakeroot	western rattlesnakeroot, white lettuce	species
Nabalus racemosus	glaucous rattlesnakeroot	glaucous rattlesnakeroot, glaucous white lettuce	species
Nabalus sagittatus	purple rattlesnakeroot	arrow-leaved rattlesnakeroot, purple rattlesnakeroot	species
Najas	naiad	naiad	genus
Najas flexilis	slender naiad	slender naiad	species
Najas guadalupensis	southern naiad	southern naiad	species
Nassella	needlegrass	needlegrass	genus
Nassella viridula	green needlegrass	green needlegrass, green needle grass	species
Nasturtium	watercress	watercress	genus
Nasturtium officinale	watercress	watercress, water cress	species
Navarretia	navarretia	navarretia	genus
Navarretia leucocephala	whiteflower navarretia	whiteflower navarretia, white-flowered navarretia	species
Nemophila	baby-blue-eyes	baby-blue-eyes	genus
Nemophila breviflora	small baby-blue-eyes	Great Basin nemophila, small baby-blue-eyes	species
Neoholmgrenia	evening-primrose	evening-primrose	genus
Neoholmgrenia andina	upland evening-primrose	upland evening primose, upland evening-primrose	species
Neottia	twayblade	twayblade	genus
Neottia banksiana	western twayblade	northwestern twayblade, western twayblade	species
Neottia borealis	northern twayblade	northern twayblade	species
Neottia convallarioides	broadlip twayblade	broad-lip twayblade, broad-lipped twayblade	species
Neottia cordata	heartleaf twayblade	heart-leaved twayblade	species
Nepeta	catnip	catnip	genus
Nepeta cataria	catnip	catnip	species
Neslia	ballmustard	ballmustard	genus
Neslia paniculata	yellow ballmustard	yellow ball-mustard, ball mustard	species
Nonea	monkswort	monkswort	genus
Nonea vesicaria	red monkswort	red monkswort, red monk's-wort	species
Nothocalais	false-dandelion	false-dandelion	genus
Nothocalais cuspidata	prairie false-dandelion	wavy-leaved prairie dandelion, prairie false dandelion	species
Nuphar	pondlily	pondlily	genus
Nuphar variegata	variegated pondlily	variegated pond-lily, yellow pond-lily	species
Nuttallanthus	toadflax	toadflax	genus
Nuttallanthus texanus	Texas toadflax	Texas toadflax, Canada toad-flax	species
Nyctaginaceae	four-o'clock family	four-o'clock family	family

ALPHABETICAL SCIENTIFIC NAMES

Scientific Name	Suggested Common Name	VASCAN and/or ACIMS Common Name(s)	Rank
Nymphaea	waterlily	waterlily	genus
Nymphaea leibergii	dwarf waterlily	dwarf water-lily, pygmy water-lily	species
Nymphaea tetragona	pygmy waterlily	pygmy water-lily, white water-lily	species
Nymphaeaceae	waterlily family	waterlily family	family
Odontarrhena	yellowtuft	yellowtuft	genus
Odontarrhena murale	yellowtuft	wall alyssum, yellow alyssum	species
Odontites	bartsia	bartsia	genus
Odontites vulgaris	red bartsia	red bartsia, late-flowering eyebright	species
Oenothera	evening-primrose, beeblossom	evening-primrose, beeblossom	genus
Oenothera biennis	common evening-primrose	common evening-primrose, yellow evening-primrose	species
Oenothera cespitosa	tufted evening-primrose	tufted evening-primrose, butte-primrose	species
Oenothera flava	low yellow evening-primrose	low yellow evening-primrose	species
Oenothera nuttallii	white evening-primrose	white evening-primrose	species
Oenothera serrulata	shrubby evening-primrose	serrate-leaved evening-primrose, shrubby evening-primrose	species
Oenothera suffrutescens	scarlet beeblossom	scarlet gaura/beeblossom, scarlet butterflyweed	species
Oenothera villosa	hairy evening-primrose	hairy evening-primrose	species
Oleaceae	olive family	olive family	family
Onagraceae	evening-primrose family	evening-primrose family	family
Onobrychis	sainfoin	sainfoin	genus
Onobrychis viciifolia	sainfoin	common sainfoin, sainfoin	species
Onocleaceae	sensitive-fern family	sensitive-fern family	family
Ononis	restharrow	restharrow	genus
Ononis spinosa	spiny restharrow	spiny restharrow, common rest-harrow	species
Ophioglossaceae	addertongue family	adder's-tongue family	family
Oplopanax	devil's-club	devil's-club	genus
Oplopanax horridus	devil's-club	devil's club, devil's-club	species
Opuntia	pricklypear	pricklypear	genus
Opuntia fragilis	brittle pricklypear	brittle prickly-pear cactus, brittle prickly-pear	species
Opuntia polyacantha	plains pricklypear	plains prickly-pear cactus, prickly-pear	species
Orchidaceae	orchid family	orchid family	family
Orobanchaceae	broomrape family	broomrape family	family
Orobanche	broomrape	broomrape, cancer-root	genus
Orthilia	one-sided wintergreen	one-sided wintergreen	genus
Orthilia secunda	oneside wintergreen	one-sided wintergreen	species

ALPHABETICAL SCIENTIFIC NAMES

Scientific Name	Suggested Common Name	VASCAN and/or ACIMS Common Name(s)	Rank
Orthocarpus	owlclover	owlclover	genus
Orthocarpus luteus	yellow owlclover	yellow owl's-clover, owl-clover	species
Oryzopsis	ricegrass	ricegrass	genus
Oryzopsis asperifolia	roughleaf ricegrass	rough-leaved mountain rice, white-grained mountain rice grass	species
Osmorhiza	sweet-cicely	sweet-cicely	genus
Osmorhiza berteroi	bluntfruit sweet-cicely	mountain sweet cicely, blunt-fruited sweet cicely	species
Osmorhiza depauperata	spreading sweet-cicely	blunt sweet cicely, spreading sweet cicely	species
Osmorhiza longistylis	smooth sweet-cicely	smooth sweet cicely	species
Osmorhiza occidentalis	western sweet-cicely	western sweet cicely	species
Osmorhiza purpurea	purple sweet-cicely	purple sweet cicely	species
Oxalidaceae	woodsorrel family	woodsorrel family	family
Oxalis	woodsorrel	woodsorrel	genus
Oxalis stricta	European woodsorrel	European wood-sorrel	species
Oxybasis	sourfoot		genus
Oxybasis glauca	oakleaf goosefoot	oak-leaved goosefoot	species
Oxybasis rubra	red goosefoot	red goosefoot	species
Oxyria	mountain-sorrel	mountain-sorrel	genus
Oxyria digyna	mountain-sorrel	mountain-sorrel, mountain sorrel	species
Oxytropis	locoweed	locoweed	genus
Oxytropis borealis	boreal locoweed	boreal locoweed	species
Oxytropis campestris	field locoweed	field locoweed, northern locoweed	species
Oxytropis deflexa	pendantpodlocoweed	pendant-pod locoweed, reflexed locoweed	species
Oxytropis lagopus	harefoot locoweed	hare's-foot locoweed, hare-footed locoweed	species
Oxytropis podocarpa	inflated locoweed	inflated locoweed, inflated oxytrope	species
Oxytropis sericea	silky locoweed	silky locoweed, early yellow locoweed	species
Oxytropis splendens	showy locoweed	showy locoweed	species
Packera	butterweed	groundsel	genus
Packera cana	woolly groundsel	woolly groundsel, prairie groundsel	species
Packera contermina	northwestern groundsel	northwestern groundsel, Arctic butterweed	species
Packera heterophylla	dwarf arctic groundsel	dwarf arctic groundsel	species
Packera indecora	rayless groundsel	rayless mountain groundsel, rayless ragwort	species
Packera pauciflora	fewflower groundsel	few-flowered groundsel, few-flowered ragwort	species
Packera paupercula	balsam groundsel	balsam groundsel	species

ALPHABETICAL SCIENTIFIC NAMES

Scientific Name	Suggested Common Name	VASCAN and/or ACIMS Common Name(s)	Rank
Packera pseudaurea	streambank groundsel	streambank groundsel, thin-leaved ragwort	species
Packera streptanthifolia	Rocky Mountain groundsel	Rocky Mountain groundsel, northern ragwort	species
Packera subnuda	alpine meadow groundsel	alpine meadow groundsel	species
Panicum	panicgrass	panicgrass	genus
Panicum capillare	panicgrass	common panicgrass, witch grass	species
Panicum miliaceum	proso millet	proso millet, broomcorn millet	species
Papaver	poppy	poppy	genus
Papaver kluanense	Kluane poppy	Kluane poppy, alpine poppy	species
Papaver nudicaule	Iceland poppy	ice poppy, Iceland poppy	species
Papaver pygmaeum	dwarf alpine poppy	dwarf alpine poppy	species
Papaver rhoeas	corn poppy	corn poppy	species
Papaver somniferum	opium poppy	opium poppy	species
Papaveraceae	poppy family	poppy family	family
Parietaria	pellitory	pellitory	genus
Parietaria pensylvanica	Pennsylvania pellitory	Pennsylvania pellitory, American pellitory	species
Parnassia	grass-of-parnassus	grass-of-parnassus	genus
Parnassia fimbriata	fringed grass-of-parnassus	fringed grass-of-Parnassus	species
Parnassia kotzebuei	small grass-of-parnassus	Kotzebue's grass-of-Parnassus, small grass-of-parnassus	species
Parnassia palustris	marsh grass-of-parnassus	marsh grass-of-Parnassus, northern grass-of-parnassus	species
Parnassia parviflora	smallflower grass-of-parnassus	small-flowered grass-of-Parnassus, small northern grass-of-parnassus	species
Paronychia	nailwort	nailwort	genus
Paronychia sessiliflora	creeping nailwort	creeping nailwort	species
Pascopyrum	western-wheatgrass	western-wheatgrass	genus
Pascopyrum smithii	western-wheatgrass	western wheatgrass, western wheat grass	species
Pastinaca	parsnip	parsnip	genus
Pastinaca sativa	wild parsnip	wild parsnip, parsnip	species
Paxistima	mountain-lover	mountain-lover	genus
Paxistima myrsinites	mountain-lover	falsebox, mountain-lover	species
Pedicularis	lousewort	lousewort	genus
Pedicularis bracteosa	bracted lousewort	bracted lousewort, western lousewort	species
Pedicularis capitata	capitate lousewort	capitate lousewort, large-flowered lousewort	species
Pedicularis contorta	coiled lousewort	coiled-beaked lousewort, coiled-beak lousewort	species

ALPHABETICAL SCIENTIFIC NAMES

Scientific Name	Suggested Common Name	VASCAN and/or ACIMS Common Name(s)	Rank
Pedicularis flammea	flame lousewort	red-tipped lousewort, flame-colored lousewort	species
Pedicularis groenlandica	elephanthead lousewort	elephant's-head lousewort, elephant's-head	species
Pedicularis labradorica	Labrador lousewort	Labrador lousewort	species
Pedicularis lanata	woolly lousewort	woolly lousewort	species
Pedicularis langsdorffii	Langsdorff lousewort	Langsdorff's lousewort, arctic lousewort	species
Pedicularis oederi	Oeder lousewort	Oeder's lousewort	species
Pedicularis parviflora	smallflower lousewort	small-flowered lousewort, swamp lousewort	species
Pedicularis racemosa	sickletop lousewort	sickletop lousewort, leafy lousewort	species
Pedicularis sudetica	Sudeten lousewort	Sudeten lousewort, purple rattle	species
Pediomelum	breadroot	breadroot	genus
Pediomelum argophyllum	silverleaf breadroot	silver-leaved Indian breadroot, silverleaf psoralea	species
Pediomelum esculentum	large breadroot	large Indian breadroot, Indian breadroot	species
Pellaea	cliffbrake	cliffbrake	genus
Pellaea gastonyi	Gastony cliffbrake	Gastony's cliffbrake, Gaston's cliff brake	species
Pellaea glabella	smooth cliffbrake	smooth cliffbrake, smooth cliff brake	species
Penstemon	beardtongue	beardtongue	genus
Penstemon albertinus	Alberta beardtongue	Alberta beardtongue, blue beardtongue	species
Penstemon albidus	white beardtongue	white beardtongue	species
Penstemon confertus	yellow beardtongue	lesser yellow beardtongue, yellow beardtongue	species
Penstemon ellipticus	rocky-ledge beardtongue	elliptic-leaved beardtongue, rocky-ledge penstemon	species
Penstemon eriantherus	fuzzytongue beardtongue	fuzzy-tongue beardtongue, crested beardtongue	species
Penstemon fruticosus	shrubby beardtongue	shrubby beardtongue	species
Penstemon gracilis	lilac beardtongue	slender beardtongue, lilac-flowered beardtongue	species
Penstemon lyallii	Lyall beardtongue	Lyall's beardtongue, large-flowered beardtongue	species
Penstemon nitidus	waxleaf beardtongue	wax-leaved beardtongue, smooth blue beardtongue	species
Penstemon procerus	smallflower beardtongue	small-flowered beardtongue, slender blue beardtongue	species
Perideridia	yampah	yampah	genus
Perideridia gairdneri	Gairdner yampah	Gairdner's yampah, common yampah	species

ALPHABETICAL SCIENTIFIC NAMES

Scientific Name	Suggested Common Name	VASCAN and/or ACIMS Common Name(s)	Rank
Peritoma	beeplant	beeplant	genus
Peritoma serrulata	Rocky Mountain beeplant	Rocky Mountain beeplant, bee plant	species
Persicaria	smartweed	smartweed	genus
Persicaria amphibia	water smartweed	water smartweed	species
Persicaria hydropiper	marshpepper smartweed	marshpepper smartweed	species
Persicaria lapathifolia	pale smartweed	pale smartweed, pale persicaria	species
Persicaria maculosa	lady's-thumb smartweed	spotted lady's-thumb, lady's-thumb	species
Petasites	sweet-coltsfoot	sweet-coltsfoot	genus
Petasites frigidus	arctic sweet-coltsfoot	arctic sweet coltsfoot, coltsfoot	species
Phacelia	scorpionweed	scorpionweed	genus
Phacelia campanularia	desert phacelia	desert phacelia	species
Phacelia franklinii	Franklin scorpionweed	Franklin's phacelia, Franklin's scorpionweed	species
Phacelia hastata	silverleaf scorpionweed	silver-leaved phacelia, silver-leaved scorpionweed	species
Phacelia linearis	linearleaf scorpionweed	thread-leaved phacelia, linear-leaved scorpionweed	species
Phacelia lyallii	Lyall scorpionweed	Lyall's phacelia, Lyall's scorpionweed	species
Phacelia sericea	silky scorpionweed	silky phacelia, silky scorpionweed	species
Phalaris	canarygrass	canarygrass	genus
Phalaris arundinacea	reed canarygrass	reed canarygrass, reed canary grass	species
Phalaris canariensis	annual canarygrass	annual canarygrass, canary grass	species
Phegopteris	beechfern	beechfern	genus
Phegopteris connectilis	northern beechfern	northern beech fern	species
Philadelphus	mockorange	mockorange	genus
Philadelphus lewisii	Lewis mockorange	Lewis' mock-orange, mock orange	species
Phleum	timothy	timothy	genus
Phleum alpinum	alpine timothy	alpine timothy, mountain timothy	species
Phleum pratense	common timothy	common timothy, timothy	species
Phlox	phlox	phlox	genus
Phlox alyssifolia	blue phlox	blue phlox	species
Phlox hoodii	Hood phlox	Hood's phlox, moss phlox	species
Phragmites	reed	reed	genus
Phragmites australis	common reed	common reed	species
Phrymaceae	lopseed family	lopseed family	family
Phyllodoce	mountainheath	mountainheath	genus
Phyllodoce empetriformis	pink mountainheath	pink mountain heather, red heather	species

ALPHABETICAL SCIENTIFIC NAMES

Scientific Name	Suggested Common Name	VASCAN and/or ACIMS Common Name(s)	Rank
Phyllodoce glanduliflora	yellow mountainheath	yellow mountain heather, yellow heather	species
Physalis	groundcherry	groundcherry	genus
Physalis ixocarpa	Mexican groundcherry	Mexican ground cherry	species
Physaria	bladderpod	bladderpod	genus
Physaria arctica	arctic bladderpod	arctic bladderpod	species
Physaria arenosa	Great Plains bladderpod	Great Plains bladderpod	species
Physaria didymocarpa	double bladderpod	common twinpod, double bladderpod	species
Physaria spatulata	spatulate bladderpod	spatulate bladderpod	species
Physocarpus	ninebark	ninebark	genus
Physocarpus malvaceus	mallowleaf ninebark	mallow-leaved ninebark	species
Physostegia	false-dragonhead	false-dragonhead	genus
Physostegia ledinghamii	Ledingham false-dragonhead	Ledingham's false dragonhead, false dragonhead	species
Physostegia parviflora	western false-dragonhead	western false dragonhead, false dragonhead	species
Picea	spruce	spruce	genus
Picea engelmannii	Engelmann spruce	Engelmann spruce	species
Picea glauca	white spruce	white spruce	species
Picea mariana	black spruce	black spruce	species
Picradeniopsis	picradeniopsis	picradeniopsis	genus
Picradeniopsis oppositifolia	picradeniopsis	opposite-leaved bahia, picradeniopsis	species
Pilosella	hairy-hawkweed	hawkweed	genus
Pilosella aurantiaca	orange hawkweed	orange hawkweed	species
Pilosella caespitosa	meadow hawkweed	meadow hawkweed	species
Pilosella glomerata	yellow devil hawkweed	yellow devil hawkweed, yellow devil	species
Pilosella piloselloides	tall hawkweed	hawkweed, tall hawkweed	species
Pimpinella	burnet-saxifrage	burnet-saxifrage	genus
Pimpinella saxifraga	solidstem burnet-saxifrage	solid stem burnet-saxifrage, Burnet-saxifrage	species
Pinaceae	pine family	pine family	family
Pinguicula	butterwort	butterwort	genus
Pinguicula villosa	hairy butterwort	hairy butterwort, small butterwort	species
Pinguicula vulgaris	common butterwort	common butterwort	species
Pinus	pine	pine	genus
Pinus albicaulis	whitebark pine	whitebark pine	species
Pinus banksiana	jack pine	jack pine	species
Pinus contorta	lodgepole pine	lodgepole pine	species
Pinus flexilis	limber pine	limber pine	species
Pinus monticola	western white pine	western white pine	species

ALPHABETICAL SCIENTIFIC NAMES

Scientific Name	Suggested Common Name	VASCAN and/or ACIMS Common Name(s)	Rank
Pinus ponderosa	ponderosa pine	ponderosa pine	species
Piptatheropsis	ricegrass	ricegrass	genus
Piptatheropsis canadensis	Canada ricegrass	Canada ricegrass, Canada rice grass	species
Piptatheropsis exigua	little ricegrass	little ricegrass, little rice grass	species
Piptatheropsis micrantha	littleseed ricegrass	small-flowered ricegrass, little-seed rice grass	species
Piptatheropsis pungens	slender ricegrass	slender ricegrass, northern rice grass	species
Plagiobothrys	popcornflower	popcornflower	genus
Plagiobothrys scouleri	Scouler popcornflower	Scouler's popcornflower, Scouler's allocarya	species
Plantaginaceae	plantain family	plantain family	family
Plantago	plantain	plantain	genus
Plantago canescens	gray hairy plantain	hairy plantain, western ribgrass	species
Plantago elongata	linearleaf plantain	slender plantain, linear-leaved plantain	species
Plantago eriopoda	saline plantain	saline plantain	species
Plantago major	common plantain	common plantain	species
Plantago maritima	seaside plantain	seaside plantain, sea-side plantain	species
Plantago media	hoary plantain	hoary plantain	species
Plantago patagonica	woolly plantain	woolly plantain, Pursh's plantain	species
Platanthera	bog-orchid	bog-orchid, green-orchid	genus
Platanthera aquilonis	tall northern green-orchid	tall northern green orchid	species
Platanthera dilatata	tall white bog-orchid	tall white bog orchid	species
Platanthera huronensis	Huron green-orchid	Lake Huron green orchid, northern green bog orchid	species
Platanthera obtusata	bluntleaf bog-orchid	blunt-leaved orchid, blunt-leaved bog orchid	species
Platanthera orbiculata	lesser roundleaf bog-orchid	lesser round-leaved orchid, round-leaved bog orchid	species
Platanthera stricta	slender bog-orchid	slender bog orchid	species
Platanthera unalascensis	Alaska bog-orchid	Alaska rein orchid, Alaska bog orchid	species
Poa	bluegrass	bluegrass	genus
Poa abbreviata	short bluegrass	abbreviated bluegrass, northern bluegrass	species
Poa alpina	alpine bluegrass	alpine bluegrass	species
Poa annua	annual bluegrass	annual bluegrass	species
Poa arctica	Arctic bluegrass	arctic bluegrass	species
Poa arida	plains bluegrass	plains bluegrass	species
Poa bulbosa	bulbous bluegrass	bulbous bluegrass	species
Poa compressa	Canada bluegrass	Canada bluegrass	species

ALPHABETICAL SCIENTIFIC NAMES

Scientific Name	Suggested Common Name	VASCAN and/or ACIMS Common Name(s)	Rank
Poa cusickii	Cusick bluegrass	Cusick's bluegrass, early bluegrass	species
Poa fendleriana	Fendler bluegrass	Fendler's bluegrass	species
Poa glauca	glaucous bluegrass	glaucous bluegrass, timberline bluegrass	species
Poa interior	inland bluegrass	inland bluegrass	species
Poa laxa	lax bluegrass	lax bluegrass	species
Poa leptocoma	western bog bluegrass	western bog bluegrass, bog bluegrass	species
Poa lettermanii	Letterman bluegrass	Letterman's bluegrass	species
Poa nemoralis	wood bluegrass	Eurasian woodland bluegrass, wood bluegrass	species
Poa palustris	fowl bluegrass	fowl bluegrass	species
Poa paucispicula	fewflower bluegrass	few-flowered bluegrass	species
Poa pratensis	Kentucky bluegrass	Kentucky bluegrass	species
Poa secunda	Sandberg bluegrass	Sandberg's bluegrass, Sandberg bluegrass	species
Poa stenantha	narrowflower bluegrass	narrow-flowered bluegrass	species
Poa trivialis	rough bluegrass	rough bluegrass	species
Poa wheeleri	Wheeler bluegrass	Wheeler's bluegrass	species
Poaceae	grass family	grass family	family
Podagrostis	bentgrass	bentgrass	genus
Podagrostis humilis	low bentgrass	alpine bentgrass, low bent grass	species
Polanisia	clammyweed	clammyweed	genus
Polanisia dodecandra	common clammyweed	common clammyweed, clammyweed	species
Polemoniaceae	phlox family	phlox family	family
Polemonium	Jacob's-ladder	Jacob's-ladder	genus
Polemonium acutiflorum	tall Jacob's-ladder	tall Jacob's-ladder	species
Polemonium occidentale	Western Jacob's-ladder	western Jacob's-ladder	species
Polemonium pulcherrimum	showy Jacob's-ladder	showy Jacob's-ladder	species
Polemonium viscosum	sticky Jacob's-ladder	sticky Jacob's-ladder, skunkweed	species
Polygala	snakeroot	snakeroot	genus
Polygala senega	seneca snakeroot	Seneca snakeroot	species
Polygalaceae	milkwort family	milkwort family	family
Polygaloides	milkwort	milkwort	genus
Polygaloides paucifolia	fringed milkwort	fringed milkwort	species
Polygonaceae	buckwheat family	buckwheat family	family
Polygonum	knotweed	knotweed	genus
Polygonum achoreum	leathery knotweed	leathery knotweed	species
Polygonum austiniae	Austin knotweed	Austin's knotweed	species
Polygonum aviculare	prostrate knotweed	prostrate knotweed	species
Polygonum douglasii	Douglas knotweed	Douglas' knotweed, Douglas knotweed	species
Polygonum engelmannii	Engelmann knotweed	Engelmann's knotweed	species

ALPHABETICAL SCIENTIFIC NAMES

Scientific Name	Suggested Common Name	VASCAN and/or ACIMS Common Name(s)	Rank
Polygonum erectum	erect knotweed	erect knotweed, striate knotweed	species
Polygonum minimum	dwarf knotweed	leafy dwarf knotweed, least knotweed	species
Polygonum polygaloides	milkwort knotweed	milkwort knotweed, white-margined knotweed	species
Polygonum ramosissimum	bushy knotweed	bushy knotweed	species
Polygonum sawatchense	Sawatch knotweed	Sawatch knotweed	species
Polypodiaceae	polypody family	polypody family	family
Polypodium	polypody	polypody	genus
Polypodium hesperium	western polypody	western polypody	species
Polypodium sibiricum	Siberian polypody	Siberian polypody	species
Polypodium virginianum	rock polypody	rock polypody	species
Polypogon	rabbitfoot-grass	rabbitfoot-grass	genus
Polypogon monspeliensis	annual rabbitfoot-grass	annual rabbit's-foot grass, rabbitfoot grass	species
Polystichum	hollyfern	hollyfern	genus
Polystichum lonchitis	northern hollyfern	northern holly fern	species
Populus	poplar, cottonwood, aspen	poplar, cottonwood, aspen	genus
Populus ×acuminata	lanceleaf cottonwood	lance-leaved cottonwood	Hybrid
Populus ×jackii	Jack hybrid poplar	Jack's hybrid poplar	Hybrid
Populus angustifolia	narrowleaf cottonwood	narrow-leaved cottonwood, narrow-leaf cottonwood	species
Populus balsamifera	balsam poplar	balsam poplar	species
Populus deltoides	common cottonwood	eastern cottonwood, plains cottonwood	species
Populus tremuloides	trembling aspen	trembling aspen, aspen	species
Populus trichocarpa	black cottonwood	black cottonwood	species
Portulaca	purslane	purslane	genus
Portulaca oleracea	common purslane	common purslane, purslane	species
Portulacaceae	purslane family	purslane family	family
Potamogeton	pondweed	pondweed	genus
Potamogeton alpinus	alpine pondweed	alpine pondweed	species
Potamogeton amplifolius	largeleaf pondweed	large-leaved pondweed	species
Potamogeton berchtoldii	Berchtold pondweed	Berchtold's pondweed	species
Potamogeton crispus	curly pondweed	curly-leaved pondweed, crisp-leaved pondweed	species
Potamogeton diversifolius	waterthread pondweed	water-thread pondweed	species
Potamogeton epihydrus	ribbonleaf pondweed	ribbon-leaved pondweed	species
Potamogeton foliosus	leafy pondweed	leafy pondweed	species
Potamogeton friesii	Fries pondweed	Fries' pondweed	species
Potamogeton gramineus	grassy pondweed	grass-leaved pondweed, various-leaved pondweed	species
Potamogeton natans	floatingleaf pondweed	floating-leaved pondweed, floating-leaf pondweed	species
Potamogeton nodosus	longleaf pondweed	long-leaved pondweed, longleaf pondweed	species

ALPHABETICAL SCIENTIFIC NAMES

Scientific Name	Suggested Common Name	VASCAN and/or ACIMS Common Name(s)	Rank
Potamogeton obtusifolius	bluntleaf pondweed	blunt-leaved pondweed	species
Potamogeton praelongus	whitestem pondweed	white-stemmed pondweed, white-stem pondweed	species
Potamogeton pusillus	small pondweed	small pondweed, small-leaf pondweed	species
Potamogeton richardsonii	Richardson pondweed	Richardson's pondweed, clasping-leaf pondweed	species
Potamogeton robbinsii	Robbins pondweed	Robbins' pondweed	species
Potamogeton strictifolius	straightleaf pondweed	straight-leaved pondweed, linear-leaved pondweed	species
Potamogeton zosteriformis	flatstem pondweed	flat-stemmed pondweed	species
Potamogetonaceae	pondweed family	pondweed family	family
Potentilla	cinquefoil	cinquefoil, silverweed	genus
Potentilla anserina	silverweed	silverweed	species
Potentilla arenosa	bluff cinquefoil	bluff cinquefoil	species
Potentilla argentea	silvery cinquefoil	silvery cinquefoil	species
Potentilla biennis	biennial cinquefoil	biennial cinquefoil	species
Potentilla bimundorum	staghorn cinquefoil	staghorn cinquefoil, branched cinquefoil	species
Potentilla bipinnatifida	plains cinquefoil	bipinnate cinquefoil, plains cinquefoil	species
Potentilla concinna	early cinquefoil	early cinquefoil	species
Potentilla drummondii	Drummond cinquefoil	Drummond's cinquefoil	species
Potentilla effusa	branched cinquefoil	branched cinquefoil	species
Potentilla flabellifolia	fanleaf cinquefoil	fan-leaved cinquefoil, fanleaf cinquefoil	species
Potentilla furcata	forked cinquefoil	forked cinquefoil	species
Potentilla glaucophylla	blueleaf cinquefoil	blue-leaved cinquefoil, mountain cinquefoil	species
Potentilla gracilis	slender cinquefoil	slender cinquefoil, graceful cinquefoil	species
Potentilla hippiana	woolly cinquefoil	Hipp's cinquefoil, woolly cinquefoil	species
Potentilla hookeriana	Hooker cinquefoil	Hooker's cinquefoil	species
Potentilla hudsonii	Hudson cinquefoil	Hudson's cinquefoil	species
Potentilla hyparctica	arctic cinquefoil	arctic cinquefoil, northern cinquefoil	species
Potentilla jepsonii	Jepson cinquefoil	Jepson's cinquefoil	species
Potentilla lasiodonta	sandhills cinquefoil	sandhills cinquefoil	species
Potentilla litoralis	coast cinquefoil	coast cinquefoil, coastal cinquefoil	species
Potentilla macounii	Macoun cinquefoil	Macoun's cinquefoil	species
Potentilla multisecta	Great Basin cinquefoil	Great Basin cinquefoil, smooth-leaved cinquefoil	species
Potentilla nivea	snow cinquefoil	snow cinquefoil	species
Potentilla norvegica	rough cinquefoil	rough cinquefoil	species

ALPHABETICAL SCIENTIFIC NAMES

Scientific Name	Suggested Common Name	VASCAN and/or ACIMS Common Name(s)	Rank
Potentilla ovina	sheep cinquefoil	sheep cinquefoil	species
Potentilla pensylvanica	Pennsylvania cinquefoil	Pennsylvania cinquefoil, prairie cinquefoil	species
Potentilla plattensis	Platte River cinquefoil	Platte River cinquefoil, low cinquefoil	species
Potentilla pulcherrima	beautiful cinquefoil	beautiful cinquefoil, soft cinquefoil	species
Potentilla recta	sulphur cinquefoil	sulphur cinquefoil, rough-fruited cinquefoil	species
Potentilla rivalis	brook cinquefoil	brook cinquefoil	species
Potentilla rubricaulis	redstem cinquefoil	red-stemmed cinquefoil	species
Potentilla subgorodkovii	woolly alpine cinquefoil	Sheenjek River cinquefoil, Jurtsev's cinquefoil	species
Potentilla subjuga	Colorado cinquefoil	Colorado cinquefoil	species
Potentilla subvahliana	High Arctic cinquefoil	high arctic cinquefoil	species
Potentilla supina	bushy cinquefoil	spreading cinquefoil, bushy cinquefoil	species
Potentilla villosula	finely villous cinquefoil	finely villous cinquefoil	species
Prenanthes	rattlesnakeroot	rattlesnakeroot, white lettuce	species
Primula	primrose, shootingstar	primrose, shootingstar	genus
Primula conjugens	mountain shootingstar	slim-pod shootingstar, mountain shooting star	species
Primula egaliksensis	Greenland primrose	Greenland primrose	species
Primula incana	mealy primrose	mealy primrose	species
Primula mistassinica	Mistassini primrose	Mistassini primrose, dwarf Canadian primrose	species
Primula pauciflora	saline shootingstar	darkthroat shootingstar, saline shooting star	species
Primulaceae	primrose family	primrose family	family
Prosartes	fairybells	fairybells	genus
Prosartes hookeri	Hooker fairybells	Hooker's fairybells	species
Prosartes trachycarpa	roughfruit fairybells	rough-fruited fairybells, fairybells	species
Prunella	selfheal	selfheal	genus
Prunella vulgaris	common selfheal	common self-heal, heal-all	species
Prunus	cherry	cherry	genus
Prunus pensylvanica	pin cherry	pin cherry	species
Prunus virginiana	chokecherry	chokecherry, choke cherry	species
Psathyrostachys	Russian-wildrye	Russian-wildrye	genus
Psathyrostachys juncea	Russian-wildrye	Russian wildrye, Russian wild rye	species
Pseudognaphalium	false-cudweed	false-cudweed	genus
Pseudognaphalium macounii	Macoun false-cudweed	Macoun's cudweed	species
Pseudognaphalium thermale	slender false-cudweed	slender cudweed	species
Pseudoroegneria	wheatgrass	wheatgrass	genus
Pseudoroegneria spicata	bluebunch wheatgrass	bluebunch wheatgrass	species
Pseudotsuga	Douglas-fir	Douglas-fir	genus

ALPHABETICAL SCIENTIFIC NAMES

Scientific Name	Suggested Common Name	VASCAN and/or ACIMS Common Name(s)	Rank
Pseudotsuga menziesii	Douglas-fir	Douglas-fir	species
Psilocarphus	woollyheads	woollyheads	genus
Psilocarphus brevissimus	dwarf woollyheads	dwarf woollyheads, round woollyheads	species
Pteridaceae	maidenhair family	maidenhair family	family
Pteridium	brackenfern	brackenfern	genus
Pteridium aquilinum	brackenfern	bracken fern	species
Pterospora	pinedrops	pinedrops	genus
Pterospora andromedea	pinedrops	pinedrops, pine-drops	species
Puccinellia	alkaligrass	alkaligrass	genus
Puccinellia distans	spreading alkaligrass	spreading alkaligrass, slender salt-meadow grass	species
Puccinellia nuttalliana	Nuttall alkaligrass	Nuttall's alkaligrass, Nuttall's salt-meadow grass	species
Pulsatilla	pasqueflower	pasqueflower	genus
Pulsatilla nuttalliana	prairie pasqueflower	prairie pasqueflower, prairie crocus	species
Pulsatilla occidentalis	western pasqueflower	western pasqueflower, western anemone	species
Pyrola	wintergreen	wintergreen	genus
Pyrola asarifolia	common pink wintergreen	pink pyrola, common pink wintergreen	species
Pyrola chlorantha	greenflower wintergreen	green-flowered pyrola, greenish-flowered wintergreen	species
Pyrola elliptica	white wintergreen	shinleaf, white wintergreen	species
Pyrola grandiflora	arctic wintergreen	arctic pyrola, Arctic wintergreen	species
Pyrola minor	lesser wintergreen	lesser pyrola, lesser wintergreen	species
Pyrola picta	whitevein wintergreen	white-veined pyrola, white-veined wintergreen	species
Pyrrocoma	goldenweed	goldenweed	genus
Pyrrocoma lanceolata	lanceleaf goldenweed	lance-leaved goldenweed, lance-leaved ironplant	species
Pyrrocoma uniflora	oneflower goldenweed	one-flowered goldenweed, one-flowered ironplant	species
Quercus	oak	oak	genus
Quercus macrocarpa	bur oak	bur oak, burr oak	species
Ranunculaceae	buttercup family	buttercup family	family
Ranunculus	buttercup	buttercup	genus
Ranunculus abortivus	smallflower buttercup	kidney-leaved buttercup, small-flowered buttercup	species
Ranunculus acris	tall buttercup	common buttercup, tall buttercup	species
Ranunculus aquatilis	threadleaf water-buttercup	thread-leaved water-crowfoot, large-leaved white water crowfoot	species

ALPHABETICAL SCIENTIFIC NAMES

Scientific Name	Suggested Common Name	VASCAN and/or ACIMS Common Name(s)	Rank
Ranunculus arcticus	northern buttercup	northern buttercup	species
Ranunculus cardiophyllus	heartleaf buttercup	heart-leaved buttercup	species
Ranunculus eschscholtzii	Eschscholtz buttercup	Eschscholtz's buttercup, mountain buttercup	species
Ranunculus flabellaris	yellow water-buttercup	yellow water buttercup, yellow water-crowfoot	species
Ranunculus flammula	creeping spearwort	lesser spearwort, creeping spearwort	species
Ranunculus glaberrimus	sagebrush buttercup	sagebrush buttercup, early buttercup	species
Ranunculus gmelinii	Gmelin water-buttercup	Gmelin's buttercup, yellow water crowfoot	species
Ranunculus grayi	Gray buttercup	Gray's buttercup	species
Ranunculus hyperboreus	far-north buttercup	far-northern buttercup, boreal buttercup	species
Ranunculus inamoenus	graceful buttercup	graceful buttercup	species
Ranunculus longirostris	longbeak water-buttercup	long-beaked water-buttercup, large-leaved white water crowfoot	species
Ranunculus macounii	Macoun buttercup	Macoun's buttercup	species
Ranunculus nivalis	snow buttercup	snow buttercup	species
Ranunculus occidentalis	western buttercup	western buttercup	species
Ranunculus pensylvanicus	Pennsylvania buttercup	Pennsylvania buttercup, bristly buttercup	species
Ranunculus pygmaeus	pygmy buttercup	pygmy buttercup, dwarf buttercup	species
Ranunculus repens	creeping buttercup	creeping buttercup	species
Ranunculus rhomboideus	prairie buttercup	prairie buttercup	species
Ranunculus sceleratus	celeryleaf buttercup	cursed buttercup, celery-leaved buttercup	species
Ranunculus uncinatus	hooked buttercup	hooked buttercup, hairy buttercup	species
Raphanus	radish	radish	genus
Raphanus raphanistrum	wild radish	wild radish	species
Ratibida	prairie-coneflower	prairie-coneflower	genus
Ratibida columnifera	upright prairie-coneflower	upright prairie coneflower, prairie coneflower	species
Reynoutria	giant-knotweed	giant-knotweed	genus
Reynoutria japonica	Japanese knotweed	Japanese knotweed	species
Rhamnaceae	buckthorn family	buckthorn family	family
Rhamnus	buckthorn	buckthorn	genus
Rhamnus alnifolia	alderleaf-buckthorn	alder-leaved buckthorn	species
Rhamnus cathartica	European buckthorn	European buckthorn, common buckthorn	species
Rhaponticum	Russian-knapweed	Russian-knapweed	genus
Rhaponticum repens	Russian-knapweed	Russian knapweed	species

ALPHABETICAL SCIENTIFIC NAMES

Scientific Name	Suggested Common Name	VASCAN and/or ACIMS Common Name(s)	Rank
Rheum	rhubarb	rhubarb	genus
Rheum rhabarbarum	rhubarb	rhubarb	species
Rhinanthus	yellowrattle	yellowrattle	genus
Rhinanthus minor	little yellowrattle	little yellow rattle, yellow rattle	species
Rhodiola	roseroot	roseroot	genus
Rhodiola integrifolia	western roseroot	entire-leaved stonecrop, rose-root	species
Rhododendron	rhododendron, Labrador-tea	rhododendron, Labrador-tea	genus
Rhododendron albiflorum	whiteflower rhododendron	white-flowered rhododendron	species
Rhododendron groenlandicum	common Labrador-tea	common Labrador tea	species
Rhododendron lapponicum	Lapland rosebay	Lapland rosebay, Lapland rose-bay	species
Rhododendron neoglandulosum	glandular Labrador-tea	western Labrador tea, glandular Labrador tea	species
Rhododendron tomentosum	northern Labrador-tea	northern Labrador tea	species
Rhus	sumac	sumac	genus
Rhus aromatica	fragrant sumac	fragrant sumac, skunkbush	species
Rhynchospora	beakrush	beakrush	genus
Rhynchospora capillacea	slender beakrush	slender beakrush, slender beak-rush	species
Ribes	currant, gooseberry	currant, gooseberry	genus
Ribes americanum	America black currant	American black currant, wild black currant	species
Ribes aureum	golden currant	golden currant	species
Ribes cereum	wax currant	wax currant	species
Ribes glandulosum	skunk currant	skunk currant	species
Ribes hirtellum	hairy gooseberry	swamp gooseberry, wild gooseberry	species
Ribes hudsonianum	northern black currant	northern black currant	species
Ribes inerme	whitestem gooseberry	white-stemmed gooseberry, mountain gooseberry	species
Ribes lacustre	bristly black currant	bristly black currant	species
Ribes laxiflorum	trailing black currant	trailing black currant, mountain currant	species
Ribes oxyacanthoides	Canada gooseberry	Canada gooseberry, northern gooseberry	species
Ribes triste	red currant	swamp red currant, wild red currant	species
Ribes viscosissimum	sticky currant	sticky currant	species
Ribes watsonianum	Watson gooseberry	Watson's gooseberry, spring gooseberry	species
Romanzoffia	mistmaiden	mistmaiden	genus
Romanzoffia sitchensis	Sitka mistmaiden	Sitka mistmaiden, Sitka romanzoffia	species

ALPHABETICAL SCIENTIFIC NAMES

Scientific Name	Suggested Common Name	VASCAN and/or ACIMS Common Name(s)	Rank
Rorippa	yellowcress	yellowcress	genus
Rorippa austriaca	Austrian yellowcress	Austrian yellowcress, Austrian cress	species
Rorippa curvipes	bluntleaf yellowcress	blunt-leaved watercress	species
Rorippa palustris	marsh yellowcress	marsh yellowcress, marsh yellow cress	species
Rorippa sinuata	spreading yellowcress	spreading yellowcress, spreading yellow cress	species
Rorippa sylvestris	creeping yellowcress	creeping yellowcress, creeping yellow cress	species
Rorippa tenerrima	slender yellowcress	slender yellowcress, slender cress	species
Rosa	rose	rose	genus
Rosa acicularis	prickly rose	prickly rose	species
Rosa arkansana	prairie rose	prairie rose	species
Rosa woodsii	Woods rose	Woods' rose, common wild rose	species
Rosaceae	rose family	rose family	family
Rubiaceae	bedstraw family	bedstraw family	family
Rubus	raspberry	raspberry	genus
Rubus arcticus	arctic raspberry	arctic raspberry, dwarf raspberry	species
Rubus chamaemorus	cloudberry	cloudberry	species
Rubus idaeus	wild red raspberry	red raspberry, wild red raspberry	species
Rubus parviflorus	western thimbleberry	western thimbleberry, thimbleberry	species
Rubus pedatus	fiveleaf dwarf-bramble	five-leaved dwarf bramble, dwarf bramble	species
Rubus pubescens	dwarf raspberry	dwarf raspberry, dewberry	species
Rudbeckia	black-eyed-Susan	black-eyed-Susan	genus
Rudbeckia hirta	black-eyed-Susan	black-eyed Susan	species
Rumex	dock, sorrel	dock, sorrel	genus
Rumex acetosa	garden sorrel	garden sorrel, green sorrel	species
Rumex acetosella	sheep sorrel	sheep sorrel	species
Rumex britannica	water dock	greater water dock, water dock	species
Rumex confertus	Asiatic dock	Asiatic dock, dock	species
Rumex crispus	curled dock	curled dock	species
Rumex dentatus	toothed dock	toothed dock	species
Rumex fueginus	golden dock	Tierra del Fuego dock, American golden dock	species
Rumex lapponicus	Lapland sorrel	Lapland sorrel	species
Rumex longifolius	longleaf dock	long-leaved dock	species
Rumex occidentalis	western dock	western dock	species
Rumex paucifolius	alpine sheep sorrel	alpine sheep sorrel	species
Rumex pseudonatronatus	field dock	field dock	species
Rumex stenophyllus	narrowleaf field dock	narrow-leaved field dock	species
Rumex triangulivalvis	triangular-valve dock	triangular-valve dock, narrow-leaved dock	species

ALPHABETICAL SCIENTIFIC NAMES

Scientific Name	Suggested Common Name	VASCAN and/or ACIMS Common Name(s)	Rank
Rumex utahensis	Utah dock	Utah dock	species
Rumex venosus	veiny dock	veined dock, wild begonia	species
Ruppia	widgeongrass	widgeongrass	genus
Ruppia cirrhosa	spiral widgeongrass	spiral ditchgrass, widgeon-grass	species
Ruppiaceae	widgeongrass family	widgeongrass family	family
Sabulina	stitchwort	stitchwort	genus
Sabulina austromontana	mountain stitchwort	Rocky Mountain stitchwort, green alpine sandwort	species
Sabulina dawsonensis	Dawson stitchwort	Dawson's stitchwort, Dawson sandwort	species
Sabulina elegans	elegant stitchwort	elegant stitchwort, purple alpine sandwort	species
Sabulina nuttallii	Nuttall stitchwort	Nuttall's stitchwort, Nuttall's sandwort	species
Sabulina rubella	reddish stitchwort	reddish stitchwort, red-seeded sandwort	species
Sagina	pearlwort	pearlwort	genus
Sagina decumbens	spreading pearlwort	spreading pearlwort	species
Sagina nivalis	snow pearlwort	snow pearlwort, pearlwort	species
Sagina nodosa	knotted pearlwort	knotted pearlwort, pearlwort	species
Sagina saginoides	alpine pearlwort	alpine pearlwort, mountain pearlwort	species
Sagittaria	arrowhead	arrowhead	genus
Sagittaria cuneata	arumleaf arrowhead	northern arrowhead, arum-leaved arrowhead	species
Sagittaria latifolia	broadleaf arrowhead	broad-leaved arrowhead	species
Salicaceae	willow family	willow family	family
Salicornia	glasswort	glasswort	genus
Salicornia rubra	red glasswort	red glasswort, samphire	species
Salix	willow	willow	genus
Salix alaxensis	Alaska willow	Alaska willow	species
Salix amygdaloides	peachleaf willow	peach-leaved willow	species
Salix arbusculoides	littletree willow	little-tree willow, shrubby willow	species
Salix arctica	Arctic willow	arctic willow	species
Salix athabascensis	Athabasca willow	Athabasca willow	species
Salix barclayi	Barclay willow	Barclay's willow	species
Salix barrattiana	Barratt willow	Barratt's willow	species
Salix bebbiana	Bebb willow	Bebb's willow, beaked willow	species
Salix boothii	Booth willow	Booth's willow	species
Salix brachycarpa	short-capsule willow	short-capsuled willow	species
Salix calcicola	woolly willow	limestone willow, woolly willow	species
Salix candida	sage willow	sage willow, hoary willow	species
Salix commutata	undergreen willow	under-green willow, changeable willow	species

ALPHABETICAL SCIENTIFIC NAMES

Scientific Name	Suggested Common Name	VASCAN and/or ACIMS Common Name(s)	Rank
Salix daphnoides	daphne willow	violet willow, Daphne's willow	species
Salix discolor	pussy willow	pussy willow	species
Salix drummondiana	Drummond willow	Drummond's willow	species
Salix exigua	narrowleaf willow	coyote willow, narrow-leaf willow	species
Salix famelica	hungry willow	starved willow, hungry willow	species
Salix farriae	Farr willow	Farr's willow	species
Salix glauca	greyleaf willow	grey-leaved willow, smooth willow	species
Salix interior	sandbar willow	sandbar willow	species
Salix lasiandra	Pacific shining willow	Pacific willow, shining willow	species
Salix maccalliana	MacCalla willow	MacCalla's willow, velvet-fruited willow	species
Salix melanopsis	dusky willow	dusky willow	species
Salix myrtillifolia	blueberryleaf willow	low blueberry willow, myrtle-leaved willow	species
Salix nivalis	snow willow	dwarf snow willow, snow willow	species
Salix pedicellaris	bog willow	bog willow	species
Salix pentandra	laurel willow	laurel willow	species
Salix petiolaris	meadow willow	meadow willow, basket willow	species
Salix petrophila	alpine willow	Rocky Mountain willow, alpine willow	species
Salix planifolia	tealeaf willow	tea-leaved willow, flat-leaved willow	species
Salix prolixa	Mackenzie willow	Mackenzie's willow	species
Salix pseudomonticola	false mountain willow	false mountain willow	species
Salix pseudomyrsinites	tall blueberry willow	tall blueberry willow	species
Salix pyrifolia	balsam willow	balsam willow	species
Salix raupii	Raup willow	Raup's willow	species
Salix reticulata	netvein willow	net-veined willow	species
Salix scouleriana	Scouler willow	Scouler's willow	species
Salix serissima	autumn willow	autumn willow	species
Salix sitchensis	Sitka willow	Sitka willow	species
Salix stolonifera	creeping willow	creeping willow	species
Salix tyrrellii	Tyrrell willow	Tyrrell's willow	species
Salix vestita	rock willow	hairy willow, rock willow	species
Salsola		Russian-thistle	Russian-thistle	genus
Salsola collina	slender Russian-thistle	slender Russian thistle, slender Russian-thistle	species
Salsola tragus	prickly Russian-thistle	prickly Russian thistle, Russian-thistle	species
Salvia	sage	sage	genus
Salvia nemorosa	woodland sage	woodland sage, wood sage	species
Sambucus	elderberry	elderberry	genus
Sambucus racemosa	red elderberry	red elderberry	species
Sanicula	sanicle	sanicle	genus

ALPHABETICAL SCIENTIFIC NAMES

Scientific Name	Suggested Common Name	VASCAN and/or ACIMS Common Name(s)	Rank
Sanicula marilandica	Maryland sanicle	Maryland sanicle, snakeroot	species
Santalaceae	sandalwood family	sandalwood family	family
Sapindaceae	soapberry family	soapberry family	family
Saponaria	bouncingbet	bouncingbet	genus
Saponaria officinalis	bouncingbet	bouncing-bet, soapwort	species
Sarcobatus	greasewood	greasewood	genus
Sarcobatus vermiculatus	black greasewood	black greasewood, greasewood	species
Sarracenia	pitcherplant	pitcherplant	genus
Sarracenia purpurea	purple pitcherplant	northern pitcher plant, pitcher-plant	species
Sarraceniaceae	pitcherplant family	pitcherplant family	family
Saussurea	sawwort	sawwort	genus
Saussurea amara	tall sawwort	tall sawwort	species
Saussurea americana	American sawwort	American sawwort, American saw-wort	species
Saussurea nuda	dwarf sawwort	dwarf sawwort, dwarf saw-wort	species
Saxifraga	saxifrage	saxifrage	genus
Saxifraga adscendens	wedgeleaf saxifrage	ascending saxifrage, wedge-leaved saxifrage	species
Saxifraga aizoides	yellow mountain saxifrage	yellow mountain saxifrage	species
Saxifraga austromontana	spotted saxifrage	red-spotted saxifrage, spotted saxifrage	species
Saxifraga cernua	nodding saxifrage	nodding saxifrage	species
Saxifraga cespitosa	tufted saxifrage	tufted saxifrage	species
Saxifraga flagellaris	spider saxifrage	stoloniferous saxifrage, spiderplant	species
Saxifraga hyperborea	pygmy saxifrage	pygmy saxifrage, brook saxifrage	species
Saxifraga mertensiana	Mertens saxifrage	Mertens' saxifrage, Merten's saxifrage	species
Saxifraga oppositifolia	purple saxifrage	purple mountain saxifrage, purple saxifrage	species
Saxifraga tricuspidata	threetooth saxifrage	three-toothed saxifrage	species
Saxifragaceae	saxifrage family	saxifrage family	family
Sceptridium	grapefern	grapefern	genus
Sceptridium multifidum	leather grapefern	leathery grapefern, leather grapefern	species
Sceptridium oneidense	bluntlobe grapefern	blunt-lobed grapefern, blunt-lobe grape-fern	species
Scheuchzeria	scheuchzeria	scheuchzeria	genus
Scheuchzeria palustris	scheuchzeria	marsh scheuchzeria, scheuchzeria	species
Scheuchzeriaceae	scheuchzeria family	scheuchzeria family	family
Schizachne	false-melic	false-melic	genus
Schizachne purpurascens	false-melic	purple false melic, purple oat grass	species

ALPHABETICAL SCIENTIFIC NAMES

Scientific Name	Suggested Common Name	VASCAN and/or ACIMS Common Name(s)	Rank
Schizachyrium	little-bluestem	little-bluestem	genus
Schizachyrium scoparium	little-bluestem	little bluestem	species
Schoenoplectus	bulrush	bulrush	genus
Schoenoplectus acutus	hardstem bulrush	hard-stemmed bulrush, great bulrush	species
Schoenoplectus heterochaetus	slender bulrush	slender bulrush	species
Schoenoplectus pungens	three-square bulrush	common three-square bulrush, three-square rush	species
Schoenoplectus tabernaemontani	softstem bulrush	soft-stemmed bulrush, common great bulrush	species
Scirpus	bulrush	bulrush	genus
Scirpus atrocinctus	blackgirdle bulrush	black-girdled bulrush	species
Scirpus microcarpus	smallfruit bulrush	red-tinged bulrush, small-fruited bulrush	species
Scirpus pallidus	pale bulrush	pale bulrush	species
Scleranthus	knawel	knawel	genus
Scleranthus annuus	annual knawel	annual knawel, knawel	species
Scolochloa	rivergrass	rivergrass	genus
Scolochloa festucacea	rivergrass	common rivergrass, spangletop	species
Scrophularia	figwort	figwort	genus
Scrophularia lanceolata	lanceleaf figwort	lance-leaved figwort	species
Scrophulariaceae	figwort family	figwort family	family
Scutellaria	skullcap	skullcap	genus
Scutellaria galericulata	marsh skullcap	marsh skullcap	species
Secale	rye	rye	genus
Secale cereale	common rye	common rye, rye	species
Securigera	crown-vetch	crown-vetch	genus
Securigera varia	crown-vetch	purple crown-vetch, field crown-vetch	species
Sedum	stonecrop	stonecrop	genus
Sedum acre	mossy stonecrop	mossy stonecrop	species
Sedum divergens	spreading stonecrop	spreading stonecrop	species
Sedum lanceolatum	lanceleaf stonecrop	lance-leaved stonecrop	species
Sedum stenopetalum	narrowpetal stonecrop	worm-leaved stonecrop, narrow-petaled stonecrop	species
Selaginella	spikemoss	spikemoss	genus
Selaginella densa	prairie spikemoss	prairie spikemoss, prairie selaginella	species
Selaginella rupestris	rock spikemoss	rock spikemoss, rock little club-moss	species
Selaginella scopulorum	Rocky Mountain spikemoss	Rocky Mountain spikemoss	species
Selaginella selaginoides	club spikemoss	low spikemoss, spiny-edged little club-moss	species

ALPHABETICAL SCIENTIFIC NAMES

Scientific Name	Suggested Common Name	VASCAN and/or ACIMS Common Name(s)	Rank
Selaginella standleyi	Standley spikemoss	Standley's spikemoss	species
Selaginella wallacei	Wallace spikemoss	Wallace's spikemoss, Wallace's little club-moss	species
Selaginellaceae	spikemoss family	spikemoss family	family
Senecio	ragwort	ragwort	genus
Senecio eremophilus	cutleaf ragwort	dryland ragwort, cut-leaved ragwort	species
Senecio fremontii	Fremont ragwort	Fremont's ragwort, mountain butterweed	species
Senecio hydrophiloides	sweet marsh ragwort	sweet marsh ragwort, ragwort	species
Senecio integerrimus	entireleaf ragwort	western ragwort, entire-leaved groundsel	species
Senecio lugens	blacktip ragwort	small black-tip ragwort, black-tipped groundsel	species
Senecio megacephalus	largeflower ragwort	large-flowered ragwort	species
Senecio triangularis	arrowleaf ragwort	arrow-leaved ragwort, brook ragwort	species
Senecio viscosus	sticky ragwort	sticky ragwort, sticky groundsel	species
Senecio vulgaris	common ragwort	common ragwort, common groundsel	species
Setaria	foxtail	foxtail	genus
Setaria italica	Italian foxtail	Italian foxtail	species
Setaria pumila	yellow foxtail	yellow foxtail	species
Setaria viridis	green foxtail	green foxtail	species
Shepherdia	buffaloberry	buffaloberry	genus
Shepherdia argentea	silver buffaloberry	silver buffaloberry, thorny buffaloberry	species
Shepherdia canadensis	Canada buffaloberry	soapberry, Canada buffaloberry	species
Shinnersoseris	skeletonweed	skeletonweed	genus
Shinnersoseris rostrata	annual skeletonweed	annual skeletonweed	species
Sibbaldia	sibbaldia	sibbaldia	genus
Sibbaldia procumbens	creeping sibbaldia	creeping sibbaldia, sibbaldia	species
Sibbaldia tridentata	threetooth sibbaldia	three-toothed cinquefoil	species
Silene	campion, catchfly	campion, catchfly	genus
Silene acaulis	moss campion	moss campion	species
Silene antirrhina	sleepy catchfly	sleepy catchfly	species
Silene chalcedonica	Maltese-cross	Maltese-cross campion, Maltese cross	species
Silene conoidea	large sand catchfly	conoid catchfly, large sand catchfly	species
Silene csereii	smooth catchfly	biennial campion, smooth catchfly	species
Silene drummondii	Drummond catchfly	Drummond's catchfly, Drummond's cockle	species
Silene hitchguirei	mountain catchfly	mountain catchfly, mountain campion	species

ALPHABETICAL SCIENTIFIC NAMES

Scientific Name	Suggested Common Name	VASCAN and/or ACIMS Common Name(s)	Rank
Silene involucrata	arctic catchfly	arctic catchfly, alpine bladder catchfly	species
Silene latifolia	white bladder-campion	white campion, white cockle, bladder campion	species
Silene menziesii	Menzies catchfly	Menzies' catchfly	species
Silene noctiflora	night-flowering catchfly	night-flowering catchfly	species
Silene parryi	Parry catchfly	Parry's catchfly, Parry's campion	species
Silene scouleri	Scouler catchfly	Scouler's catchfly	species
Silene uralensis	nodding catchfly	nodding catchfly, nodding campion	species
Silene vulgaris	common bladder-campion	bladder campion	species
Silybum	milkthistle	milkthistle	genus
Silybum marianum	blessed milkthistle	blessed milk thistle, milk thistle	species
Sinapis	mustard	mustard	genus
Sinapis alba	white mustard	white mustard	species
Sinapis arvensis	corn mustard	corn mustard, wild mustard	species
Sisymbrium	tumblemustard	tumblemustard	genus
Sisymbrium altissimum	tall tumblemustard	tall tumble-mustard, tumbling mustard	species
Sisymbrium linifolium	flaxleaf tumblemustard	flax-leaved plains mustard, narrow-leaved mustard	species
Sisymbrium loeselii	Loesel tumblemustard	Loesel's tumble mustard, tall hedge mustard	species
Sisymbrium officinale	common tumblemustard	common tumble mustard, hedge mustard	species
Sisyrinchium	blue-eyed-grass	blue-eyed-grass	genus
Sisyrinchium montanum	common blue-eyed-grass	strict blue-eyed grass, common blue-eyed grass	species
Sisyrinchium septentrionale	pale blue-eyed-grass	northern blue-eyed-grass, pale blue-eyed grass	species
Sium	waterparsnip	waterparsnip	genus
Sium suave	common waterparsnip	common water-parsnip, water parsnip	species
Smelowskia	smelowskia	smelowskia	genus
Smelowskia americana	American smelowskia	American smelowskia, silver rock cress	species
Solanaceae	nightshade family	nightshade family	family
Solanum	nightshade	nightshade	genus
Solanum dulcamara	climbing nightshade	bittersweet nightshade, climbing nightshade	species
Solanum nigrum	black nightshade	black nightshade	species
Solanum nitidibaccatum	hairy nightshade	hairy nightshade	species
Solanum rostratum	buffalobur nightshade	horned nightshade, buffalo-burr	species
Solanum triflorum	cutleaf nightshade	cut-leaved nightshade, wild tomato	species
Solidago	goldenrod	goldenrod	genus

ALPHABETICAL SCIENTIFIC NAMES

Scientific Name	Suggested Common Name	VASCAN and/or ACIMS Common Name(s)	Rank
Solidago altissima	tall goldenrod	tall goldenrod	species
Solidago gigantea	giant goldenrod	giant goldenrod, late goldenrod	species
Solidago lepida	elegant goldenrod	elegant goldenrod	species
Solidago missouriensis	Missouri goldenrod	Missouri goldenrod, low goldenrod	species
Solidago mollis	velvety goldenrod	velvety goldenrod	species
Solidago multiradiata	manyray goldenrod	multi-rayed goldenrod, alpine goldenrod	species
Solidago nemoralis	grey goldenrod	grey-stemmed goldenrod, showy goldenrod	species
Solidago rigida	stiff goldenrod	stiff goldenrod	species
Solidago glutinosa	sticky goldenrod	sticky goldenrod	species
Sonchus	sowthistle	sowthistle	genus
Sonchus arvensis	perennial sowthistle	field sow-thistle, perennial sow-thistle	species
Sonchus asper	prickly sowthistle	prickly sow-thistle, prickly annual sow-thistle	species
Sonchus oleraceus	common sowthistle	common sow-thistle, annual sow-thistle	species
Sorbaria	false-spiraea	false-spiraea	genus
Sorbaria sorbifolia	false-spiraea	false spiraea	species
Sorbus	mountain-ash	mountain-ash	genus
Sorbus aucuparia	European mountain-ash	European mountain-ash	species
Sorbus scopulina	western mountain-ash	Greene's mountain-ash, western mountain-ash	species
Sorbus sitchensis	Sitka mountain-ash	Sitka mountain-ash, Sitka mountain ash	species
Sparganium	burreed	burreed	genus
Sparganium americanum	American burreed	American burreed	species
Sparganium angustifolium	narrowleaf burreed	narrow-leaved burreed, narrow-leaved bur-reed	species
Sparganium emersum	greenfruit burreed	green-fruited burreed	species
Sparganium eurycarpum	broadfruit burreed	broad-fruited burreed, giant bur-reed	species
Sparganium fluctuans	floating burreed	floating burreed, floating bur-reed	species
Sparganium glomeratum	clustered burreed	clustered burreed	species
Sparganium hyperboreum	northern burreed	northern burreed, northern bur-reed	species
Sparganium natans	small burreed	small burreed, small bur-reed	species
Spartina	cordgrass	cordgrass, cord grass	genus
Spergula	sandspurry	cornspurry	genus
Spergula arvensis	cornspurry	corn spurrey, corn spurry	species
Spergularia	sandspurry	sandspurry	genus
Spergularia diandra	alkali sandspurry	alkali sand-spurrey, sand spurry	species
Spergularia salina	saltmarsh sandspurry	saltmarsh sand-spurrey, salt-marsh sand spurry	species

ALPHABETICAL SCIENTIFIC NAMES

Scientific Name	Suggested Common Name	VASCAN and/or ACIMS Common Name(s)	Rank
Sphaeralcea	globemallow	globemallow	genus
Sphaeralcea coccinea	scarlet globemallow	scarlet globe-mallow, scarlet mallow	species
Sphenopholis	wedgegrass	wedgegrass	genus
Sphenopholis intermedia	slender wedgegrass	slender wedgegrass, slender wedge grass	species
Sphenopholis obtusata	prairie wedgegrass	prairie wedgegrass, prairie wedge grass	species
Spinacia	spinach	spinach	genus
Spinacia oleracea	spinach	spinach	species
Spiraea	meadowsweet	meadowsweet	genus
Spiraea alba	white meadowsweet	white meadowsweet, narrow-leaved meadowsweet	species
Spiraea lucida	shinyleaf meadowsweet	shiny-leaved meadowsweet, white meadowsweet	species
Spiraea splendens	rose meadowsweet	subalpine meadowsweet, pink meadowsweet	species
Spiranthes	ladytresses	ladie's-tresses	genus
Spiranthes lacera	northern slender ladytresses	northern slender ladies'-tresses	species
Spiranthes romanzoffiana	hooded ladytresses	hooded ladies'-tresses	species
Spirodela	great-duckweed	great-duckweed	genus
Spirodela polyrhiza	great-duckweed	great duckweed, larger duckweed	species
Sporobolus	dropseed	dropseed, cordgrass	genus
Sporobolus cryptandrus	sand dropseed	sand dropseed	species
Sporobolus hookerianus	alkali cordgrass	alkali cordgrass, alkali cord grass	species
Sporobolus michauxianus	prairie cordgrass	prairie cordgrass, prairie cord grass	species
Sporobolus neglectus	small dropseed	small dropseed, annual dropseed	species
Sporobolus rigidus	prairie cropseed	prairie sandreed, sand grass	species
Stachys	hedgenettle	hedgenettle	genus
Stachys pilosa	hairy hedgenettle	hairy hedge-nettle, marsh hedge-nettle	species
Stellaria	starwort	starwort, chickweed	genus
Stellaria americana	American starwort	American starwort, American chickweed	species
Stellaria borealis	boreal starwort	boreal starwort	species
Stellaria calycantha	northern starwort	northern starwort, northern stitchwort	species
Stellaria crassifolia	fleshy starwort	fleshy starwort, fleshy stitchwort	species
Stellaria crispa	wavyleaf starwort	crisp starwort, wavy-leaved chickweed	species
Stellaria longifolia	longleaf starwort	long-leaved starwort, long-leaved chickweed	species
Stellaria longipes	longstalk starwort	long-stalked starwort, long-stalked chickweed	species

ALPHABETICAL SCIENTIFIC NAMES

Scientific Name	Suggested Common Name	VASCAN and/or ACIMS Common Name(s)	Rank
Stellaria media	common starwort	common chickweed	species
Stellaria nitens	shiny starwort	shiny starwort	species
Stellaria obtusa	bluntsepal starwort	blunt-sepaled starwort, chickweed	species
Stellaria umbellata	umbellate starwort	umbellate starwort, chickweed	species
Stephanomeria	wirelettuce	wirelettuce	genus
Stephanomeria runcinata	sawtooth wirelettuce	sawtooth wirelettuce, rush-pink	species
Streptopus	twistedstalk	twistedstalk	genus
Streptopus amplexifolius	clasping-leaf twisted-stalk	clasping-leaved twisted-stalk	species
Streptopus lanceolatus	rose twisted-stalk	rose twisted-stalk, rose mandarin	species
Streptopus streptopoides	small twisted-stalk	small twisted-stalk, twisted-stalk	species
Stuckenia	slender-pondweed	pondweed	genus
Stuckenia filiformis	threadleaf pondweed	thread-leaved pondweed	species
Stuckenia pectinata	sago pondweed	sago pondweed	species
Stuckenia vaginata	sheathed pondweed	big-sheathed pondweed, large-sheath pondweed	species
Suaeda	seablite	seepweed, seablite	genus
Suaeda calceoliformis	western seablite	Pursh's seepweed, western sea-blite	species
Suaeda nigra	Moquin seablite	bush seepweed, Moquin's sea-blite	species
Suckleya	suckleya	suckleya	genus
Suckleya suckleyana	poison suckleya	poison suckleya	species
Suksdorfia	suksdorfia	suksdorfia	genus
Suksdorfia ranunculifolia	buttercup suksdorfia	buttercup-leaved suksdorfia, suksdorfia	species
Suksdorfia violacea	violet suksdorfia	violet suksdorfia, blue suksdorfia	species
Symphoricarpos	snowberry	snowberry	genus
Symphoricarpos albus	thinleaf snowberry	thin-leaved snowberry, snowberry	species
Symphoricarpos occidentalis	western snowberry	western snowberry, buckbrush	species
Symphyotrichum	American-aster, aster	aster	genus
Symphyotrichum ascendens	western aster	western aster	species
Symphyotrichum boreale	northern aster	rush aster, marsh aster	species
Symphyotrichum campestre	meadow aster	western meadow aster, meadow aster	species
Symphyotrichum ciliatum	rayless aster	rayless alkali aster, rayless aster	species
Symphyotrichum ciliolatum	Lindley aster	Lindley's aster	species
Symphyotrichum cusickii	Cusick aster	Cusick's aster	species
Symphyotrichum eatonii	Eaton aster	Eaton's aster	species
Symphyotrichum ericoides	tufted white prairie-aster	white heath aster, tufted white prairie aster	species
Symphyotrichum falcatum	creeping white prairie-aster	white prairie aster, creeping white prairie aster	species
Symphyotrichum firmum	glossyleaf aster	glossy-leaved aster	species
Symphyotrichum foliaceum	leafy aster	leafy aster, leafy-bracted aster	species

ALPHABETICAL SCIENTIFIC NAMES

Scientific Name	Suggested Common Name	VASCAN and/or ACIMS Common Name(s)	Rank
Symphyotrichum laeve	smooth aster	smooth aster	species
Symphyotrichum lanceolatum	lanceleaf aster	white panicled aster, western willow aster	species
Symphyotrichum puniceum	purplestem aster	purple-stemmed aster	species
Symphyotrichum spathulatum	western mountain aster	western mountain aster	species
Symphyotrichum subspicatum	Douglas aster	Douglas' aster, leafy-bracted aster	species
Symphytum	comfrey	comfrey	genus
Symphytum officinale	common comfrey	common comfrey, comfrey	species
Syringa	lilac	lilac	genus
Syringa vulgaris	common lilac	common lilac	species
Tanacetum	tansy	tansy	genus
Tanacetum bipinnatum	dwarf tansy	dwarf tansy, Lake Huron tansy	species
Tanacetum vulgare	common tansy	common tansy	species
Taraxacum	dandelion	dandelion	genus
Taraxacum ceratophorum	horned dandelion	horned dandelion, northern dandelion	species
Taraxacum erythrospermum	redseed dandelion	red-seeded dandelion	species
Taraxacum officinale	common dandelion	common dandelion	species
Taraxacum scopulorum	alpine dandelion	alpine dandelion	species
Taraxia	taraxia	taraxia	genus
Taraxia breviflora	taraxia	short-flowered evening primrose, taraxia	species
Taxaceae	yew family	yew family	family
Taxus	yew	yew	genus
Taxus brevifolia	western yew	western yew	species
Telesonix	brookfoam	brookfoam	genus
Telesonix heucheriformis	alumroot brookfoam	alumroot brookfoam, telesonix	species
Tellima	fringecup	fringecup	genus
Tellima grandiflora	bigflower fringecup	big-flowered tellima, fringe-cups	species
Tephroseris	marsh-groundsel	marsh-groundsel	genus
Tephroseris palustris	marsh-groundsel	marsh groundsel, marsh ragwort	species
Tetraneuris	four-nerve-daisy	four-nerve-daisy	genus
Tetraneuris acaulis	stemless four-nerve-daisy	stemless four-nerved daisy, butte marigold	species
Thalictrum	meadowrue	meadowrue	genus
Thalictrum dasycarpum	purple meadowrue	purple meadow-rue, tall meadow rue	species
Thalictrum occidentale	western meadowrue	western meadow-rue, western meadow rue	species
Thalictrum sparsiflorum	fewflower meadowrue	few-flowered meadow-rue, flat-fruited meadow rue	species

ALPHABETICAL SCIENTIFIC NAMES

Scientific Name	Suggested Common Name	VASCAN and/or ACIMS Common Name(s)	Rank
Thalictrum venulosum	veiny meadowrue	veiny meadow-rue, veiny meadow rue	species
Thelesperma	Navajo-tea, greenthread	Navajo tea, greenthread	genus
Thelesperma subnudum	hairless greenthread	Navajo tea, greenthread	species
Thelypteridaceae	marshfern family	marshfern family	family
Thermopsis	goldenbean	goldenbean	genus
Thermopsis rhombifolia	prairie goldenbean	prairie golden bean, golden bean	species
Thesium	thesium	thesium	genus
Thesium ramosum	thesium	field thesium, thesium	species
Thinopyrum	wheatgrass	wheatgrass	genus
Thinopyrum intermedium	intermediate wheatgrass	intermediate wheatgrass	species
Thinopyrum ponticum	tall wheatgrass	tall wheatgrass, rush wheatgrass	species
Thlaspi	pennycress	pennycress	genus
Thlaspi arvense	field pennycress	field pennycress, stinkweed	species
Thuja	red-cedar	red-cedar	genus
Thuja plicata	western red-cedar	western red cedar	species
Tiarella	foamflower	foamflower	genus
Tiarella trifoliata	threeleaf foamflower	three-leaved foamflower, laceflower	species
Tofieldia	false-asphodel	false-asphodel	genus
Tofieldia pusilla	dwarf false-asphodel	small tofieldia, dwarf false asphodel	species
Tofieldiaceae	false-asphodel family	false-asphodel family	family
Tomostima	creeping-draba	creeping-draba	genus
Tomostima reptans	creeping-draba	creeping draba	species
Tonestus	serpentweed	serpentweed	genus
Tonestus lyallii	Lyall serpentweed	Lyall's serpentweed, Lyall's ironplant	species
Torreyochloa	false-mannagrass	false-mannagrass	genus
Torreyochloa pallida	pale false-mannagrass	pale false mannagrass	species
Townsendia	townsendia	townsendia	genus
Townsendia condensata	alpine townsendia	alpine townsendia	species
Townsendia exscapa	stemless townsendia	stemless townsendia, low townsendia	species
Townsendia hookeri	Hooker townsendia	Hooker's townsendia	species
Townsendia parryi	Parry townsendia	Parry's townsendia	species
Toxicodendron	poison-ivy	poison-ivy	genus
Toxicodendron radicans	poison-ivy	poison ivy	species
Toxicoscordion	meadow-deathcamas	meadow-deathcamas	genus
Toxicoscordion venenosum	meadow-deathcamas	meadow death camas, death camas	species
Tradescantia	spiderwort	spiderwort	genus
Tradescantia occidentalis	western spiderwort	western spiderwort	species
Tragopogon	goatsbeard	goatsbeard	genus

ALPHABETICAL SCIENTIFIC NAMES

Scientific Name	Suggested Common Name	VASCAN and/or ACIMS Common Name(s)	Rank
Tragopogon dubius	common goatsbeard	yellow goatsbeard, common goat's-beard	species
Tragopogon porrifolius	purple goatsbeard	purple goatsbeard, common salsify	species
Tragopogon pratensis	meadow goatsbeard	meadow goatsbeard, meadow goat's-beard	species
Transberingia	fissurewort	fissurewort, mouse-ear-cress	species
Triantha	sticky false-asphodel	false-asphodel	genus
Triantha glutinosa	Scotch false-asphodel	sticky tofieldia, sticky false asphodel	species
Triantha occidentalis	western false-asphodel	western tofieldia, western false asphodel	species
Trichophorum	clubrush	clubrush	genus
Trichophorum alpinum	alpine clubrush	alpine clubrush, Hudson Bay bulrush	species
Trichophorum cespitosum	tufted clubrush	tufted clubrush, tufted bulrush	species
Trichophorum clintonii	Clinton clubrush	Clinton's clubrush, Clinton's bulrush	species
Trichophorum pumilum	dwarf clubrush	dwarf clubrush, dwarf bulrush	species
Trifolium	clover	clover	genus
Trifolium aureum	yellow clover	yellow clover	species
Trifolium hybridum	alsike clover	alsike clover	species
Trifolium pratense	red clover	red clover	species
Trifolium repens	white clover	white clover	species
Triglochin	arrowgrass	arrowgrass, flowering-quillwort	genus
Triglochin maritima	seaside arrowgrass	seaside arrowgrass, seaside arrow-grass	species
Triglochin palustris	marsh arrowgrass	marsh arrowgrass, slender arrow-grass	species
Triglochin scilloides	flowering-quillwort	flowering-quillwort	species
Trigonella	fenugreek	fenugreek	genus
Trigonella caerulea	blue fenugreek	blue fenugreek, trigonella	species
Trillium	trillium	trillium	genus
Trillium ovatum	western trillium	western trillium, western wakerobin	species
Tripleurospermum	chamomile	chamomile	genus
Tripleurospermum inodorum	scentless chamomile	scentless chamomile	species
Tripterocalyx	sand-verbena	sand-verbena	genus
Tripterocalyx micranthus	smallflower sand-verbena	small-flowered sand-verbena, sand verbena	species
Trisetum	trisetum	trisetum	genus
Trisetum cernuum	nodding trisetum	nodding trisetum	species
Trisetum flavescens	yellow trisetum	yellow false oat, yellow trisetum	species
Trisetum spicatum	spike trisetum	spike trisetum	species
Trisetum wolfii	Wolf trisetum	Wolf's trisetum, awnless trisetum	species
Triticum	wheat	wheat	genus

ALPHABETICAL SCIENTIFIC NAMES

Scientific Name	Suggested Common Name	VASCAN and/or ACIMS Common Name(s)	Rank
Triticum aestivum	common wheat	common wheat	species
Triticum durum	durum wheat	durum wheat	species
Trollius	globeflower	globeflower	genus
Trollius albiflorus	white globeflower	white globeflower, globeflower	species
Tsuga	hemlock	hemlock	genus
Tsuga heterophylla	western hemlock	western hemlock	species
Turritis	towermustard	towermustard	genus
Turritis glabra	towermustard	tower mustard	species
Typha	cattail	cattail	genus
Typha latifolia	broadleaf cattail	broad-leaved cattail, common cattail	species
Typhaceae	cattail family	cattail family	family
Ulmaceae	elm family	elm family	family
Ulmus	elm	elm	genus
Ulmus americana	American elm	white elm, American elm	species
Urtica	nettle	nettle	genus
Urtica dioica	stinging nettle	stinging nettle, common nettle	species
Urtica urens	burning nettle	burning nettle, small nettle	species
Urticaceae	nettle family	nettle family	family
Utricularia	bladderwort	bladderwort	genus
Utricularia cornuta	horned bladderwort	horned bladderwort	species
Utricularia intermedia	flatleaf bladderwort	flat-leaved bladderwort	species
Utricularia minor	lesser bladderwort	lesser bladderwort, small bladderwort	species
Utricularia ochroleuca	yellowish-white bladderwort	yellowish-white bladderwort, northern bladderwort	species
Utricularia vulgaris	common bladderwort	common bladderwort	species
Vaccaria	cowcockle	cowcockle	genus
Vaccaria hispanica	cowcockle	cowcockle, cow cockle	species
Vaccinium	blueberry, bilberry, cranberry	blueberry, bilberry, cranberry	genus
Vaccinium cespitosum	dwarf bilberry	dwarf bilberry	species
Vaccinium membranaceum	tall bilberry	mountain huckleberry, tall bilberry	species
Vaccinium microcarpum	small bog cranberry	small bog cranberry	species
Vaccinium myrtilloides	velvetleaf blueberry	velvet-leaved blueberry, common blueberry	species
Vaccinium myrtillus	low bilberry	myrtle whortleberry, low bilberry	species
Vaccinium ovalifolium	ovalleaf blueberry	oval-leaved blueberry	species
Vaccinium oxycoccos	small cranberry	small cranberry, small bog cranberry	species
Vaccinium scoparium	grouse bilberry	grouseberry	species
Vaccinium uliginosum	bog blueberry	bog bilberry	species
Vaccinium vitis-idaea	mountain cranberry	mountain cranberry, bog cranberry	species

ALPHABETICAL SCIENTIFIC NAMES

Scientific Name	Suggested Common Name	VASCAN and/or ACIMS Common Name(s)	Rank
Vahlodea	hairgrass	hairgrass	genus
Vahlodea atropurpurea	mountain hairgrass	mountain hairgrass, mountain hair grass	species
Valeriana	valerian	valerian	genus
Valeriana dioica	northern valerian	marsh valerian, northern valerian	species
Valeriana sitchensis	Sitka valerian	Sitka valerian, mountain valerian	species
Ventenata	North-Africa-grass	North-Africa-grass	genus
Ventenata dubia	North-Africa-grass	ventenata	species
Veratrum	false-hellebore	false-hellebore	genus
Veratrum viride	green false-hellebore	green false hellebore	species
Verbascum	mullein	mullein	genus
Verbascum nigrum	black mullein	black mullein	species
Verbascum phlomoides	orange mullein	clasping mullein, orange mullein, woolly mullein	species
Verbascum thapsus	common mullein	common mullein	species
Verbena	vervain	vervain	genus
Verbena bracteata	bracted vervain	large-bracted vervain, carpet vervain	species
Verbenaceae	vervain family	vervain family	family
Veronica	speedwell, kittentails	speedwell, kittentails	genus
Veronica agrestis	field speedwell	field speedwell, prostrate speedwell	species
Veronica americana	American speedwell	American speedwell, American brooklime	species
Veronica anagallis-aquatica	water speedwell	water speedwell, speedwell	species
Veronica catenata	stalkless water speedwell		species
Veronica chamaedrys	germander speedwell	germander speedwell	species
Veronica longifolia	longleaf speedwell	long-leaved speedwell, spiked speedwell	species
Veronica nutans	alpine speedwell	Wormskjold's alpine speedwell, alpine speedwell	species
Veronica peregrina	hairy speedwell	purslane speedwell, hairy speedwell	species
Veronica persica	birdeye speedwell	bird's-eye speedwell, bird's-eye	species
Veronica scutellata	marsh speedwell	marsh speedwell	species
Veronica serpyllifolia	thymeleaf speedwell	thyme-leaved speedwell	species
Veronica verna	spring speedwell	spring speedwell	species
Veronica wyomingensis	kittentails	Wyoming kitten-tails, kittentails	species
Viburnum	bush-cranberry	bush-cranberry	genus
Viburnum edule	low bush-cranberry	squashberry, low-bush cranberry	species
Viburnum opulus	high bush-cranberry	cranberry viburnum, high-bush cranberry	species
Vicia	vetch	vetch	genus

ALPHABETICAL SCIENTIFIC NAMES

Scientific Name	Suggested Common Name	VASCAN and/or ACIMS Common Name(s)	Rank
Vicia americana	America vetch	American vetch, wild vetch	species
Vicia cracca	tufted vetch	tufted vetch	species
Viola	violet, pansy	violet, pansy	genus
Viola adunca	early blue violet	hooked violet, early blue violet	species
Viola arvensis	European field pansy	European field pansy	species
Viola canadensis	Canada violet	Canada violet, western Canada violet	species
Viola epipsila	northern marsh violet	northern marsh violet	species
Viola glabella	yellow wood violet	stream violet, yellow wood violet	species
Viola macloskeyi	small white violet	Macloskey's violet, small white violet	species
Viola nephrophylla	northern bog violet	northern bog violet, bog violet	species
Viola nuttallii	Nuttall violet	Nuttall's violet, yellow prairie violet	species
Viola orbiculata	evergreen violet	western round-leaved violet, evergreen violet	species
Viola palustris	marsh violet	alpine marsh violet, marsh violet	species
Viola pedatifida	crowfoot violet	prairie violet, crowfoot violet	species
Viola praemorsa	canary violet	yellow montane violet, canary violet, broad leaved yellow prairie violet	species
Viola renifolia	kidneyleaf violet	kidney-leaved violet	species
Viola selkirkii	Selkirk violet	Selkirk's violet, great-spurred violet	species
Viola tricolor	pansy violet	Johnny-jump-up, pansy	species
Viola vallicola	valley violet	valley violet	species
Violaceae	violet family	violet family	family
Vulpia	six-week-fescue	six-week-fescue	genus
Vulpia octoflora	six-week-fescue	eight-flowered fescue, six-weeks fescue	species
Wolffia	watermeal	watermeal	genus
Wolffia borealis	northern watermeal	northern watermeal	species
Wolffia columbiana	Columbia watermeal	Columbia watermeal	species
Woodsia	woodsia	woodsia	genus
Woodsia glabella	smooth woodsia	smooth woodsia	species
Woodsia ilvensis	rusty woodsia	rusty woodsia	species
Woodsia oregana	Oregon woodsia	Oregon woodsia	species
Woodsia scopulina	mountain woodsia	mountain woodsia	species
Woodsiaceae	cliff-fern family	cliff-fern family	family
Xanthisma	ironplant	ironplant	genus
Xanthisma grindelioides	toothed ironplant	rayless tansy-aster, toothed ironplant	species
Xanthisma spinulosum	spiny ironplant	lacy tansy-aster, spiny ironplant	species
Xanthium	cocklebur	cocklebur	genus
Xanthium strumarium	rough cocklebur	rough cockleburr, cocklebur	species

ALPHABETICAL SCIENTIFIC NAMES

Scientific Name	Suggested Common Name	VASCAN and/or ACIMS Common Name(s)	Rank
Xerophyllum	beargrass	beargrass	genus
Xerophyllum tenax	beargrass	beargrass	species
Yucca	yucca	yucca	genus
Yucca glauca	soapweed yucca	soapweed yucca, soapweed	species
Zannichellia	horned-pondweed	horned-pondweed	genus
Zannichellia palustris	horned-pondweed	horned pondweed	species
Zizania	wildrice	wildrice	genus
Zizania aquatica	annual wildrice	southern wildrice, wild rice	species
Zizania palustris	northern wildrice	northern wildrice, northern wild rice	species
Zizia	alexanders	alexanders	genus
Zizia aptera	heartleaf alexanders	heart-leaved alexanders	species

ALPHABETIZED* COMMON NAMES

Suggested Common Name	VASCAN &/or ACIMS Common Name(s)	Scientific Name	Rank
* Suggested Common Names for species are presented with the second name followed by a comma and then the first name, to simplify the alphabetical listing.			
adder's-mouth	adder's-mouth	Malaxis	genus
adder's-mouth, bog	bog adder's-mouth	Malaxis paludosa	species
adder's-mouth, white	white adder's-mouth	Malaxis monophyllos	species
adder's-tongue family	adder's-tongue family	Ophioglossaceae	family
agrimony	agrimony	Agrimonia	genus
agrimony, woodland	woodland agrimony, agrimony	Agrimonia striata	species
alder	alder	Alnus	genus
alder, green	green alder	Alnus alnobetula/viridis	species
alder, grey	grey alder, alder	Alnus incana	species
alderleaf-buckthorn	alderleaved buckthorn	Endotropis	genus
alderleaf-buckthorn	alder-leaved buckthorn	Endotropis alnifolia	species
alexanders	alexanders	Zizia	genus
alexanders, heartleaf	heart-leaved alexanders	Zizia aptera	species
alfalfa	alfalfa, medick	Medicago	genus
alfalfa	alfalfa	Medicago sativa	species
alkaligrass	alkaligrass	Puccinellia	genus
alkaligrass, Nuttall	Nuttall's alkaligrass, Nuttall's salt-meadow grass	Puccinellia nuttalliana	species
alkaligrass, spreading	spreading alkaligrass, slender salt-meadow grass	Puccinellia distans	species
alpine-bearberry	alpine-bearberry	Arctous	genus
alpine-bearberry	red bearberry, alpine bearberry	Arctous rubra	species
alumroot	alumroot	Heuchera	genus
alumroot, alpine	smooth alumroot, alpine alumroot	Heuchera glabra	species
alumroot, littleleaf	little-leaved alumroot, small-leaved alumroot	Heuchera parvifolia	species
alumroot, Richardson	Richardson's alumroot	Heuchera richardsonii	species
alumroot, roundleaf	round-leaved alumroot, sticky alumroot	Heuchera cylindrica	species
alyssum	alyssum	Alyssum	genus
alyssum, desert	desert alyssum	Alyssum desertorum	species
alyssum, desert	desert alyssum	Alyssum turkestanicum	species
alyssum, small	small alyssum	Alyssum alyssoides	species
amaranth	amaranth	Amaranthus	genus
amaranth family	amaranth family	Amaranthaceae	family
amaranth, Californian	California amaranth, Californian amaranth	Amaranthus californicus	species
amaranth, Powell	Powell's amaranth	Amaranthus powellii	species
amaranth, prostrate	prostrate amaranth	Amaranthus blitoides	species
amaranth, redroot	redroot amaranth, red-root pigweed	Amaranthus retroflexus	species
amaranth, white	white amaranth	Amaranthus albus	species
amaryllis family	amaryllis family	Amaryllidaceae	family

ALPHABETIZED* COMMON NAMES

Suggested Common Name	VASCAN &/or ACIMS Common Name(s)	Scientific Name	Rank
American-aster	American-aster, aster	Symphyotrichum	genus
anemone	anemone	Anemonastrum	genus
anemone	anemone	Anemone	genus
anemone, Canada	Canada anemone	Anemonastrum canadense	species
anemone, Canada	Canada anemone	Anemone canadensis	species
anemone, candle	long-headed anemone, candle anemone	Anemone cylindrica	species
anemone, cutleaf	cut-leaved anemone	Anemone multifida	species
anemone, Drummond	Drummond's anemone	Anemone drummondii	species
anemone, narcissus	one-flowered anemone, narcissus anemone	Anemonastrum sibiricum	species
anemone, narcissus	one-flowered anemone, narcissus anemone	Anemone narcissiflora	species
anemone, smallflower	small-flowered anemone, small wood anemone	Anemone parviflora	species
anemone, tall	tall anemone, Virginia anemone	Anemone virginiana	species
anemone, wood	wood anemone	Anemone quinquefolia	species
anemone, yellow	Richardson's anemone, yellow anemone	Anemonastrum richardsonii	species
anemone, yellow	Richardson's anemone, yellow anemone	Anemone richardsonii	species
angelica	angelica	Angelica	genus
angelica, Dawson	Dawson's angelica, yellow angelica	Angelica dawsonii	species
angelica, kneeling	kneeling angelica	Angelica genuflexa	species
angelica, white	sharp-toothed angelica, white angelica	Angelica arguta	species
arnica	arnica	Arnica	genus
arnica, alpine	narrow-leaved arnica, alpine arnica	Arnica angustifolia	species
arnica, broadleaf	broad-leaved arnica	Arnica latifolia	species
arnica, Chamisso	Chamisso's arnica, leafy arnica	Arnica chamissonis	species
arnica, graceful	slender arnica, graceful arnica	Arnica gracilis	species
arnica, hairy	hairy arnica, cordilleran arnica	Arnica mollis	species
arnica, heartleaf	heart-leaved arnica	Arnica cordifolia	species
arnica, Lake Louise	Lake Louise arnica	Arnica louiseana	species
arnica, lanceleaf	lance-leaved arnica, lanceleaf arnica	Arnica lanceolata	species
arnica, longleaf	long-leaved arnica	Arnica longifolia	species
arnica, Parry	Parry's arnica, nodding arnica	Arnica parryi	species
arnica, Rydberg	Rydberg's arnica, narrow-leaved arnica	Arnica rydbergii	species
arnica, shining	hillside arnica, shining arnica	Arnica fulgens	species
arnica, spearleaf	spear-leaved arnica	Arnica lonchophylla	species

ALPHABETIZED* COMMON NAMES

Suggested Common Name	VASCAN &/or ACIMS Common Name(s)	Scientific Name	Rank
arnica, sticky	sticky arnica, lawless arnica	Arnica ovata	species
arnica, twin	twin arnica	Arnica sororia	species
arrowgrass	arrowgrass, flowering-qullwort	Triglochin	genus
arrowgrass family	arrowgrass family	Juncaginaceae	family
arrowgrass, marsh	marsh arrowgrass, slender arrow-grass	Triglochin palustris	species
arrowgrass, seaside	seaside arrowgrass, seaside arrow-grass	Triglochin maritima	species
arrowhead	arrowhead	Sagittaria	genus
arrowhead, arumleaf	northern arrowhead, arum-leaved arrowhead	Sagittaria cuneata	species
arrowhead, broadleaf	broad-leaved arrowhead	Sagittaria latifolia	species
arum family	arum family	Araceae	family
ash	ash	Fraxinus	genus
ash, green	red ash, green ash	Fraxinus pennsylvanica	species
asparagus	asparagus	Asparagus	genus
asparagus family	asparagus family	Asparagaceae	family
asparagus, garden	garden asparagus, asparagus	Asparagus officinalis	species
aspen	aspen, poplar, cottonwood	Populus	genus
aspen, trembling	trembling aspen, aspen	Populus tremuloides	species
aster	aster	Aster	genus
aster	aster	Eucephalus	genus
aster	aster, American-aster	Symphyotrichum	genus
aster family	aster family	Asteraceae	family
aster, alpine	alpine aster	Aster alpinus	species
aster, Cusick	Cusick's aster	Symphyotrichum cusickii	species
aster, Douglas	Douglas' aster, leafy-bracted aster	Symphyotrichum subspicatum	species
aster, Eaton	Eaton's aster	Symphyotrichum eatonii	species
aster, Engelmann	Engelmann's aster, elegant aster	Eucephalus engelmannii	species
aster, glossyleaf	glossy-leaved aster	Symphyotrichum firmum	species
aster, lanceleaf	white panicled aster, western willow aster	Symphyotrichum lanceolatum	species
aster, leafy	leafy aster, leafy-bracted aster	Symphyotrichum foliaceum	species
aster, Lindley	Lindley's aster	Symphyotrichum ciliolatum	species
aster, meadow	western meadow aster, meadow aster	Symphyotrichum campestre	species
aster, northern	rush aster, marsh aster	Symphyotrichum boreale	species
aster, purplestem	purple-stemmed aster	Symphyotrichum puniceum	species
aster, rayless	rayless alkali aster, rayless aster	Symphyotrichum ciliatum	species
aster, smooth	smooth aster	Symphyotrichum laeve	species
aster, western	western aster	Symphyotrichum ascendens	species
aster, western mountain	western mountain aster	Symphyotrichum spathulatum	species

ALPHABETIZED* COMMON NAMES

Suggested Common Name	VASCAN &/or ACIMS Common Name(s)	Scientific Name	Rank
avens	avens	Geum	genus
avens, largeleaf	large-leaved avens, large-leaved yellow avens	Geum macrophyllum	species
avens, purple	water avens, purple avens	Geum rivale	species
avens, threeflower	three-flowered avens	Geum triflorum	species
avens, yellow	yellow avens	Geum aleppicum	species
baby-blue-eyes	baby-blue-eyes	Nemophila	genus
baby-blue-eyes, small	Great Basin nemophila, small baby-blue-eyes	Nemophila breviflora	species
baby's-breath	baby's-breath	Gypsophila	genus
baby's-breath, annual	showy baby's-breath, annual baby's-breath	Gypsophila elegans	species
baby's-breath, glandular	glandular baby's-breath, pink baby's-breath	Gypsophila scorzonerifolia	species
baby's-breath, tall	tall baby's-breath, common baby's-breath	Gypsophila paniculata	species
ballmustard	ballmustard	Neslia	genus
ballmustard, yellow	yellow ball-mustard, ball mustard	Neslia paniculata	species
balsam family	balsam family	Balsaminaceae	family
balsamroot	balsamroot	Balsamorhiza	genus
balsamroot, arrowleaf	arrow-leaved balsamroot,	Balsamorhiza sagittata	species
baneberry	baneberry	Actaea	genus
baneberry, red	red baneberry, red and white baneberry	Actaea rubra	species
barberry	barberry	Berberis	genus
barberry	barberry	Mahonia	genus
barberry family	barberry family	Berberidaceae	family
barberry, common	common barberry	Berberis vulgaris	species
barberry, creeping	creeping barberry, creeping mahonia	Mahonia repens	species
barley	barley	Hordeum	genus
barley, common	common barley, cultivated barley	Hordeum vulgare	species
barley, foxtail	foxtail barley	Hordeum jubatum	species
barley, little	little barley	Hordeum pusillum	species
barley, meadow	meadow barley	Hordeum brachyantherum	species
barley, mouse	mouse barley	Hordeum murinum	species
barnyardgrass	barnyardgrass	Echinochloa	genus
barnyardgrass, large	large barnyard grass, barnyard grass	Echinochloa crus-galli	species
barnyardgrass, rough	rough barnyard grass, rough barnyard grass	Echinochloa muricata	species
bartsia	bartsia	Odontites	genus
bartsia, red	red bartsia, late-flowering eyebright	Odontites vulgaris	species
bassia	bassia, summer-cypress	Bassia	genus

ALPHABETIZED* COMMON NAMES

Suggested Common Name	VASCAN &/or ACIMS Common Name(s)	Scientific Name	Rank
bassia, fivehook	five-hooked bassia, five-hook bassia	Bassia hyssopifolia	species
bastard-toadflax	bastard-toadflax	Comandra	genus
bastard-toadflax	bastard toadflax, common comandra	Comandra umbellata	species
beakrush	beakrush	Rhynchospora	genus
beakrush, slender	slender beakrush, slender beak-rush	Rhynchospora capillacea	species
bearberry	bearberry	Arctostaphylos	genus
bearberry, common	common bearberry	Arctostaphylos uva-ursi	species
beardtongue	beardtongue	Penstemon	genus
beardtongue, Alberta	Alberta beardtongue, blue beardtongue	Penstemon albertinus	species
beardtongue, fuzzytongue	fuzzy-tongue beardtongue, crested beardtongue	Penstemon eriantherus	species
beardtongue, lilac	slender beardtongue, lilac-flowered beardtongue	Penstemon gracilis	species
beardtongue, Lyall	Lyall's beardtongue, large-flowered beardtongue	Penstemon lyallii	species
beardtongue, rocky-ledge	elliptic-leaved beardtongue, rocky-ledge penstemon	Penstemon ellipticus	species
beardtongue, shrubby	shrubby beardtongue	Penstemon fruticosus	species
beardtongue, smallflower	small-flowered beardtongue, slender blue beardtongue	Penstemon procerus	species
beardtongue, waxleaf	wax-leaved beardtongue, smooth blue beardtongue	Penstemon nitidus	species
beardtongue, white	white beardtongue	Penstemon albidus	species
beardtongue, yellow	lesser yellow beardtongue, yellow beardtongue	Penstemon confertus	species
beargrass	beargrass	Xerophyllum	genus
beargrass	beargrass	Xerophyllum tenax	species
bedstraw	bedstraw	Galium	genus
bedstraw family	bedstraw family	Rubiaceae	family
bedstraw, cleavers	common bedstraw, cleavers	Galium aparine	species
bedstraw, Labrador	Labrador bedstraw	Galium labradoricum	species
bedstraw, northern	northern bedstraw	Galium boreale	species
bedstraw, sweetscented	three-flowered bedstraw, sweet-scented bedstraw	Galium triflorum	species
bedstraw, threepetal	three-petalled bedstraw, small bedstraw	Galium trifidum	species
bedstraw, twinleaf	thin-leaved bedstraw, two-leaved bedstraw	Galium bifolium	species
bedstraw, yellow	yellow bedstraw	Galium verum	species
beeblossom	evening-primrose, beeblossom	Oenothera	genus
beeblossom, scarlet	scarlet gaura/beeblossom, scarlet butterflyweed	Oenothera suffrutescens	species

ALPHABETIZED* COMMON NAMES

Suggested Common Name	VASCAN &/or ACIMS Common Name(s)	Scientific Name	Rank
beechfern	beechfern	Phegopteris	genus
beechfern, northern	northern beech fern	Phegopteris connectilis	species
beeplant	beeplant	Peritoma	genus
beeplant, Rocky Mountain	Rocky Mountain beeplant, bee plant	Peritoma serrulata	species
beggarticks	beggarticks	Bidens	genus
beggarticks, devil	devil's beggarticks, common beggarticks	Bidens frondosa	species
beggarticks, nodding	nodding beggarticks	Bidens cernua	species
beggarticks, tall	tall beggarticks	Bidens vulgata	species
beggarticks, threepart	three-parted beggarticks, tall beggarticks	Bidens tripartita	species
bellflower	bellflower	Campanula	genus
bellflower family	bellflower family	Campanulaceae	family
bellflower, Alaska	Alaska bellflower, harebell	Campanula alaskana	species
bellflower, clustered	clustered bellflower	Campanula glomerata	species
bellflower, creeping	creeping bellflower	Campanula rapunculoides	species
bellflower, marsh	marsh bellflower	Campanula aparinoides	species
bellflower, mountain	mountain bellflower, Alaska harebell	Campanula lasiocarpa	species
bentgrass	bentgrass	Agrostis	genus
bentgrass	bentgrass	Podagrostis	genus
bentgrass, creeping	creeping bentgrass, redtop	Agrostis stolonifera	species
bentgrass, giant	redtop, giant bentgrass	Agrostis gigantea	species
bentgrass, low	alpine bentgrass, low bent grass	Podagrostis humilis	species
bentgrass, mountain	mountain bentgrass, alpine redtop	Agrostis variabilis	species
bentgrass, northern	northern bentgrass, northern bent grass	Agrostis mertensii	species
bentgrass, rough	rough bentgrass, rough hair grass	Agrostis scabra	species
bentgrass, spike	spike bentgrass, spike redtop	Agrostis exarata	species
bergamot	bergamot	Monarda	genus
bergamot, wild	wild bergamot	Monarda fistulosa	species
bilberry	bilberry, blueberry, cranberry	Vaccinium	genus
bilberry, dwarf	dwarf bilberry	Vaccinium cespitosum	species
bilberry, grouse	grouseberry	Vaccinium scoparium	species
bilberry, low	myrtle whortleberry, low bilberry	Vaccinium myrtillus	species
bilberry, tall	mountain huckleberry, tall bilberry	Vaccinium membranaceum	species
bindweed	bindweed	Convolvulus	genus
bindweed family	bindweed family	Convolvulaceae	family
bindweed, field	field bindweed	Convolvulus arvensis	species
birch	birch	Betula	genus
birch family	birch family	Betulaceae	family
birch, Alaska paper	Alaska paper birch, Alaska birch	Betula neoalaskana	species

222

ALPHABETIZED* COMMON NAMES

Suggested Common Name	VASCAN &/or ACIMS Common Name(s)	Scientific Name	Rank
birch, arctic dwarf	arctic dwarf birch	Betula nana	species
birch, dwarf	bog birch, dwarf birch	Betula pumila	species
birch, glandular	glandular birch, bog birch	Betula glandulosa	species
birch, paper	paper birch, white birch	Betula papyrifera	species
birch, water	water birch	Betula occidentalis	species
birdsfoot-trefoil	birdsfoot-trefoil	Lotus	genus
birdsfoot-trefoil	garden bird's-foot trefoil, bird's-foot trefoil	Lotus corniculatus	species
bistort	bistort	Bistorta	genus
bistort, alpine	alpine bistort	Bistorta vivipara	species
bistort, western	western bistort	Bistorta bistortoides	species
bittercress	bittercress	Cardamine	genus
bittercress, alpine	alpine bittercress, alpine bitter cress	Cardamine bellidifolia	species
bittercress, northern field	Nyman's bittercress, northern field bittercress	Cardamine polemonoides	species
bittercress, Pennsylvania	Pennsylvania bittercress	Cardamine pensylvanica	species
bittercress, smallflower	small-flowered bittercress, small bittercress	Cardamine parviflora	species
bittercress, toothed	toothed bittercress	Cardamine dentata	species
bittercress, umbel	umbel bittercress, mountain cress	Cardamine umbellata	species
bittersweet family	bittersweet family	Celastraceae	family
bitterweed	bitterweed	Hymenoxys	genus
bitterweed, Richardson	Richardson's bitterweed, Colorado rubber-plant	Hymenoxys richardsonii	species
black-eyed-Susan	black-eyed-Susan	Rudbeckia	genus
black-eyed-Susan	black-eyed Susan	Rudbeckia hirta	species
bladder-campion, common	bladder campion	Silene vulgaris	species
bladder-campion, white	white campion, white cockle, bladder campion	Silene latifolia	species
bladderfern	bladderfern	Cystopteris	genus
bladderfern family	bladderfern family	Cystopteridaceae	family
bladderfern, fragile	fragile fern, fragile bladder fern	Cystopteris fragilis	species
bladderfern, mountain	mountain bladder fern	Cystopteris montana	species
bladderpod	bladderpod	Physaria	genus
bladderpod, arctic	arctic bladderpod	Physaria arctica	species
bladderpod, double	common twinpod, double bladderpod	Physaria didymocarpa	species
bladderpod, Great Plains	Great Plains bladderpod	Physaria arenosa	species
bladderpod, spatulate	spatulate bladderpod	Physaria spatulata	species
bladderwort	bladderwort	Utricularia	genus
bladderwort family	bladderwort family	Lentibulariaceae	family
bladderwort, common	common bladderwort	Utricularia vulgaris	species
bladderwort, flatleaf	flat-leaved bladderwort	Utricularia intermedia	species

ALPHABETIZED* COMMON NAMES

Suggested Common Name	VASCAN &/or ACIMS Common Name(s)	Scientific Name	Rank
bladderwort, horned	horned bladderwort	Utricularia cornuta	species
bladderwort, lesser	lesser bladderwort, small bladderwort	Utricularia minor	species
bladderwort, yellow-white	yellowish-white bladderwort, northern bladderwort	Utricularia ochroleuca	species
blanketflower	blanketflower	Gaillardia	genus
blanketflower, great	great blanketflower, gaillardia	Gaillardia aristata	species
blazingstar	blazingstar	Liatris	genus
blazingstar	blazingstar	Mentzelia	genus
blazingstar, dotted	dotted blazing-star, dotted blazingstar	Liatris punctata	species
blazingstar, meadow	meadow blazing-star, meadow blazingstar	Liatris ligulistylis	species
blazingstar, tenpetal	ten-petalled blazing star, sand-lily	Mentzelia decapetala	species
bluebells	bluebells	Mertensia	genus
bluebells, lanceleaf	lance-leaved bluebells, lance-leaved lungwort	Mertensia lanceolata	species
bluebells, longflower	long-flowered bluebells, large-flowered lungwort	Mertensia longiflora	species
bluebells, tall	tall bluebells, tall lungwort	Mertensia paniculata	species
blueberry	blueberry, bilberry, cranberry	Vaccinium	genus
blueberry, bog	bog bilberry	Vaccinium uliginosum	species
blueberry, ovalleaf	oval-leaved blueberry	Vaccinium ovalifolium	species
blueberry, velvetleaf	velvet-leaved blueberry, common blueberry	Vaccinium myrtilloides	species
blue-eyed-grass	blue-eyed-grass	Sisyrinchium	genus
blue-eyed-grass, common	strict blue-eyed grass, common blue-eyed grass	Sisyrinchium montanum	species
blue-eyed-grass, pale	northern blue-eyed-grass, pale blue-eyed grass	Sisyrinchium septentrionale	species
blue-eyed-Mary	blue-eyed-Mary	Collinsia	genus
blue-eyed-Mary, smallflower	small-flowered blue-eyed Mary, blue-eyed Mary	Collinsia parviflora	species
bluegrass	bluegrass	Poa	genus
bluegrass, alpine	alpine bluegrass	Poa alpina	species
bluegrass, annual	annual bluegrass	Poa annua	species
bluegrass, Arctic	arctic bluegrass	Poa arctica	species
bluegrass, bulbous	bulbous bluegrass	Poa bulbosa	species
bluegrass, Canada	Canada bluegrass	Poa compressa	species
bluegrass, Cusick	Cusick's bluegrass, early bluegrass	Poa cusickii	species
bluegrass, Fendler	Fendler's bluegrass	Poa fendleriana	species
bluegrass, fewflower	few-flowered bluegrass	Poa paucispicula	species
bluegrass, fowl	fowl bluegrass	Poa palustris	species

ALPHABETIZED* COMMON NAMES

Suggested Common Name	VASCAN &/or ACIMS Common Name(s)	Scientific Name	Rank
bluegrass, glaucous	glaucous bluegrass, timberline bluegrass	Poa glauca	species
bluegrass, inland	inland bluegrass	Poa interior	species
bluegrass, Kentucky	Kentucky bluegrass	Poa pratensis	species
bluegrass, lax	lax bluegrass	Poa laxa	species
bluegrass, Letterman	Letterman's bluegrass	Poa lettermanii	species
bluegrass, narrowflower	narrow-flowered bluegrass	Poa stenantha	species
bluegrass, plains	plains bluegrass	Poa arida	species
bluegrass, rough	rough bluegrass	Poa trivialis	species
bluegrass, Sandberg	Sandberg's bluegrass, Sandberg bluegrass	Poa secunda	species
bluegrass, short	abbreviated bluegrass, northern bluegrass	Poa abbreviata	species
bluegrass, western bog	western bog bluegrass, bog bluegrass	Poa leptocoma	species
bluegrass, Wheeler	Wheeler's bluegrass	Poa wheeleri	species
bluegrass, wood	Eurasian woodland bluegrass, wood bluegrass	Poa nemoralis	species
blue-lettuce	blue-lettuce	Mulgedium	genus
blue-lettuce	blue lettuce, common blue lettuce	Mulgedium pulchellum	species
blue-mustard	blue-mustard	Chorispora	genus
blue-mustard	blue mustard	Chorispora tenella	species
bluets	bluets	Houstonia	genus
bluets, longleaf	long-leaved bluets	Houstonia longifolia	species
bog-clubmoss	bog-clubmoss	Lycopodiella	genus
bog-clubmoss, flooded	northern bog clubmoss, bog club-moss	Lycopodiella inundata	species
bog-orchid	rein orchid, bog orchid	Platanthera	genus
bog-orchid, Alaska	Alaska rein orchid, Alaska bog orchid	Platanthera unalascensis	species
bog-orchid, bluntleaf	blunt-leaved orchid, blunt-leaved bog orchid	Platanthera obtusata	species
bog-orchid, lesser roundleaf	lesser round-leaved orchid, round-leaved bog orchid	Platanthera orbiculata	species
bog-orchid, slender	slender bog orchid	Platanthera stricta	species
bog-orchid, tall white	tall white bog orchid	Platanthera dilatata	species
bog-rosemary	bog-rosemary	Andromeda	genus
bog-rosemary	bog rosemary	Andromeda polifolia	species
bogsedge, mousetail	mouse-tail bog sedge, bog-sedge	Carex myosuroides	species
bog-sedge, simple	simple bog sedge, simple bog-sedge	Carex simpliciuscula	species
borage	borage	Borago	genus
borage family	borage family	Boraginaceae	family
borage, common	common borage, oxtongue	Borago officinalis	species

ALPHABETIZED* COMMON NAMES

Suggested Common Name	VASCAN &/or ACIMS Common Name(s)	Scientific Name	Rank
bouncingbet	bouncingbet	Saponaria	genus
bouncingbet	bouncing-bet, soapwort	Saponaria officinalis	species
brackenfern	brackenfern	Pteridium	genus
brackenfern	bracken fern	Pteridium aquilinum	species
brackenfern family	brackenfern family	Dennstaedtiaceae	family
braya	braya	Braya	genus
braya, low	low braya	Braya humilis	species
braya, purple	purple braya	Braya purpurascens	species
braya, smooth	smooth braya	Braya glabella	species
breadroot	breadroot	Pediomelum	genus
breadroot, large	large Indian breadroot, Indian breadroot	Pediomelum esculentum	species
breadroot, silverleaf	silver-leaved Indian breadroot, silverleaf psoralea	Pediomelum argophyllum	species
brickellia	brickellia	Brickellia	genus
brickellia, largeflower	large-flowered brickellia	Brickellia grandiflora	species
brome	brome	Bromus	genus
brome, broadglume	broad-glumed brome, Canada brome	Bromus latiglumis	species
brome, Columbia	Columbia brome, woodland brome	Bromus vulgaris	species
brome, corn	corn brome, field brome	Bromus squarrosus	species
brome, downy	downy brome	Bromus tectorum	species
brome, fringed	fringed brome	Bromus ciliatus	species
brome, great	great brome	Bromus diandrus	species
brome, hairy	hairy brome, hairy chess	Bromus commutatus	species
brome, Japanese	Japanese brome, Japanese chess	Bromus japonicus	species
brome, meadow	Asian meadow brome	Bromus riparius	species
brome, Porter	Porter's brome	Bromus porteri	species
brome, Pumpelly	Pumpelly's brome, Pumpelly brome	Bromus pumpellianus	species
brome, Richardson	Richardson's brome	Bromus richardsonii	species
brome, rye	rye brome, rye chess	Bromus secalinus	species
brome, Sitka	Sitka brome, Alaska brome, keeled brome, mountain brome	Bromus sitchensis	species
brome, smooth	smooth brome	Bromus inermis	species
brome, soft	soft brome, soft chess	Bromus hordeaceus	species
bronzebells	bronzebells, deathcamas	Anticlea	genus
bronzebells, western	western mountain-bells, bronzebells	Anticlea occidentalis	species
brookfoam	brookfoam	Telesonix	genus
brookfoam, alumroot	alumroot brookfoam, telesonix	Telesonix heucheriformis	species
broomrape	broomrape	Aphyllon	genus
broomrape family	broomrape family	Orobanchaceae	family

226

ALPHABETIZED* COMMON NAMES

Suggested Common Name	VASCAN &/or ACIMS Common Name(s)	Scientific Name	Rank
broomrape, clustered	clustered broomrape, clustered broom-rape	Aphyllon fasciculatum	species
broomrape, Louisiana	Louisiana broomrape, Louisiana broom-rape	Aphyllon ludovicianum	species
broomrape, western oneflower	western one-flowered broomrape, one-flowered cancer-root	Aphyllon purpureum	species
buckbean	buckbean	Menyanthes	genus
buckbean	bog buckbean, buck-bean	Menyanthes trifoliata	species
buckbean family	buckbean family	Menyanthaceae	family
buckthorn	buckthorn	Rhamnus	genus
buckthorn family	buckthorn family	Rhamnaceae	family
buckthorn, European	European buckthorn, common buckthorn	Rhamnus cathartica	species
buckwheat	buckwheat	Eriogonum	genus
buckwheat	buckwheat	Fagopyrum	genus
buckwheat family	buckwheat family	Polygonaceae	family
buckwheat, common	common buckwheat	Fagopyrum esculentum	species
buckwheat, cushion	cushion buckwheat, silver-plant	Eriogonum ovalifolium	species
buckwheat, fewflower	few-flowered buckwheat, few-flower buckwheat	Eriogonum pauciflorum	species
buckwheat, nodding	nodding buckwheat, nodding umbrella-plant	Eriogonum cernuum	species
buckwheat, rockjasmine	androsace buckwheat, cushion umbrella-plant	Eriogonum androsaceum	species
buckwheat, sulphur	sulphur-flowered buckwheat, subalpine umbrellaplant	Eriogonum umbellatum	species
buckwheat, Tartary	Tartarian buckwheat, tartary buckwheat	Fagopyrum tataricum	species
buckwheat, yellow	yellow buckwheat, yellow umbrella-plant	Eriogonum flavum	species
buffaloberry	buffaloberry	Shepherdia	genus
buffaloberry, Canada	soapberry, Canada buffaloberry	Shepherdia canadensis	species
buffaloberry, silver	silver buffaloberry, thorny buffaloberry	Shepherdia argentea	species
buffalograss	buffalograss	Munroa	genus
buffalograss, FALSE	false buffalograss, false buffalo grass	Munroa squarrosa	species
bugseed	bugseed	Corispermum	genus
bugseed, American	American bugseed	Corispermum americanum	species
bugseed, hairy	hairy bugseed	Corispermum villosum	species
bugseed, Hooker	Hooker's bugseed	Corispermum hookeri	species
bugseed, Pallas	Pallas' bugseed	Corispermum pallasii	species
bulrush	bulrush	Amphiscirpus	genus
bulrush	bulrush	Bolboschoenus	genus
bulrush	bulrush	Schoenoplectus	genus

ALPHABETIZED* COMMON NAMES

Suggested Common Name	VASCAN &/or ACIMS Common Name(s)	Scientific Name	Rank
bulrush	bulrush	Scirpus	genus
bulrush, alkali	saltmarsh bulrush, alkali bulrush	Bolboschoenus maritimus	species
bulrush, blackgirdle	black-girdled bulrush	Scirpus atrocinctus	species
bulrush, hardstem	hard-stemmed bulrush, great bulrush	Schoenoplectus acutus	species
bulrush, Nevada	Nevada bulrush	Amphiscirpus nevadensis	species
bulrush, pale	pale bulrush	Scirpus pallidus	species
bulrush, river	river bulrush	Bolboschoenus fluviatilis	species
bulrush, slender	slender bulrush	Schoenoplectus heterochaetus	species
bulrush, smallfruit	red-tinged bulrush, small-fruited bulrush	Scirpus microcarpus	species
bulrush, softstem	soft-stemmed bulrush, common great bulrush	Schoenoplectus tabernaemontani	species
bulrush, three-square	common three-square bulrush, three-square rush	Schoenoplectus pungens	species
bunchberry	bunchberry, dogwood	Cornus	genus
bunchberry, Alaska	Alaska bunchberry, western bunchberry	Cornus unalaschkensis	species
bunchberry, Canada	bunchberry	Cornus canadensis	species
burdock	burdock	Arctium	genus
burdock, common	common burdock	Arctium minus	species
burdock, great	great burdock	Arctium lappa	species
burdock, woolly	woolly burdock	Arctium tomentosum	species
burnet-saxifrage	burnet-saxifrage	Pimpinella	genus
burnet-saxifrage, solidstem	solid stem burnet-saxifrage, Burnet-saxifrage	Pimpinella saxifraga	species
burreed	burreed	Sparganium	genus
burreed, American	American burreed	Sparganium americanum	species
burreed, broadfruit	broad-fruited burreed, giant bur-reed	Sparganium eurycarpum	species
burreed, clustered	clustered burreed	Sparganium glomeratum	species
burreed, floating	floating burreed, floating bur-reed	Sparganium fluctuans	species
burreed, greenfruit	green-fruited burreed	Sparganium emersum	species
burreed, narrowleaf	narrow-leaved burreed, narrow-leaved bur-reed	Sparganium angustifolium	species
burreed, northern	northern burreed, northern bur-reed	Sparganium hyperboreum	species
burreed, small	small burreed, small bur-reed	Sparganium natans	species
bush-cranberry	bush-cranberry	Viburnum	genus
bush-cranberry, high	cranberry viburnum, high-bush cranberry	Viburnum opulus	species
bush-cranberry, low	squashberry, low-bush cranberry	Viburnum edule	species
buttercup	buttercup	Ranunculus	genus
buttercup family	buttercup family	Ranunculaceae	family

ALPHABETIZED* COMMON NAMES

Suggested Common Name	VASCAN &/or ACIMS Common Name(s)	Scientific Name	Rank
buttercup, celeryleaf	cursed buttercup, celery-leaved buttercup	Ranunculus sceleratus	species
buttercup, creeping	creeping buttercup	Ranunculus repens	species
buttercup, Eschscholtz	Eschscholtz's buttercup, mountain buttercup	Ranunculus eschscholtzii	species
buttercup, far-north	far-northern buttercup, boreal buttercup	Ranunculus hyperboreus	species
buttercup, graceful	graceful buttercup	Ranunculus inamoenus	species
buttercup, Gray	Gray's buttercup	Ranunculus grayi	species
buttercup, heartleaf	heart-leaved buttercup	Ranunculus cardiophyllus	species
buttercup, hooked	hooked buttercup, hairy buttercup	Ranunculus uncinatus	species
buttercup, Macoun	Macoun's buttercup	Ranunculus macounii	species
buttercup, northern	northern buttercup	Ranunculus arcticus	species
buttercup, Pennsylvania	Pennsylvania buttercup, bristly buttercup	Ranunculus pensylvanicus	species
buttercup, prairie	prairie buttercup	Ranunculus rhomboideus	species
buttercup, pygmy	pygmy buttercup, dwarf buttercup	Ranunculus pygmaeus	species
buttercup, sagebrush	sagebrush buttercup, early buttercup	Ranunculus glaberrimus	species
buttercup, smallflower	kidney-leaved buttercup, small-flowered buttercup	Ranunculus abortivus	species
buttercup, snow	snow buttercup	Ranunculus nivalis	species
buttercup, tall	common buttercup, tall buttercup	Ranunculus acris	species
buttercup, western	western buttercup	Ranunculus occidentalis	species
butterwort	butterwort	Ceratocephala	genus
butterwort	butterwort	Pinguicula	genus
butterwort, common	common butterwort	Pinguicula vulgaris	species
butterwort, curveseed	horn-seed buttercup, curveseed butterwort	Ceratocephala testiculata	species
butterwort, hairy	hairy butterwort, small butterwort	Pinguicula villosa	species
cactus family	cactus family	Cactaceae	family
calicoflower	calicoflower	Downingia	genus
calicoflower, Great Basin	Great Basin downingia, downingia	Downingia laeta	species
California-poppy	California-poppy	Eschscholtzia	genus
California-poppy	California poppy	Eschscholzia californica	species
calla	calla	Calla	genus
calla, wild	wild calla, water arum	Calla palustris	species
calypso	calypso	Calypso	genus
calypso	calypso, Venus'-slipper	Calypso bulbosa	species
camas	camas	Camassia	genus
camas, blue	common camas, blue camas	Camassia quamash	species
campion	campion, catchfly	Silene	genus
campion, moss	moss campion	Silene acaulis	species

ALPHABETIZED* COMMON NAMES

Suggested Common Name	VASCAN &/or ACIMS Common Name(s)	Scientific Name	Rank
canarygrass	canarygrass	Phalaris	genus
canarygrass, annual	annual canarygrass, canary grass	Phalaris canariensis	species
canarygrass, reed	reed canarygrass, reed canary grass	Phalaris arundinacea	species
caragana	caragana	Caragana	genus
caragana, common	Siberian pea shrub, common caragana	Caragana arborescens	species
caraway	caraway	Carum	genus
caraway, wild	wild caraway, caraway	Carum carvi	species
carpetweed	carpetweed	Mollugo	genus
carpetweed family	carpetweed family	Molluginaceae	family
carpetweed, green	green carpetweed	Mollugo verticillata	species
carrot	carrot	Daucus	genus
carrot family	carrot family	Apiaceae	family
carrot, wild	wild carrot	Daucus carota	species
catchfly	catchfly, campion	Silene	genus
catchfly, arctic	arctic catchfly, alpine bladder catchfly	Silene involucrata	species
catchfly, Drummond	Drummond's catchfly, Drummond's cockle	Silene drummondii	species
catchfly, large sand	conoid catchfly, large sand catchfly	Silene conoidea	species
catchfly, Menzies	Menzies' catchfly	Silene menziesii	species
catchfly, mountain	mountain catchfly, mountain campion	Silene hitchguirei	species
catchfly, night-flowering	night-flowering catchfly	Silene noctiflora	species
catchfly, nodding	nodding catchfly, nodding campion	Silene uralensis	species
catchfly, Parry	Parry's catchfly, Parry's campion	Silene parryi	species
catchfly, Scouler	Scouler's catchfly	Silene scouleri	species
catchfly, sleepy	sleepy catchfly	Silene antirrhina	species
catchfly, smooth	biennial campion, smooth catchfly	Silene csereii	species
catnip	catnip	Nepeta	genus
catnip	catnip	Nepeta cataria	species
cattail	cattail	Typha	genus
cattail family	cattail family	Typhaceae	family
cattail, broadleaf	broad-leaved cattail, common cattail	Typha latifolia	species
ceanothus	ceanothus	Ceanothus	genus
ceanothus, snowbrush	snowbrush ceanothus	Ceanothus velutinus	species
celandine	celandine	Chelidonium	genus
celandine	rose chamaerhodos, greater celandine	Chelidonium majus	species
chaffweed.	chaffweed, loosestrife, starflower, milkwort	Lysimachia	genus
chaffweed	chaffweed	Lysimachia minima	species

ALPHABETIZED* COMMON NAMES

Suggested Common Name	VASCAN &/or ACIMS Common Name(s)	Scientific Name	Rank
chamomile	chamomile	Matricaria	genus
chamomile	chamomile	Tripleurospermum	genus
chamomile, scentless	scentless chamomile	Tripleurospermum inodorum	species
chamomile, wild	wild chamomile	Matricaria chamomilla	species
cherry	cherry	Prunus	genus
cherry, pin	pin cherry	Prunus pensylvanica	species
chickweed	chickweed	Cerastium	genus
chickweed	chickweed, starwort	Stellaria	genus
chickweed family, water	water chickweed family	Montiaceae	family
chickweed, Bering	Bering Sea chickweed, alpine mouse-ear chickweed	Cerastium beeringianum	species
chickweed, common	common mouse-ear chickweed	Cerastium fontanum	species
chickweed, common	common chickweed	Stellaria media	species
chickweed, field	field chickweed, field mouse-ear chickweed	Cerastium arvense	species
chickweed, nodding	nodding chickweed, long-stalked mouse-ear chickweed	Cerastium nutans	species
chickweed, shortstalk	short-stalked chickweed, short-stalk mouse-ear chickweed	Cerastium brachypodum	species
chicory	chicory	Cichorium	genus
chicory, wild	wild chicory, chicory	Cichorium intybus	species
chives, wild	wild chives	Allium schoenoprasum	species
chokecherry	chokecherry, choke cherry	Prunus virginiana	species
cinquefoil	cinquefoil, silverweed	Potentilla	genus
cinquefoil, arctic	arctic cinquefoil, northern cinquefoil	Potentilla hyparctica	species
cinquefoil, beautiful	beautiful cinquefoil, soft cinquefoil	Potentilla pulcherrima	species
cinquefoil, biennial	biennial cinquefoil	Potentilla biennis	species
cinquefoil, blueleaf	blue-leaved cinquefoil, mountain cinquefoil	Potentilla glaucophylla	species
cinquefoil, bluff	bluff cinquefoil	Potentilla arenosa	species
cinquefoil, branched	branched cinquefoil	Potentilla effusa	species
cinquefoil, brook	brook cinquefoil	Potentilla rivalis	species
cinquefoil, bushy	spreading cinquefoil, bushy cinquefoil	Potentilla supina	species
cinquefoil, coast	coast cinquefoil, coastal cinquefoil	Potentilla litoralis	species
cinquefoil, Colorado	Colorado cinquefoil	Potentilla subjuga	species
cinquefoil, Drummond	Drummond's cinquefoil	Potentilla drummondii	species
cinquefoil, early	early cinquefoil	Potentilla concinna	species
cinquefoil, fanleaf	fan-leaved cinquefoil, fanleaf cinquefoil	Potentilla flabellifolia	species
cinquefoil, finely villous	finely villous cinquefoil	Potentilla villosula	species
cinquefoil, forked	forked cinquefoil	Potentilla furcata	species

ALPHABETIZED* COMMON NAMES

Suggested Common Name	VASCAN &/or ACIMS Common Name(s)	Scientific Name	Rank
cinquefoil, Great Basin	Great Basin cinquefoil, smooth-leaved cinquefoil	Potentilla multisecta	species
cinquefoil, High Arctic	high arctic cinquefoil	Potentilla subvahliana	species
cinquefoil, Hooker	Hooker's cinquefoil	Potentilla hookeriana	species
cinquefoil, Hudson	Hudson's cinquefoil	Potentilla hudsonii	species
cinquefoil, Jepson	Jepson's cinquefoil	Potentilla jepsonii	species
cinquefoil, Macoun	Macoun's cinquefoil	Potentilla macounii	species
cinquefoil, Pennsylvania	Pennsylvania cinquefoil, prairie cinquefoil	Potentilla pensylvanica	species
cinquefoil, plains	bipinnate cinquefoil, plains cinquefoil	Potentilla bipinnatifida	species
cinquefoil, Platte River	Platte River cinquefoil, low cinquefoil	Potentilla plattensis	species
cinquefoil, redstem	red-stemmed cinquefoil	Potentilla rubricaulis	species
cinquefoil, rough	rough cinquefoil	Potentilla norvegica	species
cinquefoil, sandhills	sandhills cinquefoil	Potentilla lasiodonta	species
cinquefoil, sheep	sheep cinquefoil	Potentilla ovina	species
cinquefoil, silvery	silvery cinquefoil	Potentilla argentea	species
cinquefoil, slender	slender cinquefoil, graceful cinquefoil	Potentilla gracilis	species
cinquefoil, snow	snow cinquefoil	Potentilla nivea	species
cinquefoil, staghorn	staghorn cinquefoil, branched cinquefoil	Potentilla bimundorum	species
cinquefoil, sulphur	sulphur cinquefoil, rough-fruited cinquefoil	Potentilla recta	species
cinquefoil, woolly	Hipp's cinquefoil, woolly cinquefoil	Potentilla hippiana	species
cinquefoil, woolly alpine	Sheenjek River cinquefoil, Jurtsev's cinquefoil	Potentilla subgorodkovii	species
clammyweed	clammyweed	Polanisia	genus
clammyweed, common	common clammyweed, clammyweed	Polanisia dodecandra	species
cleavers, false	false cleavers	Galium spurium	species
clematis	clematis	Clematis	genus
clematis, golden	golden clematis, yellow clematis	Clematis tangutica	species
clematis, purple	purple clematis	Clematis occidentalis	species
clematis, western white	western white clematis, western clematis	Clematis ligusticifolia	species
cliffbrake	cliffbrake	Pellaea	genus
cliffbrake, Gastony	Gastony's cliffbrake, Gaston's cliff brake	Pellaea gastonyi	species
cliffbrake, smooth	smooth cliffbrake, smooth cliff brake	Pellaea glabella	species
cliff-fern family	cliff-fern family	Woodsiaceae	family
clintonia	clintonia	Clintonia	genus

ALPHABETIZED* COMMON NAMES

Suggested Common Name	VASCAN &/or ACIMS Common Name(s)	Scientific Name	Rank
clintonia, singleflower	single-flowered clintonia, corn lily	Clintonia uniflora	species
cloudberry	raspberry, cloudberry, dwarf-bramble, thimbleberry	Rubus	genus
cloudberry	cloudberry	Rubus chamaemorus	species
clover	clover	Trifolium	genus
clover, alsike	alsike clover	Trifolium hybridum	species
clover, red	red clover	Trifolium pratense	species
clover, white	white clover	Trifolium repens	species
clover, yellow	yellow clover	Trifolium aureum	species
clubmoss	clubmoss	Lycopodium	genus
clubmoss family	clubmoss family	Lycopodiaceae	family
clubmoss, onecone	one-cone clubmoss	Lycopodium lagopus	species
clubmoss, stiff	stiff clubmoss, stiff club-moss	Lycopodium annotinum	species
clubrush	clubrush	Trichophorum	genus
clubrush, alpine	alpine clubrush, Hudson Bay bulrush	Trichophorum alpinum	species
clubrush, Clinton	Clinton's clubrush, Clinton's bulrush	Trichophorum clintonii	species
clubrush, dwarf	dwarf clubrush, dwarf bulrush	Trichophorum pumilum	species
clubrush, tufted	tufted clubrush, tufted bulrush	Trichophorum cespitosum	species
cocklebur	cocklebur	Xanthium	genus
cocklebur, rough	rough cockleburr, cocklebur	Xanthium strumarium	species
collomia	collomia	Collomia	genus
collomia, narrowleaf	narrow-leaved collomia	Collomia linearis	species
columbine	columbine	Aquilegia	genus
columbine, blue	blue columbine	Aquilegia brevistyla	species
columbine, Jones	Jones' columbine	Aquilegia jonesii	species
columbine, western	western columbine, Sitka columbine	Aquilegia formosa	species
columbine, yellow	yellow columbine	Aquilegia flavescens	species
comfrey	comfrey	Symphytum	genus
comfrey, common	common comfrey, comfrey	Symphytum officinale	species
coralroot	coralroot	Corallorhiza	genus
coralroot, Merten	Pacific coralroot, Merten coralroot	Corallorhiza mertensiana	species
coralroot, pale	early coralroot, pale coralroot	Corallorhiza trifida	species
coralroot, spotted	spotted coralroot	Corallorhiza maculata	species
coralroot, striped	striped coralroot	Corallorhiza striata	species
cordgrass, alkali	alkali cordgrass, alkali cord grass	Sporobolus hookerianus	species
cordgrass	cordgrass, dropseed	Sporobolus	genus
cordgrass, prairie	prairie cordgrass, prairie cord grass	Sporobolus michauxianus	species
corncockle	corncockle	Agrostemma	genus
corncockle, common	common corncockle	Agrostemma githago	species

ALPHABETIZED* COMMON NAMES

Suggested Common Name	VASCAN &/or ACIMS Common Name(s)	Scientific Name	Rank
cornflower,	cornflower, knapweed, starthistle	Centaurea	species
cornflower, garden	bachelor's button, cornflower	Centaurea cyanus	species
cornflower, mountain	mountain cornflower, mountain star-thistle	Centaurea montana	species
cornspurry	cornspurry	Spergula	genus
cornspurry	corn spurrey, corn spurry	Spergula arvensis	species
corydalis	corydalis	Corydalis	genus
corydalis, golden	golden corydalis	Corydalis aurea	species
cotoneaster	cotoneaster	Cotoneaster	genus
cotoneaster, shiny	shiny cotoneaster, Peking cotoneaster	Cotoneaster lucidus	species
cottongrass	cottongrass	Eriophorum	genus
cottongrass, beautiful	beautiful cottongrass, russett cotton grass	Eriophorum callitrix	species
cottongrass, closed-sheath	closed-sheathed cottongrass, close-sheathed cotton grass	Eriophorum brachyantherum	species
cottongrass, greenkeel	green-keeled cottongrass, thin-leaved cotton grass	Eriophorum viridicarinatum	species
cottongrass, narrowleaf	narrow-leaved cottongrass, narrowleaf cotton-grass	Eriophorum angustifolium	species
cottongrass, russet	russet cottongrass, slender cotton grass	Eriophorum russeolum	species
cottongrass, Scheuchzer	Scheuchzer's cottongrass, one-spike cotton grass	Eriophorum scheuchzeri	species
cottongrass, slender	slender cottongrass, beautiful cotton grass	Eriophorum gracile	species
cottongrass, tussock	tussock cottongrass, sheathed cotton grass	Eriophorum vaginatum	species
cottonwood	cottonwood, poplar, aspen	Populus	genus
cottonwood, black	black cottonwood	Populus trichocarpa	species
cottonwood, common	eastern cottonwood, plains cottonwood	Populus deltoides	species
cottonwood, lanceleaf	lance-leaved cottonwood	Populus ×acuminata	Hybrid
cottonwood, narrowleaf	narrow-leaved cottonwood, narrow-leaf cottonwood	Populus angustifolia	species
cowcockle	cowcockle	Vaccaria	genus
cowcockle	cowcockle, cow cockle	Vaccaria hispanica	species
cowparsnip	cowparsnip	Heracleum	genus
cowparsnip, American	American cow parsnip, cow parsnip	Heracleum maximum	species
cow-wheat	cow-wheat	Melampyrum	genus
cow-wheat, narrowleaf	American cow-wheat, cow-wheat	Melampyrum lineare	species
crabapple	crabapple	Malus	genus
crabapple	crabapple	Malus sp.	species

ALPHABETIZED* COMMON NAMES

Suggested Common Name	VASCAN &/or ACIMS Common Name(s)	Scientific Name	Rank
crabgrass	crabgrass	Digitaria	genus
crabgrass, hairy	hairy crabgrass, crabgrass	Digitaria sanguinalis	species
crabgrass, smooth	smooth crabgrass	Digitaria ischaemum	species
cranberry	cranberry, bilberry, blueberry	Vaccinium	genus
cranberry, mountain	mountain cranberry, bog cranberry	Vaccinium vitis-idaea	species
cranberry, small	small cranberry, small bog cranberry	Vaccinium oxycoccos	species
cranberry, small bog	small bog cranberry	Vaccinium microcarpum	species
creeping-draba	creeping-draba	Tomostima	genus
creeping-draba	creeping draba	Tomostima reptans	species
cross-thistle	cross-thistle	Eryngium	genus
cross-thistle	plains eryngo, cross-thistle	Eryngium planum	species
crowberry	crowberry	Empetrum	genus
crowberry	black crowberry, crowberry	Empetrum nigrum	species
crown-vetch	crown-vetch	Securigera	genus
crown-vetch	purple crown-vetch, field crown-vetch	Securigera varia	species
cryptantha	cryptantha	Cryptantha	genus
cryptantha, cock's-comb	cock's-comb cryptantha	Cryptantha celosioides	species
cryptantha, Fendler	Fendler's cryptantha, Fendler's cryptanthe	Cryptantha fendleri	species
cryptantha, Kelsey	Kelsey's cryptantha, Kelsey's cat's eye	Cryptantha kelseyana	species
cryptantha, tiny	tiny cryptantha	Cryptantha minima	species
cudweed	cudweed	Gnaphalium	genus
cudweed, low	low cudweed	Gnaphalium uliginosum	species
cudweed, marsh	western marsh cudweed, marsh cudweed	Gnaphalium palustre	species
currant	currant, gooseberry	Ribes	genus
currant family	currant family	Grossulariaceae	family
currant, America black	American black currant, wild black currant	Ribes americanum	species
currant, bristly black	bristly black currant	Ribes lacustre	species
currant, golden	golden currant	Ribes aureum	species
currant, northern black	northern black currant	Ribes hudsonianum	species
currant, red	swamp red currant, wild red currant	Ribes triste	species
currant, skunk	skunk currant	Ribes glandulosum	species
currant, sticky	sticky currant	Ribes viscosissimum	species
currant, trailing black	trailing black currant, mountain currant	Ribes laxiflorum	species
currant, wax	wax currant	Ribes cereum	species
cushion-cactus	pincushion cactus, cushion cactus	Coryphantha vivipara	species
cushion-cactus	cushion-cactus	Escobaria	genus

ALPHABETIZED* COMMON NAMES

Suggested Common Name	VASCAN &/or ACIMS Common Name(s)	Scientific Name	Rank
cypress family	cypress family	Cupressaceae	family
daisy	daisy	Leucanthemum	genus
daisy, oxeye	oxeye daisy, ox-eye daisy	Leucanthemum vulgare	species
dame's-rocket	dame's-rocket	Hesperis	genus
dame's-rocket	dame's rocket	Hesperis matronalis	species
dandelion	dandelion	Taraxacum	genus
dandelion, alpine	alpine dandelion	Taraxacum scopulorum	species
dandelion, common	common dandelion	Taraxacum officinale	species
dandelion, horned	horned dandelion, northern dandelion	Taraxacum ceratophorum	species
dandelion, redseed	red-seeded dandelion	Taraxacum erythrospermum	species
deadnettle	deadnettle	Lamium	genus
deadnettle, henbit	common dead-nettle, henbit	Lamium amplexicaule	species
death-camas	death-camas, bronzebells	Anticlea	genus
death-camas, white	mountain death camas, white camas	Anticlea elegans	species
desert-parsley	desert-parsley	Lomatium	genus
desert-parsley, biscuitroot	cous-root desert-parsley, biscuit-root	Lomatium cous	species
desert-parsley, fernleaf	fern-leaved desert-parsley	Lomatium dissectum	species
desert-parsley, Great Basin	Great Basin desert-parsley	Lomatium simplex	species
desert-parsley, hairyfruit	fennel-leaved desert-parsley, hairy-fruited wild parsley	Lomatium foeniculaceum	species
desert-parsley, largefruit	large-fruited desert-parsley, long-fruited wild parsley	Lomatium macrocarpum	species
desert-parsley, nineleaf	nine-leaved desert-parsley, western wild parsley	Lomatium triternatum	species
desert-parsley, Sandberg	Sandberg's desert-parsley, Sandberg's wild parsley	Lomatium sandbergii	species
devil's-club	devil's-club	Oplopanax	genus
devil's-club	devil's club, devil's-club	Oplopanax horridus	species
dill	dill	Anethum	genus
dill	dill	Anethum graveolens	species
dock	dock, sorrel	Rumex	genus
dock, Asiatic	Asiatic dock, dock	Rumex confertus	species
dock, curled	curled dock	Rumex crispus	species
dock, field	field dock	Rumex pseudonatronatus	species
dock, golden	Tierra del Fuego dock, American golden dock	Rumex fueginus	species
dock, longleaf	long-leaved dock	Rumex longifolius	species
dock, narrowleaf field	narrow-leaved field dock	Rumex stenophyllus	species
dock, toothed	toothed dock	Rumex dentatus	species
dock, triangle-valve	triangular-valve dock, narrow-leaved dock	Rumex triangulivalvis	species
dock, Utah	Utah dock	Rumex utahensis	species

ALPHABETIZED* COMMON NAMES

Suggested Common Name	VASCAN &/or ACIMS Common Name(s)	Scientific Name	Rank
dock, veiny	veined dock, wild begonia	Rumex venosus	species
dock, water	greater water dock, water dock	Rumex britannica	species
dock, western	western dock	Rumex occidentalis	species
dodder	dodder	Cuscuta	genus
dodder, bigfruit	large-fruit dodder, big-fruit dodder	Cuscuta umbrosa	species
dodder, swamp	swamp dodder	Cuscuta gronovii	species
dogbane	dogbane	Apocynum	genus
dogbane, hemp	hemp dogbane, Indian hemp	Apocynum cannabinum	species
dogbane, spreading	spreading dogbane	Apocynum androsaemifolium	species
dogmustard	dogmustard	Erucastrum	genus
dogmustard, common	common dog mustard, dog mustard	Erucastrum gallicum	species
dogwood	dogwood, bunchberry	Cornus	genus
dogwood family	dogwood family	Cornaceae	family
dogwood, red-osier	red-osier dogwood	Cornus sericea	species
Douglas-fir	Douglas-fir	Pseudotsuga	genus
Douglas-fir	Douglas-fir	Pseudotsuga menziesii	species
draba	draba	Draba	genus
draba, Alaska	Alaska draba	Draba stenoloba	species
draba, Austrian	Austrian draba	Draba fladnizensis	species
draba, boreal	boreal draba	Draba borealis	species
draba, coast mountain	coast mountain draba	Draba ruaxes	species
draba, denseleaf	dense-leaved draba	Draba densifolia	species
draba, fewseed	few-seed draba	Draba oligosperma	species
draba, golden	golden draba	Draba aurea	species
draba, hoary	hoary draba	Draba cana	species
draba, lancepod	lance-pod draba	Draba lonchocarpa	species
draba, longstalk	long-stalked draba	Draba juvenilis	species
draba, Macoun	Macoun's draba	Draba macounii	species
draba, Mt. Olympic	Mt. Olympic draba	Draba novolympica	species
draba, Payson	Payson's draba	Draba paysonii	species
draba, Porsild	Porsild's draba	Draba porsildii	species
draba, slender	slender draba	Draba albertina	species
draba, smooth	smooth draba	Draba glabella	species
draba, snow	snow draba	Draba nivalis	species
draba, snowbed	snowbed draba	Draba crassifolia	species
draba, spring	spring draba	Draba verna	species
draba, tall	tall draba	Draba praealta	species
draba, Wind River	Wind River draba	Draba ventosa	species
draba, woodland	woodland draba	Draba nemorosa	species
draba, Yellowstone	Yellowstone draba	Draba incerta	species
dragonhead	dragonhead	Dracocephalum	genus

ALPHABETIZED* COMMON NAMES

Suggested Common Name	VASCAN &/or ACIMS Common Name(s)	Scientific Name	Rank
dragonhead, American	American dragonhead	Dracocephalum parviflorum	species
dragonhead, thymeflower	thyme-flowered dragonhead, thyme-leaved dragonhead	Dracocephalum thymiflorum	species
dragon's-mouth	dragon's-mouth	Arethusa	genus
dragon's-mouth	dragon's-mouth, dragon's mouth	Arethusa bulbosa	species
dropseed	dropseed, cordgrass	Sporobolus	genus
dropseed, prairie	prairie sandreed, sand grass	Sporobolus rigidus	species
dropseed, sand	sand dropseed	Sporobolus cryptandrus	species
dropseed, small	small dropseed, annual dropseed	Sporobolus neglectus	species
duckweed	duckweed	Lemna	genus
duckweed, common	turion duckweed	Lemna turionifera	species
duckweed, star	star duckweed, ivy-leaved duckweed	Lemna trisulca	species
dunegrass	dunegrass	Leymus	genus
dunegrass, American	sea lymegrass, American dunegrass	Leymus mollis	species
Dutchman's-pipe family	Dutchman's-pipe family	Aristolochiaceae	family
dwarf-bramble	raspberry, cloudberry, dwarf-bramble, thimbleberry	Rubus	genus
dwarf-bramble, fiveleaf	five-leaved dwarf bramble, dwarf bramble	Rubus pedatus	species
dwarf-gentian, autumn	autumn dwarf gentian, felwort	Gentianella amarella	species
dwarf-gentian, four-part	four-parted gentian	Gentianella propinqua	species
dwarf-gentiana	dwarf-gentiana	Gentianella	genus
dwarf-mistletoe	dwarf-mistletoe	Arceuthobium	genus
dwarf-mistletoe, American	lodgepole pine dwarf mistletoe, dwarf mistletoe	Arceuthobium americanum	species
dwarf-primrose	dwarf-primrose	Douglasia	genus
dwarf-primrose, mountain	Rocky Mountain dwarf primrose, mountain dwarf-primula	Douglasia montana	species
dwarf-snapdragon	dwarf snapdragon	Chaenorhinum minus	species
dwarf-snapdragon	dwarf-snapdragon	Chaenorrhinum	genus
elderberry	elderberry	Sambucus	genus
elderberry, red	red elderberry	Sambucus racemosa	species
elm	elm	Ulmus	genus
elm family	elm family	Ulmaceae	family
elm, American	white elm, American elm	Ulmus americana	species
enchanters-nightshade	enchanters-nightshade	Circaea	genus
enchanter's-nightshade, small	small enchanter's nightshade	Circaea alpina	species
evening-primrose	evening-primrose	Neoholmgrenia	genus
evening-primrose	evening-primrose, beeblossom	Oenothera	genus
evening-primrose family	evening-primrose family	Onagraceae	family
evening-primrose, common	common evening-primrose, yellow evening-primrose	Oenothera biennis	species
evening-primrose, hairy	hairy evening-primrose	Oenothera villosa	species

ALPHABETIZED* COMMON NAMES

Suggested Common Name	VASCAN &/or ACIMS Common Name(s)	Scientific Name	Rank
evening-primrose, low yellow	low yellow evening-primrose	Oenothera flava	species
evening-primrose, shrubby	serrate-leaved evening-primrose, shrubby evening-primrose	Oenothera serrulata	species
evening-primrose, tufted	tufted evening-primrose, butte-primrose	Oenothera cespitosa	species
evening-primrose, upland	upland evening primose, upland evening-primrose	Neoholmgrenia andina	species
evening-primrose, white	white evening-primrose	Oenothera nuttallii	species
everlasting	everlasting	Anaphalis	genus
everlasting, pearly	pearly everlasting	Anaphalis margaritacea	species
eyebright	eyebright	Euphrasia	genus
eyebright, common	common eyebright	Euphrasia nemorosa	species
eyebright, Hudson Bay	Hudson Bay eyebright, eyebright	Euphrasia hudsoniana	species
eyebright, subarctic	subarctic eyebright	Euphrasia subarctica	species
fairybells	fairybells	Prosartes	genus
fairybells, Hooker	Hooker's fairybells	Prosartes hookeri	species
fairybells, roughfruit	rough-fruited fairybells, fairybells	Prosartes trachycarpa	species
fairy-candelabra	fairy-candelabra	Androsace	genus
fairy-candelabra, northern	northern fairy-candelabra, northern fairy candelabra	Androsace septentrionalis	species
fairy-candelabra, sweetflower	sweet-flowered fairy-candelabra, sweet-flowered androsace	Androsace chamaejasme	species
fairy-candelabra, western	western fairy-candelabra, western fairy candelabra	Androsace occidentalis	species
false-asphodel	false-asphodel	Tofieldia	genus
false-asphodel	false-asphodel	Triantha	genus
false-asphodel family	false-asphodel family	Tofieldiaceae	family
false-asphodel, dwarf	small tofieldia, dwarf false asphodel	Tofieldia pusilla	species
false-asphodel, Scotch	sticky tofieldia, sticky false asphodel	Triantha glutinosa	species
false-asphodel, western	western tofieldia, western false asphodel	Triantha occidentalis	species
false-azalea	false-azalea	Menziesia	genus
false-azalea	false azalea	Menziesia ferruginea	species
false-bindweed	false-bindweed	Calystegia	genus
false-bindweed, hedge	hedge false bindweed, wild morning-glory	Calystegia sepium	species
false-bindweed, Macoun	Macoun's false bindweed	Calystegia macounii	species
false-buckwheat, black	Eurasian black bindweed, wild buckwheat	Fallopia convolvulus	species
false-buckwheat, climbing	climbing false buckwheat	Fallopia scandens	species
false-cudweed	false-cudweed	Pseudognaphalium	genus

239

ALPHABETIZED* COMMON NAMES

Suggested Common Name	VASCAN &/or ACIMS Common Name(s)	Scientific Name	Rank
false-cudweed, Macoun	Macoun's cudweed	Pseudognaphalium macounii	species
false-cudweed, slender	slender cudweed	Pseudognaphalium thermale	species
false-dandelion	false-dandelion	Agoseris	genus
false-dandelion	false-dandelion	Nothocalais	genus
false-dandelion, orange	orange agoseris, orange false dandelion	Agoseris aurantiaca	species
false-dandelion, prairie	wavy-leaved prairie dandelion, prairie false dandelion	Nothocalais cuspidata	species
false-dandelion, yellow	pale agoseris, yellow false dandelion	Agoseris glauca	species
false-dragonhead	false-dragonhead	Physostegia	genus
false-dragonhead, Ledingham	Ledingham's false dragonhead, false dragonhead	Physostegia ledinghamii	species
false-dragonhead, western	western false dragonhead, false dragonhead	Physostegia parviflora	species
falseflax	falseflax	Camelina	genus
falseflax, flatseed	flat-seed false-flax	Camelina alyssum	species
falseflax, largeseed	large-seeded false flax	Camelina sativa	species
falseflax, smallseed	small-seeded false flax	Camelina microcarpa	species
false-groundcherry	false-groundcherry	Leucophysalis	genus
false-groundcherry, large	large false ground-cherry, large white ground-cherry	Leucophysalis grandiflora	species
false-hellebore	false-hellebore	Veratrum	genus
false-hellebore, green	green false hellebore	Veratrum viride	species
false-mannagrass	false-mannagrass	Torreyochloa	genus
false-mannagrass, pale	pale false mannagrass	Torreyochloa pallida	species
false-melic	false-melic	Schizachne	genus
false-melic	purple false melic, purple oat grass	Schizachne purpurascens	species
false-pennyroyal	false-pennyroyal	Hedeoma	genus
false-pennyroyal, rough	rough false-pennyroyal, pennyroyal	Hedeoma hispida	species
false-ragweed	false-ragweed	Cyclachaena	genus
false-ragweed	false ragweed	Cyclachaena xanthiifolia	species
false-Solomon-seal	false Solomon's seal, lily-of-the-valley	Maianthemum	Genus
false-Solomon-seal, starflower	star-flowered false Solomon's seal, star-flowered Solomon's-seal	Maianthemum stellatum	species
false-Solomon-seal, threeleaf	three-leaved false Solomon's seal, three-leaved Solomon's-seal	Maianthemum trifolium	species
false-Solomon-seal, western	western false Solomon's seal, false Solomon's-seal	Maianthemum amplexicaule	species
false-spiraea	false-spiraea	Sorbaria	genus
false-spiraea	false spiraea	Sorbaria sorbifolia	species
false-toadflax	false-toadflax	Geocaulon	genus
false-toadflax	northern comandra, northern bastard toadflax	Geocaulon lividum	species

ALPHABETIZED* COMMON NAMES

Suggested Common Name	VASCAN &/or ACIMS Common Name(s)	Scientific Name	Rank
false-wheatgrass	false-wheatgrass	Eremopyrum	genus
false-wheatgrass, annual	annual false wheatgrass, annual wheat grass	Eremopyrum triticeum	species
falsle-buckwheat	falsle-buckwheat	Fallopia	genus
fenugreek	fenugreek	Trigonella	genus
fenugreek, blue	blue fenugreek, trigonella	Trigonella caerulea	species
fescue	fescue	Festuca	genus
fescue, alpine	short-leaved fescue, alpine fescue	Festuca brachyphylla	species
fescue, Baffin	Baffin Island fescue, Arctic fescue	Festuca baffinensis	species
fescue, bearded	bearded fescue	Festuca subulata	species
fescue, hard	hard fescue	Festuca trachyphylla	species
fescue, Idaho	Idaho fescue, bluebunch fescue	Festuca idahoensis	species
fescue, red	red fescue	Festuca rubra	species
fescue, Rocky Mountain	Rocky Mountain fescue	Festuca saximontana	species
fescue, sheep	sheep fescue	Festuca ovina	species
fescue, smallflower	small-flowered fescue, tiny-flowered fescue	Festuca minutiflora	species
fescue, steppe	steppe fescue	Festuca valesiaca	species
fescue, viviparous	viviparous fescue	Festuca viviparoidea	species
fescue, western	western fescue	Festuca occidentalis	species
fetid-dogweed	fetid-dogweed	Dyssodia	genus
fetid-dogweed	fetid dogweed	Dyssodia papposa	species
fiddleneck	fiddleneck	Amsinckia	genus
fiddleneck, Menzies	Menzies' fiddleneck, fiddle-neck	Amsinckia menziesii	species
figwort	figwort	Scrophularia	genus
figwort family	figwort family	Scrophulariaceae	family
figwort, lanceleaf	lance-leaved figwort	Scrophularia lanceolata	species
fir	fir	Abies	genus
fir, balsam	balsam fir	Abies balsamea	species
fir, subalpine	Rocky Mountain alpine fir, subalpine fir	Abies bifolia	species
fireweed	fireweed	Chamaenerion	genus
fireweed, broadleaf	river beauty, broad-leaved fireweed	Chamaenerion latifolium	species
fireweed, common	fireweed, common fireweed	Chamaenerion angustifolium	species
firmoss	firmoss	Huperzia	genus
firmoss, continental	continental firmoss, alpine firmoss	Huperzia continentalis	species
firmoss, northern	northern firmoss, mountain club-moss	Huperzia selago	species
firmoss, western	western firmoss	Huperzia occidentalis	species
fissurewort	fissurewort	Crucihimalaya, Transberingia	genus
fissurewort, twiggy	twiggy fissurewort, slender mouse-ear-cress	Crucihimalaya virgata	species
flatsedge	flatsedge	Cyperus	genus
flatsedge, awned	awned flatsedge, awned nut-grass	Cyperus squarrosus	species

241

ALPHABETIZED* COMMON NAMES

Suggested Common Name	VASCAN &/or ACIMS Common Name(s)	Scientific Name	Rank
flatsedge, Schweinitz	Schweinitz's flatsedge, sand nut-grass	Cyperus schweinitzii	species
flax	flax	Linum	genus
flax family	flax family	Linaceae	family
flax, common	common flax	Linum usitatissimum	species
flax, compact	compact flax	Linum compactum	species
flax, Lewis blue	Lewis' wild blue flax, wild blue flax	Linum lewisii	species
flax, stiff yellow	large-flowered yellow flax, yellow flax	Linum rigidum	species
fleabane	fleabane	Erigeron	genus
fleabane, annual	annual fleabane, whitetop	Erigeron annuus	species
fleabane, bitter	bitter fleabane, northern daisy fleabane	Erigeron acris	species
fleabane, buff	buff fleabane	Erigeron ochroleucus	species
fleabane, creeping	trailing fleabane, creeping fleabane	Erigeron flagellaris	species
fleabane, cutleaf	cut-leaved fleabane	Erigeron compositus	species
fleabane, diffuse	diffuse fleabane	Erigeron divergens	species
fleabane, golden	golden fleabane	Erigeron aureus	species
fleabane, horseweed	Canada horseweed, horseweed	Conyza canadensis	species
fleabane, hyssopleaf	hyssop-leaved fleabane, wild daisy fleabane	Erigeron hyssopifolius	species
fleabane, Lackschewitz	Lackschewitz's fleabane, front-range fleabane	Erigeron lackschewitzii	species
fleabane, largeflower	large-flowered fleabane	Erigeron grandiflorus	species
fleabane, low	low fleabane, purple fleabane	Erigeron humilis	species
fleabane, pale alpine	pale fleabane, pale alpine fleabane	Erigeron pallens	species
fleabane, Philadelphia	Philadelphia fleabane	Erigeron philadelphicus	species
fleabane, rough	rough fleabane	Erigeron strigosus	species
fleabane, shaggy	shaggy fleabane, hairy fleabane	Erigeron pumilus	species
fleabane, shortray	short-rayed fleabane	Erigeron lonchophyllus	species
fleabane, showy	showy fleabane	Erigeron speciosus	species
fleabane, smooth	streamside fleabane, smooth fleabane	Erigeron glabellus	species
fleabane, snow	snow fleabane	Erigeron nivalis	species
fleabane, subalpine	subalpine fleabane	Erigeron glacialis	species
fleabane, tall	swamp fleabane, tall fleabane	Erigeron elatus	species
fleabane, taproot	taproot fleabane, dwarf fleabane	Erigeron radicatus	species
fleabane, threelobe	three-lobed fleabane, trifid-leaved fleabane	Erigeron trifidus	species
fleabane, tufted	tufted fleabane	Erigeron caespitosus	species
fleabane, wandering	wandering fleabane, wandering daisy	Erigeron peregrinus	species
fleabane, woolly	woolly fleabane	Erigeron lanatus	species
flowering-quillwort	flowering-quillwort, arrowgrass	Triglochin	genus

ALPHABETIZED* COMMON NAMES

Suggested Common Name	VASCAN &/or ACIMS Common Name(s)	Scientific Name	Rank
flowering-quillwort	flowering-quillwort	Triglochin scilloides	species
flowering-rush	flowering-rush	Butomus	genus
flowering-rush	flowering-rush	Butomus umbellatus	species
flowering-rush family	flowering-rush family	Butomaceae	family
fluffweed	fluffweed	Logfia	genus
fluffweed, field	field cottonrose, field fluffweed	Logfia arvensis	species
fly-honeysuckle, mountain	mountain fly-honeysuckle, mountain fly-honeysuckle	Lonicera villosa	species
foamflower	foamflower	Tiarella	genus
foamflower, threeleaf	three-leaved foamflower, laceflower	Tiarella trifoliata	species
forget-me-not	forget-me-not	Myosotis	genus
forget-me-not, alpine	Asian forget-me-not, alpine forget-me-not	Myosotis asiatica	species
forget-me-not, field	field forget-me-not	Myosotis arvensis	species
forget-me-not, small	small forget-me-not	Myosotis laxa	species
forget-me-not, upright	upright forget-me-not, forget-me-not	Myosotis stricta	species
four-nerve-daisy	four-nerve-daisy	Tetraneuris	genus
four-nerve-daisy, stemless	stemless four-nerved daisy, butte marigold	Tetraneuris acaulis	species
four-o'clock family	four-o'clock family	Nyctaginaceae	family
four-o'clock	four-o'clock	Mirabilis	genus
four-o'clock, hairy	hairy four-o'clock, hairy umbrellawort	Mirabilis albida	species
four-o'clock, heartleaf	heart-leaved four-o'clock, heart-leaved umbrellawort	Mirabilis nyctaginea	species
four-o'clock, narrowleaf	narrow-leaved four-o'clock, narrowleaf umbrella-wort	Mirabilis linearis	species
foxtail	foxtail	Alopecurus	genus
foxtail	foxtail	Setaria	genus
foxtail, alpine	alpine foxtail	Alopecurus magellanicus	species
foxtail, Carolina	tufted foxtail, Carolina foxtail	Alopecurus carolinianus	species
foxtail, creeping	creeping foxtail	Alopecurus arundinaceus	species
foxtail, green	green foxtail	Setaria viridis	species
foxtail, Italian	Italian foxtail	Setaria italica	species
foxtail, meadow	meadow foxtail	Alopecurus pratensis	species
foxtail, shortawn	short-awned foxtail	Alopecurus aequalis	species
foxtail, water	water foxtail	Alopecurus geniculatus	species
foxtail, yellow	yellow foxtail	Setaria pumila	species
fringecup	fringecup	Tellima	genus
fringecup, bigflower	big-flowered tellima, fringe-cups	Tellima grandiflora	species
fringed-gentian	fringed-gentian	Gentianopsis	genus
fringed-gentian, Macoun	lesser fringed gentian, Macoun's gentian	Gentianopsis virgata	species

ALPHABETIZED* COMMON NAMES

Suggested Common Name	VASCAN &/or ACIMS Common Name(s)	Scientific Name	Rank
fringed-gentian, northern	sheared gentian, northern fringed gentian	Gentianopsis detonsa	species
fritillary	fritillary	Fritillaria	genus
fritillary, yellow	yellow fritillary, yellowbell	Fritillaria pudica	species
frog-bit family	frog-bit family	Hydrocharitaceae	family
frog-orchid	frog-orchid	Coeloglossum	genus
frog-orchid	frog orchid, bracted bog orchid	Coeloglossum viride	species
fumitory	fumitory	Fumaria	genus
fumitory, common	common fumitory, fumitory	Fumaria officinalis	species
galinsoga	galinsoga	Galinsoga	genus
galinsoga, hairy	hairy galinsoga, galinsoga	Galinsoga quadriradiata	species
gardenrocket	gardenrocket	Eruca	genus
gardenrocket	garden rocket	Eruca vesicaria	species
garlic-mustard	garlic-mustard	Alliaria	genus
garlic-mustard	garlic mustard	Alliaria petiolata	species
gentian	gentian	Gentiana	genus
gentian family	gentian family	Gentianaceae	family
gentian, lowly	lowly gentian, marsh gentian	Gentiana fremontii	species
gentian, moss	moss gentian	Gentiana prostrata	species
gentian, mountain	mountain bog gentian, mountain gentian	Gentiana calycosa	species
gentian, pale	pale gentian, alpine gentian	Gentiana glauca	species
gentian, pleated	pleated gentian, prairie gentian	Gentiana affinis	species
gentian, yellow	yellow gentian	Gentiana lutea	species
geranium	geranium	Geranium	genus
geranium family	geranium family	Geraniaceae	family
geranium, Bicknell	Bicknell's geranium	Geranium bicknellii	species
geranium, Carolina	Carolina geranium, Carolina wild geranium	Geranium carolinianum	species
geranium, meadow	meadow geranium, meadow crane's-bill	Geranium pratense	species
geranium, sticky purple	sticky purple geranium	Geranium viscosissimum	species
geranium, white	white geranium, wild white geranium	Geranium richardsonii	species
geranium, woolly	woolly geranium	Geranium erianthum	species
giant-hyssop	giant-hyssop	Agastache	genus
giant-hyssop, blue	blue giant hyssop, giant hyssop	Agastache foeniculum	species
giant-knotweed	giant-knotweed	Reynoutria	genus
ginseng family	ginseng family	Araliaceae	family
glacier-lily	glacier-lily	Erythronium	genus
glacier-lily, yellow	yellow glacier lily, glacier lily	Erythronium grandiflorum	species
glasswort	glasswort	Salicornia	genus
glasswort, red	red glasswort, samphire	Salicornia rubra	species
globeflower	globeflower	Trollius	genus
globeflower, white	white globeflower, globeflower	Trollius albiflorus	species

ALPHABETIZED* COMMON NAMES

Suggested Common Name	VASCAN &/or ACIMS Common Name(s)	Scientific Name	Rank
globemallow	globemallow	Sphaeralcea	genus
globemallow, scarlet	scarlet globe-mallow, scarlet mallow	Sphaeralcea coccinea	species
goatsbeard	goatsbeard	Aruncus	genus
goatsbeard	goatsbeard	Tragopogon	genus
goatsbeard, common	common goatsbeard	Aruncus dioicus	species
goatsbeard, common	yellow goatsbeard, common goat's-beard	Tragopogon dubius	species
goatsbeard, meadow	meadow goatsbeard, meadow goat's-beard	Tragopogon pratensis	species
goatsbeard, purple	purple goatsbeard, common salsify	Tragopogon porrifolius	species
golden-aster	golden-aster	Heterotheca	genus
golden-aster, hairy	hairy goldenaster, golden aster	Heterotheca villosa	species
goldenbean	goldenbean	Thermopsis	genus
goldenbean, prairie	prairie golden bean, golden bean	Thermopsis rhombifolia	species
goldenrod	goldenrod	Solidago	genus
goldenrod, elegant	elegant goldenrod	Solidago lepida	species
goldenrod, giant	giant goldenrod, late goldenrod	Solidago gigantea	species
goldenrod, grey	grey-stemmed goldenrod, showy goldenrod	Solidago nemoralis	species
goldenrod, manyray	multi-rayed goldenrod, alpine goldenrod	Solidago multiradiata	species
goldenrod, Missouri	Missouri goldenrod, low goldenrod	Solidago missouriensis	species
goldenrod, sticky	sticky goldenrod	Solidago glutinosa	species
goldenrod, stiff	stiff goldenrod	Solidago rigida	species
goldenrod, tall	tall goldenrod	Solidago altissima	species
goldenrod, velvety	velvety goldenrod	Solidago mollis	species
golden-saxifrage	golden-saxifrage	Chrysosplenium	genus
golden-saxifrage, Iowa	Iowa golden-saxifrage, golden saxifrage	Chrysosplenium iowense	species
golden-saxifrage, northern	northern golden-saxifrage, green saxifrage	Chrysosplenium tetrandrum	species
goldentop	goldentop	Euthamia	genus
goldentop, common	grass-leaved goldenrod, flat-topped goldenrod	Euthamia graminifolia	species
goldenweed	goldenweed	Pyrrocoma	genus
goldenweed, lanceleaf	lance-leaved goldenweed, lance-leaved ironplant	Pyrrocoma lanceolata	species
goldenweed, oneflower	one-flowered goldenweed, one-flowered ironplant	Pyrrocoma uniflora	species
goldthread	goldthread	Coptis	genus
goldthread	goldthread	Coptis trifolia	species
gooseberry	gooseberry, currant	Ribes	genus

ALPHABETIZED* COMMON NAMES

Suggested Common Name	VASCAN &/or ACIMS Common Name(s)	Scientific Name	Rank
gooseberry, Canada	Canada gooseberry, northern gooseberry	Ribes oxyacanthoides	species
gooseberry, hairy	swamp gooseberry, wild gooseberry	Ribes hirtellum	species
gooseberry, Watson	Watson's gooseberry, spring gooseberry	Ribes watsonianum	species
gooseberry, whitestem	white-stemmed gooseberry, mountain gooseberry	Ribes inerme	species
goosefoot	goosefoot, strawberry-blite	Blitum	genus
goosefoot	goosefoot	Chenopodiastrum	genus
goosefoot	goosefoot, lamb's-quarters	Chenopodium	genus
goosefoot	goosefoot	Oxybasis	genus
goosefoot, aridland	aridland goosefoot	Chenopodium desiccatum	species
goosefoot, Berlandier	Berlandier's goosefoot, Berlandier goosefoot	Chenopodium berlandieri	species
goosefoot, darkgreen	dark-green goosefoot	Chenopodium atrovirens	species
goosefoot, Fremont	Fremont's goosefoot	Chenopodium fremontii	species
goosefoot, gaping	gaping goosefoot	Chenopodium hians	species
goosefoot, mapleleaf	maple-leaved goosefoot	Chenopodiastrum simplex	species
goosefoot, meadow	meadow goosefoot	Chenopodium pratericola	species
goosefoot, mealy	mealy goosefoot	Chenopodium incanum	species
goosefoot, oakleaf	oak-leaved goosefoot	Oxybasis glauca	species
goosefoot, red	red goosefoot	Oxybasis rubra	species
goosefoot, slimleaf	slim-leaved goosefoot, narrow-leaved goosefoot	Chenopodium leptophyllum	species
goosefoot, smooth	smooth goosefoot	Chenopodium subglabrum	species
goosefoot, Watson	Watson's goosefoot	Chenopodium watsonii	species
gourd family	gourd family	Cucurbitaceae	family
grama	grama	Bouteloua	genus
grama, blue	blue grama	Bouteloua gracilis	species
grama, side-oats	side-oats grama	Bouteloua curtipendula	species
grapefern	grapefern	Sceptridium	genus
grapefern, bluntlobe	blunt-lobed grapefern, blunt-lobe grape-fern	Sceptridium oneidense	species
grapefern, leather	leathery grapefern, leather grapefern	Sceptridium multifidum	species
grass family	grass family	Poaceae	family
grass-of-parnassus	grass-of-parnassus	Parnassia	genus
grass-of-parnassus, fringed	fringed grass-of-Parnassus	Parnassia fimbriata	species
grass-of-parnassus, marsh	marsh grass-of-Parnassus, northern grass-of-parnassus	Parnassia palustris	species
grass-of-parnassus, small	Kotzebue's grass-of-Parnassus, small grass-of-parnassus	Parnassia kotzebuei	species

ALPHABETIZED* COMMON NAMES

Suggested Common Name	VASCAN &/or ACIMS Common Name(s)	Scientific Name	Rank
grass-of-parnassus, smallflower	small-flowered grass-of-Parnassus, small northern grass-of-parnassus	Parnassia parviflora	species
greasewood	greasewood	Sarcobatus	genus
greasewood, black	black greasewood, greasewood	Sarcobatus vermiculatus	species
great-duckweed	great-duckweed	Spirodela	genus
great-duckweed	great duckweed, larger duckweed	Spirodela polyrhiza	species
green-orchid	bog-orchid, green-orchid	Platanthera	genus
green-orchid, Huron	Lake Huron green orchid, northern green bog orchid	Platanthera huronensis	species
green-orchid, tall northern	tall northern green orchid	Platanthera aquilonis	species
greenthread, hairless	Navajo tea, greenthread	Thelesperma subnudum	species
gromwell	gromwell	Lithospermum	genus
gromwell, narrowleaf	narrow-leaved puccoon	Lithospermum incisum	species
gromwell, western false	western false gromwell	Lithospermum occidentale	species
gromwell, woolly	western puccoon, woolly gromwell	Lithospermum ruderale	species
groundcedar	groundcedar	Diphasiastrum	genus
groundcedar, alpine	alpine clubmoss, alpine club-moss	Diphasiastrum alpinum	species
groundcedar, northern	northern ground-cedar, ground-cedar	Diphasiastrum complanatum	species
groundcedar, Sitka	Sitka ground-cedar, ground-fir	Diphasiastrum sitchense	species
groundcherry	groundcherry	Physalis	genus
groundcherry, Mexican	Mexican ground cherry	Physalis ixocarpa	species
groundcone	groundcone	Boschniakia	genus
groundcone, northern	northern groundcone, ground-cone	Boschniakia rossica	species
ground-ivy	ground-ivy	Glechoma	genus
ground-ivy	ground-ivy, ground ivy	Glechoma hederacea	species
groundpine	groundpine	Dendrolycopodium	genus
groundpine	round-branched tree-clubmoss, ground-pine	Dendrolycopodium dendroideum	species
groundsel	groundsel	Packera	genus
groundsel, alpine meadow	alpine meadow groundsel	Packera subnuda	species
groundsel, balsam	balsam groundsel	Packera paupercula	species
groundsel, dwarf arctic	dwarf arctic groundsel	Packera heterophylla	species
groundsel, fewflower	few-flowered groundsel, few-flowered ragwort	Packera pauciflora	species
groundsel, northwestern	northwestern groundsel, Arctic butterweed	Packera contermina	species
groundsel, rayless	rayless mountain groundsel, rayless ragwort	Packera indecora	species
groundsel, Rocky Mountain	Rocky Mountain groundsel, northern ragwort	Packera streptanthifolia	species

ALPHABETIZED* COMMON NAMES

Suggested Common Name	VASCAN &/or ACIMS Common Name(s)	Scientific Name	Rank
groundsel, streambank	streambank groundsel, thin-leaved ragwort	Packera pseudaurea	species
groundsel, woolly	woolly groundsel, prairie groundsel	Packera cana	species
groundsmoke	groundsmoke	Gayophytum	genus
groundsmoke, racemose	racemose groundsmoke	Gayophytum racemosum	species
gumweed	gumweed	Grindelia	genus
gumweed, curlycup	curly-cup gumweed	Grindelia squarrosa	species
gumweed, hairy	hairy gumweed	Grindelia hirsutula	species
hairgrass	hairgrass	Deschampsia	genus
hairgrass	hairgrass	Vahlodea	genus
hairgrass, mountain	mountain hairgrass, mountain hair grass	Vahlodea atropurpurea	species
hairgrass, slender	slender hairgrass, slender hair grass	Deschampsia elongata	species
hairgrass, tufted	tufted hairgrass, tufted hair grass	Deschampsia cespitosa	species
harebell, alpine	arctic bellflower, alpine harebell	Campanula uniflora	species
hare's-ear-mustard	hare's-ear-mustard	Conringia	genus
hare's-ear-mustard	hare's ear mustard	Conringia orientalis	species
hawksbeard	hawksbeard	Askellia	genus
hawksbeard	hawksbeard	Crepis	genus
hawksbeard, dandelion	dandelion hawksbeard, scapose hawk's-beard	Crepis runcinata	species
hawksbeard, dwarf	dwarf hawksbeard, dwarf hawk's-beard	Askellia pygmaea	species
hawksbeard, elegant	elegant hawksbeard	Askellia elegans	species
hawksbeard, intermediate	limestone hawksbeard, intermediate hawk's-beard	Crepis intermedia	species
hawksbeard, narrowleaf	narrow-leaved hawksbeard, annual hawk's-beard	Crepis tectorum	species
hawksbeard, slender	slender hawksbeard, slender hawk's-beard	Crepis atribarba	species
hawksbeard, smooth	smooth hawksbeard, green hawk's-beard	Crepis capillaris	species
hawksbeard, western	western hawksbeard, small-flowered hawk's-beard	Crepis occidentalis	species
hawkweed	hawkweed	Hieracium	genus
hawkweed	hawkweed	Pilosella	genus
hawkweed, meadow	meadow hawkweed	Pilosella caespitosa	species
hawkweed, orange	orange hawkweed	Pilosella aurantiaca	species
hawkweed, Scouler	Scouler's hawkweed, woolly hawkweed	Hieracium scouleri	species
hawkweed, slender	woolly hawkweed, slender hawkweed	Hieracium triste	species
hawkweed, tall	hawkweed, tall hawkweed	Pilosella piloselloides	species

ALPHABETIZED* COMMON NAMES

Suggested Common Name	VASCAN &/or ACIMS Common Name(s)	Scientific Name	Rank
hawkweed, umbellate	umbellate hawkweed, narrow-leaved hawkweed	Hieracium umbellatum	species
hawkweed, white	white hawkweed	Hieracium albiflorum	species
hawkweed, yellow devil	yellow devil hawkweed, yellow devil	Pilosella glomerata	species
hawthorn	hawthorn	Crataegus	genus
hawthorn, Adams Creek	Adams Creek hawthorn	Crataegus rivuloadamensis	species
hawthorn, Battle Creek	Battle Creek hawthorn	Crataegus rivulopugnensis	species
hawthorn, bearpaw	bear's paw hawthorn	Crataegus ursopedensis	species
hawthorn, Castlegar	Castlegar hawthorn, Castlegar hawthorn	Crataegus castlegarensis	species
hawthorn, Cypress Hills	Cypress Hills hawthorn	Crataegus cupressocollina	species
hawthorn, Douglas	Douglas' hawthorn, Douglas hawthorn	Crataegus douglasii	species
hawthorn, Elkwater	Elkwater hawthorn	Crataegus aquacervensis	species
hawthorn, fireberry	fireberry hawthorn, round-leaved hawthorn	Crataegus chrysocarpa	species
hawthorn, Great Plains	Great Plains hawthorn	Crataegus sheridana	species
hawthorn, largethorn	large-thorned hawthorn, western hawthorn	Crataegus macracantha	species
hawthorn, redbract	red bracteole hawthorn	Crataegus rubribracteolata	species
hazelnut	hazelnut	Corylus	genus
hazelnut, beaked	beaked hazelnut	Corylus cornuta	species
heath family	heath family	Ericaceae	family
hedge-hyssop	hedge-hyssop	Gratiola	genus
hedge-hyssop, clammy	clammy hedge-hyssop	Gratiola neglecta	species
hedgenettle	hedgenettle	Stachys	genus
hedgenettle, hairy	hairy hedge-nettle, marsh hedge-nettle	Stachys pilosa	species
hedysarum	hedysarum	Hedysarum	genus
hedysarum, alpine	alpine hedysarum	Hedysarum americanum	species
hedysarum, northern	northern hedysarum	Hedysarum boreale	species
hedysarum, yellow	yellow hedysarum	Hedysarum sulphurescens	species
heliotrope	heliotrope	Heliotropium	genus
heliotrope family	heliotrope family	Heliotropiaceae	family
heliotrope, salt	salt heliotrope, spatulate-leaved heliotrope	Heliotropium curassavicum	species
hemlock	hemlock	Tsuga	genus
hemlock, western	western hemlock	Tsuga heterophylla	species
hemp	hemp	Cannabis	genus
hemp	hemp	Cannabis sativa	species
hemp family	hemp family	Cannabaceae	family
hempnettle	hempnettle	Galeopsis	genus
hempnettle, common	common hemp-nettle, hemp-nettle	Galeopsis tetrahit	species

ALPHABETIZED* COMMON NAMES

Suggested Common Name	VASCAN &/or ACIMS Common Name(s)	Scientific Name	Rank
hempnettle, largeflower	large-flowered hemp-nettle, yellow hemp-nettle	Galeopsis speciosa	species
henbane	henbane	Hyoscyamus	genus
henbane, black	black henbane	Hyoscyamus niger	species
hoary-alyssum	hoary-alyssum	Berteroa	genus
hoary-alyssum	hoary alyssum	Berteroa incana	species
hoary-aster	hoary-aster	Dieteria	genus
hoary-aster	hoary aster	Dieteria canescens	species
hoarycress	peppergrass, hoarycress	Lepidium	genus
hoarycress, globepod	globe-pod hoarycress, globe-podded hoary cress	Lepidium appelianum	species
hoarycress, heartpod	heart-pod hoarycress, heart-podded hoary cress	Lepidium draba	species
hoarycress, lenspod	lens-pod hoarycress	Lepidium chalepense	species
hollyfern	hollyfern	Polystichum	genus
hollyfern, northern	northern holly fern	Polystichum lonchitis	species
honeysuckle	honeysuckle	Lonicera	genus
honeysuckle family	honeysuckle family	Caprifoliaceae	family
honeysuckle, bracted	bracted honeysuckle	Lonicera involucrata	species
honeysuckle, tatarian	Tatarian honeysuckle	Lonicera tatarica	species
honeysuckle, twining	limber honeysuckle, twining honeysuckle	Lonicera dioica	species
honeysuckle, Utah	Utah honeysuckle, red twinberry	Lonicera utahensis	species
hop	hop	Humulus	genus
hop, common	common hop	Humulus lupulus	species
horned-pondweed	horned-pondweed	Zannichellia	genus
horned-pondweed	horned pondweed	Zannichellia palustris	species
hornwort	hornwort	Ceratophyllum	genus
hornwort family	hornwort family	Ceratophyllaceae	family
hornwort, common	common hornwort, hornwort	Ceratophyllum demersum	species
horseradish	horseradish	Armoracia	genus
horseradish	horseradish, horse-radish	Armoracia rusticana	species
horsetail	horsetail, scouringrush	Equisetum	genus
horsetail family	horsetail family	Equisetaceae	family
horsetail, field	field horsetail, common horsetail	Equisetum arvense	species
horsetail, marsh	marsh horsetail	Equisetum palustre	species
horsetail, meadow	meadow horsetail	Equisetum pratense	species
horsetail, water	water horsetail, swamp horsetail	Equisetum fluviatile	species
horsetail, woodland	woodland horsetail	Equisetum sylvaticum	species
hound's-tongue	hound's-tongue	Cynoglossum	genus
hound's-tongue, common	common hound's-tongue, hound's-tongue	Cynoglossum officinale	species
hydrangea family	hydrangea family	Hydrangeaceae	family
hymenopappus	hymenopappus	Hymenopappus	genus

ALPHABETIZED* COMMON NAMES

Suggested Common Name	VASCAN &/or ACIMS Common Name(s)	Scientific Name	Rank
hymenopappus, fineleaf	fine-leaved hymenopappus, tufted hymenopappus	Hymenopappus filifolius	species
Indianpipe	Indianpipe	Monotropa	genus
Indianpipe	Indian pipe, Indian-pipe	Monotropa uniflora	species
iris	iris	Iris	genus
iris family	iris family	Iridaceae	family
iris, western blue	western blue iris, western blue flag	Iris missouriensis	species
iris, yellow	yellow iris	Iris pseudacorus	species
ironplant	ironplant	Xanthisma	genus
ironplant, spiny	lacy tansy-aster, spiny ironplant	Xanthisma spinulosum	species
ironplant, toothed	rayless tansy-aster, toothed ironplant	Xanthisma grindelioides	species
Jacob's-ladder	Jacob's-ladder	Polemonium	genus
Jacob's-ladder, showy	showy Jacob's-ladder	Polemonium pulcherrimum	species
Jacob's-ladder, sticky	sticky Jacob's-ladder, skunkweed	Polemonium viscosum	species
Jacob's-ladder, tall	tall Jacob's-ladder	Polemonium acutiflorum	species
Jacob's-ladder, Western	western Jacob's-ladder	Polemonium occidentale	species
jewelweed	jewelweed	Impatiens	genus
jewelweed, purple	purple jewelweed, Himalayan balsam	Impatiens glandulifera	species
jewelweed, spotted	spotted jewelweed, spotted touch-me-not	Impatiens capensis	species
jewelweed, western	western jewelweed	Impatiens noli-tangere	species
jimsonweed	jimsonweed	Datura	genus
jimsonweed	jimsonweed	Datura stramonium	species
Joe-Pye-weed	Joe-Pye-weed	Eutrochium	genus
Joe-Pye-weed, spotted	spotted Joe Pye weed, spotted Joe-pye weed	Eutrochium maculatum	species
junegrass	junegrass	Koeleria	genus
junegrass, prairie	prairie junegrass, June grass	Koeleria macrantha	species
juniper	juniper	Juniperus	genus
juniper, common	common juniper, ground juniper	Juniperus communis	species
juniper, creeping	creeping juniper	Juniperus horizontalis	species
juniper, Rocky Mountain	Rocky Mountain juniper	Juniperus scopulorum	species
kidney-vetch	kidney-vetch	Anthyllis	genus
kidney-vetch, common	common kidney-vetch	Anthyllis vulneraria	species
kittentails	Wyoming kitten-tails, kittentails	Veronica wyomingensis	species
knapweed	knapweed, cornflower, starthistle	Centaurea	genus
knapweed, bighead	globe knapweed, bighead knapweed	Centaurea macrocephala	species
knapweed, brown	brown knapweed	Centaurea jacea	species
knapweed, diffuse	diffuse knapweed	Centaurea diffusa	species
knapweed, spotted	spotted knapweed	Centaurea stoebe	species
knawel	knawel	Scleranthus	genus

ALPHABETIZED* COMMON NAMES

Suggested Common Name	VASCAN &/or ACIMS Common Name(s)	Scientific Name	Rank
knawel, annual	annual knawel, knawel	Scleranthus annuus	species
knotweed	knotweed	Polygonum	genus
knotweed, Austin	Austin's knotweed	Polygonum austiniae	species
knotweed, bushy	bushy knotweed	Polygonum ramosissimum	species
knotweed, Douglas	Douglas' knotweed, Douglas knotweed	Polygonum douglasii	species
knotweed, dwarf	leafy dwarf knotweed, least knotweed	Polygonum minimum	species
knotweed, Engelmann	Engelmann's knotweed	Polygonum engelmannii	species
knotweed, erect	erect knotweed, striate knotweed	Polygonum erectum	species
knotweed, Japanese	Japanese knotweed	Reynoutria japonica	species
knotweed, leathery	leathery knotweed	Polygonum achoreum	species
knotweed, milkwort	milkwort knotweed, white-margined knotweed	Polygonum polygaloides	species
knotweed, prostrate	prostrate knotweed	Polygonum aviculare	species
knotweed, Sawatch	Sawatch knotweed	Polygonum sawatchense	species
koenigia	koenigia	Koenigia	genus
koenigia, island	Iceland purslane, koenigia	Koenigia islandica	species
Labrador-tea	Labrador-tea, rhododendron	Rhododendron	genus
Labrador-tea, common	common Labrador tea	Rhododendron groenlandicum	species
Labrador-tea, glandular	western Labrador tea, glandular Labrador tea	Rhododendron neoglandulosum	species
Labrador-tea, northern	northern Labrador tea	Rhododendron tomentosum	species
ladie's-tresses	ladie's-tresses	Spiranthes	genus
ladies'-tresses, hooded	hooded ladies'-tresses	Spiranthes romanzoffiana	species
ladies'-tresses, slender	northern slender ladies'-tresses	Spiranthes lacera	species
ladyfern	ladyfern	Athyrium	genus
ladyfern family	ladyfern family	Athyriaceae	family
ladyfern, alpine	alpine lady fern	Athyrium distentifolium	species
ladyfern, common	common lady fern, lady fern	Athyrium filix-femina	species
ladyslipper	ladyslipper	Cypripedium	genus
ladyslipper, mountain	mountain lady's-slipper	Cypripedium montanum	species
ladyslipper, pink	pink lady's-slipper, stemless lady's-slipper	Cypripedium acaule	species
ladyslipper, sparrowegg	sparrow's-egg lady's-slipper	Cypripedium passerinum	species
ladyslipper, yellow	yellow lady's-slipper	Cypripedium parviflorum	species
lamb's-quarters	lamb's-quarters, goosefoot	Chenopodium	genus
lamb's-quarters	common lamb's-quarters, lamb's-quarters	Chenopodium album	species
Lapland-buttercup	Lapland-buttercup	Coptidium	genus
Lapland-buttercup	Lapland buttercup	Coptidium lapponicum	species
larch	larch	Larix	genus
larch, subalpine	subalpine larch	Larix lyallii	species

ALPHABETIZED* COMMON NAMES

Suggested Common Name	VASCAN &/or ACIMS Common Name(s)	Scientific Name	Rank
larch, western	western larch	Larix occidentalis	species
larkspur	larkspur	Delphinium	genus
larkspur, little	flathead larkspur, low larkspur	Delphinium bicolor	species
larkspur, Nuttall	upland larkspur, Nuttall's larkspur	Delphinium nuttallianum	species
larkspur, tall	tall larkspur	Delphinium glaucum	species
laurel	laurel	Kalmia	genus
laurel, alpine	alpine azalea	Kalmia procumbens	species
laurel, pale	pale bog laurel, northern laurel	Kalmia polifolia	species
laurel, western	western bog laurel, mountain laurel	Kalmia microphylla	species
leatherleaf	leatherleaf	Chamaedaphne	genus
leatherleaf	leatherleaf	Chamaedaphne calyculata	species
leatherleaf-saxifrage	leatherleaf-saxifrage	Leptarrhena	genus
leatherleaf-saxifrage	leather-leaved saxifrage	Leptarrhena pyrolifolia	species
legume family	legume family	Fabaceae	family
lentil	lentil	Lens	genus
lentil	lentil	Lens culinaris	species
lettuce	lettuce	Lactuca	genus
lettuce, prickly	prickly lettuce	Lactuca serriola	species
lettuce, tall blue	tall blue lettuce	Lactuca biennis	species
lewisia	lewisia	Lewisia	genus
lewisia, alpine	alpine lewisia	Lewisia pygmaea	species
lewisia, bitterroot	Oregon bitterroot, bitter-root	Lewisia rediviva	species
lilac	lilac	Syringa	genus
lilac, common	common lilac	Syringa vulgaris	species
lily	lily	Lilium	genus
lily family	lily family	Liliaceae	family
lily, wood	wood lily, western wood lily	Lilium philadelphicum	species
lily-of-the-valley	lily-of-the-valley	Convallaria	genus
lily-of-the-valley	lily-of-the-valley, false-Solomon-seal	Maianthemum	genus
lily-of-the-valley, European	European lily-of-the-valley	Convallaria majalis	species
lily-of-the-valley, wild	wild lily-of-the-valley	Maianthemum canadense	species
linanthus	linanthus	Leptosiphon	genus
linanthus, northern	northern linanthus	Leptosiphon septentrionalis	species
lipfern	lipfern	Myriopteris	genus
lipfern, lace	lace lip fern, lace fern	Myriopteris gracillima	species
lipfern, slender	slender lip fern	Myriopteris gracilis	species
little-bluestem	little-bluestem	Schizachyrium	genus
little-bluestem	little bluestem	Schizachyrium scoparium	species
little-rose	little-rose	Chamaerhodos	genus
little-rose	rose chamaerhodos, chamaerhodos	Chamaerhodos erecta	species
lobelia	lobelia	Lobelia	genus

253

ALPHABETIZED* COMMON NAMES

Suggested Common Name	VASCAN &/or ACIMS Common Name(s)	Scientific Name	Rank
lobelia, Kalm	Kalm's lobelia	Lobelia kalmii	species
lobelia, spiked	pale-spike lobelia, spiked lobelia	Lobelia spicata	species
lobelia, water	water lobelia	Lobelia dortmanna	species
locoweed	locoweed	Oxytropis	genus
locoweed, boreal	boreal locoweed	Oxytropis borealis	species
locoweed, field	field locoweed, northern locoweed	Oxytropis campestris	species
locoweed, harefoot	hare's-foot locoweed, hare-footed locoweed	Oxytropis lagopus	species
locoweed, inflated	inflated locoweed, inflated oxytrope	Oxytropis podocarpa	species
locoweed, pendantpod	pendant-pod locoweed, reflexed locoweed	Oxytropis deflexa	species
locoweed, showy	showy locoweed	Oxytropis splendens	species
locoweed, silky	silky locoweed, early yellow locoweed	Oxytropis sericea	species
loosestrife	loosestrife, starflower, milkwort, chaffweed,	Lysimachia	genus
loosestrife	loosestrife	Lythrum	genus
loosestrife family	loosestrife family	Lythraceae	family
loosestrife, fringed	fringed yellow loosestrife, fringed loosestrife	Lysimachia ciliata	species
loosestrife, lowland yellow	lowland yellow loosestrife, lance-leaved loosestrife	Lysimachia hybrida	species
loosestrife, purple	purple loosestrife	Lythrum salicaria	species
loosestrife, tufted	tufted yellow loosestrife, tufted loosestrife	Lysimachia thyrsiflora	species
lopseed family	lopseed family	Phrymaceae	family
lousewort	lousewort	Pedicularis	genus
lousewort, bracted	bracted lousewort, western lousewort	Pedicularis bracteosa	species
lousewort, capitate	capitate lousewort, large-flowered lousewort	Pedicularis capitata	species
lousewort, coiled	coiled-beaked lousewort, coiled-beak lousewort	Pedicularis contorta	species
lousewort, elephanthead	elephant's-head lousewort, elephant's-head	Pedicularis groenlandica	species
lousewort, flame	red-tipped lousewort, flame-colored lousewort	Pedicularis flammea	species
lousewort, Labrador	Labrador lousewort	Pedicularis labradorica	species
lousewort, Langsdorff	Langsdorff's lousewort, arctic lousewort	Pedicularis langsdorffii	species
lousewort, Oeder	Oeder's lousewort	Pedicularis oederi	species
lousewort, sickletop	sickletop lousewort, leafy lousewort	Pedicularis racemosa	species
lousewort, smallflower	small-flowered lousewort, swamp lousewort	Pedicularis parviflora	species
lousewort, Sudeten	Sudeten lousewort, purple rattle	Pedicularis sudetica	species

ALPHABETIZED* COMMON NAMES

Suggested Common Name	VASCAN &/or ACIMS Common Name(s)	Scientific Name	Rank
lousewort, woolly	woolly lousewort	Pedicularis lanata	species
lovage	lovage	Levisticum	genus
lovage, garden	garden lovage, lovage	Levisticum officinale	species
lupine	lupine	Lupinus	genus
lupine, dwarf	dwarf lupine, alpine lupine	Lupinus lepidus	species
lupine, largeleaf	large-leaved lupine	Lupinus polyphyllus	species
lupine, least	least lupine	Lupinus minimus	species
lupine, low	low lupine, annual lupine	Lupinus pusillus	species
lupine, Nootka	Nootka lupine	Lupinus nootkatensis	species
lupine, silky	silky lupine, silky perennial lupine	Lupinus sericeus	species
lupine, silvery	silvery lupine, silvery perennial lupine	Lupinus argenteus	species
lupine, Wyeth	Wyeth's lupine	Lupinus wyethii	species
lymegrass	lymegrass	Leymus	genus
lymegrass, downy	downy lymegrass, hairy wild rye	Leymus innovatus	species
lymegrass, Great Basin	Great Basin lymegrass, giant wild rye	Leymus cinereus	species
madwort	madwort	Asperugo	genus
madwort, German	German madwort, madwort	Asperugo procumbens	species
maidenhair	maidenhair	Adiantum	genus
maidenhair family	maidenhair family	Pteridaceae	family
maidenhair, Aleutian	Aleutian maidenhair fern, western maidenhair fern	Adiantum aleuticum	species
mallow	mallow	Malva	genus
mallow family	mallow family	Malvaceae	family
mallow, common	common mallow, round-leaved mallow	Malva neglecta	species
mallow, high	high mallow	Malva sylvestris	species
mallow, low	small mallow, round-leaved mallow	Malva pusilla	species
mallow, smallflower	small-flowered mallow	Malva parviflora	species
mallow, whorled	whorled mallow	Malva verticillata	species
Maltese-cross	Maltese-cross campion, Maltese cross	Silene chalcedonica	species
mannagrass	mannagrass	Glyceria	genus
mannagrass, fowl	fowl mannagrass, fowl manna grass	Glyceria striata	species
mannagrass, graceful	graceful mannagrass, graceful manna grass	Glyceria pulchella	species
mannagrass, northern	boreal mannagrass, northern manna grass	Glyceria borealis	species
mannagrass, tall	tall mannagrass, common tall manna grass	Glyceria grandis	species
mannagrass, tufted tall	tufted tall mannagrass, tufted tall manna grass	Glyceria elata	species
maple	maple	Acer	genus

ALPHABETIZED* COMMON NAMES

Suggested Common Name	VASCAN &/or ACIMS Common Name(s)	Scientific Name	Rank
maple, Manitoba	Manitoba maple	Acer negundo	species
maple, mountain	Rocky Mountain maple, mountain maple	Acer glabrum	species
mare's-tail	mare's-tail	Hippuris	genus
mare's-tail, common	common mare's-tail	Hippuris vulgaris	species
mare's-tail, mountain	mountain mare's-tail	Hippuris montana	species
mariposa-lily	mariposa-lily	Calochortus	genus
mariposa-lily, three-spot	three-spot mariposa lily, mariposa lily	Calochortus apiculatus	species
marsh-aster	marsh-aster	Almutaster	genus
marsh-aster, fewflower	marsh alkali aster, few-flowered aster	Almutaster pauciflorus	species
marsh-cinquefoil	marsh-cinquefoil	Comarum	genus
marsh-cinquefoil	marsh cinquefoil	Comarum palustre	species
marsh-felwort	marsh-felwort	Lomatogonium	genus
marsh-felwort	marsh felwort	Lomatogonium rotatum	species
marshfern family	marshfern family	Thelypteridaceae	family
marsh-groundsel	marsh-groundsel	Tephroseris	genus
marsh-groundsel	marsh groundsel, marsh ragwort	Tephroseris palustris	species
marshmarigold	marshmarigold	Caltha	genus
marshmarigold, floating	floating marsh marigold, floating marsh-marigold	Caltha natans	species
marshmarigold, white	white marsh marigold, mountain marsh-marigold	Caltha leptosepala	species
marshmarigold, yellow	yellow marsh marigold, marsh-marigold	Caltha palustris	species
matrimony-vine	matrimony-vine	Lycium	genus
matrimony-vine	common matrimony vine, matrimony vine	Lycium barbarum	species
meadow-deathcamas	meadow-deathcamas	Toxicoscordion	genus
meadow-deathcamas	meadow death camas, death camas	Toxicoscordion venenosum	species
meadowrue	meadowrue	Thalictrum	genus
meadowrue, fewflower	few-flowered meadow-rue, flat-fruited meadow rue	Thalictrum sparsiflorum	species
meadowrue, purple	purple meadow-rue, tall meadow rue	Thalictrum dasycarpum	species
meadowrue, veiny	veiny meadow-rue, veiny meadow rue	Thalictrum venulosum	species
meadowrue, western	western meadow-rue, western meadow rue	Thalictrum occidentale	species
meadowsweet	meadowsweet	Spiraea	genus
meadowsweet, rose	subalpine meadowsweet, pink meadowsweet	Spiraea splendens	species
meadowsweet, shinyleaf	shiny-leaved meadowsweet, white meadowsweet	Spiraea lucida	species

ALPHABETIZED* COMMON NAMES

Suggested Common Name	VASCAN &/or ACIMS Common Name(s)	Scientific Name	Rank
meadowsweet, white	white meadowsweet, narrow-leaved meadowsweet	Spiraea alba	species
medick	medick, alfalfa	Medicago	genus
medick, black	black medick	Medicago lupulina	species
microseris	microseris	Microseris	genus
microseris, nodding	nodding microseris	Microseris nutans	species
milkthistle	milkthistle	Silybum	genus
milkthistle, blessed	blessed milk thistle, milk thistle	Silybum marianum	species
milkvetch	milkvetch	Astragalus	genus
milkvetch, alpine	alpine milk-vetch, alpine milkvetch	Astragalus alpinus	species
milkvetch, American	American milk-vetch, American milk vetch	Astragalus americanus	species
milkvetch, bentflower	bent-flowered milk-vetch, few-flowered milkvetch	Astragalus vexilliflexus	species
milkvetch, Bodin	Bodin's milk-vetch, Bodin's milk vetch	Astragalus bodinii	species
milkvetch, Bourgov	Bourgov's milk-vetch, Bourgov's milk vetch	Astragalus bourgovii	species
milkvetch, Canada	Canada milk-vetch, Canadian milkvetch	Astragalus canadensis	species
milkvetch, chickpea	chickpea milk-vetch, cicer milk vetch	Astragalus cicer	species
milkvetch, Drummond	Drummond's milk-vetch, Drummond's milk vetch	Astragalus drummondii	species
milkvetch, elegant	elegant milk-vetch	Astragalus eucosmus	species
milkvetch, flexible	flexible milk-vetch, slender milkvetch	Astragalus flexuosus	species
milkvetch, ground-plum	ground plum milk-vetch, ground-plum	Astragalus crassicarpus	species
milkvetch, Laxmann	Laxmann's milk-vetch, ascending purple milk-vetch	Astragalus laxmannii	species
milkvetch, looseflower	loose-flowered milk-vetch, loose-flowered milk vetch	Astragalus tenellus	species
milkvetch, lotus	lotus milk-vetch, low milk vetch	Astragalus lotiflorus	species
milkvetch, Missouri	Missouri milk-vetch, Missouri milkvetch	Astragalus missouriensis	species
milkvetch, narrowleaf	narrow-leaved milk-vetch, narrow-leaved milk vetch	Astragalus pectinatus	species
milkvetch, plains	plains milk-vetch, cushion milkvetch	Astragalus gilviflorus	species
milkvetch, purple	field milk-vetch, purple milk vetch	Astragalus agrestis	species
milkvetch, Pursh	Pursh's milk-vetch, Pursh's milkvetch	Astragalus purshii	species
milkvetch, Robbins	Robbins' milk-vetch, Robbins' milk vetch	Astragalus robbinsii	species

ALPHABETIZED* COMMON NAMES

Suggested Common Name	VASCAN &/or ACIMS Common Name(s)	Scientific Name	Rank
milkvetch, southern	southern milk-vetch, Indian milkvetch	Astragalus australis	species
milkvetch, spiny	spiny milk-vetch, prickly milk vetch	Astragalus kentrophyta	species
milkvetch, timber	timber milk-vetch, timber milkvetch	Astragalus miser	species
milkvetch, tufted	tufted milk-vetch, tufted milk vetch	Astragalus spatulatus	species
milkvetch, twogroove	two-grooved milk-vetch, two-grooved milkvetch	Astragalus bisulcatus	species
milkweed	milkweed	Asclepias	genus
milkweed family	milkweed family; dogbane family	Apocynaceae	family
milkweed, green	green comet milkweed, green milkweed	Asclepias viridiflora	species
milkweed, ovalleaf	oval-leaved milkweed, low milkweed	Asclepias ovalifolia	species
milkweed, showy	showy milkweed	Asclepias speciosa	species
milkwort.	milkwort, loosestrife, starflower, chaffweed	Lysimachia	genus
milkwort	milkwort	Polygaloides	genus
milkwort family	milkwort family	Polygalaceae	family
milkwort, fringed	fringed milkwort	Polygaloides paucifolia	species
milkwort, sea	sea milkwort	Lysimachia maritima	species
millet	millet, panicgrass	Panicum	genus
millet, proso	proso millet, broomcorn millet	Panicum miliaceum	species
mint	mint	Mentha	genus
mint family	mint family	Lamiaceae	family
mint, wild	Canada mint, wild mint	Mentha canadensis/ Mentha arvensis	species
mistletoe family	mistletoe family	Loranthaceae	family
mistmaiden	mistmaiden	Romanzoffia	genus
mistmaiden, Sitka	Sitka mistmaiden, Sitka romanzoffia	Romanzoffia sitchensis	species
mitrewort	mitrewort	Conimitella	genus
mitrewort	mitrewort	Mitella	genus
mitrewort, Brewer	Brewer's mitrewort, Brewer's bishop's-cap	Mitella breweri	species
mitrewort, fivestamen	five-stamen mitrewort, bishop's-cap	Mitella pentandra	species
mitrewort, naked	naked mitrewort, bishop's-cap	Mitella nuda	species
mitrewort, Pacific	Pacific mitrewort, bishop's-cap	Mitella trifida	species
mitrewort, Williams	Williams' mitrewort, conimitella	Conimitella williamsii	species
mockorange	mockorange	Philadelphus	genus
mockorange, Lewis	Lewis' mock-orange, mock orange	Philadelphus lewisii	species
monkeyflower	monkeyflower	Erythranthe	genus

ALPHABETIZED* COMMON NAMES

Suggested Common Name	VASCAN &/or ACIMS Common Name(s)	Scientific Name	Rank
monkeyflower	monkeyflower	Mimulus	genus
monkeyflower, Brewer	Brewer's monkeyflower	Erythranthe breweri	species
monkeyflower, Geyer	Geyer's yellow monkeyflower, smooth monkeyflower	Erythranthe geyeri	species
monkeyflower, Lewis	Lewis' monkeyflower, red monkeyflower	Erythranthe lewisii	species
monkeyflower, musk	musk monkeyflower	Erythranthe moschatus	species
monkeyflower, seep	seep monkeyflower, yellow monkeyflower	Erythranthe guttata	species
monkeyflower, small yellow	purple-stemmed monkeyflower, small yellow monkeyflower	Erythranthe floribunda	species
monkeyflower, squarestem	square-stemmed monkeyflower, square-stem monkeyflower	Mimulus ringens	species
monkeyflower, Tiling	Tiling's monkeyflower, large mountain monkeyflower	Erythranthe tilingii	species
monkshood	monkshood	Aconitum	genus
monkshood, mountain	mountain monkshood, monkshood	Aconitum delphiniifolium	species
monkswort	monkswort	Nonea	genus
monkswort, red	red monkswort, red monk's-wort	Nonea vesicaria	species
montia	montia	Montia	genus
montia, littleleaf	small-leaved montia	Montia parvifolia	species
montia, narrowleaf	narrow-leaved montia, linear-leaved montia	Montia linearis	species
moonwort	moonwort	Botrychium	genus
moonwort, ascending	upswept moonwort, ascending grape fern	Botrychium ascendens	species
moonwort, chamomile	daisy-leaved moonwort, chamomile grape-fern	Botrychium matricariifolium	species
moonwort, common	common moonwort, moonwort	Botrychium lunaria	species
moonwort, field	prairie moonwort, field grape fern	Botrychium campestre	species
moonwort, least	least moonwort, dwarf grape fern	Botrychium simplex	species
moonwort, Michigan	Michigan moonwort, Michigan grapefern	Botrychium michiganense	species
moonwort, Mingan	Mingan moonwort, Mingan grape fern	Botrychium minganense	species
moonwort, North America	North American moonwort	Botrychium neolunaria	species
moonwort, northwestern	northwestern moonwort, northwestern grapefern	Botrychium pinnatum	species
moonwort, pale	pale moonwort	Botrychium pallidum	species
moonwort, paradox	paradox moonwort, paradoxical grape fern	Botrychium paradoxum	species
moonwort, scalloped	dainty moonwort, scalloped grapefern	Botrychium crenulatum	species
moonwort, slender	slender moonwort, straight-leaf moonwort	Botrychium lineare	species

ALPHABETIZED* COMMON NAMES

Suggested Common Name	VASCAN &/or ACIMS Common Name(s)	Scientific Name	Rank
moonwort, spatula	spatulate moonwort, spatulate grape fern	Botrychium spathulatum	species
moonwort, stalked	stalked moonwort, stalked grape fern	Botrychium pedunculosum	species
moonwort, triangle	triangle moonwort	Botrychium lanceolatum	species
moonwort, Tunux	Tunux' moonwort, moosewort	Botrychium tunux	species
moonwort, Waterton	Waterton moonwort, Waterton grapefern	Botrychium ×watertonense	Hybrid
moonwort, western	western moonwort, western grape fern	Botrychium hesperium	species
moschatel family	moschatel family	Adoxaceae	family
motherwort	motherwort	Leonurus	genus
motherwort	common motherwort, motherwort	Leonurus cardiaca	species
mountain-ash	mountain-ash	Sorbus	genus
mountain-ash, European	European mountain-ash	Sorbus aucuparia	species
mountain-ash, Sitka	Sitka mountain-ash, Sitka mountain ash	Sorbus sitchensis	species
mountain-ash, western	Greene's mountain-ash, western mountain-ash	Sorbus scopulina	species
mountain-avens	mountain-avens	Dryas	genus
mountain-avens, Drummond	Drummond's mountain avens, yellow mountain avens	Dryas drummondii	species
mountain-avens, entireleaf	entire-leaved mountain avens, northern white mountain avens	Dryas integrifolia	species
mountain-avens, Hooker	Hooker's mountain avens, white mountain avens	Dryas hookeriana	species
mountainheath	mountainheath	Phyllodoce	genus
mountainheath, pink	pink mountain heather, red heather	Phyllodoce empetriformis	species
mountainheath, yellow	yellow mountain heather, yellow heather	Phyllodoce glanduliflora	species
mountain-heather	mountain-heather	Cassiope	genus
mountain-heather, fourangle	four-angled mountain heather, white mountain-heather	Cassiope tetragona	species
mountain-heather, western	white mountain heather, western mountain-heather	Cassiope mertensiana	species
mountain-lover	mountain-lover	Paxistima	genus
mountain-lover	falsebox, mountain-lover	Paxistima myrsinites	species
mountain-sorrel	mountain-sorrel	Oxyria	genus
mountain-sorrel	mountain-sorrel, mountain sorrel	Oxyria digyna	species
mousetail	mousetail	Myosurus	genus
mousetail, bristly	bristly mousetail	Myosurus apetalus	species
mousetail, tiny	tiny mousetail, least mousetail	Myosurus minimus	species
mudwort	mudwort	Limosella	genus
mudwort, water	water mudwort, mudwort	Limosella aquatica	species

ALPHABETIZED* COMMON NAMES

Suggested Common Name	VASCAN &/or ACIMS Common Name(s)	Scientific Name	Rank
muhly	muhly	Muhlenbergia	genus
muhly, alkali	alkali muhly, scratch grass	Muhlenbergia asperifolia	species
muhly, marsh	marsh muhly	Muhlenbergia racemosa	species
muhly, mat	mat muhly	Muhlenbergia richardsonis	species
muhly, plains	plains muhly	Muhlenbergia cuspidata	species
muhly, spike	spike muhly, bog muhly	Muhlenbergia glomerata	species
muhly, tumblegrass	prairie tumblegrass, tumble grass	Muhlenbergia paniculata	species
mullein	mullein	Verbascum	genus
mullein, black	black mullein	Verbascum nigrum	species
mullein, common	common mullein	Verbascum thapsus	species
mullein, orange	clasping mullein, orange mullein, woolly mullein	Verbascum phlomoides	species
muskroot	muskroot	Adoxa	genus
muskroot	muskroot, moschatel	Adoxa moschatellina	species
mustard	mustard	Brassica	genus
mustard	mustard	Sinapis	genus
mustard family	mustard family	Brassicaceae	family
mustard, black	black mustard	Brassica nigra	species
mustard, Chinese	Chinese mustard, Indian mustard	Brassica juncea	species
mustard, corn	corn mustard, wild mustard	Sinapis arvensis	species
mustard, field	field mustard, Bird's rape	Brassica rapa	species
mustard, rapeseed	rapeseed, rutabaga	Brassica napus	species
mustard, white	white mustard	Sinapis alba	species
naiad	naiad	Najas	genus
naiad, slender	slender naiad	Najas flexilis	species
naiad, southern	southern naiad	Najas guadalupensis	species
nailwort	nailwort	Paronychia	genus
nailwort, creeping	creeping nailwort	Paronychia sessiliflora	species
Navajo-tea, greenthread	Navajo tea, greenthread	Thelesperma	genus
navarretia	navarretia	Navarretia	genus
navarretia, whiteflower	whiteflower navarretia, white-flowered navarretia	Navarretia leucocephala	species
needle-and-thread	needle-and-thread grass, needle-and-thread	Hesperostipa comata	species
needlegrass	needlegrass	Achnatherum	genus
needlegrass	needlegrass	Nassella	genus
needlegrass, green	green needlegrass, green needle grass	Nassella viridula	species
needlegrass, Nelson	Nelson's needlegrass	Achnatherum nelsonii	species
needlegrass, Richardson	Richardson's needlegrass, Richardson needle grass	Achnatherum richardsonii	species
nettle	nettle	Urtica	genus
nettle family	nettle family	Urticaceae	family
nettle, burning	burning nettle, small nettle	Urtica urens	species
nettle, stinging	stinging nettle, common nettle	Urtica dioica	species

261

ALPHABETIZED* COMMON NAMES

Suggested Common Name	VASCAN &/or ACIMS Common Name(s)	Scientific Name	Rank
nightshade	nightshade	Solanum	genus
nightshade family	nightshade family	Solanaceae	family
nightshade, black	black nightshade	Solanum nigrum	species
nightshade, buffalobur	horned nightshade, buffalo-burr	Solanum rostratum	species
nightshade, climbing	bittersweet nightshade, climbing nightshade	Solanum dulcamara	species
nightshade, cutleaf	cut-leaved nightshade, wild tomato	Solanum triflorum	species
nightshade, hairy	hairy nightshade	Solanum nitidibaccatum	species
ninebark	ninebark	Physocarpus	genus
ninebark, mallowleaf	mallow-leaved ninebark	Physocarpus malvaceus	species
nipplewort	nipplewort	Lapsana	genus
nipplewort	common nipplewort, nipplewort	Lapsana communis	species
North-Africa-grass	North-Africa-grass	Ventenata	genus
North-Africa-grass	ventenata	Ventenata dubia	species
northern-aster	northern-aster	Canadanthus	genus
northern-aster, large	great northern aster, large northern aster	Canadanthus modestus	species
oak	oak	Quercus	genus
oak, bur	bur oak, burr oak	Quercus macrocarpa	species
oakfern	oakfern	Gymnocarpium	genus
oakfern, common	common oak fern, oak fern	Gymnocarpium dryopteris	species
oakfern, Nahanni	Nahanni oak fern, northern oak fern	Gymnocarpium continentale	species
oakfern, Pacific	Pacific oak fern, western oak fern	Gymnocarpium disjunctum	species
oat	oat	Avena	genus
oat, cultivated	cultivated oats, cultivated oat	Avena sativa	species
oat, wild	common wild oats, wild oat	Avena fatua	species
oatgrass	oatgrass	Danthonia	genus
oatgrass	oatgrass	Helictochloa	genus
oatgrass, California	California oatgrass, California oat grass	Danthonia californica	species
oatgrass, Hooker	Hooker's oatgrass, Hooker's oat grass	Helictochloa hookeri	species
oatgrass, onespike	one-spike oatgrass, one-spike oat grass	Danthonia unispicata	species
oatgrass, Parry	Parry's oatgrass, Parry oat grass	Danthonia parryi	species
oatgrass, poverty	poverty oatgrass, poverty oat grass	Danthonia spicata	species
oatgrass, timber	timber oatgrass, intermediate oat grass	Danthonia intermedia	species
oleaster family	oleaster family	Elaeagnaceae	family
oneflower-wintergreen	oneflower-wintergreen	Moneses	genus
oneflower-wintergreen	one-flowered wintergreen	Moneses uniflora	species
onion	onion	Allium	genus

ALPHABETIZED* COMMON NAMES

Suggested Common Name	VASCAN &/or ACIMS Common Name(s)	Scientific Name	Rank
onion, Geyer	Geyer's onion	Allium geyeri	species
onion, nodding	nodding onion	Allium cernuum	species
onion, prairie	prairie onion	Allium textile	species
oniongrass	oniongrass	Melica	genus
oniongrass, Alaska	Alaska oniongrass, Alaska onion grass	Melica subulata	species
oniongrass, purple	purple oniongrass, onion grass	Melica spectabilis	species
oniongrass, Smith	Smith's oniongrass	Melica smithii	species
orchardgrass	orchardgrass	Dactylis	genus
orchardgrass	orchard grass	Dactylis glomerata	species
orchid family	orchid family	Orchidaceae	family
ostrich-fern	ostrich-fern	Matteuccia	genus
ostrich-fern	ostrich fern	Matteuccia struthiopteris	species
owlclover	owlclover	Orthocarpus	genus
owlclover, yellow	yellow owl's-clover, owl-clover	Orthocarpus luteus	species
oxtongue	oxtongue	Helminthotheca	genus
oxtongue, bristly	bristly oxtongue	Helminthotheca echioides	species
paintbrush	paintbrush	Castilleja	genus
paintbrush, Cusick	Cusick's paintbrush, yellow paintbrush	Castilleja cusickii	species
paintbrush, downy	downy paintbrush	Castilleja sessiliflora	species
paintbrush, elegant	elegant paintbrush	Castilleja elegans	species
paintbrush, great red	great red paintbrush, common red paintbrush	Castilleja miniata	species
paintbrush, harsh	harsh paintbrush, hispid paintbrush	Castilleja hispida	species
paintbrush, northeastern	northeastern paintbrush	Castilleja septentrionalis	species
paintbrush, purple	purple paintbrush	Castilleja purpurascens	species
paintbrush, Raup	Raup's paintbrush, purple paintbrush	Castilleja raupii	species
paintbrush, smallflower	small-flowered paintbrush, small-flowered Indian paintbrush	Castilleja parviflora	species
paintbrush, splitleaf	rhexia-leaved paintbrush, alpine red paintbrush	Castilleja rhexiifolia	species
paintbrush, stiff yellow	stiff yellow paintbrush	Castilleja lutescens	species
paintbrush, western	western paintbrush, lance-leaved paintbrush	Castilleja occidentalis	species
panicgrass	panicgrass	Dichanthelium	genus
panicgrass	panicgrass, millet	Panicum	genus
panicgrass, common	common panicgrass, witch grass	Panicum capillare	species
panicgrass, fewflower	few-flowered panicgrass, sand millet	Dichanthelium oligosanthes	species
panicgrass, Geyser	Geyser panicgrass	Dichanthelium thermale	species
panicgrass, Leiberg	Leiberg's panicgrass, Leiberg's millet	Dichanthelium leibergii	species
panicgrass, Wilcox	Wilcox's panicgrass	Dichanthelium wilcoxianum	species

ALPHABETIZED* COMMON NAMES

Suggested Common Name	VASCAN &/or ACIMS Common Name(s)	Scientific Name	Rank
panicgrass, woolly	woolly panicgrass, hairy panicgrass	Dichanthelium lanuginosum	species
pansy	pansy, violet	Viola	genus
pansy, European field	European field pansy	Viola arvensis	species
parsnip	parsnip	Pastinaca	genus
parsnip, wild	wild parsnip, parsnip	Pastinaca sativa	species
partridgefoot	partridgefoot	Luetkea	genus
partridgefoot	partridgefoot	Luetkea pectinata	species
pasqueflower	pasqueflower	Pulsatilla	genus
pasqueflower, prairie	prairie pasqueflower, prairie crocus	Anemone patens	species
pasqueflower, western	western pasqueflower, western anemone	Anemone occidentalis	species
pathfinder	pathfinder	Adenocaulon	genus
pathfinder	pathfinder	Adenocaulon bicolor	species
pearlwort	pearlwort	Sagina	genus
pearlwort, alpine	alpine pearlwort, mountain pearlwort	Sagina saginoides	species
pearlwort, knotted	knotted pearlwort, pearlwort	Sagina nodosa	species
pearlwort, snow	snow pearlwort, pearlwort	Sagina nivalis	species
pearlwort, spreading	spreading pearlwort	Sagina decumbens	species
pellitory	pellitory	Parietaria	genus
pellitory, Pennsylvania	Pennsylvania pellitory, American pellitory	Parietaria pensylvanica	species
pennycress	pennycress	Thlaspi	genus
pennycress, field	field pennycress, stinkweed	Thlaspi arvense	species
peppergrass	peppergrass, hoarycress	Lepidium	genus
peppergrass, branched	branched peppergrass, branched pepper-grass	Lepidium ramosissimum	species
peppergrass, broadleaf	broad-leaved peppergrass, broad-leaved pepper-grass	Lepidium latifolium	species
peppergrass, claspingleaf	clasping-leaved peppergrass, perfoliate pepper-grass	Lepidium perfoliatum	species
peppergrass, common	common peppergrass, common pepper-grass	Lepidium densiflorum	species
peppergrass, field	field peppergrass, cow cress	Lepidium campestre	species
peppergrass, garden	garden peppergrass, garden cress	Lepidium sativum	species
peppergrass, roadside	roadside peppergrass	Lepidium ruderale	species
phacelia, desert	desert phacelia	Phacelia campanularia	species
phlox	phlox	Phlox	genus
phlox family	phlox family	Polemoniaceae	family
phlox, blue	blue phlox	Phlox alyssifolia	species
phlox, Hood	Hood's phlox, moss phlox	Phlox hoodii	species
picradeniopsis	picradeniopsis	Picradeniopsis	genus

ALPHABETIZED* COMMON NAMES

Suggested Common Name	VASCAN &/or ACIMS Common Name(s)	Scientific Name	Rank
picradeniopsis	opposite-leaved bahia, picradeniopsis	Picradeniopsis oppositifolia	species
pincushion	pincushion	Chaenactis	genus
pincushion, hoary	hoary pincushion	Chaenactis douglasii	species
pine	pine	Pinus	genus
pine family	pine family	Pinaceae	family
pine, jack	jack pine	Pinus banksiana	species
pine, limber	limber pine	Pinus flexilis	species
pine, lodgepole	lodgepole pine	Pinus contorta	species
pine, ponderosa	ponderosa pine	Pinus ponderosa	species
pine, western white	western white pine	Pinus monticola	species
pine, whitebark	whitebark pine	Pinus albicaulis	species
pineappleweed	pineappleweed	Matricaria discoidea	species
pinedrops	pinedrops	Pterospora	genus
pinedrops	pinedrops, pine-drops	Pterospora andromedea	species
pinesap	pinesap	Hypopitys	genus
pinesap	pinesap	Hypopitys monotropa	species
pink	pink	Dianthus	genus
pink family	pink family	Caryophyllaceae	family
pink, garden	garden pink	Dianthus plumarius	species
pink, grass	Deptford pink, grass pink	Dianthus armeria	species
pink, maiden	maiden pink	Dianthus deltoides	species
pink, ragged	ragged pink, European pink	Dianthus seguieri	species
pinweed	pinweed	Lechea	genus
pinweed, largepod	large-pod pinweed, narrowleaf pinweed	Lechea intermedia	species
pipsissewa	pipsissewa	Chimaphila	genus
pipsissewa	common pipsissewa, prince's-pine	Chimaphila umbellata	species
pitcherplant	pitcherplant	Sarracenia	genus
pitcherplant family	pitcherplant family	Sarraceniaceae	family
pitcherplant, purple	northern pitcher plant, pitcher-plant	Sarracenia purpurea	species
plantain	plantain	Plantago	genus
plantain family	plantain family	Plantaginaceae	family
plantain, common	common plantain	Plantago major	species
plantain, gray hairy	hairy plantain, western ribgrass	Plantago canescens	species
plantain, hoary	hoary plantain	Plantago media	species
plantain, linearleaf	slender plantain, linear-leaved plantain	Plantago elongata	species
plantain, saline	saline plantain	Plantago eriopoda	species
plantain, seaside	seaside plantain, sea-side plantain	Plantago maritima	species
plantain, woolly	woolly plantain, Pursh's plantain	Plantago patagonica	species
plumeless-thistle	plumeless-thistle	Carduus	genus

ALPHABETIZED* COMMON NAMES

Suggested Common Name	VASCAN &/or ACIMS Common Name(s)	Scientific Name	Rank
plumeless-thistle, spiny	spiny plumeless thistle, plumeless thistle	Carduus acanthoides	species
poison-hemlock	poison-hemlock	Conium	genus
poison-hemlock	poison-hemlock, poison hemlock	Conium maculatum	species
poison-ivy	poison-ivy	Toxicodendron	genus
poison-ivy	poison ivy	Toxicodendron radicans	species
polargrass	polargrass	Arctagrostis	genus
polargrass, wideleaf	wide-leaved polargrass	Arctagrostis latifolia	species
polypody	polypody	Polypodium	genus
polypody family	polypody family	Polypodiaceae	family
polypody, rock	rock polypody	Polypodium virginianum	species
polypody, Siberian	Siberian polypody	Polypodium sibiricum	species
polypody, western	western polypody	Polypodium hesperium	species
pondlily	pondlily	Nuphar	genus
pondlily, variegated	variegated pond-lily, yellow pond-lily	Nuphar variegata	species
pondweed	pondweed	Potamogeton	genus
pondweed	pondweed	Stuckenia	genus
pondweed family	pondweed family	Potamogetonaceae	family
pondweed, alpine	alpine pondweed	Potamogeton alpinus	species
pondweed, Berchtold	Berchtold's pondweed	Potamogeton berchtoldii	species
pondweed, bluntleaf	blunt-leaved pondweed	Potamogeton obtusifolius	species
pondweed, curly	curly-leaved pondweed, crisp-leaved pondweed	Potamogeton crispus	species
pondweed, flatstem	flat-stemmed pondweed	Potamogeton zosteriformis	species
pondweed, floatingleaf	floating-leaved pondweed, floating-leaf pondweed	Potamogeton natans	species
pondweed, Fries	Fries' pondweed	Potamogeton friesii	species
pondweed, grassy	grass-leaved pondweed, various-leaved pondweed	Potamogeton gramineus	species
pondweed, largeleaf	large-leaved pondweed	Potamogeton amplifolius	species
pondweed, leafy	leafy pondweed	Potamogeton foliosus	species
pondweed, longleaf	long-leaved pondweed, longleaf pondweed	Potamogeton nodosus	species
pondweed, ribbonleaf	ribbon-leaved pondweed	Potamogeton epihydrus	species
pondweed, Richardson	Richardson's pondweed, clasping-leaf pondweed	Potamogeton richardsonii	species
pondweed, Robbins	Robbins' pondweed	Potamogeton robbinsii	species
pondweed, sago	sago pondweed	Stuckenia pectinata	species
pondweed, sheathed	big-sheathed pondweed, large-sheath pondweed	Stuckenia vaginata	species
pondweed, small	small pondweed, small-leaf pondweed	Potamogeton pusillus	species
pondweed, straightleaf	straight-leaved pondweed, linear-leaved pondweed	Potamogeton strictifolius	species

ALPHABETIZED* COMMON NAMES

Suggested Common Name	VASCAN &/or ACIMS Common Name(s)	Scientific Name	Rank
pondweed, threadleaf	thread-leaved pondweed	Stuckenia filiformis	species
pondweed, waterthread	water-thread pondweed	Potamogeton diversifolius	species
pondweed, whitestem	white-stemmed pondweed, white-stem pondweed	Potamogeton praelongus	species
popcornflower	popcornflower	Plagiobothrys	genus
popcornflower, Scouler	Scouler's popcornflower, Scouler's allocarya	Plagiobothrys scouleri	species
poplar	poplar, cottonwood, aspen	Populus	genus
poplar, balsam	balsam poplar	Populus balsamifera	species
poplar, Jack hybrid	Jack's hybrid poplar	Populus ×jackii	Hybrid
poppy	poppy	Papaver	genus
poppy family	poppy family	Papaveraceae	family
poppy, corn	corn poppy	Papaver rhoeas	species
poppy, dwarf alpine	dwarf alpine poppy	Papaver pygmaeum	species
poppy, Iceland	ice poppy, Iceland poppy	Papaver nudicaule	species
poppy, Kluane	Kluane poppy, alpine poppy	Papaver kluanense	species
poppy, opium	opium poppy	Papaver somniferum	species
porcupinegrass, needle-and-thread	needle-and-thread, porcupinegrass	Hesperostipa	genus
porcupinegrass, northern	northern porcupine grass, western porcupine grass	Hesperostipa curtiseta	species
porcupinegrass, plains	plains porcupine grass, porcupine grass	Hesperostipa spartea	species
povertyweed	povertyweed	Iva	genus
povertyweed	povertyweed	Iva axillaris	species
povertyweed, Nuttall	Nuttall's povertyweed, spear-leaved goosefoot	Blitum nuttallianum	species
prairie-aster, creeping white	white prairie aster, creeping white prairie aster	Symphyotrichum falcatum	species
prairie-aster, tufted white	white heath aster, tufted white prairie aster	Symphyotrichum ericoides	species
prairieclover	prairieclover	Dalea	genus
prairieclover, purple	purple prairie-clover	Dalea purpurea	species
prairieclover, white	white prairie-clover	Dalea candida	species
prairie-coneflower	prairie-coneflower	Ratibida	genus
prairie-coneflower, upright	upright prairie coneflower, prairie coneflower	Ratibida columnifera	species
pricklypear	pricklypear	Opuntia	genus
pricklypear, brittle	brittle prickly-pear cactus, brittle prickly-pear	Opuntia fragilis	species
pricklypear, plains	plains prickly-pear cactus, prickly-pear	Opuntia polyacantha	species
primrose	primrose, shootingstar	Primula	genus
primrose family	primrose family	Primulaceae	family
primrose, Greenland	Greenland primrose	Primula egaliksensis	species

ALPHABETIZED* COMMON NAMES

Suggested Common Name	VASCAN &/or ACIMS Common Name(s)	Scientific Name	Rank
primrose, mealy	mealy primrose	Primula incana	species
primrose, Mistassini	Mistassini primrose, dwarf Canadian primrose	Primula mistassinica	species
purslane	purslane	Portulaca	genus
purslane family	purslane family	Portulacaceae	family
purslane, common	common purslane, purslane	Portulaca oleracea	species
pussytoes	pussytoes	Antennaria	genus
pussytoes, alpine	alpine pussytoes, alpine everlasting	Antennaria alpina	species
pussytoes, broadleaf	field pussytoes, broad-leaved everlasting	Antennaria neglecta	species
pussytoes, cushion	low pussytoes, cushion everlasting	Antennaria dimorpha	species
pussytoes, flat-top	flat-top pussytoes, corymbose everlasting	Antennaria corymbosa	species
pussytoes, Howell	Howell's pussytoes, small pussytoes	Antennaria howellii	species
pussytoes, littleleaf	little-leaved pussytoes, littleleaf pussytoes	Antennaria microphylla	species
pussytoes, onehead	pygmy pussytoes, one-headed everlasting	Antennaria monocephala	species
pussytoes, pearly	pearly pussytoes, tall everlasting	Antennaria anaphaloides	species
pussytoes, racemose	racemose pussytoes, racemose everlasting	Antennaria racemosa	species
pussytoes, Rocky-Mountain	Rocky Mountain pussytoes	Antennaria media	species
pussytoes, rosy	rosy pussytoes, rosy everlasting	Antennaria rosea	species
pussytoes, scented	scented pussytoes	Antennaria aromatica	species
pussytoes, showy	showy pussytoes, showy everlasting	Antennaria pulcherrima	species
pussytoes, smallleaf	small-leaved pussytoes, small-leaved everlasting	Antennaria parvifolia	species
pussytoes, umber	umber pussytoes, brown-bracted mountain everlasting	Antennaria umbrinella	species
pussytoes, woodrush	woodrush pussytoes, silvery everlasting	Antennaria luzuloides	species
pussytoes, woolly	woolly pussytoes, woolly everlasting	Antennaria lanata	species
quackgrass	quackgrass	Elymus repens	species
quaking-grass	quaking-grass	Briza	genus
quaking-grass, big	big quaking grass	Briza maxima	species
quillwort	quillwort	Isoetes, Isoëtes	genus
quillwort family	quillwort family	Isoetaceae	family
quillwort, Bolander	Bolander's quillwort	Isoetes bolanderi	species
quillwort, coastal	coastal quillwort	Isoetes maritima	species
quillwort, spinyspore	spiny-spored quillwort, northern quillwort	Isoetes echinospora	species
quillwort, western	western quillwort	Isoetes occidentalis	species

ALPHABETIZED* COMMON NAMES

Suggested Common Name	VASCAN &/or ACIMS Common Name(s)	Scientific Name	Rank
rabbitbrush, rubber	rubber rabbitbrush, rabbitbrush	Ericameria nauseosa	species
rabbitbush	rabbitbush	Ericameria	genus
rabbitfoot-grass	rabbitfoot-grass	Polypogon	genus
rabbitfoot-grass, annual	annual rabbit's-foot grass, rabbitfoot grass	Polypogon monspeliensis	species
radish	radish	Raphanus	genus
radish, wild	wild radish	Raphanus raphanistrum	species
ragweed	ragweed	Ambrosia	genus
ragweed, bur	burr ragweed, bur ragweed	Ambrosia acanthicarpa	species
ragweed, common	common ragweed	Ambrosia artemisiifolia	species
ragweed, great	great ragweed	Ambrosia trifida	species
ragweed, perennial	perennial ragweed	Ambrosia psilostachya	species
ragwort	ragwort	Senecio	genus
ragwort, arrowleaf	arrow-leaved ragwort, brook ragwort	Senecio triangularis	species
ragwort, blacktip	small black-tip ragwort, black-tipped groundsel	Senecio lugens	species
ragwort, common	common ragwort, common groundsel	Senecio vulgaris	species
ragwort, cutleaf	dryland ragwort, cut-leaved ragwort	Senecio eremophilus	species
ragwort, entireleaf	western ragwort, entire-leaved groundsel	Senecio integerrimus	species
ragwort, Fremont	Fremont's ragwort, mountain butterweed	Senecio fremontii	species
ragwort, largeflower	large-flowered ragwort	Senecio megacephalus	species
ragwort, sticky	sticky ragwort, sticky groundsel	Senecio viscosus	species
ragwort, sweet marsh	sweet marsh ragwort, ragwort	Senecio hydrophiloides	species
raspberry	raspberry, cloudberry, dwarf-bramble, thimbleberry	Rubus	genus
raspberry, arctic	arctic raspberry, dwarf raspberry	Rubus arcticus	species
raspberry, dwarf	dwarf raspberry, dewberry	Rubus pubescens	species
raspberry, wild red	red raspberry, wild red raspberry	Rubus idaeus	species
rattlesnake-fern	rattlesnake-fern	Botrypus	genus
rattlesnake-fern	rattlesnake fern, Virginia grape fern	Botrypus virginianus	species
rattlesnake-plantain	rattlesnake-plantain	Goodyera	genus
rattlesnake-plantain, dwarf	dwarf rattlesnake-plantain, lesser rattlesnake plantain	Goodyera repens	species
rattlesnake-plantain, Menzies	Menzies' rattlesnake-plantain, rattlesnake plantain	Goodyera oblongifolia	species
rattlesnakeroot	rattlesnakeroot	Nabalus	genus
rattlesnakeroot, glaucous	glaucous rattlesnakeroot, glaucous white lettuce	Nabalus racemosus	species

ALPHABETIZED* COMMON NAMES

Suggested Common Name	VASCAN &/or ACIMS Common Name(s)	Scientific Name	Rank
rattlesnakeroot, purple	arrow-leaved rattlesnakeroot, purple rattlesnakeroot	Nabalus sagittatus	species
rattlesnakeroot, western	western rattlesnakeroot, white lettuce	Nabalus alatus	species
red-bulrush	red-bulrush	Blysmopsis	genus
red-bulrush	red bulrush	Blysmopsis rufa	species
red-cedar	red-cedar	Thuja	genus
red-cedar, western	western red cedar	Thuja plicata	species
reed	reed	Phragmites	genus
reed, common	common reed	Phragmites australis	species
reedgrass	reedgrass	Calamagrostis	genus
reedgrass, bluejoint	bluejoint reedgrass, bluejoint	Calamagrostis canadensis	species
reedgrass, chee	chee reedgrass	Calamagrostis epigeios	species
reedgrass, Lapland	Lapland reedgrass, Lapland reed grass	Calamagrostis lapponica	species
reedgrass, pine	pine reedgrass, pine reed grass	Calamagrostis rubescens	species
reedgrass, plains	plains reedgrass, plains reed grass	Calamagrostis montanensis	species
reedgrass, purple	purple reedgrass, purple reed grass	Calamagrostis purpurascens	species
reedgrass, slimstem	slim-stemmed reedgrass, narrow reed grass	Calamagrostis stricta	species
restharrow	restharrow	Ononis	genus
restharrow, spiny	spiny restharrow, common rest-harrow	Ononis spinosa	species
rhododendron	rhododendron, Labrador-tea	Rhododendron	genus
rhododendron, whiteflower	white-flowered rhododendron	Rhododendron albiflorum	species
rhubarb	rhubarb	Rheum	genus
rhubarb	rhubarb	Rheum rhabarbarum	species
ricegrass	ricegrass	Eriocoma	genus
ricegrass	ricegrass	Oryzopsis	genus
ricegrass	ricegrass	Piptatheropsis	genus
ricegrass, Canada	Canada ricegrass, Canada rice grass	Piptatheropsis canadensis	species
ricegrass, Indian	Indian ricegrass, Indian rice grass	Eriocoma hymenoides	species
ricegrass, little	little ricegrass, little rice grass	Piptatheropsis exigua	species
ricegrass, littleseed	small-flowered ricegrass, little-seed rice grass	Piptatheropsis micrantha	species
ricegrass, roughleaf	rough-leaved mountain rice, white-grained mountain rice grass	Oryzopsis asperifolia	species
ricegrass, slender	slender ricegrass, northern rice grass	Piptatheropsis pungens	species
rivergrass	rivergrass	Scolochloa	genus
rivergrass	common rivergrass, spangletop	Scolochloa festucacea	species
rockbrake	rockbrake	Cryptogramma	genus

270

ALPHABETIZED* COMMON NAMES

Suggested Common Name	VASCAN &/or ACIMS Common Name(s)	Scientific Name	Rank
rockbrake, American	American rockbrake, parsley fern	Cryptogramma acrostichoides	species
rockbrake, Steller	Steller's rockbrake, Steller's rock brake	Cryptogramma stelleri	species
rockcress	rockcress	Arabidopsis	genus
rockcress	rockcress	Arabis	genus
rockcress	rockcress	Boechera	genus
rockcress, Calder	Calder's rockcress	Boechera calderi	species
rockcress, Collins	Collins' rockcress	Boechera collinsii	species
rockcress, danglepod	dangle-pod rockcress	Boechera pendulocarpa	species
rockcress, Drummond	Drummond's rockcress, Drummond's rock cress	Boechera stricta	species
rockcress, Eschscholtz	Eschscholtz's rockcress	Arabis eschscholtziana	species
rockcress, Graham	Graham's rockcress, limestone rockcress	Boechera grahamii	species
rockcress, hairy	cream-flowered rockcress, hairy rockcress	Arabis pycnocarpa	species
rockcress, Lemmon	Lemmon's rockcress	Boechera lemmonii	species
rockcress, Lyall	Lyall's rockcress	Boechera lyallii	species
rockcress, lyreleaf	lyre-leaved rockcress, lyreleaf rockcress	Arabidopsis lyrata	species
rockcress, Nuttall	Nuttall's rockcress, Nuttall's rock cress	Arabis nuttallii	species
rockcress, reflexed	reflexed rockcress	Boechera retrofracta	species
rockcress, soldier	soldier rockcress	Boechera drepanoloba	species
rock-harlequin	rock-harlequin	Capnoides	genus
rock-harlequin	rock harlequin, pink corydalis	Capnoides sempervirens	species
rockrose family	rockrose family	Cistaceae	family
rose	rose	Rosa	genus
rose family	rose family	Rosaceae	family
rose, prairie	prairie rose	Rosa arkansana	species
rose, prickly	prickly rose	Rosa acicularis	species
rose, Woods	Woods' rose, common wild rose	Rosa woodsii	species
rosebay, Lapland	Lapland rosebay, Lapland rose-bay	Rhododendron lapponicum	species
roseroot	roseroot	Rhodiola	genus
roseroot, western	entire-leaved stonecrop, rose-root	Rhodiola integrifolia	species
rough-fescue, mountain	mountain rough fescue	Festuca campestris	species
rough-fescue, northern	northern rough fescue	Festuca altaica	species
rough-fescue, plains	plains rough fescue	Festuca hallii	species
roundleaf-orchid	roundleaf-orchid	Galearis	genus
roundleaf-orchid	small round-leaved orchid, round-leaved orchid	Galearis rotundifolia	species
rush	rush	Juncus	genus
rush family	rush family	Juncaceae	family

ALPHABETIZED* COMMON NAMES

Suggested Common Name	VASCAN &/or ACIMS Common Name(s)	Scientific Name	Rank
rush, alpine	alpine rush	Juncus alpinoarticulatus	species
rush, chestnut	chestnut rush	Juncus castaneus	species
rush, Drummond	Drummond's rush	Juncus drummondii	species
rush, Dudley	Dudley's rush	Juncus dudleyi	species
rush, fewflower	Colorado rush, few-flowered rush	Juncus confusus	species
rush, knotted	knotted rush	Juncus nodosus	species
rush, longstyle	long-styled rush	Juncus longistylis	species
rush, Merten	Merten's rush, slender-stemmed rush	Juncus mertensianus	species
rush, moor	moor rush	Juncus stygius	species
rush, Nevada	Sierra rush, Nevada rush	Juncus nevadensis	species
rush, Parry	Parry's rush	Juncus parryi	species
rush, path	path rush, slender rush	Juncus tenuis	species
rush, Regel	Regel's rush	Juncus regelii	species
rush, Rocky Mountain	Rocky Mountain rush	Juncus saximontanus	species
rush, shorttail	short-tailed rush, short-tail rush	Juncus brevicaudatus	species
rush, swordleaf	dagger-leaved rush, equitant-leaved rush	Juncus ensifolius	species
rush, thread	thread rush	Juncus filiformis	species
rush, threeflower	three-flowered rush, white rush	Juncus triglumis	species
rush, toad	toad rush	Juncus bufonius	species
rush, Torrey	Torrey's rush	Juncus torreyi	species
rush, twoglume	two-glumed rush	Juncus biglumis	species
rush, Vasey	Vasey's rush, big-head rush	Juncus vaseyi	species
rush, wire	Baltic rush, wire rush	Juncus balticus	species
Russian-knapweed	Russian-knapweed	Rhaponticum	genus
Russian-knapweed	Russian knapweed	Rhaponticum repens	species
Russian-olive	Russian-olive, wolfwillow	Elaeagnus	genus
Russian-olive	Russian olive	Elaeagnus angustifolia	species
Russian-pigweed	Russian-pigweed	Axyris	genus
Russian-pigweed	Russian pigweed	Axyris amaranthoides	species
Russian-thistle	Russian-thistle	Salsola	genus
Russian-thistle, prickly	prickly Russian thistle, Russian-thistle	Salsola tragus	species
Russian-thistle, slender	slender Russian thistle, slender Russian-thistle	Salsola collina	species
Russian-wildrye	Russian-wildrye	Psathyrostachys	genus
Russian-wildrye	Russian wildrye, Russian wild rye	Psathyrostachys juncea	species
rye	rye	Secale	genus
rye, common	common rye, rye	Secale cereale	species
ryegrass	ryegrass	Lolium	genus
ryegrass, annual	annual ryegrass, Italian ryegrass	Lolium multiflorum	species
ryegrass, darnel	bearded ryegrass, darnel	Lolium temulentum	species
ryegrass, meadow	meadow ryegrass, meadow fescue	Lolium pratense	species

ALPHABETIZED* COMMON NAMES

Suggested Common Name	VASCAN &/or ACIMS Common Name(s)	Scientific Name	Rank
ryegrass, perennial	perennial ryegrass	Lolium perenne	species
ryegrass, Persian	Persian ryegrass, Persian darnel	Lolium persicum	species
ryegrass, tall	tall ryegrass, tall fescue	Lolium arundinaceum	species
safflower	safflower	Carthamus	genus
safflower	safflower	Carthamus tinctorius	species
sage	sage	Salvia	genus
sage, woodland	woodland sage, wood sage	Salvia nemorosa	species
sagebrush,	sagebrush, sagewort, wormwood	Artemisia	genus
sagebrush, big	big sagebrush	Artemisia tridentata	species
sagebrush, silver	silver wormwood, silver sagebrush	Artemisia cana	species
sagebrush, wormwood	wormwood, sagebrush	Artemisia	genus
sainfoin	sainfoin	Onobrychis	genus
sainfoin	common sainfoin, sainfoin	Onobrychis viciifolia	species
saltbush	saltbush	Atriplex	genus
saltbush, creeping	creeping saltbush, prostrate saltbush	Atriplex prostrata	species
saltbush, fourwing	four-wing saltbush	Atriplex canescens	species
saltbush, garden	garden saltbush, garden orache	Atriplex hortensis	species
saltbush, Gardner	Gardner's saltbush	Atriplex gardneri	species
saltbush, glabrous	glabrous saltbush, glabrous orach	Atriplex glabriuscula	species
saltbush, oblongleaf	oblong-leaved saltbush, saltbush	Atriplex oblongifolia	species
saltbush, Powell	Powell's saltbush	Atriplex powellii	species
saltbush, redscale	redscale saltbush, red scale saltbush	Atriplex rosea	species
saltbush, Russian	Russian saltbush, Russian atriplex	Atriplex heterosperma	species
saltbush, saline	saline saltbush	Atriplex dioica	species
saltbush, silver	silver saltbush	Atriplex argentea	species
saltbush, spear	spear saltbush, spear orach	Atriplex patula	species
saltbush, Suckley	Suckley's saltbush, endolepis	Atriplex suckleyi	species
saltbush, wedgescale	wedgescale saltbush, saltbush	Atriplex truncata	species
saltgrass	saltgrass	Distichlis	genus
saltgrass	saltgrass	Distichlis spicata	species
saltwater-cress	saltwater-cress	Eutrema	genus
saltwater-cress	saltwater-cress, mouse-ear cress	Eutrema salsugineum	species
sandalwood family	sandalwood family	Santalaceae	family
sandgrass	sandgrass	Calamovilfa	genus
sandheather	sandheather	Hudsonia	genus
sandheather, woolly	woolly beach-heather, sand heather	Hudsonia tomentosa	species
sandspurry	sandspurry	Spergularia	genus
sandspurry, alkali	alkali sand-spurrey, sand spurry	Spergularia diandra	species
sandspurry, saltmarsh	saltmarsh sand-spurrey, salt-marsh sand spurry	Spergularia salina	species
sand-verbena	sand-verbena	Tripterocalyx	genus

ALPHABETIZED* COMMON NAMES

Suggested Common Name	VASCAN &/or ACIMS Common Name(s)	Scientific Name	Rank
sand-verbena, smallflower	small-flowered sand-verbena, sand verbena	Tripterocalyx micranthus	species
sandwort	sandwort	Arenaria	genus
sandwort	sandwort	Eremogone	genus
sandwort	sandwort	Moehringia	genus
sandwort, ballhead	ballhead sandwort, rocky-ground sandwort	Eremogone congesta	species
sandwort, bluntleaf	grove sandwort, blunt-leaved sandwort	Moehringia lateriflora	species
sandwort, longstem	long-stemmed sandwort, sandwort	Arenaria longipedunculata	species
sandwort, threadleaf	thread-leaved sandwort, linear-leaved sandwort	Eremogone capillaris	species
sandwort, thymeleaf	thyme-leaved sandwort	Arenaria serpyllifolia	species
sanicle	sanicle	Sanicula	genus
sanicle, Maryland	Maryland sanicle, snakeroot	Sanicula marilandica	species
sarsaparilla	sarsaparilla	Aralia	genus
sarsaparilla, wild	wild sarsaparilla	Aralia nudicaulis	species
saskatoon	saskatoon, serviceberry	Amelanchier	genus
saskatoon	saskatoon	Amelanchier alnifolia	species
sawwort	sawwort	Saussurea	genus
sawwort, American	American sawwort, American saw-wort	Saussurea americana	species
sawwort, dwarf	dwarf sawwort, dwarf saw-wort	Saussurea nuda	species
sawwort, tall	tall sawwort	Saussurea amara	species
saxifrage	saxifrage	Micranthes	genus
saxifrage	saxifrage	Saxifraga	genus
saxifrage family	saxifrage family	Saxifragaceae	family
saxifrage, alpine	snow saxifrage, alpine saxifrage	Micranthes nivalis	species
saxifrage, brook	streambank saxifrage, brook saxifrage	Micranthes odontoloma	species
saxifrage, heartleaf	Nelson's saxifrage, cordate-leaved saxifrage	Micranthes nelsoniana	species
saxifrage, Mertens	Mertens' saxifrage, Merten's saxifrage	Saxifraga mertensiana	species
saxifrage, nodding	nodding saxifrage	Saxifraga cernua	species
saxifrage, purple	purple mountain saxifrage, purple saxifrage	Saxifraga oppositifolia	species
saxifrage, pygmy	pygmy saxifrage, brook saxifrage	Saxifraga hyperborea	species
saxifrage, redstem	red-stemmed saxifrage	Micranthes lyallii	species
saxifrage, rusty	rusty saxifrage	Micranthes ferruginea	species
saxifrage, spider	stoloniferous saxifrage, spiderplant	Saxifraga flagellaris	species
saxifrage, spotted	red-spotted saxifrage, spotted saxifrage	Saxifraga austromontana	species
saxifrage, threetooth	three-toothed saxifrage	Saxifraga tricuspidata	species

ALPHABETIZED* COMMON NAMES

Suggested Common Name	VASCAN &/or ACIMS Common Name(s)	Scientific Name	Rank
saxifrage, tufted	tufted saxifrage	Saxifraga cespitosa	species
saxifrage, wedgeleaf	ascending saxifrage, wedge-leaved saxifrage	Saxifraga adscendens	species
saxifrage, western	western saxifrage, rhomboid-leaved saxifrage	Micranthes occidentalis	species
saxifrage, yellow mountain	yellow mountain saxifrage	Saxifraga aizoides	species
scabious	scabious	Knautia	genus
scabious, field	field scabious	Knautia arvensis	species
scheuchzeria	scheuchzeria	Scheuchzeria	genus
scheuchzeria	marsh scheuchzeria, scheuchzeria	Scheuchzeria palustris	species
scheuchzeria family	scheuchzeria family	Scheuchzeriaceae	family
scorpionweed	scorpionweed	Phacelia	genus
scorpionweed, Franklin	Franklin's phacelia, Franklin's scorpionweed	Phacelia franklinii	species
scorpionweed, linearleaf	thread-leaved phacelia, linear-leaved scorpionweed	Phacelia linearis	species
scorpionweed, Lyall	Lyall's phacelia, Lyall's scorpionweed	Phacelia lyallii	species
scorpionweed, silky	silky phacelia, silky scorpionweed	Phacelia sericea	species
scorpionweed, silverleaf	silver-leaved phacelia, silver-leaved scorpionweed	Phacelia hastata	species
scouringrush	scouring-rush, horsetail	Equisetum	species
scouringrush, common	common scouring-rush	Equisetum hyemale	species
scouringrush, dwarf	dwarf scouring-rush	Equisetum scirpoides	species
scouringrush, smooth	smooth scouring-rush	Equisetum laevigatum	species
scouringrush, variegated	variegated scouring-rush, variegated horsetail	Equisetum variegatum	species
scurfpea	scurfpea	Ladeania	genus
scurfpea, lanceleaf	lance-leaved scurf-pea, scurf pea	Ladeania lanceolata	species
seablite, Moquin	bush seepweed, Moquin's sea-blite	Suaeda nigra	species
seablite	seablite, seepweed	Suaeda	genus
seablite, western	Pursh's seepweed, western sea-blite	Suaeda calceoliformis	species
sea-buckthorn	sea-buckthorn	Hippophae	genus
sea-buckthorn	sea buckthorn	Hippophae rhamnoides	species
seaside-buttercup	seaside-buttercup	Halerpestes	genus
seaside-buttercup	seaside buttercup	Halerpestes cymbalaria	species
sedge	sedge	Carex	genus
sedge family	sedge family	Cyperaceae	family
sedge, awlfruit	awl-fruited sedge	Carex stipata	species
sedge, Back	Back's sedge	Carex backii	species
sedge, bald	deep-green sedge, bald sedge	Carex tonsa	species
sedge, beaked	swollen beaked sedge, beaked sedge	Carex rostrata	species

ALPHABETIZED* COMMON NAMES

Suggested Common Name	VASCAN &/or ACIMS Common Name(s)	Scientific Name	Rank
sedge, Bebb	Bebb's sedge	Carex bebbii	species
sedge, bent northern	bent northern sedge, bent sedge	Carex deflexa	species
sedge, black alpine	black alpine sedge	Carex nigricans	species
sedge, black-and-white	black-and-white-scale sedge, black-and-white sedge	Carex albonigra	species
sedge, blackened	blackened sedge	Carex epapillosa	species
sedge, blister	inflated sedge, blister sedge	Carex vesicaria	species
sedge, blunt	blunt sedge	Carex obtusata	species
sedge, boreal bog	boreal bog sedge, bog sedge	Carex magellanica	species
sedge, bottle	northern beaked sedge, small bottle sedge	Carex utriculata	species
sedge, bristleleaf	bristle-leaved sedge	Carex eburnea	species
sedge, bristlestalk	bristle-stalked sedge	Carex leptalea	species
sedge, bronze	bronze sedge, silvery-flowered sedge	Carex foenea	species
sedge, broom	pointed broom sedge, broom sedge	Carex scoparia	species
sedge, brownish	brownish sedge	Carex brunnescens	species
sedge, Buxbaum	Buxbaum's sedge, brown sedge	Carex buxbaumii	species
sedge, capitate	capitate sedge	Carex capitata	species
sedge, clustered field	clustered field sedge, graceful sedge	Carex praegracilis	species
sedge, cordillera	cordilleran sedge	Carex cordillerana	species
sedge, Crawe	Crawe's sedge	Carex crawei	species
sedge, Crawford	Crawford's sedge	Carex crawfordii	species
sedge, creeping	creeping sedge, prostrate sedge	Carex chordorrhiza	species
sedge, curved-spike	curved-spike sedge	Carex incurviformis	species
sedge, cyperus	cyperus-like sedge	Carex pseudocyperus	species
sedge, Dewey	Dewey's sedge	Carex deweyana	species
sedge, Douglas	Douglas' sedge, Douglas sedge	Carex douglasii	species
sedge, dryspike	dry-spike sedge, hay sedge	Carex siccata	species
sedge, dunhead	dunhead sedge, head-like sedge	Carex phaeocephala	species
sedge, Enander	Enander's sedge	Carex enanderi	species
sedge, fewflower	few-flowered sedge	Carex pauciflora	species
sedge, fewseed	few-seeded sedge, few-fruited sedge	Carex oligosperma	species
sedge, fewseed fen	few-seeded fen sedge, short-awned sedge	Carex microglochin	species
sedge, fox	fox sedge	Carex vulpinoidea	species
sedge, Garber	Garber's sedge, elk sedge	Carex garberi	species
sedge, Geyer	Geyer's sedge	Carex geyeri	species
sedge, glacier	glacier sedge	Carex glacialis	species
sedge, golden	golden sedge	Carex aurea	species
sedge, green	greenish sedge, green sedge	Carex viridula	species
sedge, hair	hair-like sedge	Carex capillaris	species

ALPHABETIZED* COMMON NAMES

Suggested Common Name	VASCAN &/or ACIMS Common Name(s)	Scientific Name	Rank
sedge, Hayden	cloud sedge, Hayden's sedge	Carex haydeniana	species
sedge, hoary	hoary sedge	Carex canescens	species
sedge, Hood	Hood's sedge	Carex hoodii	species
sedge, Hooker	Hooker's sedge	Carex hookeriana	species
sedge, Houghton	Houghton's sedge, sand sedge	Carex houghtoniana	species
sedge, Hudson Bay	Hudson Bay sedge	Carex heleonastes	species
sedge, inland	inland sedge	Carex interior	species
sedge, intermediate	intermediate sedge	Carex media	species
sedge, Kellogg	Kellogg's sedge	Carex kelloggii	species
sedge, Lachenal	Lachenal's sedge, two-parted sedge	Carex lachenalii	species
sedge, lake	lake sedge, lakeshore sedge	Carex lacustris	species
sedge, Lake Tahoe	Lake Tahoe sedge	Carex tahoensis	species
sedge, lakeshore	lenticular sedge, shore sedge	Carex lenticularis	species
sedge, Lapland	Lapland sedge	Carex lapponica	species
sedge, lesser blackscale	lesser black-scale sedge, dark-scaled sedge	Carex atrosquama	species
sedge, lesser brown	lesser brown sedge, browned sedge	Carex adusta	species
sedge, livid	livid sedge	Carex livida	species
sedge, longstalk	long-stalked sedge, stalked sedge	Carex pedunculata	species
sedge, long-stolon	long-stolon sedge	Carex inops	species
sedge, Mackenzie		Carex mackenziei	species
sedge, manyhead	many-headed sedge, long-beaked sedge	Carex sychnocephala	species
sedge, meadow	northern meadow sedge, meadow sedge	Carex praticola	species
sedge, Mertens	Mertens' sedge, purple sedge	Carex mertensii	species
sedge, mimic	mimic sedge	Carex simulata	species
sedge, mountain	Holm's Rocky Mountain sedge	Carex scopulorum	species
sedge, mud	mud sedge	Carex limosa	species
sedge, Nebraska	Nebraska sedge	Carex nebrascensis	species
sedge, needleleaf	needle-leaved sedge, low sedge	Carex duriuscula	species
sedge, northern bog	northern bog sedge	Carex gynocrates	species
sedge, northern capitate		Carex arctogena	species
sedge, northern cluster	northern clustered sedge, narrow sedge	Carex arcta	species
sedge, northern elegant	northern elegant sedge, beautiful sedge	Carex concinna	species
sedge, northwest	northwestern sedge, low northern sedge	Carex concinnoides	species
sedge, open	open sedge	Carex aperta	species
sedge, Parry	Parry's sedge	Carex parryana	species
sedge, pasture	pasture sedge	Carex petasata	species
sedge, Payson	Payson's sedge	Carex paysonis	species

ALPHABETIZED* COMMON NAMES

Suggested Common Name	VASCAN &/or ACIMS Common Name(s)	Scientific Name	Rank
sedge, Peck	Peck's sedge	Carex peckii	species
sedge, porcupine	porcupine sedge	Carex hystericina	species
sedge, prairie	prairie sedge	Carex prairea	species
sedge, Presl	Presl's sedge, Presl sedge	Carex preslii	species
sedge, Raynolds	Raynolds' sedge, Raynold's sedge	Carex raynoldsii	species
sedge, Richardson	Richardson's sedge	Carex richardsonii	species
sedge, rock	rock sedge	Carex rupestris	species
sedge, rock	russet sedge, rocky-ground sedge	Carex saxatilis	species
sedge, Rocky Mountain	Rocky Mountain sedge	Carex saximontana	species
sedge, Ross	Ross' sedge	Carex rossii	species
sedge, ryegrass	ryegrass sedge, rye-grass sedge	Carex loliacea	species
sedge, Sartwell	Sartwell's sedge	Carex sartwellii	species
sedge, scabrous black	scabrous black sedge	Carex atratiformis	species
sedge, seaside	seaside sedge	Carex maritima	species
sedge, sheathed	sheathed sedge	Carex vaginata	species
sedge, sheep	sheep sedge, small-headed sedge	Carex illota	species
sedge, shortbeak	short-beaked sedge, slender-beaked sedge	Carex brevior	species
sedge, shortleaf	short-leaved sedge, nodding sedge	Carex fuliginosa	species
sedge, shortstalk	graceful mountain sedge, alpine sedge	Carex podocarpa	species
sedge, showy	showy sedge	Carex spectabilis	species
sedge, singlespike	single-spike sedge, rush-like sedge	Carex scirpoidea	species
sedge, slenderbeak	slender-beaked sedge, long-bracted sedge	Carex athrostachya	species
sedge, smallroot	small-rooted sedge, spiked sedge	Carex micropoda	species
sedge, smallwing	small-winged sedge	Carex microptera	species
sedge, sparseflower	sparse-flowered sedge, thin-flowered sedge	Carex tenuiflora	species
sedge, spikenard	nard sedge, fragrant sedge	Carex nardina	species
sedge, Sprengel	Sprengel's sedge	Carex sprengelii	species
sedge, star	star sedge, little prickly sedge	Carex echinata	species
sedge, stone	rock-dwelling sedge, stone sedge	Carex petricosa	species
sedge, tender	tender sedge, broad-fruited sedge	Carex tenera	species
sedge, thickhead	thick-headed sedge, sedge	Carex pachystachya	species
sedge, thickspike	Falkland Island sedge, thick-spike sedge	Carex macloviana	species
sedge, threadleaf	thread-leaved sedge	Carex filifolia	species
sedge, threeseed	three-seeded sedge	Carex trisperma	species
sedge, tinged	tinged sedge	Carex tincta	species
sedge, Torrey	Torrey's sedge	Carex torreyi	species
sedge, turned	retrorse sedge, turned sedge	Carex retrorsa	species
sedge, two-color	two-coloured sedge, two-color sedge	Carex bicolor	species
sedge, twoseed	two-seeded sedge	Carex disperma	species

ALPHABETIZED* COMMON NAMES

Suggested Common Name	VASCAN &/or ACIMS Common Name(s)	Scientific Name	Rank
sedge, twostamen	lesser panicled sedge, two-stamened sedge	Carex diandra	species
sedge, umbellate	umbellate sedge	Carex umbellata	species
sedge, water	water sedge	Carex aquatilis	species
sedge, weak arctic	weak arctic sedge, weak sedge	Carex supina	species
sedge, weaknerve	weak-nerved sedge	Carex infirminervia	species
sedge, wheat	wheat sedge, awned sedge	Carex atherodes	species
sedge, whitescale	dryland sedge, white-scaled sedge	Carex xerantica	species
sedge, woolly	woolly sedge	Carex pellita	species
sedge, woollyfruit	woolly-fruit sedge, hairy-fruited sedge	Carex lasiocarpa	species
sedge, yellow	yellow sedge	Carex flava	species
seepweed	seepweed, seablite	Suaeda	genus
selfheal	selfheal	Prunella	genus
selfheal, common	common self-heal, heal-all	Prunella vulgaris	species
sensitive-fern family	sensitive-fern family	Onocleaceae	family
serpentweed	serpentweed	Tonestus	genus
serpentweed, Lyall	Lyall's serpentweed, Lyall's ironplant	Tonestus lyallii	species
serviceberry, saskatoon	saskatoon, serviceberry	Amelanchier	genus
shepherd's-purse	shepherd's-purse	Capsella	genus
shepherd's-purse	common shepherd's purse	Capsella bursa-pastoris	species
shootingstar	shootingstar, primrose	Primula	genus
shootingstar, mountain	slim-pod shootingstar, mountain shooting star	Primula conjugens	species
shootingstar, saline	darkthroat shootingstar, saline shooting star	Primula pauciflora	species
shrubby-cinquefoil	shrubby-cinquefoil	Dasiphora	genus
shrubby-cinquefoil	shrubby cinquefoil	Dasiphora fruticosa	species
sibbaldia	sibbaldia	Sibbaldia	genus
sibbaldia, creeping	creeping sibbaldia, sibbaldia	Sibbaldia procumbens	species
sibbaldia, threetooth	three-toothed cinquefoil	Sibbaldia tridentata	species
silverweed	silverweed, cinquefoil	Potentilla	genus
silverweed	silverweed	Potentilla anserina	species
silverweed, cinquefoil	cinquefoil, silverweed	Potentilla	genus
six-week-fescue	six-week-fescue	Vulpia	genus
six-week-fescue	eight-flowered fescue, six-weeks fescue	Vulpia octoflora	species
skeletonplant	skeletonplant	Lygodesmia	genus
skeletonplant, rush	rush skeletonplant, skeletonweed	Lygodesmia juncea	species
skeletonweed	skeletonweed	Shinnersoseris	genus
skeletonweed, annual	annual skeletonweed	Shinnersoseris rostrata	species
skullcap	skullcap	Scutellaria	genus
skullcap, marsh	marsh skullcap	Scutellaria galericulata	species
slender-phlox	slender-phlox	Microsteris	genus

279

ALPHABETIZED* COMMON NAMES

Suggested Common Name	VASCAN &/or ACIMS Common Name(s)	Scientific Name	Rank
slender-phlox	slender phlox	Microsteris gracilis	species
sloughgrass	sloughgrass	Beckmannia	genus
sloughgrass, American	American sloughgrass, slough grass	Beckmannia syzigachne	species
smartweed	smartweed	Persicaria	genus
smartweed, lady's-thumb	spotted lady's-thumb, lady's-thumb	Persicaria maculosa	species
smartweed, marshpepper	marshpepper smartweed	Persicaria hydropiper	species
smartweed, pale	pale smartweed, pale persicaria	Persicaria lapathifolia	species
smartweed, water	water smartweed	Persicaria amphibia	species
smelowskia	smelowskia	Smelowskia	genus
smelowskia, American	American smelowskia, silver rock cress	Smelowskia americana	species
snakekroot	snakekroot	Polygala	genus
snakeroot, seneca	Seneca snakeroot	Polygala senega	species
snakeweed	snakeweed	Gutierrezia	genus
snakeweed, broom	broom snakeweed, broomweed	Gutierrezia sarothrae	species
sneezeweed	sneezeweed	Helenium	genus
sneezeweed	common sneezeweed, sneezeweed	Helenium autumnale	species
snowberry	snowberry	Symphoricarpos	genus
snowberry, creeping	creeping snowberry	Gaultheria hispidula	species
snowberry, thinleaf	thin-leaved snowberry, snowberry	Symphoricarpos albus	species
snowberry, western	western snowberry, buckbrush	Symphoricarpos occidentalis	species
soapberry family	soapberry family	Sapindaceae	family
sorrel	sorrel, dock	Rumex	genus
sorrel, alpine sheep	alpine sheep sorrel	Rumex paucifolius	species
sorrel, garden	garden sorrel, green sorrel	Rumex acetosa	species
sorrel, Lapland	Lapland sorrel	Rumex lapponicus	species
sorrel, sheep	sheep sorrel	Rumex acetosella	species
sowthistle	sowthistle	Sonchus	genus
sowthistle, common	common sow-thistle, annual sow-thistle	Sonchus oleraceus	species
sowthistle, perennial	field sow-thistle, perennial sow-thistle	Sonchus arvensis	species
sowthistle, prickly	prickly sow-thistle, prickly annual sow-thistle	Sonchus asper	species
spearmint	spearmint	Mentha spicata	species
spearwort, creeping	lesser spearwort, creeping spearwort	Ranunculus flammula	species
speedwell	speedwell	Veronica	genus
speedwell, alpine	Wormskjold's alpine speedwell, alpine speedwell	Veronica nutans	species
speedwell, American	American speedwell, American brooklime	Veronica americana	species

ALPHABETIZED* COMMON NAMES

Suggested Common Name	VASCAN &/or ACIMS Common Name(s)	Scientific Name	Rank
speedwell, birdeye	bird's-eye speedwell, bird's-eye	Veronica persica	species
speedwell, field	field speedwell, prostrate speedwell	Veronica agrestis	species
speedwell, germander	germander speedwell	Veronica chamaedrys	species
speedwell, hairy	purslane speedwell, hairy speedwell	Veronica peregrina	species
speedwell, longleaf	long-leaved speedwell, spiked speedwell	Veronica longifolia	species
speedwell, marsh	marsh speedwell	Veronica scutellata	species
speedwell, spring	spring speedwell	Veronica verna	species
speedwell, stalkless water		Veronica catenata	species
speedwell, thymeleaf	thyme-leaved speedwell	Veronica serpyllifolia	species
speedwell, water	water speedwell, speedwell	Veronica anagallis-aquatica	species
spiderflower family	spiderflower family	Cleomaceae	family
spiderwort	spiderwort	Tradescantia	genus
spiderwort family	spiderwort family	Commelinaceae	family
spiderwort, western	western spiderwort	Tradescantia occidentalis	species
spikemoss	spikemoss	Selaginella	genus
spikemoss family	spikemoss family	Selaginellaceae	family
spikemoss, club	low spikemoss, spiny-edged little club-moss	Selaginella selaginoides	species
spikemoss, prairie	prairie spikemoss, prairie selaginella	Selaginella densa	species
spikemoss, rock	rock spikemoss, rock little club-moss	Selaginella rupestris	species
spikemoss, Rocky Mountain	Rocky Mountain spikemoss	Selaginella scopulorum	species
spikemoss, Standley	Standley's spikemoss	Selaginella standleyi	species
spikemoss, Wallace	Wallace's spikemoss, Wallace's little club-moss	Selaginella wallacei	species
spikerush	spikerush	Eleocharis	genus
spikerush, bald	red-stemmed spikerush, bald spikerush	Eleocharis erythropoda	species
spikerush, common	common spikerush, creeping spike-rush	Eleocharis palustris	species
spikerush, elliptic	elliptic spikerush, slender spikerush	Eleocharis elliptica	species
spikerush, Engelmann	Engelmann's spikerush, Engelmann's spike-rush	Eleocharis engelmannii	species
spikerush, fewflower	few-flowered spikerush, few-flowered spike-rush	Eleocharis quinqueflora	species
spikerush, flatstem	flat-stemmed spikerush, flat-stem spikerush	Eleocharis compressa	species
spikerush, longhead	long-headed spikerush, creeping spikerush	Eleocharis macrostachya	species
spikerush, needle	needle spikerush, needle spike-rush	Eleocharis acicularis	species

ALPHABETIZED* COMMON NAMES

Suggested Common Name	VASCAN &/or ACIMS Common Name(s)	Scientific Name	Rank
spikerush, oneglume	single-glumed spikerush, creeping spikerush	Eleocharis uniglumis	species
spikerush, ovate	ovate spikerush, ovate spikerush	Eleocharis ovata	species
spikerush, softstem	soft-stemmed spikerush, spike-rush	Eleocharis mamillata	species
spikerush, Suksdorf	Suksdorf's spikerush	Eleocharis suksdorfiana	species
spinach	spinach	Spinacia	genus
spinach	spinach	Spinacia oleracea	species
spleenwort	spleenwort	Asplenium	genus
spleenwort family	spleenwort family	Aspleniaceae	family
spleenwort, green	green spleenwort	Asplenium viride	species
springbeauty	springbeauty	Claytonia	genus
springbeauty, alpine	alpine spring beauty	Claytonia megarhiza	species
springbeauty, western	western spring beauty	Claytonia lanceolata	species
spring-parsley	spring-parsley	Cymopterus	genus
spring-parsley, plains	plains spring parsley	Cymopterus glomeratus	species
spruce	spruce	Picea	genus
spruce, black	black spruce	Picea mariana	species
spruce, Engelmann	Engelmann spruce	Picea engelmannii	species
spruce, white	white spruce	Picea glauca	species
spurge	spurge	Euphorbia	genus
spurge family	spurge family	Euphorbiaceae	family
spurge, field	field spurge	Euphorbia agraria	species
spurge, leafy	leafy spurge	Euphorbia virgata	species
spurge, petty	petty spurge	Euphorbia peplus	species
spurge, ridgeseed	ridge-seeded spurge	Euphorbia glyptosperma	species
spurge, sun	sun spurge, wartweed	Euphorbia helioscopia	species
spurge, thymeleaf	thyme-leaved spurge	Euphorbia serpillifolia	species
spurred-gentian	spurred-gentian	Halenia	genus
spurred-gentian, American	American spurred-gentian, spurred gentian	Halenia deflexa	species
St. John's-wort	St. John's-wort	Hypericum	genus
St. John's-wort family	St. John's-wort family	Hypericaceae	family
St. John's-wort, common	common St. John's-wort, St. John's-wort	Hypericum perforatum	species
St. John's-wort, Fraser	Fraser's St. John's-wort, Fraser's Marsh-St. John's-wort	Hypericum fraseri	species
St. John's-wort, large	large St. John's-wort, large Canada St. John's-wort	Hypericum majus	species
St. John's-wort, Scouler	Scouler's St. John's-wort, western St. John's-wort	Hypericum scouleri	species
starflower	starflower, loosestrife, milkwort, chaffweed,	Lysimachia	genus
starflower, Arctic	arctic starflower	Lysimachia europaea	species

ALPHABETIZED* COMMON NAMES

Suggested Common Name	VASCAN &/or ACIMS Common Name(s)	Scientific Name	Rank
starflower, broadleaf	broad-leaved starflower, northern starflower	Lysimachia latifolia	species
starthistle	starthistle, cornflower, knapweed	Centaurea	genus
starthistle, yellow	yellow starthistle, yellow star-thistle	Centaurea solstitialis	species
starwort	starwort, chickweed	Stellaria	genus
starwort, American	American starwort, American chickweed	Stellaria americana	species
starwort, bluntsepal	blunt-sepaled starwort, chickweed	Stellaria obtusa	species
starwort, boreal	boreal starwort	Stellaria borealis	species
starwort, fleshy	fleshy starwort, fleshy stitchwort	Stellaria crassifolia	species
starwort, longleaf	long-leaved starwort, long-leaved chickweed	Stellaria longifolia	species
starwort, longstalk	long-stalked starwort, long-stalked chickweed	Stellaria longipes	species
starwort, northern	northern starwort, northern stitchwort	Stellaria calycantha	species
starwort, shiny	shiny starwort	Stellaria nitens	species
starwort, umbellate	umbellate starwort, chickweed	Stellaria umbellata	species
starwort, wavyleaf	crisp starwort, wavy-leaved chickweed	Stellaria crispa	species
stickleaf family	stickleaf family	Loasaceae	family
stickseed	stickseed	Hackelia	genus
stickseed	stickseed	Lappula	genus
stickseed, bristly	bristly stickseed, bluebur	Lappula squarrosa	species
stickseed, Jessica	blue stickseed, Jessica's stickseed	Hackelia micrantha	species
stickseed, manyflower	many-flowered stickseed, large-flowered stickseed	Hackelia floribunda	species
stickseed, nodding	nodding stickseed, northern stickseed	Hackelia deflexa	species
stickseed, western	western stickseed, western bluebur	Lappula occidentalis	species
stinkgrass	stinkgrass	Eragrostis	genus
stinkgrass	stinkgrass, skunk-grass	Eragrostis cilianensis	species
stinking-chamomile	stinking-chamomile	Anthemis	genus
stinking-chamomile	stinking chamomile, mayweed	Anthemis cotula	species
stitchwort	stitchwort	Cherleria/Minuartia	genus
stitchwort	stitchwort	Sabulina	genus
stitchwort, alpine	alpine stitchwort, Arctic sandwort	Cherleria obtusiloba	species
stitchwort, Dawson	Dawson's stitchwort, Dawson sandwort	Sabulina dawsonensis	species
stitchwort, elegant	elegant stitchwort, purple alpine sandwort	Sabulina elegans	species

ALPHABETIZED* COMMON NAMES

Suggested Common Name	VASCAN &/or ACIMS Common Name(s)	Scientific Name	Rank
stitchwort, mountain	mountain stitchwort, dwarf alpine sandwort	Cherleria biflora	species
stitchwort, mountain	Rocky Mountain stitchwort, green alpine sandwort	Sabulina austromontana	species
stitchwort, Nuttall	Nuttall's stitchwort, Nuttall's sandwort	Sabulina nuttallii	species
stitchwort, reddish	reddish stitchwort, red-seeded sandwort	Sabulina rubella	species
stock	stock	Matthiola	genus
stock, night-scented	night-scented stock	Matthiola longipetala	species
stonecrop	stonecrop	Sedum	genus
stonecrop family	stonecrop family	Crassulaceae	family
stonecrop, lanceleaf	lance-leaved stonecrop	Sedum lanceolatum	species
stonecrop, mossy	mossy stonecrop	Sedum acre	species
stonecrop, narrowpetal	worm-leaved stonecrop, narrow-petaled stonecrop	Sedum stenopetalum	species
stonecrop, spreading	spreading stonecrop	Sedum divergens	species
storksbill	storksbill	Erodium	genus
storksbill, common	common storksbill	Erodium cicutarium	species
strawberry	strawberry	Fragaria	genus
strawberry, wild	wild strawberry	Fragaria virginiana	species
strawberry, woodland	woodland strawberry	Fragaria vesca	species
strawberry-blite	strawberry-blite, goosefoot	Blitum	genus
strawberry-blite	strawberry-blite, strawberry blite	Blitum capitatum	species
suckleya	suckleya	Suckleya	genus
suckleya, poison	poison suckleya	Suckleya suckleyana	species
suksdorfia	suksdorfia	Suksdorfia	genus
suksdorfia, buttercup	buttercup-leaved suksdorfia, suksdorfia	Suksdorfia ranunculifolia	species
suksdorfia, violet	violet suksdorfia, blue suksdorfia	Suksdorfia violacea	species
sumac	sumac	Rhus	genus
sumac family	sumac family	Anacardiaceae	family
sumac, fragrant	fragrant sumac, skunkbush	Rhus aromatica	species
summer-cypress	summer-cypress, bassia	Bassia	genus
summer-cypress	summer-cypress, bassia	Bassia scoparia	species
sundew	sundew	Drosera	genus
sundew family	sundew family	Droseraceae	family
sundew, English	English sundew, oblong-leaved sundew	Drosera anglica	species
sundew, roundleaf	round-leaved sundew	Drosera rotundifolia	species
sundew, slenderleaf	slender-leaved sundew	Drosera linearis	species
sunflower	sunflower	Helianthus	genus
sunflower, common	common sunflower, common annual sunflower	Helianthus annuus	species

ALPHABETIZED* COMMON NAMES

Suggested Common Name	VASCAN &/or ACIMS Common Name(s)	Scientific Name	Rank
sunflower, Maximilian	Maximilian sunflower, narrow-leaved sunflower	Helianthus maximilianii	species
sunflower, Nuttall	Nuttall's sunflower, common tall sunflower	Helianthus nuttallii	species
sunflower, prairie	prairie sunflower	Helianthus petiolaris	species
sunflower, stiff	stiff sunflower	Helianthus pauciflorus	species
sweet-cicely	sweet-cicely	Osmorhiza	genus
sweet-cicely, bluntfruit	mountain sweet cicely, blunt-fruited sweet cicely	Osmorhiza berteroi	species
sweet-cicely, purple	purple sweet cicely	Osmorhiza purpurea	species
sweet-cicely, smooth	smooth sweet cicely	Osmorhiza longistylis	species
sweet-cicely, spreading	blunt sweet cicely, spreading sweet cicely	Osmorhiza depauperata	species
sweet-cicely, western	western sweet cicely	Osmorhiza occidentalis	species
sweetclover	sweetclover	Melilotus	genus
sweetclover, white	white sweet-clover	Melilotus albus	species
sweetclover, yellow	yellow sweet-clover	Melilotus officinalis	species
sweet-coltsfoot	sweet-coltsfoot	Petasites	genus
sweet-coltsfoot, arctic	arctic sweet coltsfoot, coltsfoot	Petasites frigidus	species
sweetflag	sweetflag	Acorus	genus
sweetflag family	sweetflag family	Acoraceae	family
sweetflag, American	American sweetflag, sweet flag	Acorus americanus	species
sweetgale	sweetgale	Myrica	genus
sweetgale	sweet gale	Myrica gale	species
sweetgrass	sweetgrass	Anthoxanthum	genus
sweetgrass, alpine	alpine sweetgrass	Anthoxanthum monticola	species
sweetgrass, common	hairy sweetgrass, sweet grass	Anthoxanthum hirtum	species
sweet-William	sweet-William	Atocion	genus
sweet-William	sweet William catchfly	Atocion armeria	species
tamarack	tamarack	Larix laricina	species
tansy	tansy	Tanacetum	genus
tansy, common	common tansy	Tanacetum vulgare	species
tansy, dwarf	dwarf tansy, Lake Huron tansy	Tanacetum bipinnatum	species
tansy-aster	tansy-aster	Machaeranthera	genus
tansy-aster	Tahoka daisy, tansy aster	Machaeranthera tanacetifolia	species
tansymustard	tansymustard	Descurainia	genus
tansymustard, flixweed	flixweed	Descurainia sophia	species
tansymustard, green	green tansy mustard	Descurainia pinnata	species
tansymustard, grey	grey tansy mustard	Descurainia incana	species
tansymustard, mountain	mountain tansy mustard	Descurainia incisa	species
tansymustard, northern	northern tansy mustard, northern tansy-mustard	Descurainia sophioides	species
taraxia	taraxia	Taraxia	genus
taraxia	short-flowered evening primrose, taraxia	Taraxia breviflora	species

ALPHABETIZED* COMMON NAMES

Suggested Common Name	VASCAN &/or ACIMS Common Name(s)	Scientific Name	Rank
tarweed	tarweed	Madia	genus
tarweed, clustered	clustered tarweed, tarweed	Madia glomerata	species
thesium	thesium	Thesium	genus
thesium	field thesium, thesium	Thesium ramosum	species
thimbleberry	raspberry, cloudberry, dwarf-bramble, thimbleberry	Rubus	genus
thimbleberry, western	western thimbleberry, thimbleberry	Rubus parviflorus	species
thistle	thistle	Cirsium	genus
thistle, bull	bull thistle	Cirsium vulgare	species
thistle, creeping	Canada thistle, creeping thistle	Cirsium arvense	species
thistle, Drummond	Drummond's thistle	Cirsium drummondii	species
thistle, Flodman	Flodman's thistle	Cirsium flodmanii	species
thistle, Hooker	Hooker's thistle, white thistle	Cirsium hookerianum	species
thistle, leafy	leafy thistle	Cirsium foliosum	species
thistle, marsh	marsh thistle	Cirsium palustre	species
thistle, meadow	meadow thistle	Cirsium scariosum	species
thistle, nodding	nodding thistle	Carduus nutans	species
thistle, wavyleaf	wavy-leaved thistle	Cirsium undulatum	species
thoroughwax	thoroughwax	Bupleurum	genus
thoroughwax, American	American thoroughwax, thorough-wax	Bupleurum americanum	species
three-awn	three-awn	Aristida	genus
three-awn, purple	purple threeawn grass, red three-awn	Aristida purpurea	species
tickseed	tickseed	Coreopsis	genus
tickseed, golden	golden tickseed, common tickseed	Coreopsis tinctoria	species
timothy	timothy	Phleum	genus
timothy, alpine	alpine timothy, mountain timothy	Phleum alpinum	species
timothy, common	common timothy, timothy	Phleum pratense	species
toadflax	toadflax	Linaria	genus
toadflax	toadflax	Nuttallanthus	genus
toadflax, common	butter-and-eggs, common toadflax	Linaria vulgaris	species
toadflax, Dalmatian	Dalmatian toadflax	Linaria dalmatica	species
toadflax, Morocco	Moroccan toadflax, Morocco toadflax	Linaria maroccana	species
toadflax, Texas	Texas toadflax, Canada toad-flax	Nuttallanthus texanus	species
towermustard	towermustard	Turritis	genus
towermustard	tower mustard	Turritis glabra	species
townsendia	townsendia	Townsendia	genus
townsendia, alpine	alpine townsendia	Townsendia condensata	species
townsendia, Hooker	Hooker's townsendia	Townsendia hookeri	species
townsendia, Parry	Parry's townsendia	Townsendia parryi	species

ALPHABETIZED* COMMON NAMES

Suggested Common Name	VASCAN &/or ACIMS Common Name(s)	Scientific Name	Rank
townsendia, stemless	stemless townsendia, low townsendia	Townsendia exscapa	species
trillium	trillium	Trillium	genus
trillium family	trillium family	Melanthiaceae	family
trillium, western	western trillium, western wakerobin	Trillium ovatum	species
trisetum	trisetum	Trisetum	genus
trisetum, nodding	nodding trisetum	Trisetum cernuum	species
trisetum, spike	spike trisetum	Trisetum spicatum	species
trisetum, Wolf	Wolf's trisetum, awnless trisetum	Trisetum wolfii	species
trisetum, yellow	yellow false oat, yellow trisetum	Trisetum flavescens	species
tumblemustard	tumblemustard	Sisymbrium	genus
tumblemustard, common	common tumble mustard, hedge mustard	Sisymbrium officinale	species
tumblemustard, flaxleaf	flax-leaved plains mustard, narrow-leaved mustard	Sisymbrium linifolium	species
tumblemustard, Loesel	Loesel's tumble mustard, tall hedge mustard	Sisymbrium loeselii	species
tumblemustard, tall	tall tumble-mustard, tumbling mustard	Sisymbrium altissimum	species
twayblade	twayblade	Liparis	genus
twayblade	twayblade	Neottia	genus
twayblade, broadlip	broad-lip twayblade, broad-lipped twayblade	Neottia convallarioides	species
twayblade, heartleaf	heart-leaved twayblade	Neottia cordata	species
twayblade, Loesel	Loesel's twayblade	Liparis loeselii	species
twayblade, northern	northern twayblade	Neottia borealis	species
twayblade, western	northwestern twayblade, western twayblade	Neottia banksiana	species
twinflower	twinflower	Linnaea	genus
twinflower	twinflower	Linnaea borealis	species
twistedstalk	twistedstalk	Streptopus	genus
twistedstalk, claspingleaf	clasping-leaved twisted-stalk	Streptopus amplexifolius	species
twistedstalk, rose	rose twisted-stalk, rose mandarin	Streptopus lanceolatus	species
twistedstalk, small	small twisted-stalk, twisted-stalk	Streptopus streptopoides	species
valerian	valerian	Valeriana	genus
valerian, northern	marsh valerian, northern valerian	Valeriana dioica	species
valerian, Sitka	Sitka valerian, mountain valerian	Valeriana sitchensis	species
velvetleaf	velvetleaf	Abutilon	genus
velvetleaf	velvetleaf	Abutilon theophrasti	species
vervain	vervain	Verbena	genus
vervain family	vervain family	Verbenaceae	family
vervain, bracted	large-bracted vervain, carpet vervain	Verbena bracteata	species
vetch	vetch	Vicia	genus

ALPHABETIZED* COMMON NAMES

Suggested Common Name	VASCAN &/or ACIMS Common Name(s)	Scientific Name	Rank
vetch, America	American vetch, wild vetch	Vicia americana	species
vetch, tufted	tufted vetch	Vicia cracca	species
vetchling	vetchling	Lathyrus	genus
vetchling, creamy	cream-colored vetchling	Lathyrus ochroleucus	species
vetchling, marsh	marsh vetchling	Lathyrus palustris	species
vetchling, veiny	veiny vetchling, purple peavine	Lathyrus venosus	species
violet	violet, pansy	Viola	genus
violet family	violet family	Violaceae	family
violet, Canada	Canada violet, western Canada violet	Viola canadensis	species
violet, canary	yellow montane violet, canary violet, broad leaved yellow prairie violet	Viola praemorsa	species
violet, crowfoot	prairie violet, crowfoot violet	Viola pedatifida	species
violet, early blue	hooked violet, early blue violet	Viola adunca	species
violet, evergreen	western round-leaved violet, evergreen violet	Viola orbiculata	species
violet, kidneyleaf	kidney-leaved violet	Viola renifolia	species
violet, marsh	alpine marsh violet, marsh violet	Viola palustris	species
violet, northern bog	northern bog violet, bog violet	Viola nephrophylla	species
violet, northern marsh	northern marsh violet	Viola epipsila	species
violet, Nuttall	Nuttall's violet, yellow prairie violet	Viola nuttallii	species
violet, pansy	Johnny-jump-up, pansy	Viola tricolor	species
violet, Selkirk	Selkirk's violet, great-spurred violet	Viola selkirkii	species
violet, small white	Macloskey's violet, small white violet	Viola macloskeyi	species
violet, valley	valley violet	Viola vallicola	species
violet, yellow wood	stream violet, yellow wood violet	Viola glabella	species
viper's-bugloss	viper's-bugloss	Echium	genus
viper's-bugloss, common	common viper's bugloss, blueweed	Echium vulgare	species
wallflower	wallflower	Erysimum	genus
wallflower, crowded	crowded wormseed mustard	Erysimum coarctatum	species
wallflower, Pallas	Pallas' wallflower, purple alpine rocket	Erysimum pallasii	species
wallflower, prairie	prairie rocket	Erysimum asperum	species
wallflower, smallflower	small-flowered wallflower, small-flowered rocket	Erysimum inconspicuum	species
wallflower, wormseed	wormseed wallflower, wormseed mustard	Erysimum cheiranthoides	species
wallrocket	wallrocket	Diplotaxis	genus
wallrocket, annual	annual wall rocket, sand rocket	Diplotaxis muralis	species
water-buttercup, Gmelin	Gmelin's buttercup, yellow water crowfoot	Ranunculus gmelinii	species

ALPHABETIZED* COMMON NAMES

Suggested Common Name	VASCAN &/or ACIMS Common Name(s)	Scientific Name	Rank
water-buttercup, longbeak	long-beaked water-crowfoot, large-leaved white water crowfoot	Ranunculus longirostris	species
water-buttercup, threadleaf	thread-leaved water-crowfoot, large-leaved white water crowfoot	Ranunculus aquatilis	species
water-buttercup, yellow	yellow water buttercup, yellow water-crowfoot	Ranunculus flabellaris	species
waterclover	waterclover	Marsilea	genus
water-clover family	water-clover family	Marsileaceae	family
waterclover, hairy	hairy water-clover, hairy pepperwort	Marsilea vestita	species
watercress	watercress	Nasturtium	genus
watercress	watercress, water cress	Nasturtium officinale	species
water-hemlock	water-hemlock	Cicuta	genus
water-hemlock, bulbous	bulbous water-hemlock, bulb-bearing water-hemlock	Cicuta bulbifera	species
water-hemlock, narrowleaf	northern water-hemlock, narrow-leaved water-hemlock	Cicuta virosa	species
water-hemlock, spotted	spotted water-hemlock, water-hemlock	Cicuta maculata	species
water-horehound	water-horehound	Lycopus	genus
water-horehound, American	American water-horehound	Lycopus americanus	species
water-horehound, northern	northern water-horehound	Lycopus uniflorus	species
water-horehound, rough	rough water-horehound, western water-horehound	Lycopus asper	species
water-hyssop	water-hyssop	Bacopa	genus
water-hyssop, disc	round-leaved water hyssop, water hyssop	Bacopa rotundifolia	species
waterleaf	waterleaf	Hydrophyllum	genus
waterleaf family	waterleaf family	Hydrophyllaceae	family
waterleaf, ballhead	ballhead waterleaf, woollen-breeches	Hydrophyllum capitatum	species
waterlily	waterlily	Nymphaea	genus
waterlily family	waterlily family	Nymphaeaceae	family
waterlily, dwarf	dwarf water-lily, pygmy water-lily	Nymphaea leibergii	species
waterlily, pygmy	pygmy water-lily, white water-lily	Nymphaea tetragona	species
watermeal	watermeal	Wolffia	genus
watermeal, Columbia	Columbia watermeal	Wolffia columbiana	species
watermeal, northern	northern watermeal	Wolffia borealis	species
watermilfoil	watermilfoil	Myriophyllum	genus
watermilfoil family	watermilfoil family	Haloragaceae	family
watermilfoil, Eurasian	Eurasian water-milfoil	Myriophyllum spicatum	species
watermilfoil, Siberian	Siberian water-milfoil, spiked water-milfoil	Myriophyllum sibiricum	species
watermilfoil, whorled	whorled water-milfoil, water-milfoil	Myriophyllum verticillatum	species

ALPHABETIZED* COMMON NAMES

Suggested Common Name	VASCAN &/or ACIMS Common Name(s)	Scientific Name	Rank
waterparsnip	waterparsnip	Sium	genus
waterparsnip, common	common water-parsnip, water parsnip	Sium suave	species
waterplantain	waterplantain	Alisma	genus
water-plantain family	water-plantain family	Alismataceae	family
water-plantain, broadleaf	northern water-plantain, broad-leaved water-plantain	Alisma triviale	species
water-plantain, narrowleaf	grass-leaved water-plantain, narrow-leaved water-plantain	Alisma gramineum	species
waterpod	waterpod	Ellisia	genus
waterpod	waterpod	Ellisia nyctelea	species
watershield	watershield	Brasenia	genus
watershield	watershield	Brasenia schreberi	species
watershield family	watershield family	Cabombaceae	family
water-starwort	water-starwort	Callitriche	genus
water-starwort, narrow-wing	narrow-winged water-starwort	Callitriche stenoptera	species
water-starwort, northern	northern water-starwort	Callitriche hermaphroditica	species
water-starwort, spring	spring water-starwort	Callitriche palustris	species
waterthyme	waterthyme	Hydrilla	genus
waterthyme	waterthyme	Hydrilla verticillata	species
waterweed	waterweed	Elodea	genus
waterweed, Canada	Canada waterweed	Elodea canadensis	species
waterweed, Nuttall	Nuttall's waterweed	Elodea nuttallii	species
waterweed, twoleaf	two-leaved waterweed	Elodea bifoliata	species
waterwort	waterwort	Elatine	genus
waterwort family	waterwort family	Elatinaceae	family
waterwort, threestamen	three-stamened waterwort, waterwort	Elatine triandra	species
wax-myrtle family	wax-myrtle family	Myricaceae	family
wedgegrass	wedgegrass	Sphenopholis	genus
wedgegrass, prairie	prairie wedgegrass, prairie wedge grass	Sphenopholis obtusata	species
wedgegrass, slender	slender wedgegrass, slender wedge grass	Sphenopholis intermedia	species
western-wheatgrass	western-wheatgrass	Pascopyrum	genus
western-wheatgrass	western wheatgrass, western wheat grass	Pascopyrum smithii	species
wheat	wheat	Triticum	genus
wheat, common	common wheat	Triticum aestivum	species
wheat, durum	durum wheat	Triticum durum	species
wheatgrass	wheatgrass	Agropyron	genus
wheatgrass	wheatgrass	Pseudoroegneria	genus
wheatgrass	wheatgrass	Thinopyrum	genus
wheatgrass, bluebunch	bluebunch wheatgrass	Pseudoroegneria spicata	species
wheatgrass, crested	crested wheatgrass	Agropyron cristatum	species

ALPHABETIZED* COMMON NAMES

Suggested Common Name	VASCAN &/or ACIMS Common Name(s)	Scientific Name	Rank
wheatgrass, intermediate	intermediate wheatgrass	Thinopyrum intermedium	species
wheatgrass, Siberian	Siberian wheatgrass	Agropyron fragile	species
wheatgrass, tall	tall wheatgrass, rush wheatgrass	Thinopyrum ponticum	species
white-aster	white-aster	Doellingeria	genus
white-aster, flattop	flat-top white aster, flat-topped white aster	Doellingeria umbellata	species
whorlgrass	whorlgrass	Catabrosa	genus
whorlgrass, water	water whorlgrass, brook grass	Catabrosa aquatica	species
widgeongrass	widgeongrass	Ruppia	genus
widgeongrass family	widgeongrass family	Ruppiaceae	family
widgeongrass, spiral	spiral ditchgrass, widgeon-grass	Ruppia cirrhosa	species
wild-comfrey	wild-comfrey	Andersonglossum	genus
wild-comfrey, northern	northern wild comfrey, wild comfrey	Cynoglossum virginianum	species
wild-cucumber	wild-cucumber	Echinocystis	genus
wild-cucumber	wild cucumber	Echinocystis lobata	species
wild-ginger	wild-ginger	Asarum	genus
wild-ginger, Canada	Canada wild ginger	Asarum canadense	species
wild-hollyhock	wild-hollyhock	Iliamna	genus
wild-hollyhock, streambank	streambank globe-mallow, mountain hollyhock	Iliamna rivularis	species
wild-licorice	wild-licorice	Glycyrrhiza	genus
wild-licorice	wild licorice	Glycyrrhiza lepidota	species
wild-parsley	wild-parsley	Musineon	genus
wild-parsley, leafy	leafy wild parsley, leafy musineon	Musineon divaricatum	species
wildrice	wildrice	Zizania	genus
wildrice, annual	southern wildrice, wild rice	Zizania aquatica	species
wildrice, northern	northern wildrice, northern wild rice	Zizania palustris	species
wildrye	wildrye	Elyhordeum	genus
wildrye	wildrye	Elymus	genus
wildrye, awnless	awnless wildrye	Elymus curvatus	species
wildrye, blue	blue wildrye, smooth wild rye	Elymus glaucus	species
wildrye, Canada	Canada wildrye	Elymus canadensis	species
wildrye, high	high wildrye	Elymus violaceus	species
wildrye, Macoun	Macoun's wildrye, Macoun's wild rye	Elyhordeum ×macounii	Hybrid
wildrye, northern	Montana wildrye, awned northern wheat grass	Elymus albicans	species
wildrye, Scribner	Scribner's wildrye, Scribner's wheat grass	Elymus scribneri	species
wildrye, slender	slender wildrye, slender wheatgrass	Elymus trachycaulus	species
wildrye, squirreltail	long-bristled wildrye, squirreltail	Elymus elymoides	species

ALPHABETIZED* COMMON NAMES

Suggested Common Name	VASCAN &/or ACIMS Common Name(s)	Scientific Name	Rank
wildrye, thickspike	thick-spike wildrye, northern wheat grass	Elymus lanceolatus	species
wildrye, Virginia	Virginia wildrye	Elymus virginicus	species
William, sweet	sweet William	Dianthus barbatus	species
willow	willow	Salix	genus
willow family	willow family	Salicaceae	family
willow, Alaska	Alaska willow	Salix alaxensis	species
willow, alpine	Rocky Mountain willow, alpine willow	Salix petrophila	species
willow, Arctic	arctic willow	Salix arctica	species
willow, Athabasca	Athabasca willow	Salix athabascensis	species
willow, autumn	autumn willow	Salix serissima	species
willow, balsam	balsam willow	Salix pyrifolia	species
willow, Barclay	Barclay's willow	Salix barclayi	species
willow, Barratt	Barratt's willow	Salix barrattiana	species
willow, Bebb	Bebb's willow, beaked willow	Salix bebbiana	species
willow, blueberryleaf	low blueberry willow, myrtle-leaved willow	Salix myrtillifolia	species
willow, bog	bog willow	Salix pedicellaris	species
willow, Booth	Booth's willow	Salix boothii	species
willow, creeping	creeping willow	Salix stolonifera	species
willow, daphne	violet willow, Daphne's willow	Salix daphnoides	species
willow, Drummond	Drummond's willow	Salix drummondiana	species
willow, dusky	dusky willow	Salix melanopsis	species
willow, false mountain	false mountain willow	Salix pseudomonticola	species
willow, Farr	Farr's willow	Salix farriae	species
willow, greyleaf	grey-leaved willow, smooth willow	Salix glauca	species
willow, hungry	starved willow, hungry willow	Salix famelica	species
willow, laurel	laurel willow	Salix pentandra	species
willow, littletree	little-tree willow, shrubby willow	Salix arbusculoides	species
willow, MacCalla	MacCalla's willow, velvet-fruited willow	Salix maccalliana	species
willow, Mackenzie	Mackenzie's willow	Salix prolixa	species
willow, meadow	meadow willow, basket willow	Salix petiolaris	species
willow, narrowleaf	coyote willow, narrow-leaf willow	Salix exigua	species
willow, netvein	net-veined willow	Salix reticulata	species
willow, Pacific shining	Pacific willow, shining willow	Salix lasiandra	species
willow, peachleaf	peach-leaved willow	Salix amygdaloides	species
willow, pussy	pussy willow	Salix discolor	species
willow, Raup	Raup's willow	Salix raupii	species
willow, rock	hairy willow, rock willow	Salix vestita	species
willow, sage	sage willow, hoary willow	Salix candida	species
willow, sandbar	sandbar willow	Salix interior	species

ALPHABETIZED* COMMON NAMES

Suggested Common Name	VASCAN &/or ACIMS Common Name(s)	Scientific Name	Rank
willow, Scouler	Scouler's willow	Salix scouleriana	species
willow, short-capsule	short-capsuled willow	Salix brachycarpa	species
willow, Sitka	Sitka willow	Salix sitchensis	species
willow, snow	dwarf snow willow, snow willow	Salix nivalis	species
willow, tall blueberry	tall blueberry willow	Salix pseudomyrsinites	species
willow, tealeaf	tea-leaved willow, flat-leaved willow	Salix planifolia	species
willow, Tyrrell	Tyrrell's willow	Salix tyrrellii	species
willow, undergreen	under-green willow, changeable willow	Salix commutata	species
willow, woolly	limestone willow, woolly willow	Salix calcicola	species
willowherb	willowherb	Epilobium	genus
willowherb, alpine	alpine willowherb	Epilobium anagallidifolium	species
willowherb, annual	tall annual willowherb, annual willowherb	Epilobium brachycarpum	species
willowherb, club	club-fruited willowherb, club willowherb	Epilobium clavatum	species
willowherb, glaucous	glaucous willowherb	Epilobium glaberrimum	species
willowherb, hairystem	hairy-stemmed willowherb	Epilobium mirabile	species
willowherb, Hall	Hall's willowherb	Epilobium hallianum	species
willowherb, Hornemann	Hornemann's willowherb	Epilobium hornemannii	species
willowherb, little	little willowherb	Epilobium minutum	species
willowherb, marsh	marsh willowherb	Epilobium palustre	species
willowherb, narrowleaf	narrow-leaved willowherb	Epilobium leptophyllum	species
willowherb, northern	northern willowherb	Epilobium ciliatum	species
willowherb, Rocky Mountain	Rocky Mountain willowherb	Epilobium saximontanum	species
willowherb, slenderfruit	slender-fruited willowherb, slender-fruit willowherb	Epilobium leptocarpum	species
willowherb, smooth	smooth willowherb, smooth boisduvalia	Epilobium campestre	species
willowherb, whiteflower	white-flowered willowherb	Epilobium lactiflorum	species
willowherb, yellow	yellow willowherb	Epilobium luteum	species
wintercress	wintercress	Barbarea	genus
wintercress, American	erect-fruit wintercress, American winter cress	Barbarea orthoceras	species
wintercress, bitter	bitter wintercress, yellow rocket	Barbarea vulgaris	species
winterfat	winterfat	Krascheninnikovia	genus
winterfat	winterfat, winter-fat	Krascheninnikovia lanata	species
wintergreen	wintergreen	Gaultheria	genus
wintergreen	wintergreen	Pyrola	genus
wintergreen, alpine	alpine wintergreen	Gaultheria humifusa	species
wintergreen, arctic	arctic pyrola, Arctic wintergreen	Pyrola grandiflora	species
wintergreen, common pink	pink pyrola, common pink wintergreen	Pyrola asarifolia	species
wintergreen, greenflower	green-flowered pyrola, greenish-flowered wintergreen	Pyrola chlorantha	species

ALPHABETIZED* COMMON NAMES

Suggested Common Name	VASCAN &/or ACIMS Common Name(s)	Scientific Name	Rank
wintergreen, lesser	lesser pyrola, lesser wintergreen	Pyrola minor	species
wintergreen, oneside	one-sided wintergreen	Orthilia secunda	species
wintergreen, one-sided	one-sided wintergreen	Orthilia	genus
wintergreen, white	shinleaf, white wintergreen	Pyrola elliptica	species
wintergreen, whitevein	white-veined pyrola, white-veined wintergreen	Pyrola picta	species
wirelettuce	wirelettuce	Stephanomeria	genus
wirelettuce, sawtooth	sawtooth wirelettuce, rush-pink	Stephanomeria runcinata	species
woad	woad	Isatis	genus
woad, dyer	dyer's woad	Isatis tinctoria	species
wolfwillow	wolfwillow, Russian-olive	Elaeagnus	genus
wolfwillow	wolf-willow, silverberry	Elaeagnus commutata	species
wood-aster	aster	Eurybia	genus
wood-aster, showy	western showy aster, showy aster	Eurybia conspicua	species
wood-aster, Siberian	Siberian aster, Arctic aster	Eurybia sibirica	species
woodbeauty	woodbeauty	Drymocallis	genus
woodbeauty, sticky	false rock-loving cinquefoil, sticky cinquefoil	Drymocallis pseudorupestris	species
woodbeauty, tall	tall wood beauty, white cinquefoil	Drymocallis arguta	species
woodfern	woodfern	Dryopteris	genus
woodfern family	woodfern family	Dryopteridaceae	family
woodfern, crested	crested wood fern, crested shield fern	Dryopteris cristata	species
woodfern, fragrant	fragrant wood fern, fragrant shield fern	Dryopteris fragrans	species
woodfern, male	male fern	Dryopteris filix-mas	species
woodfern, spinulose	spinulose wood fern, narrow spinulose shield fern	Dryopteris carthusiana	species
woodfern, spreading	spreading wood fern, broad spinulose shield fern	Dryopteris expansa	species
woodland-star	woodland-star	Lithophragma	genus
woodland-star, bulbous	smooth woodland-star, rockstar	Lithophragma glabrum	species
woodland-star, smallflower	small-flowered woodland-star, small-flowered rockstar	Lithophragma parviflorum	species
woodnettle	woodnettle	Laportea	genus
woodnettle, Canada	Canada wood nettle, Canada wood-nettle	Laportea canadensis	species
woodreed	woodreed	Cinna	genus
woodreed, drooping	drooping woodreed, drooping wood-reed	Cinna latifolia	species
woodruff	woodruff	Asperula	genus
woodruff, blue	blue woodruff, quinsywort	Asperula arvensis	species
woodrush	woodrush	Luzula	genus
woodrush, curved	curved woodrush, curved wood rush	Luzula arcuata	species
woodrush, Greenland	Greenland woodrush, wood-rush	Luzula groenlandica	species

ALPHABETIZED* COMMON NAMES

Suggested Common Name	VASCAN &/or ACIMS Common Name(s)	Scientific Name	Rank
woodrush, hairy	hairy woodrush, wood-rush	Luzula acuminata	species
woodrush, Hitchcock	Hitchcock's woodrush, smooth wood-rush	Luzula hitchcockii	species
woodrush, manyflower	many-flowered woodrush, field wood-rush	Luzula multiflora	species
woodrush, Piper	Piper's woodrush, mountain wood-rush	Luzula piperi	species
woodrush, rusty	rusty woodrush, reddish wood-rush	Luzula rufescens	species
woodrush, smallflower	small-flowered woodrush, small-flowered wood-rush	Luzula parviflora	species
woodrush, spiked	spiked woodrush, spiked wood-rush	Luzula spicata	species
woodsia	woodsia	Woodsia	genus
woodsia, mountain	mountain woodsia	Woodsia scopulina	species
woodsia, Oregon	Oregon woodsia	Woodsia oregana	species
woodsia, rusty	rusty woodsia	Woodsia ilvensis	species
woodsia, smooth	smooth woodsia	Woodsia glabella	species
woodsorrel	woodsorrel	Oxalis	genus
woodsorrel family	woodsorrel family	Oxalidaceae	family
woodsorrel, European	European wood-sorrel	Oxalis stricta	species
woollyheads	woollyheads	Psilocarphus	genus
woollyheads, dwarf	dwarf woollyheads, round woollyheads	Psilocarphus brevissimus	species
wormwood	wormwood, sagebrush, sagewort	Artemisia	genus
wormwood, absinthe	absinthe wormwood	Artemisia absinthium	species
wormwood, alpine	alpine wormwood, mountain sagewort	Artemisia norvegica	species
wormwood, biennial	biennial wormwood, biennial sagewort	Artemisia biennis	species
wormwood, common	common wormwood	Artemisia vulgaris	species
wormwood, dragon	dragon wormwood, dragonwort	Artemisia dracunculus	species
wormwood, forked	forked wormwood	Artemisia hyperborea	species
wormwood, longleaf	long-leaved wormwood, long-leaved sagewort	Artemisia longifolia	species
wormwood, Michaux	Michaux's wormwood, Michaux's sagewort	Artemisia michauxiana	species
wormwood, northern	boreal wormwood, northern wormwood	Artemisia borealis	species
wormwood, pasture	prairie sagebrush, pasture sagewort	Artemisia frigida	species
wormwood, plains	field wormwood, plains wormwood	Artemisia campestris	species
wormwood, silver	silver wormwood, prairie sagewort	Artemisia ludoviciana	species

ALPHABETIZED* COMMON NAMES

Suggested Common Name	VASCAN &/or ACIMS Common Name(s)	Scientific Name	Rank
wormwood, southern	southern wormwood, southernwood	Artemisia abrotanum	species
wormwood, Tilesius	Tilesius wormwood, Herriot's sagewort	Artemisia tilesii	species
yampah	yampah	Perideridia	genus
yampah, Gairdner	Gairdner's yampah, common yampah	Perideridia gairdneri	species
yarrow	yarrow	Achillea	genus
yarrow, common	common yarrow	Achillea borealis	species
yarrow, manyflower	Siberian yarrow, many-flowered yarrow	Achillea alpina	species
yarrow, sneezewort	sneezeweed yarrow, sneezewort yarrow	Achillea ptarmica	species
yellow-chamomile	yellow-chamomile	Cota	genus
yellow-chamomile	yellow chamomile	Cota tinctoria	species
yellowcress	yellowcress	Rorippa	genus
yellowcress, Austrian	Austrian yellowcress, Austrian cress	Rorippa austriaca	species
yellowcress, bluntleaf	blunt-leaved watercress	Rorippa curvipes	species
yellowcress, creeping	creeping yellowcress, creeping yellow cress	Rorippa sylvestris	species
yellowcress, marsh	marsh yellowcress, marsh yellow cress	Rorippa palustris	species
yellowcress, slender	slender yellowcress, slender cress	Rorippa tenerrima	species
yellowcress, spreading	spreading yellowcress, spreading yellow cress	Rorippa sinuata	species
yellowrattle	yellowrattle	Rhinanthus	genus
yellowrattle, little	little yellow rattle, yellow rattle	Rhinanthus minor	species
yellowtuft	wall alyssum, yellow alyssum	Odontarrhena murale	species
yellowtuft	yellowtuft	Odontarrhena/Alyssum	genus
yew	yew	Taxus	genus
yew family	yew family	Taxaceae	family
yew, western	western yew	Taxus brevifolia	species
yucca	yucca	Yucca	genus
yucca, soapweed	soapweed yucca, soapweed	Yucca glauca	species

References

Alberta Conservation Information Management System (ACIMS). 2018. List of all Vascular Plant Taxa Confirmed for Alberta as recorded in the ACIMS database - March 2018. ACIMS, Government of Alberta, Edmonton, AB.

Backyard Gardener. 2018. Backyardgardener, Tacoma WA. Accessed 2010-2018. www.backyardgardener.com.

Baranova, A. 1971. Basic Latin for plant taxonomists. Verlag Von J. Cramer, Lehre.

Bowyer, T. 2018. Howjsay. Perth Freelance Web Development, Bowyer.co, Perth, AUS. Accessed 2018. https://howjsay.com/.

Britton, N. L. and A. Brown. 1913. An illustrated flora of the northern United States and Canada. Reprinted by Dover Publications in 1970 edition. Dover Publications, Inc., New York, New York.

Brouillet, L., F. Coursol, S.J. Meades, M. A. M. Favreau, P. Bélisle, and P. Desmet. 2010+. VASCAN, the Database of Vascular Plants of Canada. Accessed 2018. http://data.canadensys.net/vascan/.

Brown, R. W. 1956. Composition of scientific words. Smithsonian Institution Press, Washington, D.C.

Brummitt, R. K. and C. E. Powell (eds.). 1992. Authors of plant names. Royal Botanic Gardens, Kew, England.

Charters, M. L. 2018. California Plant Names: Latin and Greek Meanings and Derivations. Michael L. Charters, Sierra Madre, California. Accessed 2008-2018. http://www.calflora.net/.

Clifford, H. T. and P. D. Bostock. 2007. Etymological Dictionary of Grasses. Springer-Verlag, New York, New York.

Covington, M. A. 2005. Latin Pronunciation Demystified. Program in Linguistics, University of Georgia.

Dave's Garden. 2015. Internet Brands, El Segundo, CA. Accessed 2010-2015. https://davesgarden.com/.

Fernald, M. L. 1950. Gray's manual of botany. 8 edition. American Book Company, New York, New York.

Fletcher, K. 1998. Glossary of roots of botanical names. Accessed 2002. http://www.prairienet.org/garden-gate/botrts.htm.

Flora North America Editorial Committee. 2008-18. Flora North America website. Oxford University Press. Accessed 2014-2016. www.fna.org.

Gledhill, D. 1989. The names of plants. 2nd edition. University Press,, Cambridge, England.

Hitchcock, L. and A. Cronquist. 1973. Flora of the Pacific Northwest: An illustrated manual. University of Washington Press, Seattle, Washington.

Hulten, E. 1968. Flora of Alaska and neighbouring territories. Stanford University Press, Stanford, California.

ITIS Canada. 2011-2018. Integrated Taxonomic Information System. Agriculture and Agri-Food Canada, Ottawa, Ontario. Accessed February 2011. http://www.cbif.gc.ca/pls/itisca/taxaget?p_ifx=cbif.

Kershaw, L. 1991. The plants of northwestern Canada: With special reference to the Dempster Highway, Yukon and Northwest Territories. Linda Kershaw (unpublished manuscript), Sherwood Park, Alberta.

Kidd, D. A. 1957. Latin Dictionary. William Collins Sons & Co. Ltd., London, England.

Merriam-Webster's Vollegiate Dictionary. 1999. 10th edition. Merriam-Webster Incorporated, Springfield, MA.

Mish, F. C. and J. M. Morse, editors. 1999. Merriam-Webster's Collegiate Dictionary. 10 edition. Merriam-Webster, Incorporated., Springfield, Massachusetts.

Olivetti, E. 2003-2021. Online Latin dictionary. Olivetti Media Communcation. Accessed 2018.

Quattrocchi, U. 1999. CRC world dictionary of plant names. CRC Press, New York, New York.

Radford, A. E., W. C. Dickison, J. R. Massey, and C. R. Bell. 1974. Vascular plant systematics. Harper and Row, Publishers, New York, New York.

Robinson, B. L. and M. L. Fernald. 1908. Gray's new manual of botany. 7 edition. American Book Company, New York, New York.

Rydberg, P. A. 1932. Flora of the prairies and plains of central North America. Hafner Publishing Company, New York, New York.

Stearn, W. T. 1966. Botanical Latin. Thomas Nelson and Sons (Canada) Ltd., Don Mills, Ontario.

Stearn, W. T. 1983. Botanical Latin: History, grammar, syntax, terminology and vocabulary. 3rd edition. David and Charles, Vermont.

Sweet, M. 1962. Common edible and useful plants of the west. Naturegraph Company, Healdsburg, California.

USDA, N. 2009+. The PLANTS Database. National Plant Data Center, Baton Rouge, LA, USA. Accessed 2010-2018. http://plants.usda.gov.

Table 1: Pronunciation Symbols

Symbol	Pronunciation
a A	as in c**a**t
ä Ä	as in f**a**ther
ā Ā	as in d**a**te
b B	as in **b**at
ch CH	as in **ch**at
d D	as in **d**o**dd**er
e E	as in b**e**t
ē Ē	as in f**ee**t
f F	as in **f**i**f**ty
g G	as in **g**a**g**
h H	as in **h**at
i I	as in k**i**t
ī Ī	as in k**i**te
j J	as in **j**ay
k K	as in **k**i**ck**
l L	as in **l**i**l**y
m M	as in **m**ur**m**ur
n N	as in **n**a**nn**y
o O	as in n**o**t
ō Ō	as in n**o**te
oo OO	as in n**oo**n
õõ ÕÕ	like u in p**u**t
ou OU	as in **ou**t
p P	as in **p**o**p**
q Q	as in **q**uit
r R	as in **r**a**r**e
s S	as in **s**a**ss**y
sh SH	as in **sh**e
t T	as in **t**a**tt**er
th TH	as in **th**in
ū Ū	as in c**u**te
v V	as in **v**al**v**e
w W	as in **w**o**w**
x X	as in e**x**am
y Y	as in **y**et
z Z	as in **z**ig
ēoo	as in f**eud**
ooē	Like **ooey** in g**ooey**
tzē	Like **tzy** in ri**tzy**

Manufactured by Amazon.ca
Bolton, ON